AF673559

THE CONTEMPORARY CARIBBEAN

The Contemporary Caribbean

Issues and Challenges

Edited by
Priti Singh
M. Raymond Izarali

All right reserved. No part of this publication may be reproduced, stored in a retrival system, or transmitted in any form or by any means, electronic, mechanical, photocopying, recording or otherwise, without the prior written permission of the Publishers.

ISBN: 978-81-7541-659-8

First Published in India in 2013

The Contemporary Caribbean: Issues and Challenges

© Editors

Published by:
SHIPRA PUBLICATIONS
H.O.: LG 18-19, Pankaj Central Market, Patparganj,
I.P. Ext., Delhi-110092, Tel: 91-11-2223 5152, 2223 6152
Br.Off.: 4617/18, Ansari Road, Darya Ganj,
New Delhi-110002, Tel: 6594 6453, 9810522367
E-mail: info@shiprapublications.com
www.shiprapublications.com

Contents

Foreword

The Contemporary Caribbean: Issues and Challenges is a collection of well-researched essays on some of the critical issues that the Caribbean region faces today. It focuses on the transformative changes currently perceived in the region and the critical challenges they pose on the future. The issues the book addresses range from the micro dimensions of the Caribbean social ethos and life-style to the way the region is engaging at the macro global level. The aim of this academic enterprise by Priti Singh and Raymond Izarali is quite evident—to bring to fore the major issues that confront the region, the resolution of which call for new ways of thinking and policy-making of the themes.

While commending the authors on the choice of the themes and the competence with which they have analyzed the issues, I would like to supplement the compendium with my own thoughts in respect of the region's past, present and its future prospects. Given the history of colonialism and the imperatives of nation-building, in the wake of independence, most countries of the region pursued inward-oriented developmental strategies which among others included a high degree of state initiative and intervention in the economy. This approach may have been feasible in the 1960s and 1970s, given the state of development-thinking and the geopolitical structure of the world economy in that period, but it is no longer sustainable in my view.

For decades, the plantation economy of the hinterland has adjusted only to a persistent low-level equilibrium, resulting in lower incomes. Although the region's resource-based industries were integrated into the global economy, this resulted in economic enclaves within the domestic economy, without sufficient development benefits. Caribbean countries remain highly sensitive to exogenous forces, such as shocks, exchange-rate manipulation and crises, all of which can adversely affect their foreign exchange, their largely export-derived public revenues, and their competitiveness.

The liberalization of the global economic system and other conditions are now eroding the preferential terms of trade on which the Caribbean standard of living is built. Faced with adverse terms of trade, the need for technological advancement, stresses in the political system, and changing political and economic ties with the rest of the world, the Caribbean is confronting its most severe challenges.

Let us start by giving a synoptic account of the events that we are facing globally since 2008. In the first instance the so-called *financial crisis* surfaced in the private sector. The bubble of this sub-prime mortgage rate had surfaced as the major indicator of things that had gone wrong and in that sense the response to the crisis was a response to the search for *financial stability*. Not achieving this financial stability was perceived to be the result of market failure in the private sector and in the larger global economy. In the large countries of the world it resulted from bad regulation and poor bank capitalization.

Soon it was discovered that this was only at the surface and within the second round, the issue of *financial solvency* began to show its head, sovereign debt and fiscal deficit emerged. The locus of the articulation of this crisis moved from the private sector to the public sector. The issue moved from market failure to lack of having built-in market confidence that is currently engaging the entire global leadership. But even before a credible solution appeared, a third dimension of this crisis emerged — *financial sustainability*, which goes beyond the private and public sectors, engaging the national economies of the world. Financial sustainability goes beyond market failure and market confidence into the need for market discipline. A discussion has emerged on the exchange rate levels and regime and the phenomenon of currency realignment in response to world global imbalance. In addition, the source of exposure really comes from the imbalance between our gross assets and our gross liabilities.

How has the global financial crisis affected the Caribbean region? Clearly, the Caribbean is neither isolated nor insulated. While some have argued that the Caribbean countries are innocent bystanders in this whole phenomenon, this is not so. We do indeed live in a world that is very interconnected, and when Lehman Brothers fell in New York, so too the largest insurance company in the Caribbean, located in Trinidad and Tobago, almost collapsed. This affected over 10 per cent of the gross domestic product of Trinidad and Tobago. In the Caribbean it affected over 17 per cent of the gross domestic product.

The Latin American region however has shown resilience and the recent report from the Economic Commission for Latin America and the Caribbean (ECLAC) and the development committee of the OECD had this to say about Latin America: *"Latin America's solid economic performance since 2003 has created the possibility for transformation of the state enabling the adoption of ambitious public policies that lock in the prospects of long-term development and mitigate short term risk".*

The situation in Trinidad and Tobago and the rest of the Caribbean remains very fragile and vulnerable to external shocks; the Caribbean has always lived with external shocks. Trinidad and Tobago does have immense impact on the small Caribbean economies. Trinidad and Tobago has been able to retain solid macro-economic performance, the debt to GDP ratio is just over 36 per cent of our GDP. The relationship between reserves, international reserves and GDP is very high despite fiscal deficits. Substantial reserves in the stabilization fund have allowed the country to escape some of the problems in the first round.

Will this be just a protracted slowdown and will we have the ability to handle it, in a part of the world that is open and does not have the benefit of large domestic demand? In light of such questions, we view the protraction of this development with some concern.

But we cannot measure fiscal sustainability solely on the basis of arithmetic ratios in finance as practiced by many of the rating agencies. As we search for a way forward to deal with a potential protracted slowdown and a continuing deepening of the financial crisis in the global economy, our imperatives are three fold: the flexibility to adjust, the resilience to cope, and the capacity to employ buffers.

Unlike large economies who would have time and mass, small economies in the Caribbean have neither and therefore flexibility to adjust has to be a daily resolve. Whether adjustment involves revenue and expenditure or changes in regulatory adherence, it is important to measure financial sustainability by the capacity to have flexibility to adjust.

The resilience to cope brings into play the narrow economic and the larger political issues. The best safeguard to this resilience has to do with addressing inequality of incomes in the country. In the final analysis that is the source of resilience.

Are there enough resources put away for the rainy day? Unfortunately, many Caribbean countries are devoid of the capacity to employ buffers. However, Trinidad and Tobago, some time ago, established a heritage and stabilization fund—a wealth fund. It represents just near to 20 per cent of the GDP in active resources. Still, it is a visible buffer that provides a sense of security for the future. More important for the Caribbean region is the issue of external buffers, buffers that are put into place by institutions like the International Monetary Fund which provide lines of credit to economies facing external shocks. But such buffers are inadequate to the problems not only of the Caribbean but of many small economies worldwide.

It is for this reason that Trinidad and Tobago took the initiative recently to start a conversation within the governance of the International Monetary Fund to ensure that small economies are given an active political presence in the deliberations of such bodies. We live in an interconnected world, one in which the periphery may have significant ripple effects on the center, as Greece and Iceland have shown in recent times. The core countries are at greater risk as they are holding more of the periphery countries' assets.

The last time when there was a serious attempt by international bodies to look at the future of the global economy was in 2008. The World Bank Commission produced the Growth Report of 2008. But the Growth Report did not in any way anticipate or articulate the problems of the turbulence ahead.

There were missing links in this articulation of the global paradigm. One such missing link in the search for development was the exclusion of the politics of development. We cannot exclude the politics of development from the search for that development. Secondly, prescription to *inclusive growth* has been without a strategy for basic development. Inclusive development does not necessarily provide basic development in society.

The time has come for a new leadership to search for a new paradigm for development; one that will identify *political logic and economic logic*; one that would construct new measures for financial sustainability; and one that will design a strategy for basic development that puts equity at the center.

We know that we need to build a competitive world. How can we arrive at the global and regional compacts based on policy coordination in a period of market convergence? This is an issue that should bring together the public sector and the private sector in order to find the right compacts. Recent attempts by leaders in the European Economic Union failed to produce an enforceable fiscal compact to support the monetary union. While this is happening in Europe, global leaders in South Africa came together at the United Nations Framework Convention on Climate Change to draft a global compact on climate change following the Kyoto Protocol.

The compacts have already begun to show cracks: the UK's decision not to be party to the European Union treaty and Canada's withdrawal from the Kyoto Protocol. In spite of the challenges to such regional and global compacts, in today's world it is necessary to arrive at such compacts in order to mitigate against the risks that are globally generated.

Can we build a consensus on changing the global financial architecture and do so within a political framework like the G 20? In today's interconnected world we may find that even that wider political framework is not sufficient to build consensus. To achieve consensus is to build on the politics of the situation. The technical arguments are persuasive but the political will to adhere to such solutions is critically important. Trinidad and Tobago has begun to seek that space in the global financial architecture.

The most important question has emerged out of the Delhi Economic Conclave in 2011. Is a financial crisis really a reflection of the deeper development crisis? Are we treating the financial stability issue? Are we treating the solvency issue? Or should we treat the sustainability issue?

This requires us to drill deeper into development. This is where the real challenge lies. This conclusion should be a turning point in the intellectual pursuit of the search for that paradigm. It is useful to think out-of-the-box and search for the space within which new solutions can be found that are sustainable and anchored in the issues of inequality in our society and jobless growth.

We in the Caribbean and Latin America look to the future; we look to the countries in the Far East and countries in Asia, like China and India. Together with the advanced countries of North America and Europe, we should articulate new thinking to ensure that smaller economies like ours do not have to be mere bystanders in this scenario.

This is a global challenge in leadership, the world is waiting on its leaders to show them the way forward. Some of these ideas are explained in greater detail in *Power, Politics and Performance* by Winston Dookeran (2012, Ian Randle Publisher).

Port of Spain
26 January 2012

Winston Dookeran
Minister of Finance,
Republic of Trinidad and Tobago

Acknowledgements

The editors are pleased to acknowledge the equal contribution of each other in bringing the idea of this book on the contemporary Caribbean to completion.

Energies toward this book span a few continents and time zones with scholars of diverse expertise in an effort to map out some of the most salient issues and challenges of the contemporary Caribbean. Contributions for example come from India, China, Canada, the U.S., and the Caribbean. This has the benefit of providing international perspectives on the region.

Achieving the final product has come with immense demands, many sleepless nights, and enormous amounts of editor consultations in addressing revisions and refinements which are made even more challenging as the editors are continents apart. This has meant diversions from family time and constant re-adjustment to our schedules.

As the project has now come to completion, we acknowledge the support of the Centre for Canadian, U.S. & Latin American Studies, School of International Studies of Jawaharlal Nehru University for its various facilitations, and to Wilfrid Laurier University in accommodating research and project-related travels to the Caribbean and India.

The contributors to this book have been very understanding in addressing reviews and revisions as we demanded and so no word of acknowledgement for an edited volume can be complete without acknowledging the participation and energy of the contributors. We are also very grateful for the support of Professor Timothy Shaw (now retired), Professor Jaipaul Roopnarine (Syracuse University), Professor Ramesh Deosaran (University of Trinidad and Tobago), Professor W. Andy Knight (University of Alberta), and Professor Rhoda Reddock (University of the West Indies, St. Augustine) - all of whom were senior administrators straddling already hectic schedules with scholarship and administration at the time they were participating in this project. Indeed they are among the leading experts on the Caribbean.

We extend our gratitude also to The Honourable Winston Dookeran, Finance Minister of Trinidad and Tobago and scholar, for giving us his unstinting support and valuable time.

The publisher, Shipra Publications, has been gracious to us in addressing deadlines. Finally, we extend thanks to our families who more often than not have been the victims of our thick schedules across time zones in bringing this project to completion.

The editors express their appreciation to the referees for their useful comments and criticisms.

Introduction

Priti Singh

By most accounts, the Caribbean as a distinct region with its well-defined geo-political-economic features has come of age. What for centuries was perceived as a region in the backwaters of the United States—and so-called "American Mediterranean"—has now been catapulted almost to the centre-stage where world powers both of the West and the East are vying to have a foot-hold. During most of the 18th century, European countries were competing for a foothold in the Caribbean for the purpose of colonizing the Americas. With the United States emerging as a naval power in the second half of the 19th century, the Caribbean became even more a contested region. At the end of the twentieth century, with the relative decline of the super powers and the emergence of Asian countries, the region is now exposed to the rising economic influence of China and India.

Defining the contours of the Caribbean as a well-knit geographical region is not an easy task; neither is deconstructing its ethnic history and cultural antecedents. To identify the Caribbean as a "unified" region has been called "a figment of imagination" (Premdas 1996, 2). For one, the region is an incredibly diverse cultural mosaic by virtue of its large ethnic population who are "part-African, part-European, part-Asian, part-Native American," but yet collectively proclaim themselves as the "Caribbeans" (Nettleford 2009). That the peoples in the region identify themselves as Caribbeans, is further evident from the waves of emigration of people from the Caribbean region during the second half of the 20th century—one in the 1960s and the other in the 1990s totaling around 5 million—who today are a manifestly visible "Caribbean Diaspora" with its characteristic cultural symbols and life-style and spread widely across North America (ECLAC 2006). This diversity of peoples of all colours settled in the Caribbean and speak a multitude of languages—from Spanish, English, Dutch, and French to a number of Creole languages including Hindi, Bhojpuri, and Urdu. Most religions of the world can also be located in the Caribbean. Thus the people co-exist in combinations of race, religion, language and culture.

Delineating the Caribbean

Geographically speaking, the clusters of island-countries astride the Gulf of Mexico are recognized unquestionably as constituents of the Caribbean region. They are divided into four major groups: i) Greater Antilles consisting of Cuba, Jamaica, Dominican Republic, Haiti (in *Hispañola*) and Puerto Rico; ii) Lesser Antilles, an arc of islands that stretches from the Virgin Islands in the north to Grenada in the south; iii) the southern coastal islands such as Trinidad and Tobago, Aruba, Bonaire and Curacao; and iv) The Bahamas, an archipelago comprising some 700 islands, 2000 rocks and cays which geographically are not in the Caribbean but more in the western Atlantic Ocean. Yet neither the physical terrain nor the surrounding waters is the single defining feature of the region. Even some of the South American mainland countries such as Guyana and Suriname in the circum-Caribbean Sea claim Caribbean identity on grounds of common ethno-history and political economy while Venezuela claims the dual status of being both a South American and a Caribbean country because of its over-arching proximity as well as its security and economic interests/concerns in the region.

Despite their small size in terms of territory, in all the 28 entities of the insular Caribbean have an aggregate population of 36 million. Of them, twenty countries have population of less than one million with a regional birth rate average around 3 per cent. The region is endowed with significant mineral resources—bauxite, gold, diamonds and nickel—and also in plantation crops such as sugar cane and banana. However, these resources are not evenly spread across the region. Only Trinidad and Tobago and to a lesser extent Barbados have oil industries while exploration is under way in Cuba and Guyana. The oil refineries in these countries cater to the needs of South and North America. While bauxite is mined commercially in the Dominican Republic, Guyana, Jamaica and Suriname, Haiti's bauxite deposits are yet to be commercially exploited. Large quantities of nickel are mined in Cuba and the Dominican Republic along with marginal quantities of gold. Gold deposits in Guyana and Belize are yet to be commercially produced. Most of the countries of the Caribbean are engaged in a variety of plantation crops such as sugar cane, bananas and coconuts. In addition to the natural endowments constituting the mainstay of the Caribbean economy, over the years a booming service sector largely confined to tourism and offshore banking have become quite productive in the region. For example, apart from the Bahamas, today Barbados, Antigua, and Belize rank strong in offshore banking services.

Given their resource endowments, the economies of the Caribbean region are considerably diverse. Strong colonial influences in the past have also contributed to this diversity. Yet what marks the Caribbean region is its long history of regional cooperation. Over the past decades, the Caribbean states have made efforts to integrate their economies and increase their combined voting power in multilateral organizations. The major regional organizations are the Caribbean Community (CARICOM), the Association of Caribbean States (ACS), and the Organization of Eastern Caribbean States (OECS), a sub-regional grouping of six eastern Caribbean countries and three UK dependent territories. CARICOM is predominantly the English-speaking Caribbean plus Suriname and Haiti, comprising 15 members. The ACS represents the Greater Caribbean, consisting of 25 members (including some Central and South American countries). While CARICOM focuses on enhancing greater regional integration and a single market economy through the Caribbean Single Market and Economy (CSME), the ASC has broader aims of regional cooperation and addressing regional issues such as sustainable tourism, disaster management, transport and trade. The OECS is dedicated to economic harmonization and integration, protection of human and legal rights, and the encouragement of good governance. The future of CARICOM has been much debated in the Caribbean. With a weakened structure and economic retrenchment, CARICOM, according to some scholars, is said to be in crisis (Stoneman, Pollard and Inniss 2011, 7). At the same time, CARICOM is also seen as the only viable alternative for substantial regional benefits (Griffith, Girvan *et al.* 2012).

More important is the geo-political location of the Caribbean region. Spanning the narrow water divide between North and South America, the region is crisscrossed by a number of international sea lanes, the control and maintenance of which have always remained vital for the major powers on both sides of the Atlantic Ocean. It is no wonder therefore that the Caribbean has been of great strategic importance to the European colonizing powers in the past as it has been to the industrially advanced countries in contemporary times, each rivaling with the other to keep at least a toe-hold in the region.

Asiatic Connections of the Caribbean

It is no mere political rhetoric to state that the history of Asia's contact with the Caribbean has been long and enduring. In fact, Asia's connections with the Caribbean can be traced as far back to the turn of the 15th century when Christopher Columbus anchored off on what is today the Dominican Republic; he firmly believed that the land he touched in the voyage was the spice-rich western coast of India and on that basis assumed that the native inhabitants of the island were the Asiatic ethnic Indians.[1] In subsequent centuries, European seafarers, mostly the Dutch and the Portuguese, who carried an active ocean-going trade across the Pacific, were instrumental in establishing commercial contacts with Asia. It is these early commercial transactions that led, among others, to the spread of sugar-cane culture from India to the Caribbean (Jadeja 1988). The introduction of sugar-cane culture significantly transformed the social profile and the economic prospects of most of the Caribbean countries, and eventually paved the way following the abolition of African slavery for a new trading relationship between British India and those in the Caribbean. Notable among this was the importation of indentured agricultural labour to the Caribbean beginning in the 1830s. This system of bonded labour was eventually abolished in the first quarter of the 20th century, largely the result of the well-orchestrated political campaign launched by the Indian National Congress against the British colonial administration.[2] Today, in Guyana and Trinidad and Tobago ethnic Indians comprise about forty per cent of the population whereas in adjacent Suriname they constitute a little more than one-third.[3] Smaller percentages are found elsewhere in the region such as in Jamaica, the Bahamas and Guadeloupe.

The presence of a large number Indians had facilitated strong cultural and travel contacts between India and these Caribbean countries and contributed to the emergence of an embryonic ethnic market catering to the needs of the Indians seeking to perpetuate their native life-style in cuisines, costumes and related cultural rituals in the Caribbean. With demand for such products increasing, much of which could not be met locally, commercial relationships with India gradually evolved. During the inter-war period of 1920s and 1930s, according to some accounts, tradesmen from India primarily interested in the tourist trade had set up their businesses in some of these countries and exerted considerable commercial influence in the region (Kirpalani 1945, 103-105). In the process, new areas for business relationship with India mushroomed. Of them, one that merits mention is Indian cinema.

With the decolonization process gathering momentum in the region since the 1960s and with the subsequent establishment of diplomatic relations between India and the newly independent countries of the Caribbean, opportunity and scope for further strengthening of bilateral relations became evident. Although these had not translated into strong and sustained trade links between India and the Caribbean region, bilateral relations grew at other levels—academic exchanges and sport activities (importantly cricket).[4]

While the socio-cultural historical links are very important, recent trends show that there is a greater potential for economic links through trade that exists between India and the Caribbean. China is already a major economic player in the world including in the Caribbean, but with its growing middle class India's population is likely to surpass that of China by 2030 and therefore is a large market (ECLAC 2011, 11). Similarly, the Caribbean countries have weathered the recent world financial crisis relatively well and have recovered faster and thus should be taken more seriously as playing a larger role in the world economy. India's trade balance with Latin America and the Caribbean has averaged 117 million dollars between 2008-2010 while its trade balance with the Caribbean countries alone is 41 million dollars in the same period (ECLAC 2011, 50). India's foreign direct investment in Latin America and the Caribbean is about 4 per cent of its total, however, of this, 70 per cent has gone to the British Virgin Islands and the Cayman Islands alone (ECLAC 2011, 44). This scenario exists because the major share of these investments is directed towards tax haven countries.

Having the advantage of a sizeable Indian diasporic community in the region along with the natural complementarities of products for trade with the region, it is time that India seeks closer cooperation and explore further avenues for interaction—

both bilateral and multilateral—based on mutuality of interests and concerns with the Caribbean countries.

Towards Unravelling the Caribbean

Given the region's multifaceted importance, Indian academics and policy-makers have come to recognize the vital need to focus closer attention on the Caribbean. This recognition has become even more evident in light of the current global economic climate. While India has had some historical ties with countries south of Rio Grande, comparatively speaking, the Caribbean thus far has not received much academic attention.

The present book is a result of such line of thinking. It is an attempt to paint and project the Caribbean on a broad canvass with a few strokes that reveal, in some depth, the unexplored dimensions in order to develop a modest understanding of the region. Questions that run through at least implicitly in the different chapters of the compendium are: What are challenges that the Caribbean confronts? How vital is the Caribbean in global affairs today?

The first chapter provides a good starting point to get an idea of the many approaches to the evolving "Caribbeans" (in plural) in the present time. Here, Timothy Shaw attempts to demolish the archaic and outdated ideas about the Caribbean and points out the resilience and vulnerabilities of the region; he takes the new regionalism(s) approach to suggest a "range of possible futures" for the Caribbean which, among others, includes the informal and the illegal. In the second chapter, Andy Knight examines the myriad relationships of the contemporary Caribbean to the West; he anticipates that the Caribbean in the decades ahead will be closely linked to the West. He argues that the resulting complex network of relations will be further compounded by "the increasing levels of interdependence and the exponential increase in processes of globalization and globalism."

In the larger context of the rise of China and India, Satnarine Balkaransingh (Chapter 3) and Wang Guo-An and Nan Yang (Chapter 4) outline the current emphasis in the Caribbean's relationship with the East, which is mainly factored on trade. Balkaransingh emphasizes the manner in which Trinidad has over the decades deepened its cultural, historical and trade links with India. Wang Guo-An and Nan Yang draw attention to the role of China in the Caribbean (and Latin America), pointing out the various dimensions of trade and cooperation over time and prescribe strategies to further improve the existing relations. They predict a great potential for Sino-Caribbean economic cooperation and trade. These discussions are significant especially in the light of concerns aired by some Latin American scholars regarding the growing economic weight and influence of China and India in the world economy (Phillips 2009; Heine 2009; Lederman, Olarreaga and Perry 2009). Emerging as two giant economies both countries, it is argued, would draw very heavily on the natural resources of Latin America and the Caribbean and thereby push the countries of the region back to their traditional role of suppliers of raw materials to the industrially advancing countries. However, Latin America does have a positive balance of trade as the prices of these raw materials rise with increase in demand (Heine 2009, 129). Following China, India too is fast becoming a major importer and consumer of primary products being produced by the Latin American and Caribbean region (for details see ECLAC 2011, 27).

A perennial issue of concern for both scholars and policy makers relates to the pace and process of development in the Caribbean. Drawing especially on Guyana, in the fifth chapter, Kalowatie Deonandan argues that Foreign Direct Investments (FDI) by the Emerging Economies in megaprojects in Guyana have had a detrimental impact on the country's development. She illustrates the ways in which they undermine good governance, bring limited economic benefits to the state, harm the environment, and violate human rights. The government, she points out, is limited in its ability in some respects given the constraints of poverty and unemployment within which it has to operate. Priti Singh in Chapter 6 attempts to unravel the development-poverty nexus and associated problems, and underlines the centrality of political processes in shaping outcomes. Based on that, she implicitly underscores how the tradition of democratic governance in some of the English-speaking Caribbean countries has been able to face the challenge of underdevelopment and poverty better than the rest of the countries of the region.

Since development and economics play an important role in the Caribbean, Samantha Joseph, Martin Franklin, and Roger Hosein in Chapter 7 explore the roles Caribbean embassies can play in bridging the gap between the Caribbean diaspora and the home country to accelerate growth and investments in the region. Natasha Parkins in the eighth chapter focuses on the causal factors of emigration from the Caribbean, especially of the highly skilled labour which in recent years has reached alarming proportions. Elaborating further, she analyzes in depth the emigration trends in relation to the push and pull factors in Jamaica. In so doing, she also brings to light the inability of the state to provide adequate human security given its already abridged role and resources in order to create an environment that is secure and productive for the citizenry. Building on the importance of the diasporic community, Satya Pattnayak in Chapter 9 examines the dynamics of the diasporic ethnic identity formation of Indians in Suriname, Guyana, and Trinidad in a comparative context. He undertakes this comparison while "[k]eeping in mind the world historical significance of the past overseas migration of Indians." He argues that although all three countries went through similar historical experiences of Indian indenture labour importation by the European colonial regimes, the outcomes were very different in each case. What is more, with globalization, the Caribbean Indians, exposed to the multitude of representations of "Indianness" in other settings, are likely to engage in much exploration of comparative Indian identity.

Globalization has impacted on identities in many ways. Rhoda Reddock in Chapter 10 offers a fascinating analysis on the ways in which the processes of the current "globalization" (markedly economic in dimension) have impacted on the gender identities. She is of the view that the identities—both masculine and feminine—are constantly evolving and are at the same time inventing new and creative realities in the Caribbean region. What is important to note here according to her is that globalization of Caribbean culture is not possible on its own terms, but only through the route of the USA or to a lesser extent the United Kingdom.

Other aspects of the Caribbean that are discussed in this compendium include the role of sports as a catalyst for deepening the integration of the Caribbean countries. In Chapter 11, Roger Hosein, Jeetendra Khadan, and Nicholas Paul discuss at length the centrality of sport to the Caribbean region. They are of the view that sport is an important element of the Caribbean and for augmenting social cohesiveness and developing multilateral relations within the region the tradition of sports needs to be harnessed more effectively. Thus, the authors offer suggestions for evolving a regional policy framework for Caribbean sports.

Sustainable development calls for the positive role of the family as a social unit. In Chapter 12, Jaipaul Roopnarine and Ambika

Krishnakumar discuss in depth the evolution of the family as an institution and the socio-historical experiences of the Afro- and Indo-Caribbean families. Focusing on violence and child maltreatment at home, optimal parenting issues and mental health delivery systems, the authors are of the view that addressing these issues can have a positive impact not only on the individual but also on the family and community relationships, building solid social and economic institutions.

Familial care has assumed critical importance in policy making especially in the less developed and least developed countries, some of which are located in the Caribbean. Given that most countries have abandoned the welfare state tradition under the spell of globalization, the issue of familial care is posing a new social challenge. In Chapter 13, Linden Lewis reviews the rather unsatisfactory track record of the Caribbean region in dealing with this issue and calls for a new social contract based on the concept of gender equality so as to alleviate the burdens placed on girls and women when it comes to the burden of care.

David Gomez and Hari Nair, in Chapter 14, analyze the concept of "transculturation" derived from the works of Fernando Ortiz in the context of understanding the socio-cultural landscape of Cuba. Ortiz had explained history as a complex interaction of multiple cultures in an attempt to understand the cultural processes that took place in Cuba as well as within the larger context of the Caribbean. Thus Gomez and Nair attempt to illustrate the value and relevance of Ortiz to the contemporary context.

The book concludes with a focus on crime and security in the region, something that has been very painstaking for Caribbean people and states. Focusing on Haiti as a case study, Aparajita Gangopadhyay in Chapter 15 raises the question of what is important for Haiti—political stability and security or humanitarian concerns? She points to the "support from international donors" that Haiti requires in order to reconstruct the country, but also acknowledges Haiti's lack of "strategic value" in the current global order for powers such as the United States. The chapter thus raises the issue of the "note of despondency" and the larger challenge that is posed not just to Haiti but to regional security in the Caribbean. In Chapter 16, Ramesh Deosaran gives a succinct overview of the criminal justice system and crime in Trinidad and Tobago. Raymond Izarali, in the concluding chapter, sketches an overview of crime, violence, and terrorism in the Caribbean.

It need hardly be said that this compendium by no means claims to be a definitive and comprehensive analysis of the contemporary Caribbean. At best it is a modest contribution to a rudimentary understanding of the Caribbean region in some of its multifaceted dimensions. While certain themes have been highlighted and dealt with in some depth, it has not been possible to cover many other but no less significant dimensions of the region. Admittedly, there is an imperative need for a more exhaustive and intense effort at unraveling the multidimensionality of the Caribbean region.

Notes

1. So came into vogue the expression 'Indies'. Later when it came to be known that where Columbus had landed was not the western India, it was changed to 'West Indies'.
2. It was in May of 1838 the first shipload of Indian immigrants arrived in Guyana (then known as British Guiana). Between 1838 and 1917, when indentured labour importation to the British Caribbean ceased, about 500,000 ethnic Indians had come to the former British colonies in the region. Except for about 37,000, who landed in Jamaica, and 34,000 who landed in Suriname between 1873 and 1916, most of the rest moved to two British colonies: Guiana and Trinidad and Tobago.
3. East Indians comprised 43.5 per cent of the population of Guyana according to the 2002 census. See http://www.statisticsguyana.gov.gy/pubs Chapter2_Population_Composition.pdf. In Trinidad and Tobago, according to the 1990 government census, East Indians comprised 40.3 per cent of the population. See < http://www. populstat.info/Americas/trinidtg.htm>.
4. One of the earliest instances of such bilateral relations was the establishment of the Indian Studies "Chair" at the St. Augustine campus in mid-1960s, an initiative that owes it to an informal discussion between Trinidad's first Prime Minister Dr. Eric Williams and India's Prime Minister Jawaharlal Nehru.

1

How Many Caribbeans in 2020: Vulnerable? Resilient? Informal? and/or Illegal?

Timothy M. Shaw

> ...the circulation of commodities is one of the unifying aspects of Caribbean history... Globalization has not just happened to the Caribbean, The Caribbean has participated in the making of globalization...four things...circulate: people, capital, drugs and information.
>
> (*Bronfman* 2007, 5-6)

> What constitutes the Caribbean?...Among scholars, "the Caribbean" is a socio-historical category...it embraces the islands and parts of the adjoining mainland—and may be extended to include the Caribbean Diaspora overseas. As one scholar observes, there are many Caribbeans...
>
> In short, the definition of the Caribbean might be based on language and identity, geography, history and culture, geopolitics, geoeconomics, or organisation.
>
> (*Girvan* 2005, 304)

This chapter juxtaposes a set of "transnational" relations—families, civil societies, supply chains, crime networks and governance nexuses—with fluid definitions of "regionalisms." Both approaches include economic, ecological, social and state relations, both formal and informal; i.e., more or less recognized and recorded. Together these seem to fit or resonate in the case of today's Caribbean(s) as both perspectives develop their own compatible genres such as "transnational studies" (Keohane and Nye 1971, Khagram and Levitt 2007) and new regionalisms (Shaw, Grant and Cornelissen 2011). Together they can advance analyses of both the transnational and the regional—i.e., beyond the state and below the global—to suggest a range of possible futures for the Caribbeans before the end of the second decade of the present century as indicated in the concluding paragraphs.

Given the contemporary variety of regional visions on offer at the start of the second decade of the 21st century, the adoption of a "new" regionalisms perspective on today's Caribbean would seem to be quite sensible and compatible with transnational approaches (Shaw, Grant and Cornelissen 2011). Orthodox frameworks cannot capture the diversity and dynamism of current regional connections: not just micro-, meso- or macro-levels or inter- and non-state but also increasingly informal and illegal at all levels and in all sectors. And enquiring into the interconnections among these three or four distinct yet interrelated "regions" also challenges traditional disciplinary approaches as indicated in f) below. Furthermore, inter-regional relations are also of growing salience, however duplicative or competitive rather than compatible or cooperative, reflective of the proliferation of regions at all levels. This is especially so around the European Union (EU), such as Asia-Europe Meeting (ASEM) (Gaens 2008), Economic Partnership Agreements (EPAs) (De Lombaerde and Schulz 2009, Laursen 2010), Mediterranean (Zank 2009) etc. as reflected in analysis by the FP6 Garnet Network of Excellence and now Network on Regional Integration Studies (NETRIS) (www.garnet-eu.org; www.netris-acp.org) (accessed January 23, 2011). The distinctive, divergent character of regions has intensified as the current "global" financial crisis has impacted them differently. For example, Asia has been less affected than either the EU, North American Free Trade Agreement (NAFTA) or the North Atlantic (Shaw 2010a).

(a) Many Regionalisms; Many Caribbeans?

The "Caribbean" can be more narrowly and broadly defined, from some/all of the heterogeneous islands to islands and mainland Central America—*el gran caribe*—to the diasporas. In formal intergovernmental institutional terms, this means progressing from the Organization of Eastern Caribbean States (OECS) through the Caribbean Community (CARICOM) and UN Caribbean

Development and Cooperation Committee (CDCC) to Association of Caribbean States (ACS). But in terms of non-state actor definitions, it means Caribbean Policy Development Centre (CPDC) to Regional Coordination for Economic and Social Research (CRIES) and Caribbean Studies Association (CSA) for civil society and for the private sector from Unilever to Nestle, Republic Bank to RBC or Scotiabank, Caribbean Airlines to Copa, B-Mobile and Flow to Digicel.

Certainly the spill-over from the current crisis in the form of the demise of CLICO and Stanford corporate empires has had a continuing negative impact (ECLAC 2009). And cutting across such geospatial and economic networks are linguistic communities: anglophone, francophone, Dutch and Spanish along with several creoles. However, while some analysts have recognized such diversity in the formal political economy extending to the diasporic, few have extended their analysis to the informal and illegal. Thus arguably just two chapters out of the 37 in the encyclopedic reader on *The Caribbean Economy* by Dennis Pantin (2005) address levels of interaction/integration (#14 by Norman Girvan) or diasporas/remittances (#29 by Wendell Samuel). This chapter seeks to go beyond such orthodoxies particularly given the spill-over from the informal and illegal and especially as this spill-over takes place in a period of global economic turmoil and contraction.

The new regionalism(s) perspective (Shaw, Grant and Cornelissen 2011) has itself generated a debate about the informal and illegal with earlier and more formal analyses which at the end of the last century tended to exclude these even in its framework of new regionalism (singular!) (Hettne and Inotai 1994; Hettne, Inotai and Sunkel 1999). Here, however, I take the informal and illegal to be inseparable from the formal and legal in terms of definitions and implications of Caribbean relations in the second decade of the 21st century (Shaw 2010a).

Symbolic of the contrast between the formal and informal, the legal and illegal is the irony of *de facto* free trade in drugs and guns by contrast to myriad *de jure* restrictions on trade in legitimate goods. So the CARICOM Single Market and Economy (CSME) has been largely stillborn whereas, despite efforts of the uniformed services, organized crime flourishes. Similarly, informal sector traders—ubiquitous "higglers"—circumvent myriad obstacles even when regular supply chains cannot. As well, private security companies—both local and global, legal and otherwise—are also increasingly being substituted for ineffective official police.

The borderline between legal and illegal, formal and informal is of great importance in the Caribbean given the fine line between, say, offshore banking and money laundering (Vlcek 2008), jewelry and property development; hence the articulation and advocacy of regulation in a mistaken attempt to prevent such leakages. Such ambiguous borders are everywhere including Geneva and London and the Channel Islands between Britain and France, but it is the Caribbean islands which receive undue attention such as both British & US Virgin Islands. Hence the evolution of international efforts at regulation from OECD Harmful Tax to Financial Action Task Force (FATF) (www.fatf-gafi.org) of some 40 states including the Caribbean office of another 30 established in Trinidad and Tobago in the early-1990s (www.cfatf-gafic.org) (accessed January 23, 2011) and on to Tax Information Exchange Agreements (TIEAs). And then the mix of the Obama Administration and the global financial crisis resulted in the establishment of a Global Forum on Transparency and Exchange of Information to monitor/peer review, again as another formality or requirement. Moreover, there is a rich variety of island jurisdictions, both independent and otherwise, from Jersey and Mauritius to Barbados, Bermuda, Caymans and Trinidad and Tobago; hence the imperative of forms of compliance by the end of the first decade of the 21st century.

Non-independent Overseas Territories (OTs) like other Small Island Developing States (SIDS) seek to minimize vulnerability and maximize resilience (Bishop 2011). In parallel to small states in Central Asia and Central Europe, they have continued to proliferate in numbers, most recently on 10-10-10 the Dutch Antilles splitting into three: two "autonomous countries" in the Netherlands—Curacao and St Maarten—and a trio remaining "special municipalities" of the Netherlands: Bonaire, Saba and St Eustatius. The diplomatic status of old and new OTs is problematic but some of them do have associate status in regional or hemispheric networks like the ACS and/or UN Economic Commission for Latin America and the Caribbean (ECLAC) as well as in some Commonwealth institutions like the Commonwealth Parliamentary Association (CPA) and Commonwealth Games.

Some of the diversity of the Caribbean can be captured in several sets of contemporary regional indicators, from GDP per capita and Human Development Index (HDI) to competitiveness and homicide rates. Here I concentrate on the seven Most

Developed Countries (MDC) identified by the Caribbean Development and Cooperation Committee (CDCC) of ECLAC (www.eclac.org/portofspain) (accessed January 24, 2011): Bahamas, Barbados, Belize, Guyana, Jamaica, Suriname and Trinidad and Tobago; this sub-branch of ECLAC includes nine "associated states" from amongst the Overseas Caribbean Territories (OCTs) drawn from the British, Dutch and US islands, several of which play important communications and financial roles, both legal and otherwise.

Per capita PPP incomes in the Caribbean stretch from US$23 507 for Trinidad and Tobago to $1 155 for Haiti through Barbados at $17 966, Suriname at $7 813, Cuba at $6 876, Dominican Republic at $6 706, Jamaica at $6 079 and Guyana at $2 782. The region likewise is mid-rank along the WEF's Global Competitiveness Index (out of 133 countries ranked) (www3.weforum.org) (accessed 28 May 2011): Puerto Rico at No. 42 and Barbados at No. 44 lead with Suriname (No. 102) and Guyana (No. 104) trailing; in mid-field, Trinidad and Tobago is No. 86, Jamaica No. 91 and Dominican Republic No. 95. The region scores quite well in terms of the UNDP Human Development Index in 2009, being concentrated in the High and Medium HD categories: Barbados is the only one categorized as Very High at No. 37 out of 182; otherwise the range is Antigua and Barbuda at No. 47 to Haiti at No. 149, with Cuba at No. 51, Trinidad and Tobago at No. 64, Suriname at No. 97, Jamaica at No. 100 and Guyana at No. 114 (http://hdr.undp.org) (accessed January 23, 2011).

In terms of homicide rates, however, the region presents impressive statistics, with Jamaica's 59.5 per 100 000 in 2008 (Harriott 2003) being just below the highest one from Honduras at 60.9, while Trinidad and Tobago at 39.7 (UNODC 2010b: 27 and 237) beats out Colombia at 38.8; St Kitts at 35.32 just trails South Africa's 36.5. Other high rates are reported for Anguilla at 27.6, Dominican Republic at 21.5 and Puerto Rico at 20.4, with the lowest levels coming from the Bahamas at 13.7 and Barbados at 8.7; the US rate is 5.2 per 100000 population (www.unodc.org) (accessed May 28, 2011).

Symptomatic of the well-established yet heterogeneous transnational Caribbean in the North was a major police raid in Toronto in May 2010 by a thousand police officers leading to the arrest of some 80 alleged members of the Jamaican "Shower Posse" gang or network ahead of the month-long "battle" around Tivoli Gardens in West Kingston for the arrest and extradition of

Christopher "Dudus" Coke. He was eventually arrested and extradited to the US before the end of June 2010. In short, the diaspora contains diverse social elements from labourers and professionals to religious fundamentalists and hardened criminals though the overwhelming majority are well-established and respected members of extended transnational families.

(b) Transnational Families

> "The creation of Caribbean transnational networks rests on the foundation of a transnational family, in which migrants and their families have multiple home bases with ongoing commitments and loyalties that straddle territorial boundaries." (*Wiltshire* 2006, 175)

Contemporary as well as historical migration has been very uneven throughout the Caribbean (Reis 2004, Thomas-Hope 2009) with recent outflows being most significant from the mainland rather than islands: from Guyana to North America and from Suriname to the Netherlands (some 200-250 000 now in the Dutch diaspora versus 450 000 at home) with growing implications for "multiculturalism" in such countries and communities. There are estimated to be as many Guyanese in the US, especially NYC, and Canada, particularly Scarborough ON, as at home: +/- 700 000 each. Their presence along with technological changes has led to a dramatic rise in communications, such as phone conversations, especially using mobiles and phonecards, and airline flights, with remittances growing from $20m in 2000 to $200m mid-decade. Guyana's reliance on remittances is highest in LAC, even higher than Haiti (IDB 2009, 10): a quarter of GDP. The situation is similar for Jamaica: some one million abroad and less than three million at home, with remittances totaling $2 billion in mid-2000s, some 20 per cent of GDP (World Bank 2008). For example, in 2007, per capita remittance flows were highest to Jamaica ($790) and lowest to Trinidad and Tobago ($69); Grenada received $524 per person; Guyana $377; and Suriname $305 (UNDP 2009a, 160). Thus Western Union, Money Gram and Grace Kennedy have become ubiquitous in diasporic communities in the North and capital cities in the South even if remittance flows have been under pressure, particularly from the US because of the financial crisis at the turn of the decade.

Remittances to LAC grew throughout almost all of the first decade of the 21st century but peaked in 2006-2008, declining in 2009 back to 2005 levels as a reflection of the knock-on effects of the global financial crisis as diasporas' incomes shrank, particularly in the trans-Atlantic centres of the US and UK, causing remittance flows to likewise decline. However, when inflation is factored in, remittances in local currencies may have actually increased in 2009. Moreover, stabilization in flows is anticipated in 2010 (IDB 2009, 3).

We can deduce from the above data on remittances that transnational Caribbean families can be considered as integral to the evolution of transnational civil society focused on the region, facilitating the two-way flows of communications, ideas, events, fashions, technologies etc. (Scher 2009) so the Caribbean is rarely out of touch with metropolitan developments or *vice versa;* interaction and influence are seemless and endless, however uneven.

(c) Transnational Civil Society

> "The Caribbean is a unique and complex concatenation of virtually every ethnic group in the world...
>
> Far more interesting than the individual contributions of the various groups constituting the contemporary Caribbean is the process whereby their sociopolitical traits have been amalgamated and Eurocentric dominance has been mitigated. The region has truly been a crucible of various cultures. This blending, not only of institutions but also of ethnicity, has produced the uniquely Caribbean Creoles." (Hillman 2009, 11 and 12)

The digital revolution has transformed both the political economy and social culture of the Caribbean, which is especially evident in a trio of "transformative processes: the introduction of cellular telephones, the adoption of the Internet, and the proliferation of offshore gambling sites" (Bronfman 2007, 12); on the latter, see Andrew Cooper (2011) on *Internet Gambling Offshore* on the rise and fall of Antigua under bilateral US pressure which the World Trade Organization (WTO) has been unable to contain.

Given contemporary communications, especially the mobile phone revolution, diasporas can make powerful demands with respect to development and democracy back home constituting a potential "foreign policy" impact in the North (cf f) below). Such leverage constitutes an aspect of double "public diplomacy": both inside and about the Caribbean (see also f) below), symbolized by the last months in office as Governor General in Canada of Michaelle-Jean who was a "celebrity diplomat" for her native Haiti after its early-2010 earthquake leading to her post-retirement appointment as a UNESCO Ambassador. Note also the proliferation of myriad Home Town Associations of ordinary citizens, most active when natural disasters hit home, as in diasporic responses to the earthquake in Haiti in early-2010.

Without being too parochial or sentimental, we should recognise even as we debate, the centrality of the University of the West Indies (UWI) in keeping the foundation of CARICOM intact and reinforced even if increasingly virtually via the Open Campus (www.uwi.edu) (accessed May 28, 2011) (Brereton 2010). This is apparent in numerous UWI-CARICOM functional relations symbolized by the CARICOM-UWI project on regional development (Hall and Chuck-A-Sang 2010) which built on established Caribbean intellectual accomplishments and histories (Girvan 2006; Meeks and Girvan 2010). There are also myriad art forms and carnivals over centuries (Mohammed 2009) now being circulated through the digital revolution. In short, the mix of established and novel communities and technologies continues to advance and accelerate communication within and around transnational civil society in the Caribbeans as elsewhere—i.e., democratic processes and pressures in countries and communities of both origin and adoption (Thomas-Hope 2009; World Bank 2008).

Just as transnational Caribbean civil society has well-established historical roots, so too the region's supply chains go back centuries, including the flow of forced as well as free people.

(d) Transnational Supply Chains

> "...the circulation of commodities is one of the unifying aspects of Caribbean history. All islands are shaped by things that circulate, and more so in the recent past, when aspects of globalization have made it easier for things to circulate at greater quantities and greater speed."
>
> (*Bronfman* 2007, 5)

Supply chains around the region have evolved from barrels to containers and airfreight/couriers using cell phones and tracking devices so each brand's communications hub is quite apparent from the distinctive routing. And personal postboxes are bought in Miami to be used as offshore addresses.

Regional and global hubs rise and fall around older and newer supply chains (Gibbon, Ponte and Lazaro 2010), and are impacted by technological, infrastructural as well as security developments (e.g., expansion of the Panama Canal and associated container ports or Copa in Panama City as well as Caribbean Airlines in Port of Spain, now incorporating Air Jamaica): i.e., from spices to drugs, cutlasses to guns, pirates to gangs, gunpowder to AK47s, depending on supply and demand, regulations and enforcement. So we can identify novel forms of supply chains given the "other" side of globalization including intellectual property violations via pirated CDs and "applications" (Naim 2006). Conversely, extra-territorial EU and US rules tend to impact goods and services (Gibbon, Ponte and Lazaro 2010), compounded by diasporic demands/expectations in the North. So transnational supply chains have to negotiate between global standards and global subversion (e.g., Nollywood).

But the current global crisis has also exposed challenges of economic/corporate governance in the region given pressures of liberalization, competition, etc.: CLICO, Stanford, TCL. New forms of effective transnational governance are needed to restore financial confidence for both regional and global communities and customers.

(e) Transnational Crime Networks

> "Illicit flows of all kinds have been part of the Caribbean's history. Goods have circulated to the region, from the region, and through the region." (*Bronfman* 2007, 8)

> "Jamaica occupies a unique place in the history of illicit flows because both marijuana and cocaine move in and out of the island." (*Bronfman* 2007, 12)

Caribbean and related transnational crime have evolved from spices to drugs and cutlasses to guns, to gunpowder and AK47s: from pirates to druglords (Griffith 2004, Harriott 2003, UNODC 2010b). In turn, it has encouraged the parallel development of comparative analysis and policy at the turn of the century (Bagley and Walker 1994; Fiorentini and Peltzman 1997; Friman and Andreas 1999; Friman 2009; Madsen 2009). In response, policy discussions have generated inter-governmental institutions like CARICOM-IMPACS (Implementation Agency for Crime and Security) (www.caricomimpacs.org) (accessed January 23, 2011) and professional networks like the Association of Caribbean Commissioners of Police (ACCP) (www.accpolice.org) and Caribbean Association of Judicial Officers (CAJO) (www.thecajo.org) (both accessed January 24, 2011).

The value of drugs increases the further they are away from production, where their value is low; their value multiplies 200 times between production and retail levels especially when they move from South to North. So although the Caribbean may be of decreasing importance in such global supply chains, the value of the global drugs trade is still greater than 90 per cent of the world's national GDPs including all islands in the Caribbean (UNODC 2010a and b). Hence the spread of narcostates or shadow states into the Caribbean with their distinctive state-economy balances (Friman and Andreas 1999, Harriott 2003, Naim 2006, Naylor 2005). As noted already, legal remittances (IBRD 2006, IDB 2009) and illegal money-laundering (Naylor 2005) have together attracted G8 and OECD attention, leading to Caribbean Financial Action Task Force (CFATF) (UNODC 2010a, Vlcek 2008).

Meanwhile, as confidence in state security organizations declines, the private security sector has expanded and diversified, both national (e.g., Guardsman in Jamaica and northern Caribbean (www.guardsmangroup.com)) and global (e.g., G4S (www.g4s.com)): but who/how to regulate private security companies at national, regional and global levels?

Interestingly, the UNDP (2009b) has begun to advocate the notion of "citizen security" to advance freedom from fear in region. And the proposed 2011 regional HDR on citizen security based on end-2010 surveys should lead beyond generic notions of human security/development given threats in the region, especially the Caribbean and Central America: another, distinctive form of "new" regionalism?

Together, these underline the imperative of informed, flexible "transnational governance" responses to burgeoning transnational relations, formal/legal as well as informal/illegal.

(f) Transnational Governance

> "While private authority beyond the state has become a popular theme of academic writing, the role of stakeholders in the Southern hemisphere as objects and subjects of private transnational governance has rarely been addressed in the literature." (*Dingwerth* 2008, 607)

"Transnational studies" (Khagram and Levitt 2007) have begun to juxtapose or situate several disciplines, genres or strands: capital, civil society, class, consumption, culture, informal sectors including gangs/drugs/guns, logistics, migration/diasporas/remittances, sports, supply chains etc. A central subfield can be identified as "transnational governance," which can be considered a generic set of responses to novel and emerging "global" issues. Given its characteristic inclusion of non-state actors, it is also referred to as "private transnational governance" (Dingwerth 2008), "non-state transnational transfers" (Brown 2009) or "non-state market-driven" governance (Bernstein and Cashore 2008). It is usually "hybrid" in character, typically involving a changing range of heterogeneous actors, non-state as well as state, acting in partnerships as in the classic International Campaign to Ban Landmines (ICBL) leading to the "Ottawa Process" on landmines. The rich variety of such alliances, campaigns, certification schemes, codes, commissions, councils, initiatives, networks, partnerships and processes are captured in tables in Dingwerth (2008, 628-630) and Bernstein and Cashore (2008, 281-283).

Such transnational or "global governance" can be treated as an extension or contemporary form of established international law/organization, which remain primarily, even exclusively inter-governmental. These have evolved from the Ottawa and Kimberley "Processes" through the Forestry Stewardship Council (FSC) and Marine Stewardship Council (MSC) to Ethical Trading Initiative (ETI) and Extractive Industries Transparency Initiative (EITI) "initiatives" (Bernstein and Cashore 2008, Dingwerth 2008). Thus the rather traditional Law of the Sea (LoS)/SIDS/Alliance of Small Island States (AOSIS) at independence in the 1970s have been superceded by myriad Caribbean/global concerns including climate change in the 21st century onto FSC/MSC/EITI in the second decade of the new century (Gale and Haward 2011).

New forms of governance for the several Caribbeans may lead to alternative futures by the end of the current decade. These were anticipated in advocacy by Trinidad and Tobago of the International Criminal Court (ICC); note the role of ANR Robinson in advancing this global coalition, which has yet to include the US despite endless advocacy.

Contemporary public or network diplomacy (cf part c) above) has been adopted by SIDS to maximize leverage internationally using non-state partners such as private sector and civil society, media and culture. Thus diasporas can impact both home and host policies; hence their transnational leverage. As already noted, Small Island Developing States (SIDS) were very active around independence in LoS negotiations, though largely inter-state in character. But then it became quiet as the bipolar context yielded to multipolarity until the contemporary era of climate change when again engaged, but this time with non-state allies such as INGOs and diasporas (www.acs-aec.org, Shaw 2010a, 96-100).

New governance networks are being developed in service sectors like education, finance, health, telecommunications and tourisms. The Caribbean Association of Industry and Commerce (CAIC) advances such private innovation (cf Iheduru 2011 on private sector in ECOWAS). But tourisms and other services are also very transnational. Recognized varieties include: business, diasporic, ecology, education, medicine, sports tourisms, etc.

Moreover, the Caribbean is also active in inter-regionalisms, often as the "junior" partner, such as the not uncontroversial CARIFORUM-EPA but also links with Mercosur, the Organization of American States (OAS) (Herz 2010) and now Union of South American Nations (UNASUR) in the hemisphere (Mace, Cooper and Shaw 2010) and with the African Union (AU) and Association of Southeast Asian Nations (ASEAN) (Gaens 2008) outside the hemisphere (De Lombaerde and Schulz 2009).

In conclusion, lessons may be derived from as well as for the Caribbean for a variety of analytic perspectives along with their policy implications in addition to new regionalisms such as:

- *development studies*—proliferation of issues and actors, especially around "Asian drivers" like China and India;
- *global governance/multilateralisms*—varieties of actors and interests, especially in "soft" law arenas like fisheries and forest certification;
- *global studies*—going beyond inter- and non-governmental,

even the trans-national, towards global structures (www.theglobalsite.ac.uk), as reflected increasingly in academic programmes, publications, appointments and associations (www.globalstudiesassociation.org; www.globalstudiesfoundation.org) (accessed, May 28, 2011);

- *migration/diasporas/remittances nexus*—looking beyond the movement of people to diasporic communities and cultures, especially remittance flows and novel forms of communications from phone cards and texting (Bronfman 2007: 86-107) to financial and technological flows and Foreign Direct Investment (FDI) along with drugs and guns;
- *regionalisms, old and new*—evolving balance between old and new given post-neoliberal world and proliferating micro-, meso- and macro-level responses to uneven globalization, etc;
- *security studies*—threats to national, human and now citizen security from "old" and "new" factors such as climate change and gang culture (Bronfman 2007, 63-85); and
- *transnational studies*—heterogeneous relations between trans- and inter- and intra-national given changes in state-civil society/private sector relations everywhere leading towards innovative forms of transnational, hybrid governance (Shaw 2010b).

The kaleidoscope of Caribbeans, both contemporary and historical, advances and reinforces notions of varieties of capitalisms and civil societies as well as plurality of regionalisms, reflective of their place in contemporary history in both South and North. It continues to inform debates about the compatibility or competitiveness of such formal and informal, more macro- and more micro-regionalisms, and raises the question: what futures lie ahead for the Caribbean by the end of this decade? Such sceptical reflections should be contrasted with the ideological claims of at least one state—Trinidad and Tobago—that by then it will have become "developed" as symbolised by its assertion, "we're next"!

(g) Many Caribbeans? How Many Futures?

"...there is a need for an interdisciplinary introduction to

> the Caribbean region. Academic, business and policy interests require understanding this complex and significant area, especially in the twenty-first century. But the growing numbers of people who wish to learn about the Caribbean are not able to use narrowly focused studies. Comprehending existing theoretical analyses of the region's socioeconomic and political conditions presupposes expertise and experience." (*Hillman* 2009, 9)

Just as we may identify several Caribbeans, so we may abstract several futures, particularly along the vulnerable and resilient divide (Cooper and Shaw 2009). But this dialectic becomes more problematic or complicated when more informal and illegal—i.e., neither recorded nor taxed or even strictly subject to legal procedure—transnational relations are incorporated with diasporas and remittances becoming increasingly salient. Nevertheless, clearly only a minority of political economies are likely to achieve "developmental" status. The majority will have their prospects largely determined by a mix of regional and global fortunes, increasingly impacted by climate change.

The place and possible transitions around Cuba in the second decade of the 21st century will be quite pivotal, especially in the Northern Caribbean and for its generations of diasporas in Florida and elsewhere in the US reinforcing the "post-neo-liberal" era in the hemisphere (Macdonald and Ruckert 2009) as well as removing one focus of regional cohesion. What directions are likely given the demise of the Washington Consensus in the first decade of the new century and the global crisis at start of the second decade, let alone decline in the Floridian and other parts of the US economy and the rise of the Tea Party?

So, what regional balances exist in the wider Caribbean among macro-, meso- and/or micro-levels is in part a function of balance between the more formal versus more informal. And cycles in the global economy including balances among sectors mean that the rankings of agriculture, education, finance, fisheries, manufacturing, resources, services, trade, transportation etc. are in flux.

Developmental and democratic deficits will persist, moderated by ubiquitous connectivity facilitating continuous transnational communication. And by 2020 if not before Caribbean relations with the emerging economies—the BRICS—will come to balance if not exceed those with the North Atlantic rim. And for much of the

Caribbean, such relations will be more formal—i.e., largely inter-governmental—with China and Russia and more informal/diasporic—i.e., less exclusively inter-governmental—with Brazil and India, now extending to South Africa as it is recognized or promoted to being #5.

I conclude by echoing Girvan (2005, 315):

> If the Caribbean was an invention of the 20th century, it seems certain to be reinterpreted and perhaps transcended in the 21st. The Caribbean of tomorrow will not be an exclusively Anglophone or Hispanic conception; and it will not be tied exclusively to geographic space or definition. If it survives at all, it will be a community of shared economic, social and political interests and strategies that encompasses different languages and cultures and the Caribbean Diaspora.

In short, Caribbean development will continue to be profoundly affected by the five sets of transnational relations identified at the start of this chapter, as well as by broadly recognized and accepted inter- and non-state relations, especially the BRICS.

2

The West in the Caribbean

W. Andy Knight

The contemporary Caribbean is interwoven with the West through history, culture, colonialism, imperialism and trade. But the relationship has always been an asymmetrical one. From its early history, the Caribbean developed a dependency relationship with the Metropole. It was one which put the West at a distinct advantage over the islands of the Caribbean. This chapter begins by defining what is meant by the Caribbean and what is meant by the West. It then provides a cursory examination of the history which ties the Caribbean and the West in an interlocking, but dependency, relationship. Three case studies are used to explore further the nature of the linkages between the Caribbean and the West. The first case study deals with the sugar industry. The second examines the case of tourism. And, the third explores the subject of migration—both legal and irregular. The conclusion reached is that the Caribbean will be, for many decades to come, linked to the West and that the relationship between these two areas will become increasingly complex because of the increasing levels of interdependence and the exponential increase in processes of globalization and globalism.

Defining the Caribbean and the West

The Caribbean

Outsiders from the Caribbean region usually think of this area primarily as a haven for tourists or as a tropical paradise. This is understandable since those who make short vacation visits to that crescent shape group of islands that separate the Gulf of Mexico and Caribbean Sea to the west and south from the Atlantic Ocean to the east and north, are generally impressed by the pleasant climate, soul warming sun, crystal clear waters, and mostly white sandy beaches—all natural attributes that entice tourists to this part of the world. While this stereotypical and superficial image of the Caribbean has been held predominant in the contemporary period, the picture of this region is much more varied and complex when one takes a panoramic historical view of the area. For the purpose of this chapter, the Caribbean includes both the Greater and Lesser Antilles, as well as Guyana (formerly British Guiana) and Suriname (formerly Dutch Guiana) on the North East portion of South America, and Belize (formerly British Honduras) in Central America.[1]

The West

When we speak of "The West," we are generally referring to the Western world or Western civilization—i.e. that Occidental civilization derived from European culture. Western civilization has its roots in Greco-Roman origins, but took on an expansionist character after the commercial revolution between the 16th to 18th century which ignited the desire among Western Europeans to engage in trade and to develop vast trading networks outside of the limited European space. The commercial revolution also sparked economic expansionism, colonialism and mercantilism. This revolution more or less coincided with the scientific revolution of the 16th and 17th century which facilitated the spread of new ideas and knowledge in astronomy, biology, chemistry, medicine and physics. The spread of scientific knowledge transformed medieval views on nature and how the world operated and became the foundation for what is now known as modern science (Grant 1996). Important figures of this period, like Copernicus, Galileo, Kepler, Newton and Vesalius, helped to change the way people in Western Europe thought about their ability to control nature to reach distant lands.

Coming on the heels of the above two revolutions was the industrial revolution of the 18th and 19th century. The industrial revolution, which essentially began in Britain, saw major changes to agricultural techniques, as well as important developments in manufacturing, mining, transportation and technology. It was because of this revolution that new mass markets were created for such items as sugar, tobacco and cotton. The limited agricultural lands in Europe created a demand for lands outside of Europe. Some European countries (like Britain, France, Portugal, Spain, and the Netherlands) colonized what was then known as "the new world." Settler colonies quickly developed in the Caribbean; some changing hands from one colonial power to the next via wars.

The West, for the purposes of this chapter, therefore refers to those countries of Western Europe that colonized the peoples of the Caribbean, plus those countries such as the United States of America, Canada, New Zealand and Australia whose colonial founders had Occidental heritage.

Historical Backdrop—The West and the Caribbean: A Dependency Relationship

The new settler colonies in the Caribbean were exploited by European countries for their natural resources and agriculture, thus speeding up the capital accumulation and the development process of the colonizers. From an historical perspective, the West's relationship with respect to the Caribbean therefore became one of domination over a subaltern people. Over the years, since the late 1400s, the Caribbean became a region highly dependent on the Metropole.

In the 15th century, there were a number of papal decrees that bestowed on Spain and Portugal the "right" to colonize lands in the so-called "new World" and to convert the occupants of those lands to Christianity. This Christian proselytization coincided with the expansionism that resulted from the three revolutions mentioned above. The 1493 *Inter Cetera* papal bull, issued by Pope Alexander VI, was one of those decrees which conferred the "right" of Spain to overthrow the "barbarous nations" of the new world and subjugate the indigenous peoples to Spanish rule and convert them to the Catholic faith (Papal Decree 1493; Taliman 1994, 7-8).

When Christopher Columbus landed in the Caribbean region in 1492, he thought he had reached the western portion of the Indian sub-continent. This is why the Caribbean region is also known as the "West Indies" (Hale 2006; Williams 1984). Indeed, one can trace the influence of the "West" in the Caribbean to that early visit by Columbus. Spain was the initial conqueror of the region we call the Caribbean. The Spanish occupied the Bahamas, the island of Hispaniola (the Dominican Republic and Haiti), Jamaica, Cuba, Trinidad and Puerto Rico. But at one point, Spain had laid claim to almost all of the Caribbean. The Portuguese were equal to the task of colonization (Ferguson 2008). Portugal initially laid claim to Barbados in 1536. The British laid claim to the Bahamas, Barbados, Jamaica, the Leeward Islands — Antigua and Barbuda, Dominica, St. Kitts and Nevis, the Windward Islands — Grenada, St. Lucia, St. Vincent and the Grenadines. Eventually, Britain took possession of Barbados in 1625. The Danes laid claim to St. Thomas, St. John and St. Croix. The Duchy of Courland colonized the small island of Tobago. The French conquered Anguilla, Antigua and Barbuda, the Dominican Republic, Grenada, Montserrat, Nevis, St. Croix, St. Dominique (Haiti), St. Lucia, St. Vincent, the Grenadines, and Martinique. The Netherlands took over Aruba, Curaçao, Anegada, St. Croix, and Tortola (Ter Tholen). Sweden initially took Guadeloupe and Saint Barthélemy until these islands were conquered by the French.

Essentially, inter-colonial rivalry turned the Caribbean into a hotbed of conflict, conquest, and genocide (UNESCO 1999). These European colonizers caused tremendous upheaval amongst the indigenous peoples of the Caribbean—the Caribs and the Awaraks. The indigenous peoples, considered heathen, were either forcibly converted to Christianity or killed off by the visiting Europeans.

A. Case Study: Production of Sugar and the Slave Trade

Because of European colonization, the Caribbean became the world's largest source of sugar. The growing population in Europe during the industrial revolution created a major market for certain crops grown in the Caribbean. The climate of the Caribbean region was especially conducive to the cultivation of sugar cane. Sugar became a sought after commodity for many Europeans and North Americans. Indeed, sugar was transformed from a scarce luxury product to a mass consumption commodity. Although the Spanish initially developed sugar cane production on the island of Cuba around the 17th century, it was the British who exploited sugar cane production and turned this sweet product into a marketable, profit generating commodity (Sharpe 1998). The labour intensive nature of sugar cane cultivation required much man power, and slaves were brought into the Caribbean to work on sugar plantations because they proved more resistant to the European diseases which had all but decimated the indigenous populations of these islands. This commodity made many plantation owners throughout the Caribbean region quite wealthy, on the backs of

African slaves and some indentured servants from India. European addiction to sugar was essentially the motive that drove the plantation economy in much of the Caribbean.

Another legacy of the West in the Caribbean has been the enslavement of Africans who provided labour on sugar plantations and contributed to enriching white slave owners of European origin (Mintz 1995). African slaves on the Caribbean sugar plantations also helped to produce molasses, an extract from sugar, which was then exported to New England (the United States) to be distilled into rum.

While the sugar industry is still important in the Caribbean, its economic importance has diminished over the years. Today, sugar still accounts for over 20 per cent of the merchandise exports of countries like Belize, Guyana, and St. Kitts and Nevis. It also accounts for about 10 per cent of employment in those countries. Sugar cane fields occupy an average of 31 per cent of the cropland in the region and more than 60 per cent of the cropland in Barbados, St. Kitts and Nevis, and Trinidad and Tobago. Although the sugar cane industry has to compete with tourism on many of the islands of the Caribbean, the industry still provides jobs to many of the rural poor who may lack the skills needed to find employment in other sectors of the economy (Mitchell 2005). The sugar cane industry represents, historically, an element of the West in the Caribbean. But this industry faces many distinct challenges today.

The sugar industries of the Caribbean have been in a steady decline since the 1970s. Efforts to revitalize these industries have not been very successful for a number of reasons. The demand for sugar from sugar cane has decreased due to the alternative options available, e.g., from beet. The cost of producing sugar has increased because of rising wages, labour strikes, run down equipment, heavy rains and hurricanes, and high rates of absenteeism among the sugar cane field workers. It is difficult to get young people in the Caribbean to work in the sugar cane fields. Bringing in labour from outside is costly. The state of sugar factories in the region have deteriorated and not much effort has gone into refurbishing them. Moreover, the price of cane sugar in the European Union (EU) market was cut by 36 per cent in 2008.

All of this means that sugar production is no longer a very profitable endeavour. Indeed, as Donald Mitchell notes, "most of the Caribbean's sugar producers would not be operating without preferential access to the EU and U.S. sugar markets that pay two to three times world market prices for imports from quota holders"

(Mitchell 2005, 2). Trade preferences in sugar were granted to Caribbean states by the EU under the Lomé Convention since 1975. Similarly, the US allowed trade preferences to these countries under its sugar programme since 1982. But these preferential deals go against the global free trade rules, according to the World Trade Organization (WTO). Even with preferential access, some countries, like Barbados, are having difficulty meeting their US or EU quotas because they are just not producing enough sugar, and they have had to give up their quotas to other sugar producing countries. It should be noted that recently the Belize sugar industry had to be rescued by a bailout from the government of Belize (Caribbean News Now 2010). Other countries, like Australia, Brazil, Colombia, Guatemala, South Africa, and Thailand are able to produce sugar at a lower cost than those in the sugar industry in the Caribbean. "The combined share of world exports of these low-cost producers has increased from 24 to 52 per cent since 1980" (Mitchell 2005, 2). Yet, Caribbean export earnings for sugar was still around US$406 million during 1999-2001, and 60 per cent of these earnings came as a result of preferential access to the EU and US sugar markets (Mitchell 2005, 2).

So, another legacy of the West in the Caribbean is that a state of dependency has been sustained through the access to preferential treatment afforded to the Caribbean sugar producers by both the EU and the US. The big question is, "how long will the EU and the US continue this preferential arrangement?" The European Commission has already hinted that such preferences will be phased out. A WTO ruling in 2005 concluded that the EU's sugar programme had subsidized the Caribbean's exports of sugar way beyond the levels agreed to in the Uruguay Round Agreement on Agriculture. There are also calls for reform of the US' preferences regime.

With the prospects of the erosion of these preferences on Caribbean sugar exports, sugar producers in the region will have to find ways for the industry to improve competitiveness by reducing the costs of production and by adding value to output. This will require rationalization, i.e., the closing down of inefficient and unprofitable estates and shifting resources, equipment and expertise to the more efficient ones. Such restructuring of the sugar sector has already begun in Trinidad and Tobago. Indeed, the European Commission has allocated €41.643 million to the government of Trinidad and Tobago for the restructuring of its sugar industry. The restructuring plan involves: a move to diversify the economic base of sugar-dependent areas; mitigating the socio-economic and environmental impacts that the restructuring process might have; the development of an integrated water management plan; the implementation of a climate change adaptation strategy; and, a socio-economic assessment of labour availability and how such labour can be retrained and deployed in other sectors (EEAS 2011).

Another possible way for Caribbean states to deal with the erosion of the sugar export preference regimes is to privatize fully or partially the sugar estates. Nationally-owned sugar estates have not proven to be very efficient or profitable. One can examine the case of nationally-owned sugar operations in Jamaica under the Manley government for evidence of this during the 1970s. But privatization under the Seaga government did not fare much better.

As Donald Mitchell puts it:

> The sugar industries of the Caribbean face severe challenges in the coming years. Those that survive will need to become more competitive by better managing and operating their industries and by adding value to sugar production in any way possible. One promising alternative appears to be to produce surplus energy from sugar cane residue (bagasse) through cogeneration. This requires the installation of high-efficiency boilers which can then produce surplus electricity which can be sold to the public utility. Other alternatives such as sugar refining and ethanol production depend on the policies and market opportunities available in each country. Those producers that cannot compete will need to devote resources to retraining workers and developing sugar lands into commercial, residential and agricultural uses.
>
> (*Mitchell* 2005, 24)

B. Case Study: The West and Caribbean Tourism

Tourism is big business in the Caribbean. In fact, the Caribbean basin is considered the most tourist-dependent region in the world, and according to the Caribbean Tourism Organization (CTO) this industry employs about one million people (Kindred 2011). Certainly, the tourist industry in the Caribbean has now outpaced the sugar industry as the primary engine of growth in most

Caribbean islands. It is estimated that tourism travel accounts for about $21.5 billion per year in the Caribbean (Gmelch 2003, 6-8; Vaughan 2011). This sector has a significant impact not only on the economies of Caribbean countries but also on the ecosystems and the cultures of this region.

British tourists tend to habitually visit countries in the English Caribbean, such as Barbados, Jamaica, and Nevis. French tourists are generally drawn to the islands in the French Caribbean, such as Martinique and Guadeloupe. Dutch tourists usually spend their holiday time in the Dutch Caribbean islands such as Curaçao and Aruba. Being able to speak the language of the island seems to be a factor in helping people of the West decide which island to visit on their holidays. But, in addition, special festivals, carnivals, concerts, fairs attract tourists from the West to these islands. One should also note the increasing popularity of cruises which bring hundreds of thousands of tourists into the Caribbean Sea each year.

To accommodate tourists from the West, Caribbean governments spend large sums of money on infrastructure (roads, international airports, ports) and Western-style amenities (tap water, sewage treatment plants, landfills, electricity, telephones, televisions, etc.) (Pattullo 1996). The variety of accommodations from small bed and breakfast joints to high-end luxury resorts ensures that visitors from every social stratum can visit these islands and enjoy the sun, sea and surf. Caribbean beaches are hot spots for students in the West who try to get away from the winter during spring breaks. But prominent A-list celebrities, entertainers and politicians from Britain, the US and Canada also choose to spend vacations in places like Barbados (Alderson 2011). Catering to Western tourists has certainly led to inflation in the price of food and land for the local people on Caribbean islands. For instance, when Oprah Winfrey bought a beach side property on the west coast of Barbados, the price of the real estate around that property skyrocketed in value.

There are other downsides of the tourist industry in the Caribbean besides the inflation of prices. The influx of Western visitors to these islands has resulted in the increase in resource consumption, strain on the environment and the ecology, damage to corals, changes in the local economy, an increase in crime, an increase in drug use, and the rapid spread of HIV/AIDS. On the latter issue, the Caribbean has a thriving sex industry that is attached informally to the tourist industry. The sex industry serves both local clients and tourists. Certain Caribbean countries like

Haiti and Jamaica have witnessed a spike in HIV prevelance among sex workers at about 5.3 per cent and 4.9 per cent respectively. In Guyana, HIV prevalence among sex workers is very high at 16.6 per cent. In the Dominican Republic, the epidemic among male sex workers is high and driven by both high unemployment rates in rural areas, which has encouraged migration to urban areas, and the profitable sex tourism industry (Padilla 2007). The same can be said of other countries in the Caribbean.

The tourist industry in the Caribbean can be quite fickle. Some years, hurricanes and major tropical storms decimate resorts and can destroy much of the hotel industry in some of these countries. The industry has also suffered from the downturn in the global economy. Since 2008, the global financial crisis has made a small dent in the Caribbean tourism industry, as the numbers of people taking winter holidays from Europe, the US and Canada have dropped slightly. The industry has also suffered somewhat because of the hike in crude oil prices which led to a decline in the number and frequency of airline flights to the region. However, recent figures indicate that tourism in the Caribbean has bounced back and remains relatively strong despite the global economic downturn. There was a 4 per cent increase in tourists to the area in 2008 (Sydelle 2011). One important point to consider on this issue, with respect to the influence of the West on the contemporary Caribbean is that foreigners own many of the hotel resorts in this region. Thus, the money made from tourism does not always stay on these islands and, in fact, is often siphoned off to the economies of the Metropole.

C. Case Study: Extra-Regional Migration Patterns

Migration is a major social phenomenon globally, with approximately 100 million migrants searching for higher wages, a better life and a secure place to live. It is also an important social issue for the contemporary Caribbean. Caribbean people, like many in the developing world, have historically moved to areas that would provide them with employment opportunities and a better life for them and their families.

After World War II both skilled and unskilled Caribbean labourers were contracted to fill labour force deficiencies in the West, particularly in the UK and the US. The main areas to which these labourers were drawn were in transport, hospitals and post-war reconstruction. Bus drivers, nurses, and construction workers coming from the Caribbean were provided with such employment opportunities in the West, particularly in the UK where there was an initial acceptance of immigrants who came from countries of the Commonwealth. After all, Commonwealth countries tend to share a lot in common with their former colonial master—including, in most cases, a loyalty to the British Crown, a roughly similar educational system, a parliamentary system that is based on the Westminster model, the English language, and sports like cricket, rugby, and polo. However, as the numbers on West Indian migrants grew in the UK, racial tensions grew to a significant degree. It was after the Notting Hill Riots of 1958 (by "New Commonwealth" immigrants) that there was a backlash against migrants from the Caribbean and other Commonwealth countries.

The obvious racist agitation by conservative factions in Britain, concerned that the country's social cohesion was at stake, resulted in the British government's decision to change the immigration laws in that country. Large scale Caribbean migration to the UK was substantially reduced by the mid-1960s because of the passage of the 1962 Commonwealth Immigrants' Act. This Act made provision for the deportation of Caribbean and other migrants who came into the country illegally, but it was designed to control and limit the inflow of non-white migrants. This Act was amended in 1968 and then superceded by the Immigration Act of 1971 (Evans 1972).

Nevertheless, the growing demand for labour in the West opened doors for skilled Caribbean workers to fill positions in selected sectors that could not be filled by nationals in the host countries. The 1970s and 1980s, for example, saw another mass exodus of educated people from several Caribbean islands to the UK, Canada and the US (ECLAC 2006). In the US, for instance, 10 per cent of all foreign nationals are from the Caribbean, with the majority coming from Cuba (34 per cent), and the Dominican Republic (24 per cent). Over 10 per cent of these Caribbean immigrants come from Haiti and Jamaica (ECLAC 2006, 2-3). This external metropolitan demand for high skilled and educated labour naturally led many Caribbean governments to be concerned about a "brain drain" (Mishra 2006). However, for some Caribbean leader the exportation of skilled labour is desirable because remittances sent back to the Caribbean can help boost some island economies. Indeed, for some Caribbean states, it would be impossible to provide the social safety nets that one finds in the West without the remittances sent home by Caribbean diaspora living in the West (Thomas-Hope 2009).

At the same time, one cannot help but view Western countries as contributors to the brain drain in certain sectors of some Caribbean countries' economies (e.g., nurses and teachers). Some scholars have argued that the siphoning off of human capital by the developed world and consequent negative impact of a severe shortage of professionals in the developing world has begun to hamper global development efforts (Schmid 1997). One wonders if this does not apply to the Caribbean as a region.

Certainly, the impact of the brain drain has been well-documented in the health sector throughout the Caribbean. One such study was conducted by the Economic Commission on Latin America and the Caribbean (ECLAC 2003). That study highlighted the push and pull factors that led to a nursing crisis in Trinidad and Tobago. There were clearly some weaknesses in the local public health system which contributed to the push factors for nurses to leave Trinidad and Tobago. Some of these were: inadequate remuneration; unfavourable working conditions; lack of proper management and leadership; insufficient training and professional development; insufficient career perspectives; under-utilization of acquired skills; burn-out due to increased workload as a consequence of resignations; and lack of recognition of the profession. With the growing shortage of nurses in the West, countries like Canada, the United States and Britain took advantage of these unfavourable conditions for nurses in the Caribbean. In effect, Western countries simply poached qualified health professionals from the Caribbean by fast-tracking the immigration process for them. The ECLAC document lists some of the pull factors that attracted Caribbean nurses to leave the islands and come to the US, the UK and Canada. Some of these pull factors were: attractive payments and benefits; modern human resources management; professional work-environment; possibility of attaining permanent residency in the receiving country; financial support for registration and immigration procedures provided by foreign employers; supportive network of family and friends; opportunities for professional development and career advancement; professional recognition; and improved quality of life for family and self.

It would seem that the time has come for the West to develop ethical recruitment practices when it comes to the health profession in the Caribbean, similar to those adopted by France with respect to the Maghreb countries. But with an aging population in most countries of the West, and with the paucity of health professionals available in those countries, one can expect that recruitment of nurses and other health professionals from the Caribbean will continue.

One issue-area that deserves further research is the impact that Caribbean migration to the West has on both children who are left behind, as well as on migrant children. These children constitute a particularly vulnerable group. In a UNICEF study done in Barbados, it was revealed that the impact of Caribbean parents' migration on children can be devastating. For one thing, this phenomenon threatens the long-term well-being and development of Caribbean adolescents into adulthood, according to the report. According to this study, Caribbean children who are affected by migration face several challenges in terms of education and health care as well as various psychosocial problems. Many children left behind suffer from depressions, low self-esteem which can lead to behavioural problems, and at increased risk of poor academic performance as well as interruption of schooling. Particular to migrant children is the access to health and education, especially when they are undocumented (Bakker, 2009, 2).

These children are often stripped of their rights to grow up in a safe and nurturing family environment. Some are abused by surrogate parents. Others are exposed to sexual exploitation as minors. And, yet others have been caught up in the seedy acitivity of human trafficking. All states that have signed on and ratified the Convention on the Rights of the Child—both those in the Caribbean and those in the West—have a legal obligation to ensure that the children left behind as well as those in transition or those who have already emigrated receive the protection of that Convention. "The fact that many migrant children are also not documented or registered is a dilemma, as it deprives these children of their fundamental rights to a nationality, a name and identity, and consequently also of the belonging to a family" (Bakker 2009, 5).

The magnitude of undocumented migration is difficult to quantify, but it is widely believed that such migration of Caribbean people is on the rise in Western countries. Part of the reason for this is the increasingly restrictive immigration policies of Western countries, euphemistically referred to as "managed immigration" (Travis 2011). In some respects, this trend is to be expected because of the economic difficulties that Western countries have been facing, particularly since the 2008 financial crisis. Natural disasters and rising poverty have exacerbated the problem, causing forced migration to the West and pressures on the socio-economic infrastructure of these developed countries. A virulent strain of xenoracism has emerged in a post-911, post-multicultural Europe of late, which increases pressure on several European governments to clamp down on immigration (Fekete 2001). This new strain of racism in the so-called post-racial societies of the West is having a negative impact on people of Caribbean origin, even those who are second generation citizens of states in Europe and North America (Lentin 2011; Lentin and Titley 2011).

Undocumented migration (irregular migration) is not only a problem for Western countries. Trafficking in people, especially women and children, has become a major concern for Caribbean states. Women and girls are sometimes trafficked as commercial sex workers from Caribbean islands to major cities in Europe and North America. Caribbean individuals involved in such criminal activity, if caught, may be deported to their place of origin. In some cases, the deportees may move back into countries of the West without documentation, i.e. illegally and reinsert themselves back into the criminal groups. This problem is difficult to resolve without the full cooperation of Caribbean and Western countries.

Conclusion

As shown above, the Caribbean region today, because of its history, is forever inextricably linked to the "West". The contemporary Caribbean has strong political, cultural, socio-economic and historical linkages to Europe, as a direct result of colonization and Western imperialism, as well as to North America (Canada and the United States) through trade, migration patterns and security arrangements. Scholars of dependency theory, writing as early as the 1950s, recognized that the underdevelopment of the Caribbean was directly associated with centre-periphery relations which ultimately disadvantaged the Caribbean as a peripheral region in the global economy. While this region produced largely primary commodities, like sugar and bauxite, for the rich industrial centres, the countries at the centre of the global political economy produced refined products and manufactured goods for themselves and the peripheral regions like the Caribbean.

As was shown in the case of sugar, the process of development depends very much on capital accumulation and surplus extraction. The rich industrial West is able to accumulate much capital from the sale of its tertiary products, and the West is thus able to extract large surpluses from profits made on those sales. In the meanwhile, Caribbean countries with their subsistence agriculture and production of primary products do not generate sufficient capital to extract surplus large enough for industrialization to take root in any significant way. Therefore, over time, this has led the Caribbean increasingly to become dependent on the countries in the West and to maintain a status of underdevelopment.

Furthermore, when the large export-oriented sugar cane plantations, found across the Caribbean region during and after the colonial period, did produce surplus, this surplus remained in the hands of plantation owners who emulated the conspicuous consumption patterns of those living in the Western industrialized countries. Surplus in the Caribbean was thus spent on luxury goods and little, if any, could be put to investment or to developing a manufacturing sector. It is this international division of labour which exacerbated the dependency situation for Caribbean states and ensured that they remained poor and underdeveloped.

This is not to say that some industrial development did not take place in the Caribbean. Indeed, during the 1960s and 70s, there were pockets of industralization in some countries in the region. However, such industralization was almost always dependent on foreign capital which largely dictated the nature of the development and the control over the domestic markets. The influence of the West in the Caribbean during that period was one in which capitalistic development favoured the centre at the expense of the periphery. Any surplus that was extracted by monopolitical capital in the Caribbean was generally not reinvested into the productive activities of these island economies. In fact, it is safe to say that most of this surplus was siphoned off and sent to the centre as profit remittances and the remainder was used to buy luxury goods by comprador political and economic elites living in the Caribbean. This form of dependency by Caribbean states on countries in the metropole was exceedingly difficult to break.

In fact, in the few cases in the Caribbean where attempts were made to break this cycle of dependency, the countries in question went through a revolution to do so, or tried to alter the relationship with Western industrial states through import substitution industrialization (ISI) (Prebisch 1959). In the latter case, ISI meant making an explicit political decision to replace foreign imported industrialized goods with locally produced goods wherever and whenever possible (Cardoso and Faletto

1970). This protectionist economic policy was followed by states like Jamaica, Cuba, and Trinidad. In such cases, those Caribbean state leaders made the argument for pursuing economic development through the nationalization of companies owned by Western foreigners, by subsidizing domestic industries, by discouraging conspicuous consumption among locals, and by increasing taxes domestically in order to fund the running of the local industries. Ultimately, however, ISI was limited because of the small size of the domestic markets in those Caribbean countries that tried it as a model of reducing dependency on the West.

Signing agreements with countries in the West with respect to preferential trade has only served to perpetuate the dependent relationship of the Caribbean and the West. So too has the shift from agriculture to tourism helped to sustain the Caribbean's dependence on the West. The advent of a complex web of interconnectedness (aided in large part by international telephone and cell-phone linkages, satellite television, fax machines, computerization, the internet and "information superhighway" and improvements to transportation technologies) has been the result of both globalization and globalism. It has often meant that an individual's life can be increasingly shaped by events occurring, and decisions made, at a great distance (Mittelman 1997). This fact has changed the very parameters of political life and calls into question the categorical distinctions that were made in the past between, for example, immigrant, diaspora, sojourner, and other migrant communities. The globalization and globalism processes have made it possible for Caribbean migrants to develop multiple loyalties and identities—to home and to host country. Communication and transportation advances have certainly made it easier for those living in Caribbean diasporic communities in the West to keep in touch with family and friends in their ancestral homeland. Electronic banking has facilitated the process of migrant remittances from the West to the Caribbean. Transnationalization of production and capital has allowed for stronger economic relations between Caribbean migrants and their country of origin.

But while globalization and globalism is changing the relationship between the West and the Caribbean, it is quite evident that the longstanding historical linkages between these two "worlds", as well as contemporary trends in trade, tourism and migration, will continue to bind these two areas together in a complex interdependent relationship for many decades to come.

Note

1. According to the World Bank's regional classification, the Caribbean includes the following countries: Antigua and Barbuda, The Bahamas, Barbados, Belize, Dominica, Dominican Republic, Grenada, Guyana, Haiti, Jamaica, Saint Kitts and Nevis, Saint Lucia, Suriname, Trinidad and Tobago, Saint Vincent and the Grenadines.

3

India-Caribbean Relations with Emphasis on Trade and Commerce between India and Trinidad and Tobago

Satnarine Balkaransingh

Some Cultural and Economic Historical Background to India in the Caribbean

India's Maritime Legacy from Ancient to Recent Times[1]

One of the earliest, and still existing, human civilization is that of the land mass referred to variously as Bharat Varsha, Bharat, Hindustan or India. Its documented history stretches back to the ancient period, the Iron Age. This is based on archaeological excavations in the Indus Valley which reveal the Mohenjo-Daro and Harappa civilizations, and on other discoveries. Moreover, history and sociology bear testimony to the fact that communities, nations and civilizations, like this one, germinated, developed roots and expanded through a number of factors including trading and commercial links. India since ancient times was a magnet for traders and conquerors because of its centres of learning, its booming trade and commerce in textiles (cotton, silks, and muslin), spices, precious metals and stones. Besides being on the established, overland, caravan routes between Europe and Eastern Asia, India also deliberately expanded its sphere of influence across its borders. A significant aspect of this expansion has been achieved through its maritime legacy. This includes the development of commercial links with the ever expanding "global economy" at various stages in the historical expansion of the "known" world. These influences included Asia, Africa, the Far East, and Europe. Within modern times its influence has spread to encompass North and South America and the Caribbean.

The Caribbean and Latin America as a Destination in this Legacy

By the 19th century almost the whole of India was under British control. Moreover, after the end of the Napoleonic wars in Europe in 1814, pressure was exerted on the Europeans to abolish the trading in human cargo. Slavery was terminated by the British in 1834 and 1838, the French in 1848 and the Dutch in 1863 (Samaroo 1999, 3). Their other dominions across the Atlantic in South America and the West Indies began to experience hardships. The ex slaves, even though offered higher terms and conditions of employment above the minimum wage set by the authorities for employing the free labour, were moving off the plantations (Riviere 1972; Look Lai 1993, 7). Exports of primary, agricultural products, especially sugar, shipped to European markets fell drastically. Incomes declined significantly. By 1866 the sugar estates of at least seven districts in Trinidad (Mayaro, Guapo, La Brea, Irois, Erin, all in the south, plus Toco and Carenage in the north) which had produced at least 8 per cent of the 1836 sugar crop, had been abandoned, sold off cheaply, or taken over by the crown (Hart 1866, 82). Crops on other plantations such as cocoa, coffee and coconut suffered. The same conditions were being experienced in other Caribbean territories whose economies were similarly structured. Alternative sources of labour had to be found to maintain planters' profits. The necessary and sufficient conditions presented themselves for the European trade to continue in human cargo, as alternative sources of replacement labour caused by this displacement of slave labour. Industrious, able bodied, hard working and malleable indentured workers from India were herded and shipped to the Americas and the Caribbean by the Portuguese (Goa to Brazil); French (Pondicherry to Guadeloupe and Martinique), Dutch (India to Suriname) and the British (to British Guiana, Jamaica, the Windward Islands and Trinidad, the southernmost island of the West Indian archipelago) (Dabydeen and Samaroo 1987; Jha 1971; La Guerre 1985).

A new trading relationship emerged between European dominions in India and those in Trinidad and the Caribbean. The colony of India, then jointly shared by the British, French and Portuguese, was a rich source of supply of Indian bonded labour. "Bong coolie" from India (and to a lesser extent, China) became an integral aspect of trade. The India-West-Indian connection, from one dominion to another, became a reality. Given that Indians were themselves in search of better livelihoods, particularly food and shelter, a new source of commerce developed between India and the Caribbean. A new classification of workers entered the labour market in India: "middlemen" recruiters of immigrants (*arkatias*). These recruiters contracted their booty by any means possible, including surreptitious, deceitful ones. Some recruits (*girmits*) were even kidnapped by these *arkatias*. They embraced and enlisted others who were running from a major oppressive socio-political situation in the country following India's First War of Independence (1857), especially from those areas where the British had experienced stiff and prolonged resistance. These included the United Provinces and Bihar, Delhi, Merut, Cawnpore (Kanpur) Jhansi, Malwa, Koonch, Gwalior, Rohilkhand, Patna, Arrah, Rajputana and Oudh (Forrest, 2006). Others were running away from oppressive domestic situations within family structures, the joint family system, internal family conflicts or indignities faced by women within the patriarchal family structures. It is from this hot, melting pot of Hindustan that the East Indians found themselves in Trinidad and the other Caribbean territories then under colonial rule. The push and pull factors created interesting statistics of immigration (Balkaransingh 2010). By 1917 (1838-1917) over four hundred thousand (400,000) East Indians had crossed the *Kala Pani* or "black water" to several Caribbean colonies as follows:

Trinidad	147,592
Guyana (Br. Guiana)	238,909
Suriname (Dutch Guiana)	31,444 (population in 1921)
Jamaica	36,412 (of which 12,109 returned to India)
Guadeloupe	40,000 plus
Martinique	25,000 (of which 11,000 returned to India)
St. Vincent and the Grenadines	2,475
St. Lucia	4,352
Grenada	3,200

Today the East Indian community in the Caribbean region, now referred to as the region washed by the Caribbean Sea, comprises about one million people (Balkaransingh 2004).

While this European trade shifted in a slightly more humane way, from that of slaves to one of bonded labour, it nonetheless remained basically a trade in human bodies. While the concept of trade in human resources and human capital was to develop much later, entrepreneurial and technical expertise were actually being shipped across frontiers, almost to the other side of the world. An additional category of British maritime trade emerged simultaneously, that of other cargo across the Indian and Atlantic Ocean and into the Caribbean Sea. The ships most frequently used were those operated by the James Nourse Ltd., Sandback, Tinne and Company, and G.D. Tyser and Company. But it was Nourse and Company who later controlled this lucrative trade (Samaroo 1999, 11-13).[2] The ships would bring Indian immigrants and other supplies including rice to South America (British and Dutch Guiana [Guyana and Suriname]) to the Caribbean, pick up sugar, rum, molasses, pitch (asphalt), annatto, and timber and offload these in Europe. It was not unusual for the ships to bring both workers and rice on the same voyage (Samaroo 1999, 14).[3]

In the early days of Indian immigration there was no other Indian commerce to the Caribbean, except that of the ships' cargo of people and grains. However consumer items arrived with the immigrants. Literary, musical, textile and handicraft items travelled across the *Kala Pani* with the *jahajis* and *jahajins* in their *jahaji* bundles, their total worldly possessions tied in cloth sacks suspended either on their backs or on their heads, or worn on their persons. The bundles also included spices, apparel and decorative crafts (jewellery etc), handicrafts, portable artisanal equipment, herbs, shrubs and other plants, including marijuana (*ganja*), used for medicinal and religious purposes. The spices were necessary ingredients for their culinary fare. They included *jeera* (cumin), *dhania* (coriander), *methi* (fenugreek), clove, *elaichi* (cardamom), cinnamon, black pepper, chillies and *adrak* (ginger). Then there were the musical instruments. The percussion instruments included majeera (small brass cymbal), dandataal (iron rod struck with another curved iron), *jhaal* (medium-sized, brass cymbal), *jhanj* (large brass cymbal), *kartaal*, *dhol* (bass drum), *tassa* (small kettle drum), tabla, *dholak* (double mouthed, hand drum), *tappu* (single faced rhythmic instrument of the tambourine [daff] family, played with a pair of sticks) and *dhap* ([daff] of the tambourine family but played with fingers). There were the string instruments of sitar, sarangi, bulbul, mandolin and wind instruments of harmonium, accordion and bansuri (flute).

The Indians brought their books on religion and philosophy—the Valmiki's *Ramayana,* Tulsidasa's *Ramcharitmanas,* the *Sukhsagar, Mahabharata,* the *Puranas,* the *Vedas* and *the* Upanishads, the Koran and the Bible.

These are some of the unique characteristics of a migrant people, moving from a culturally and geographically familiar environment into a new alien environment, far removed from the original one, where a new education system, literacy patterns, religious beliefs and socio-cultural forms are imposed on them. The above articles were therefore necessary for the immigrants' maintenance of their way of life and cultural continuity in this new and "hostile" environment where they found themselves at the bottom of the socio-economic ladder. The Trinidadian society, even before the entry of the Indians, was heavily stratified, with the Whites at the top followed by the Coloureds and "free negroes." Portuguese and Syrians were lower down the social ladder. This was the society that the Indian indentured immigrant encountered in the Caribbean, but particularly in Trinidad. They kept to themselves in their plantations. Later, following the expiration of their contracts, those who opted to remain in Trinidad founded their own villages, purchasing abandoned and swamp lands from the State and developing these into productive agriculture.[4] Many who returned to India faced significant socio-economic and cultural challenges including the loss of caste and social ostracism for having crossed the *Kala Pani* (black water). India which had previously had a daring history and legacy of its people engaging in maritime journeys had now adopted new social patterns. A fundamental change of attitude had taken place which led Pandit Jawaharlal Nehru to comment:

> The urge to adventure and an overflowing life which had led to vast schemes of distant colonisation and the transplantation of Indian culture in far-off lands: all these fade away and a narrow orthodoxy taboos even the crossing of high seas. (Nehru 1973, 54)

From the late Middle Ages, this new orthodoxy had replaced the liberalism of the earlier period. But the very problem itself created new dynamics for trade and commerce. The "returnees" to India were undaunted. In many instances, when faced with hostile reception, they promptly made about turns, renewed their contracts and took the next available boat back to the Caribbean. They adapted themselves to the new environment and commenced the transformation of the region, indirectly redefining West Indian society, especially those countries in which they were in large numbers—British and Dutch Guiana (Guyana, Suriname) and Trinidad and to a lesser extent Jamaica, Guadeloupe and Martinique. In Trinidad they refashioned the physical, socio-economic, trading, commercial, financial and political imperatives, perpetuating their cultural traditions, rituals and festivities through the performing, creative, literary and culinary arts. They brought and planted trees, shrubs and herbs of religious, medicinal, agricultural or culinary value; rice, peas (*dhall-matar, moong,* and *urdi,*) till (*bene*), various types of spinach (*poi, saijan, guma, chowrai, and sarson* [mustard]). They planted ginger (*adrak*), saffron (*hardi/ haldi*), pomegranate (*anar*) and several varieties of mango (*aam*), coriander (*dhania*), cardamom (*elaichi*), bitter gourd (*caraille*), egg plant (*baigan*), curry leaves (*karapille*), and several varieties of pepper (*mirchi*). For religious purposes, betel nut (*supari*), basel (*tulsi*) and marigold (*gainde*r) were introduced into the local flora (Dabydeen and Samaroo 1987; Jha 1971). In agriculture water buffaloes (bhaisa), zebu cattle and mongoose (to kill the snakes) were imported and introduced into the landscape. By the end of indentureship not only over half of a million Indians (543,596) had been moved from India to the Caribbean with 143,939 to Trinidad alone, its flora and fauna had commenced a refashioning (Look Lai 1993, 276).

Following the termination of indentureship, the potters (*kohars*) returned to their trade in pottery, manufacturing, decorating and selling earthen goblets and water jugs. While none of the above products and food items was initially traded, the demand for them, including fabrics, other textiles, musical instruments and items for religious worship later developed into full scale, lucrative trade and commerce with India.

From the sociological perspective, there continued to be socio-economic stratification within the Indian community, in the form of the caste system. This stratification existed within and parallel with that of the wider society. Within the larger society of Trinidad the all embracing social stratification persisted, long after the end of indentureship. Sociologist Lloyd Braithwaite records that even up to the 1950s, "Upper class discriminated against lower class and lower class discriminated against coolie." Braithwaite's (1975,

41) instructive study in the 1950s in the study of societal patterns of behaviour in Trinidad noted that:

> The existence of a large variety of ethnic groups has led, not to the development of an eclectic cosmopolitanism, but to a certain separateness of the groups and to a ranking of them in terms of superiority and inferiority, as groups...stratified very largely on racial lines....the biological division of skin colour played an important part in the differentiation of social class even within the broad bands, determined by race.

Trinidad was thus a complex society, a fact of local life. It was therefore natural that the Indians, still on the margins of national society, would perpetuate their cultural norms and behavioural patterns in food, dress, language and religious rituals and festivals. The products required for the propagation of this way of life were all consumer durables that had to be replenished. The demand could not be met at the local level. It is therefore logical that entrepreneurial trade would have to be established and that these would have been the first set of items that would be in demand. This in fact did occur. These were the first set of products that constituted trading and commercial relationships with the "mother" country.

Commencing from around the 1920s, by 1940s the British Caribbean territories and Trinidad in particular, were attracting businessmen from several exporting centres. Kirpalani *et al.* (1945, 103-105) noted that:

> During this period certain merchants from India, chiefly from Sind, Bengal and Gujerat primarily interested in the tourist trade, began to set up their business in the city of Port of Spain and at San Fernando. With the necessary training and experience in big business, and with reputable export houses behind them, they were able after a short while to command secure positions in the commercial life of the colony. The largest Indian dry goods firm in the island is a firm of Sindhi merchants—Messrs Kirpalani United Co, Ltd. New avenues for business relationship with India have been created...

It was during this period that an entirely new branch of trade between India and Trinidad emerged, the entertainment industry. In December 1935, a young and dynamic engineer and entrepreneur, Ranjit Kumar, brought the first Hindi movie to Trinidad, *Bala Joban* (Wayward Child), and entered into arrangements with Hajji Gokool, the then owner of the largest cinema hall in Trinidad, Globe Theatre, in Port of Spain. Globe, formerly named Metro, built at a cost of over eighty thousand dollars (TT $80,000) by Hajji Gokool, had a seating capacity of seventeen hundred (Gooptar 2011). The patronage to this first and other "Indian" movies that followed was astounding. The Indian cinema industry grew significantly. Film distributors included Ranjit Kumar, Murli Kirpalani (from 1936), Soral Billimoria, Sarran Teelucksingh, Timothy Roodal, India Overseas International (from early 1940s) and International Traders Ltd. (from 1946). Together with other successful entrepreneurs and cinema magnates such as Timothy Roodal, Jang Bahadur and Henry Teelucksingh, the trade in and screening of Indian movies became a very lucrative industry. A highly successful, private sector driven entertainment industry developed in tandem with the rapidly growing Indian film industry. By the 1960s Indo-Trinidadians were engaged in a building boom of cinema cum theatre halls throughout the country showing among others, movies from India's Bollywood film industry (Gooptar 2011). In 1968 these theatres/cinemas (Astor Theatre, Globe Theatre, Ascot Theatre) totalled 78 in number, of which over 70 of them screened Indian movies on a regular, weekly basis (Gooptar 2011).

Establishment of Formal India-Caribbean Relationships

Notwithstanding the complexity of the Trinidad society, for social relationships to grow and develop, for a nation to be forged, for trade and commerce to succeed across borders, a number of conditions must be fulfilled. There has to be knowledge of, sensitivity to and appreciation for the cultural norms, values, morals and ethics, behavioural patterns and values of the trading partner. These characteristics were already there between Trinidad and India. Another level of sensitivity, appreciation, mutual respect and understanding had to be initiated. At the intellectual level, by the 1950s Dr. Eric Williams, the Oxford scholar and historian, expressed keen interest in publishing the first researched Ph.D. thesis on Indian migration to Trinidad. It was entitled "East Indian

Coolies in the British West Indies 1838-1870," undertaken by Edgar Erickson in 1932 at the University of Wisconsin, U.S.A. This initiative lasted for over 4 years (1951-55), with Dr. Williams maintaining correspondence with the researcher/author on the need for sensitivity in the editing of the document for publication. Dr. Williams even engaged the interest and attention of the then Indian High Commissioner to Trinidad and Tobago, Mr. A.M. Sahay, who undertook an endorsement of the proposed publication. A literary chapter in the relationship of both countries was in the embryonic stage of development. The Indian High Commissioner's presence in Trinidad was the result of India's achievement of independence in 1947 and the subsequent establishment of diplomatic relations with several countries in the Caribbean including British Guiana, Suriname, Jamaica and Trinidad. The manuscript of the book was forwarded to the Government Printing Press of Trinidad and Tobago (T&T) for publication. Copies of the book were even booked in advance. The publication never materialized (Samaroo 2011). In 1955 Dr. Williams found himself in conflict with his employers (the Caribbean Commission, from which he was later, dismissed) and was thrust into, and got himself engrossed in, the national politics of T&T. He founded and headed the Peoples National Movement, becoming the country's first Premier, and thereafter first Prime Minister of independent Trinidad and Tobago in 1962.

Then on his initiatives, now as Prime Minister of independent Trinidad and Tobago,[5] following personal discussions with India's then Prime Minister J. Nehru, the scholarly "Chair" in Indian Studies was established at the University of the West Indies (UWI) in the mid 1960s. An intellectual element was added to India—Caribbean relations, but more so India-Trinidad relations, since the "Chair" was located at the St Augustine campus of UWI.

Around this time both countries had begun to engage in sporting activities, predominantly cricket. There were exchanges of cricketing teams from India and the Caribbean. One of India's spin bowlers, Subhas Gupte, after a successful tour of cricket matches, remained in Trinidad, married a person of Indian origin and made Trinidad his home. Through these initiatives, the trade in services had been further expanded.

From 1970s into the 21st Century

The growing commercial relationship of the two countries was fuelled by the first oil boom of the 1970s which saw Trinidad and

Tobago, an oil producing country, increasing its Gross National Product (GNP) per capita income and conspicuous consumption levels many fold, fuelling greater air travel by Indo-Trinidadians back to India with resultant changing taste patterns which increased India-Trinidad trade and commerce in consumer items. The trade in the celluloid arts that had begun in the 1930s grew by leaps and bounds. Many offshoots of this film industry developed between India and the Caribbean, but more so with Trinidad and Tobago. By the 1960s there was a regular, though predominantly one-way, trade in Indian artistic talent: the visit of screen stars, playback singers and their troupes of musicians and dancers. Those who visited and enjoyed megastar status, commanding high contractual fees, included Hemant Kumar, Mohammed Rafi, Lata Mangeshkar, Asha Bhosle, Suman Kalyanpur, C.H. Atma and Kishore Kumar. The successes of these ventures, and hence the lucrative invisible trade, were due in part to the size of the Indo-Trinidadian population and its demographic layout, their effective demand for these services and their propensity to consume, on an ongoing basis, Indian commercial and artistic offerings made popular by the Indian film industry. It is on one of Kishore Kumar's trip to Trinidad, in 1979, that he heard the *Soca* hit, *Om shanty Om,* composed and sung, in that same year, by the then popular Trinidadian Soca artiste, Ras Shorty I. The calypsonian gave the Indian playback singer a record, "a gift from one singer to the next" (Jacob 1996, 15). Kumar took the concept and used it in Hindi but the chorus was the same. The rest is history. It continues to ride the Indian airwaves. So too are some of the Bhojpuri folk songs, brought to Trinidad by indentured Indians, and later turned into pop "chutney" songs. These have been rebottled by Indian artiste Kanchan with remixes by Babla and remarketed. One such song is *Phulorie bina chutney, kaise banee.* India and Trinidad and Tobago were trading at various levels.

Towards the latter half of the 20th century, at the socio-economic and geopolitical levels, the concept of "globalization," one community, the human community without physical border, was propagated and developed. The offshoot of this was the establishment of different geopolitical, social and racial groupings into trading blocs: the European Union, the African Union, Chinese, Jews, North American and Indians. The forging of a global Indian bloc and resultant network was built on several pillars with similar characteristics: strong ethnic identity in which groups drew sustenance from common threads such as philosophies and basic principles of living, will to survive, ancestry, food, literature, religion, rituals, music, dance, feasts and festivals. There was the common need to establish and maintain linkages between home country and those of the diasporic communities for common growth prospects and survival. Based on this principle the India-Caribbean and particularly India-Trinidad and Tobago relations developed further impetus.

By 1980 the oil windfall of the 1970s had been fritted away through faulty political, socio-economic and national policies. By 1983 the T&T economy was in serious trouble, unable to balance its national budget. Expenditure outstripped income. The country was saddled with 66 State Enterprises of which 34 were wholly owned and 15 equal or majority owned. Like the majority of the others, the Iron and Steel Company of T&T Ltd was wholly owned and losing money on a daily basis (Demas 1983, 158-161). By 1990 Indian entrepreneur Lakshmi Mittal made his first major investment. He leased the floundering State-owned enterprise, the iron and steel mill (ISCOTT) in Point Lisas, renamed it (ISPAT) and commenced to develop it into a resounding success story. He subsequently bought it, paving the way for his phenomenal rise in the global iron and steel industry.

Since the initial political initiative of our founding "father" of the nation, Dr. Eric Williams, there have been exchange visits by ministers and prime ministers of both countries. Indira Gandhi visited Trinidad in 1967. Former T&T Prime Ministers George Chambers and Basdeo Panday visited India in 1980s and 1997 respectively, the latter being the Guest of Honour at India's Republic Day parade, witnessing its military might and cultural pageantry at Raj Path Delhi. Later, in 1999 the Indian Prime Minister Rt. Hon. Atal Bihari Vajpayee visited Trinidad and inaugurated a Shelter Support Centre in Trincity to provide low-cost housing to our citizenry. He also signed a number of Memoranda of Understanding (MOUs), agreements affecting trade in several sectors of the national economy and other bilateral relations.[6] One such agreement was a Double Taxation Avoidance Agreement (DTAA), thus facilitating further trading and commercial links. Each visit further advanced the potential of both countries for bilateral trade and investment.

India-T&T Current Trading Relations: Trading and Commercial Arrangements (2005-2012)

In an attempt to further expand the trading relations between the two regions and especially with Trinidad and Tobago, in 1997 a Trinidadian business delegation was presented, at the Taj Mahal hotel, New Delhi, with a proposal by the Indian Chamber of Commerce to globalize trade. A few years later, in 2003, an India–Trinidad and Tobago Association was founded in New Delhi. The membership comprised a predominance of Indians from India with a sprinkling of Trinidad and Tobagonians living, working and visiting that country. The organization was conceptualized and founded, following India's two-day meeting with its diasporic community, both people of Indian origin (PIO) and non-resident Indians (NRIs) through "Pravasi Bharatiya Divas," a fertile meeting ground for initiation and/or furtherance of trading, commercial and other cultural ties.

Yet trade in goods across borders remained a trickle. The consumer reach was not achieved as expected, partly due to high prices. In May 2004 "Indian Arrival Day" was celebrated by T&T in Delhi, a first in the history of Indian migrations across borders. The event was hosted by H.E. Pundit Maniedeo Persad, the then T&T High Commissioner to India. The event attracted a host of traders, cultural activists and exponents. This was followed up in 2005 and 2006 with Trinidad and Tobago reciprocating by hosting delegations of over 200 persons from India. In 2007 the Minister of Trade and Industry from the government of T&T, Mr Kenneth Valley, visited India, China and South Korea. Simultaneously the Minister of Public Administration, Dr Lenny Saith, himself an alumnus of the Indian Institute of Technology at Rourke, was in India, negotiating for technical experts from India to come to Trinidad to help develop its technological base.[7] Enhancing this thrust at increasing trade and commerce between India and Trinidad and Tobago, this author also contributed, in March 2007, by addressing several academics, industrialists, diplomats, nongovernmental organizations (NGOs) and business organizations in Delhi, on the investment potential of T&T.[8] By the end of 2007 India and T&T had accomplished the following: Both governments had signed a Bilateral Investment Promotion and Protection Agreement (BIPPA) Act; the Bank of Baroda was issued with a license to operate in Trinidad and Tobago; and a Memorandum of Understanding was signed by Trinidad and Tobago Chamber of Commerce and the Chamber of Indian Industries.

In 2008 the first major Trade and Investment Mission from India, comprising over 60 merchants from India, Bangladesh and

Singapore, headed by T&T High Commissioner, Pundit Persad, arrived in Trinidad. In quick succession a second Investment Mission arrived in 2009, bringing merchants from India and Sri Lanka (Ramdeen *et al.* 2009, 42). In addition the High Commission of India in Trinidad organized visits of senior executives of the EXIM (Export Import) Bank, Air India, and Indian tourism based in the USA to coincide with the visit of the Confederation of Indian Industries (CII) and the Federation of Indian Export Organizations (FIEO) to Trinidad. The CII delegation also visited Tobago and held discussions with the Tobago House of Assembly on a range of prospective trade initiatives. The delegation members later held discussion on a range of issues with Ministers and High Officials of the governments of Grenada, Suriname, Cuba and Dominica. The list of possible investments was in diverse fields of irrigation, farming, petrochemicals, Ayurveda, information technology (IT), tourism, desalination projects, engineering, and micro, small and medium-scale enterprises (MSMEs). By the end of 2009 India was "the fourth largest investor in this Caribbean twin-island nation" (Ramdeen *et al.* 2009, 17-19).

With respect to India T&T bilateral trade, from the period 2001 to 2008-9, Indian exports to T&T registered an exponential growth from US$ 8.8milion to US$ 312 million. India also set a target of reaching US$ 500 million of exports to T&T by 2010-2011. On the whole, over the period 2005-2010, India-Trinidad and Tobago bilateral trade statistics recorded significant positive changes. Exports from India to Trinidad included petroleum crude oil and products, drugs and pharmaceuticals, iron and steel, garments and other textiles, rice and other food stuff, including spices, IT services, automotive components, machinery and transportation equipment, plastic products, cosmetics, organic/inorganic chemicals, electronic goods, transport equipment, non-ferrous metals, gems and jewellery, silk, sports goods, chemicals, paints, footwear, carpets and leather goods. On the other hand, exports from Trinidad and Tobago to India comprised "scrap metals, wood and wood products, asphalt, chemicals and Liquid Natural Gas (LNG)" (Ramdeen 2009, 42-45). However trade figures between the two countries for 2009-2011decreased significantly due to global recession. T&T exports to India declined due to the fall in its exports of Liquefied Natural Gas (LNG). Trade figures are as follows:

Table 3.1: India and Trinidad Bilateral Trade Statistics in $US Million for the Period 2005-2010

Year	*India's Exports*	*India's Imports*
2005-2006	66.64	1.82
2006-2007	107.99	50.82
2007-2008	136.02	174.28
2008-2009	312.27	101.96l*
2009-2010	149.15	57.68
2010-2011	60.53	80.62

* Petroleum crude and petroleum products dropped from $172.58m in 2008 to $ 97.91M in 2009.

Source: Ministry of Commerce, New Delhi.

With the aim of further broadening and deepening their already existing bilateral trading and commercial relationships, The Hon. Prime Minister together with a delegation of governmental and private sector officials of Trinidad and Tobago visited India in January 2012 as guests of the Government of India. Negotiations were conducted in several areas and various sectors of the economy. This culminated in both countries signing Memoranda of Understanding (MOUs) in several sectors including ICT, medical and health care, tourism, fashion, film and animation plus air transport. Through a separate Memoranda of Understanding the University of the West Indies, St Augustine Campus, entered into an agreement with the Indira Gandhi National Open University (IGNOU) to introduce distance learning courses in Trinidad and Tobago. The Sri Ram Institute will also be assisting UWI in the field of research testing.

In terms of natural resources, the Gas Authority of India Ltd (GAIL) and the Oil and Natural Gas Commission of T&T entered into agreement for Trinidad and Tobago to provide India with expertise in the petroleum sector (Trinidad Express Newspaper, January 14, 2012). Trinidad has acquired significant experience in the petroleum sector, spanning over one hundred years, in drilling, crude oil refining and gas monetization.[9]

Today, Trinidad and Tobago with a land mass of approximately 2000 sq miles (Trinidad is 1864 sq miles and Tobago is 114 sq miles), a multicultural society, comprises a mosaic population of approximately 1.2 million people. Of this, approximately 40 per cent of this population is of Indian origin. It is a democratic republic with a bicameral system of government, literacy rates of over 99 per cent, with three university campuses and several other tertiary level educational and training institutions, both from North and South America operating within these shores by franchising their services. It has an excellent transport network and functioning public utilities. The country has a very vigilant press; over 37 radio stations, of which over five of them (radio stations) carry "Indian" music as their programming fare. There are several television stations and three daily newspapers, with the *lingua franca* being English. Physically and intellectually, the country possesses all the characteristics of an economy ready for take-off into achieving sustained economic growth.

With its rich oil and natural gas reserves, the country in 2010 had a high Gross Domestic Product (GDP) at current market prices of US$Mn. 20,945.3 and a GDP per capita of US$15,895.2.[10] With the energy sector being the mainstay of the economy, the petroleum sector contributed, in 2010, approximately 35.7 per cent of the country's GDP. In 2011 (January 1st to September 30) crude oil production amounted to 25,576 thousand barrels while natural gas production measured 32,023 million cubic metres (Jan-Sept 2011).[11]

Currently T&T is the largest and most vibrant economy in the Caribbean with a very stable and dynamic financial services sector. Moreover with its regional and bilateral preferential trade agreements, T&T offers excellent opportunities to exporters operating from within its geographic boundaries to access other Latin American and Caribbean markets.

Potential for Future Development: Globalization, Culture Blocks, the Digital Divide

In the 21st century, we are witnessing more countries inadvertently fraternizing and converging to form blocs in which there are common characteristics of ethnicities, common legacies, traditions and histories and in this way figuratively compressing the planet into a smaller, more assessable market place. Wars are being fought by technology which is beamed to the rest of the world in real time. In this process physical distances have become almost a non-issue. The world in which the concept of "rural" or "hinterland," or people living on the margin of information and knowledge is rapidly disappearing. The television has invaded almost all living rooms and telephone has become an indispensable feature of daily communication.

In this brave new world India has developed the competitive edge in a range of products and services: agriculture, industry, manufacturing, textiles, education, training and entertainment. It is engaged in the export of services, and the development of technology and innovative methods of production leading to the creation of a knowledge-based economy, achieving high returns on investment. In this scenario Trinidad and Tobago offers not only an attractive market for Indian goods and services but is the *entrepôt* to Latin America and the rest of the Caribbean, a captive market of over 600 million people. Being a member of the major economic blocs in the region, it assures automatic access to the Latin American and Caribbean integrated markets, and the North American economic giant which is currently experiencing some cyclical depression. This strategic location creates the avenue for Indian products to penetrate these markets from different directions thereby benefitting from economies of scale. Moreover, the scientific and technological advances facilitating the rapidity of connectivity and air travel has significantly reduced distances and provided information for real time decision making. In this regard a number of organizations and confederations, particularly those from India have begun to take advantage of these opportunities and commenced interactions with similar partners in the private sectors in T&T and its neighbours.

The year 2009 (October 6, 2009) witnessed the inauguration of the India—Trinidad and Tobago Chamber of Industry and Commerce, a not-for-profit business organization, "dedicated to the promotion of Industry and Commerce in and between the Republics of India and Trinidad and Tobago" (Gosine 2009, 5). This chamber is yet another mechanism established to both increase commercial and trading links between Asia and the West Indies, given that China and India are the two emerging Asian and global economic giants of the 21st century. Comprising a number of organizations with similar interests, the Chamber enunciated a number of plans. These included, *inter alia,* proposals to foster the collaboration necessary to enter regional markets, business ventures, technology transfers, help provide foreign direct investment in T&T, become the forum and vehicle to promote commerce, create wealth, educate and improve the lives of our people, provide member network service and brand, and position Trinidad and Tobago as a centre and gateway for regional commerce between Asia, North and South America. These are very grandiose ideas. The Chamber, in pursuing its objectives, established alliances with a number of similar federations including the Federation of Indian Commerce and Industry (FICCI), Confederation of Indian Industries (CII), Federation of Indian Export Organizations (FIEO) and the Indian Association of Tour Operations providing adequate platform and leverage to assist in the continued transformation of the respective economies.

And even as trade and commerce continue between India and the Caribbean in the established products, there are new areas being further exploited, such as the celluloid world, sports and tourism. Bollywood has been filming in Trinidad, Tobago and the Caribbean. India, over the last decade, has been contracting Trinidad and Tobago's sportsmen to join their regional sporting teams, cricket and now football, to either enhance their competitive edge or build capability in those games. These sportsmen include Robin Singh, Brian Lara, and more recently Dwayne Bravo and Kieron Pollard.

Conclusion

So much has been written and disseminated by Europeans on Indian anthropological and historical issues, from the outsider's perspective. The whole history of the impact of India's trade, commerce and other cultural influences, along with its spirituality, philosophy, religion, and the literary, creative, performing, culinary and plastic arts with the outside world now needs to be rewritten from India's perspective. This has to be viewed through land, sea and air routes, and now cyber space. It is also necessary to view these issues from an entirely fresh Western perspective so as to understand and correct distortions of facts and derive a more balanced view of human civilization and India's role in this constantly changing global dynamic environment, all the way from antiquity to the current period. To a lesser extent, this can also be said of new societies such as those of the Caribbean and Trinidad and Tobago.

Enterprise, entrepreneurship, technology and innovativeness are major attributes in the armory of assets of countries. They are major factors in the development of capital and the creation of both the wealth and wellbeing of their citizenry, in the physical and the intellectual sense. While the above attributes are plentiful in the Indian economy, they are slowly developing in Trinidad and Tobago. But the fraternal relationships, common complementarities and positioning are as important as entrepreneurship, enterprise and innovativeness. With these pillars the platform has been created for improving future trade and commerce between the Caribbean and Latin America and India.

This platform has recently been given credibility by The "Financial Times" of August/September 2011.[12] The *Financial Times* ranked five Caribbean countries including Trinidad and Tobago among the top 10 Caribbean and Central American countries of the future. Trinidad and Tobago is number one among the Caribbean countries. Costa Rica however tops the list, as the number one country in the Caribbean and Latin American countries of the future. The top five ranking, taking the Caribbean only, is listed below with the country's ranking in the top 10 in brackets: Trinidad and Tobago (3); Barbados (4); Antigua and Barbuda (6); British Virgin Islands (7); and Jamaica (10)

The rankings were created by the Foreign Direct Investment (FDI) Intelligence Division of the *Financial Times* in Britain as a benchmark of the investment attractiveness of countries and cities in more than 55 sectors for 350 locations around the world.

The Countries of the Future shortlists were created by an independent collection of data by the FDI Intelligence division across 31 Caribbean and Central American countries. Based on this survey, using data in nine categories per country, Trinidad and Tobago's rankings were as follows: Best Cost Effectiveness, 2; Best Economic Potential, 5; Best Quality of Life, 7; Best FDI (Foreign Direct Investment) Strategy, 7; Best Infrastructure, 10. The country is not ranked in the top 10 in two categories: Best Business Friendliness and Best Human Resources. In terms of world rankings as a competitive economy, the World Economic Forum Global Competiveness Report, 2011-2012 (this year) moved it up the ladder three places, to number 81. Barbados ranked 42 and Jamaica in number 107, Guyana at 109 and Suriname at 112. (*Daily Express* 2011, 10).

Given the results of the above survey, and the growing recognition by more Indian companies of the investment potential and opportunities in this country to develop and market appropriate products for hemispheric and global markets, the future for both trading partners is bright.

Given the historical antecedents that Trinidad and Tobago and the Caribbean share with India, the mutual complementarities, fraternal bonds, struggle for independence from shared colonial masters and later their South-South cooperation, their common goals within the Group of Seventy Seven, the United Nations family and their current geopolitical bilateral relationships, the future joint relationships are promising and exciting. They would only improve to the benefit of each trading partner. Moreover, in the spirit of globalization where the walls of the mind are not only being shattered but are being replaced by creative initiatives and influences by people with common legacies, the possibilities for the two regions for the 21st century are endless. Trinidad and Tobago and the Caribbean can achieve that state of sustained development, nay paradise, for in the words of Nobel Laureate Rabindranath Tagore: "Everywhere in this earth the spirit of paradise is awake and sending forth its voice. It reaches our inner ear without our knowing it. It tunes our harp of life which sends our aspirations in music beyond the finite, in pictures which are dreams made everlasting" (Tagore 1926, 13-15).

Notes

1. For this study the various periods of history are classified accordingly: Early Ancient Period (Iron Age),10th century BC to 4th-3rd century BC; Ancient Period, 3rd century BC to 4th century AD; Medieval period (early), 5th to 10th century AD; Medieval period (late), 11-17th century AD; Modern period, 17th-21st century (present); Current 1950 to 2010.
2. Some of the well known sailing ships owned by James Nourse Ltd were the *'Ailsa, Jura, Pandora, British Nation, British Statesman, Sheila, Brenda and later the Jumna, Foyle, Bann, Moy, and Avoca.* The first two ships that brought Indentured Indian immigrants to Guyana in 1838, the *Hesperus* and *Whitby* were however owned by Messers. Gillanders, Arbuthnot and Co., a Calcutta Shipping Company. The *Fath Al Razak,* a 395 tons, sail driven (*pal jahaj* manned by *laskars,* as the Indian sailors were then called), caravel built in Denmark in 1844, and owned then by a wealthy Bombay merchant, Ibrahim bin Yoosuf, landed the first batch of 225 Indian "coolies" in Port of Spain Trinidad in 1845 (Samaroo 1999,11-13).
3. The *Dahomey* carried 622 workers and 13,000 bags of rice to Jamaica and Demerara from Calcutta. See Samaroo 1999, 14.
4. Crown Lands Purchased by East Indians in Trinidad, 1885-1921.

Year	*No. of Grants To Population*	*Acreage**	*No. of Grants To Indians*	*Acreage**
1885-1889	3018	44,600	797	10,654
1890-1894	2,917	33,006	162	9,615
1895-1899	3,474	38,606	1,089	12,602

(*Contd.*)

Year	*No. of Grants To Population*	*Acreage**	*No. of Grants To Indians*	*Acreage**
1900-1904	6,969	67,626	2,733	21,920
1905-1909	5,741	51,803	2,593	18,374
1910-1914	1,975	12,356	667	3,267
1915-1920	3,358	19,481	1,055	5,334
Total	**27,452**	**267,478**	**9,096**	**81,676**

Source: 1885 to 1908-9: Gt. Britain, Parliamentary Papers 1910, XXVII (Cd.5194), Report of the Committee of Emigration from India to the Crown Colonies and Protectorates (Sanderson Commission Report), pt. 3, p. 130: 1908-9 to 1920-21: Annual reports of the Sub-Intendant for Crown Lands (Trinidad), in Trinidad Legislative Council Papers. * Acreages given in round figures.

5. The twin island State of Trinidad and Tobago received its independence from Great Britain on August 31, 1962.
6. MOUs were signed in sectors of Housing, Cultural Relations and Foreign Affairs. This author was part of the joint, small, official team from Governments of T&T and India preparing the manuscript for the MOU on Housing and Settlements. He delivered the acknowledgements at the formal opening ceremony of the Shelter Support Centre by the Prime Ministers of both countries.
7. This author was in India when both Ministers of T&T Government visited that country and was invited to meet with them.
8. The Address, made on Friday March 23, at the Ballroom of the Grand Hotel, Delhi, was entitled "Exploring Trinidad and Tobago and India's Cultural Relations With A View To Enhancing Further Co-Operation." It was organized by His Excellency, the High Commissioner for Trinidad and Tobago to India, Pundit Maniedeo Persad and the Trinidad and Tobago High Commission, India.
9. Address by Kamla Persad Bissessar, Prime Minister of The Republic of T&T, to Pravasi Bharatiya Divas 2012, Jaipur, India
10. "T&T Major Economic Indicators"; Summary Economic Indicators, Central Bank of T&T September 13, 2011.
11. "Summary of Economic Developments of Trinidad and Tobago"—Summary Economic Indicators, Central Bank of T&T, September 1, 2011.
12. Caribbean and Central American Countries of the future. www.fDiIntelligence.com. August/September 2011,26-29.

4

An Overview of Sino-Caribbean Relations

Wang Guo-An and *Nan Yang*

Since adopting the Reform and Opening-Up policies, China has made great progress in its economy. From 1978 to 2008, the annual growth rate of the gross domestic product (GDP) of China reached 9.69 per cent, which is much higher than the world's average growth rate of 3.3 per cent over the same period (see Figure 4.1). China's annual GDP of 2009 reached RMB 33.54 trillion (US$5.17 trillion), accounting for about 8 per cent of the world's total. In accounting for purchasing power, China's annual GDP for 2009 reached US$8.77 trillion, which is now ranked as the world's second largest economy, after the United States. By the end of 2009, China's foreign exchange reserve reaching US$2.4 trillion was ranked as number one in the world, thus accounting for approximately 30.7 per cent of global reserves and is 1.93 times the total of G7 reserves. Moreover, China's annual total export-import volume in 2009 reached US$2.2 trillion, giving it the second place in the world in which the annual export volume reached US$1.2 trillion and for the first time overtaking Germany as the world's largest exporter of goods; the annual import volume reached about US$1 trillion, with a trade surplus of US$196.1 billion. Thus, China has emerged as a robust economy on the world stage.

Despite the geographical distance being thousands of miles between China and the Caribbean region, the traditional friendship of the two regions has a long and enduring history. Since the first group of Chinese arrived in Trinidad and Tobago more than 200 years ago, the ethnic Chinese people have been gradually

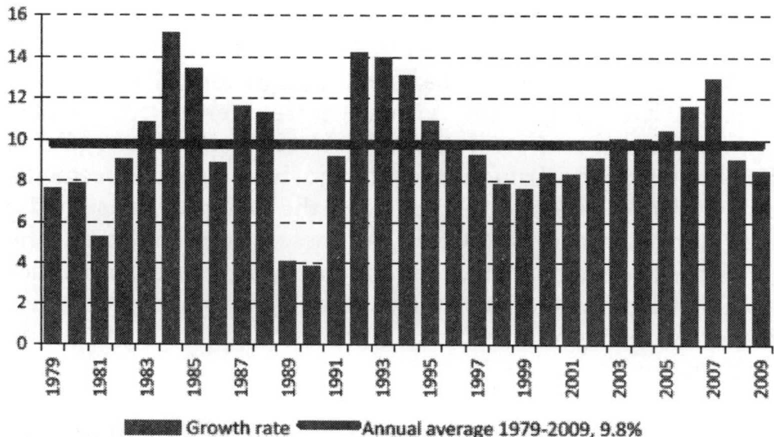

Figure 4.1: China: Annual Growth Rate, 1979-2009 (Percentage)

Source: Economic Commission for Latin America and the Caribbean (ECLAC), on the basis of information from the United Nations Commodity Trade Database (COMTRADE) and IMF Direction of Trade Statistics (DOTS).

integrated with the local Caribbean people. This integration has made a great contribution to the development of the local economy and has played the part of bridging the connection between China and the Caribbean area at the initial stage of economic and trade cooperation. However, Sino-Caribbean economic and trade relationship had been at a low level for a period of time principally because of the long geographic distance between these two regions and some related historical reasons. It was with the birth of the new China (People's Republic of China) in October 1949 that this situation saw a turning point, especially as China adopted the Reform and Opening-Up policies. In these years, with the diversification of the Chinese market, the implementation of China's "Going Out" Strategy and the gradual opening of the Caribbean market, the Sino-Caribbean economic and trade relationship developed rapidly and achieved notable progress.

In addition to the economic progression, the development of the Sino-Caribbean political relationship has helped to promote both sides' cooperation in economic and bilateral trade. Data furnished by the Chinese Foreign Ministry suggest that China has established formal diplomatic relationships with most countries in this region at present (Ministry of Foreign Affairs of the People's Republic of China 2010).[1] Among the countries having already established diplomatic relations with China, five countries (Cuba, Suriname, Jamaica, Guyana and Trinidad and Tobago) have signed trade agreements, five (Cuba, Jamaica, Barbados, Trinidad and Tobago, Guyana) have signed agreements on mutual encouragement and protection of investments, and four (Cuba, Jamaica, Barbados, Trinidad and Tobago) have signed agreements on avoidance of double taxation, and the Bahamas has signed a maritime agreement with China. All these agreements enable the two sides to develop their economic and trade relationship under a stable framework of law to facilitate the development of their respective economies (China-Caribbean Economic and Trade Cooperation Forum 2004).

Trade and Economic Cooperation between China and Latin America and the Caribbean Area

Trade between China and Latin America and the Caribbean

It need hardly be said that the Caribbean region sits alongside Latin America and that the trade relationship between China and Latin America also has a long history. Since China adopted the Reform and Opening-Up policies in late 1970s, trade between China and Latin America has entered a new promising era. Trade between China and Latin America experienced a steady growth in the 1990s (see Table 4.1). In 2000, the bilateral trade volume amounted to US$12.6 billion. Since the beginning of this century, the bilateral trade has been growing very rapidly. Especially during the period of 2003 to 2008, trade between China and Latin America appears to have accelerated (see Figure 4.2). It reached more than US$100 billion in 2007 for the first time, which met the target three years ahead of schedule as was set by Chinese President Hu Jintao in 2004 when he visited Latin America and it was a well noted point in the history of trading between China and Latin America (Tong 2009). From this perspective, China has become the third largest goods supplier for Latin America, where imports from China account for 14 per cent of the total imports for Latin America. In 2008 the trade volume between China and Latin America reached about US$150 billion, which increased by about 40 per cent in comparison to that of 2007 and represents ten times as much as that of 2000.

According to statistics from the Chinese government, in 2007 the volume of export from China to Latin America was US$51.5

Table 4.1: China: Average Annual Trade Growth with Latin America and the Caribbean, 1990-2009 (Percentage)

	1990-1995	*1995-2000*	*2000-2005*	*2005-2009*
Export	32.2	17.8	26.8	26.1
Import	14.5	12.7	37.6	22.8

Source: Economic Commission for Latin America and the Caribbean (ECLAC), on the basis of information from the United Nations Commodity Trade Database (COMTRADE) and IMF Direction of Trade Statistics (DOTS)

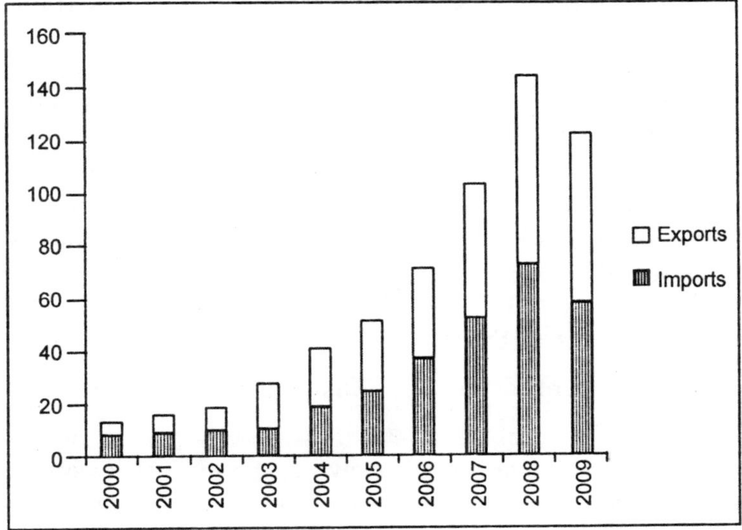

Figure 4.2: Exports, Imports with China (Billions of Dollars)

Source: National Bureau of Statistics of China. China Statistic Year Book 2000-2009.

billion, accounting for approximately 4.2 per cent of its total, while China's imports from Latin America amounted to US$51 billion, accounting for 5.3 per cent of China's total imports (Development Bureau of Ministry of Commerce, People's Republic of China 2008). Based on that, the total trade volume reached as much as over US$100 billion for the first time and Brazil had become China's 9th largest supplier of goods. This situation being so, China has become one of the most important trading partners in Latin America and the Caribbean area, and their exports to China have also been increasing so much so that, among these countries in Latin America and the Caribbean area, Chile's share of export to the Asia-Pacific region (17 countries) and China have increased from 25.8 per cent in 2001 to 33.7 per cent in 2006 (in which about 9 per cent of the growth came from its export to China). Both Peru and CSN (South American Community of Nations) (excluding Paraguay) also expanded their exports to China. Costa Rica's share of export to the Asia-Pacific region and China increased from 7.3 per cent in 2001 to 19.8 per cent in 2006, in which the export to China accounts for about 7.7 per cent. Statistics from China's General Administration of Customs show that China's trade volume with the region in 2008 amounted to US$143.4 billion, up 39.8 per cent year-on-year. Chinese exports to that region were US$71.47 billion and imports were US$71.9 billion, basically maintaining a balance of imports and exports. Exports and imports rose 38.8 per cent and 40.8 per cent year-on-year respectively (National Bureau of Statistics of China 2009). Of China's exports to the Latin American region, mechanical and electrical products accounted for about 50 per cent. High and new technology products, as well as light industrial and textile products, still made up a large proportion of exports. China's imports from Latin America were mainly mineral products, farm produce and other basic raw material products (see Figure 4.5).

Economic Cooperation between China and Latin America and the Caribbean

As the bilateral trade flow is growing, the mutual investment between China and Latin America has also been developing. Latin America is a key area of interest for China's "Going out" strategy adopted in 2004 by the Chinese government. In that year, China's foreign direct investment reached US$5.5 billion, about 32 per cent of which (US$1.76 billion) had been invested in Latin America. In 2008, China's non-financial foreign direct investment to Latin America reached US$3.07 billion. As of 2008, China's cumulative outward direct investment in Latin America was around US$24.77 billion, mainly referring to the fields of trading, engineering contracts, the exploration of oil, gas and mineral resources.

At the same time, the growing Chinese market also attracted many investors from Latin America. According to statistics from the Chinese Ministry of Commerce, by the end of 2005, there had been 17,958 investment projects in China from Latin America and the total investment volume reached US$56.9 billion. The number of investment projects from Latin America amounted to 1337 items by 2008. By the end of 2008, the total number of investing projects from Latin America had amounted to 24,976, the contracted foreign investment reached US$208.7 billion, and the actual amount of investment reached US$112.6 billion. By way of specific countries, British Virgin Islands, Cayman Islands, Barbados, Bahamas, Panama, and Brazil are the countries that had invested the most in China (National Bureau of Statistics of China 2008; Tong 2009, accessed on 15 Jan. 2011).

Shocks From the Financial Crisis and the Future for Development

The worldwide financial crisis that originated from the US subprime mortgage crisis had severe negative effects on the bilateral trade between China and Latin America, so much so that the bilateral trading volume of the first half of 2009 dropped by 26.6 per cent to US$48.941 billion, in which the export and import volumes of China to that region were respectively US$23.093 billion and US$25.847 billion, decreasing by 28.1 per cent and 25.3 per cent. Despite the strikes brought on by the financial crisis from the beginning of 2009, viewing the monthly volumes of bilateral trades between China and Latin America from a different angle, these data indicated that the monthly declining rates in the bilateral trade had been already in a gradually narrowing trend, suggesting that a restorative growth had been underway; it is considered that trade between China and Latin America has begun to stabilize without a further plunge.

Largely influenced by the liquidity caused by the international financial crisis, the investment activities from Latin America and the Caribbean decreased significantly: from January to April in 2009, the number of newly approved investment projects from the Latin America and Caribbean areas to China dropped by 52.1 per cent yearly to only 257 items, and the amount of contracted foreign investment reached US$3.058 billion while the actual investment reached US$5.154 billion, dropping respectively by 35.1 per cent and 37.1 per cent yearly. This situation being the case, Chinese enterprises had not delayed their pace in investing in Latin America: the non-financial investment in Latin America and the Caribbean region from China reached US$0.309 billion in the first quarter of 2009, increasing by 61.5 per cent yearly. The non-financial investment from China to Latin America and the Caribbean, apart from the international tax havens such as the Cayman Islands and British Virgin Islands, increased by 19.4 per cent yearly to US$15.857

million. Although the trading between China and Latin America was influenced in some degree in the context of the international financial crisis, their complementarity in economy still has a great capacity, the bilateral political relationship is still in a good condition, and the foundation of cooperation in economy and trading is still firm. With this deepening of mutual understanding and the growing interests in the business community being keen to cooperate, the developing economic and trade cooperation between China and Latin America has a good prospect with substantial potential benefit.

According to a recent report of Economic Commission for Latin America and the Caribbean (ECLAC), ("China has become a key strategic cooperator of Caribbean countries", www.people.com, Apr. 28, 2010 http://world.people.com.cn/GB/57507/11481931.html —accessed Jan 15, 2011), China has already become a strategic trading partner of Latin America and the Caribbean region, and the development potential is still huge. With the increasing export to Latin American countries, China is also expanding its investment in mining, energy, agriculture, technology, infrastructure construction in Latin America and the Caribbean area. ECLAC predicts that China is likely to become the second largest export/supply destination for the Latin America and Caribbean areas in the next 10 years. The sustainable development of China will change the traditional export markets for these Latin American countries (see Figure 4.2).

Trade and Economic Cooperation between China and the Caribbean Region

Trade between China and Caribbean Region

Under the rapid development of the Sino-Latin America trade and investment in recent years, Sino-Caribbean economic and trade relationship has also made great progress. The Caribbean region has been an important area for China's strategy of market diversification. In the past 30 years, since China's adoption of the Reform and Opening-Up policies, the economic and trade cooperation between China and the Caribbean area began with bilateral trade, then gradually evolved to the multi-level and comprehensive cooperation in various fields, such as bilateral investment, project contracting, high-tech cooperation and so on based on the enlarging trade volume. According to the statistics of China Customs, the rapid growth in bilateral trade between

China and the Caribbean area started in the 1990s. With the constant development in these two regions during this time, the economic and trade cooperation has made great progress in that the bilateral trade volume hit US$5.2 billion in 2007 from just US$0.4 billion in 1991, showing almost 13 fold increase in 16 years.

Going back to 1991, only Cuba within the Caribbean region had a bilateral trade volume of more than US$10 million with China, and even the countries with more than US$5 million of bilateral trade volume at this time included only Dominica, Trinidad and Tobago, and Jamaica. By comparison, in 2004, there were 15 of China's trade partners in the Caribbean region with bilateral trade volume of more than US$ 10 million: Cuba, Jamaica, Puerto Rico, the Dominican Republic, Antigua and Barbuda, the Bahamas, Trinidad and Tobago, Dominica, Curacao, Suriname, Belize, Guyana, Haiti, Saint Vincent and the Grenadines, Barbados, in which the bilateral trade volumes of Cuba, Jamaica, Puerto Rico, the Dominican Republic, Antigua and Barbuda all have exceeded US$100 million (Ministry of Commerce of the People's Republic of China 2006).

In 2007, the Sino-Caribbean bilateral trade volume headed to a new high of US$5.25 billion with a year-on-year growth of 19.3 per cent. This marked the first time the two regions' annual trade volume amounted to more than US$5 billion, in which the export and import trade volumes of China respectively reached US$3.77 billion and US$1.48 billion with an annual growth of 15.1 per cent and 31.5 per cent respectively. Currently, there are 9 trade partners in the Caribbean region whose bilateral trade volumes with China exceed US$100 million. These countries were Cuba (US$2.28 billion), Dominican Republic (US$613 million), Puerto Rico (US$557 million), Antigua and Barbuda (US$395 million), Jamaica (US$285 million), Trinidad and Tobago (US$284 million), Bahamas (US$181 million), the British Virgin Islands (US$116 million) and Dominica (US$104 million). Bilateral trade volumes with China of the remaining countries of the Caribbean region are neither large nor stable, in which the exports from China often accounts for the largest share. The main export products from China to the Caribbean region are currently mechanical and electrical products (ships, port equipment, household appliances, etc.), clothing and textiles, light industry products, chemical products and pharmaceutical raw materials, etc. For the long distance and the unfamiliarity of the export products from the Caribbean region, China still imports few from this region and the main importing products include aluminum, wood, and asphalt (Ministry of Commerce of the People's Republic of China 2008).

Economic Cooperation between China and Caribbean Region

In the meantime, the economic cooperation between China and the Caribbean is being continually broadened. The deepening cooperation in specialized areas such as human resource development, investment, tourism, agriculture, education, finance, and infrastructure construction has already achieved remarkable progress and has made positive contributions to the development of economic and social progress of both sides. Despite the differences in the natural conditions, social institutions and levels of development, China and the countries of the Caribbean region all belong to developing countries that are devoted to the development of their respective national economies and the improvement of people's standards of living. After entering this new century, facing all sorts of challenges brought by the complex international situation and the irresistible trend of economic globalization, China and the Caribbean countries have increasingly realized the importance and urgency in strengthening their bilateral cooperation.

More than 30 years since China adopted the Reform and Opening-Up policies, a series of multilateral or bilateral dialogue mechanisms have been set up between China and the countries of the Caribbean region, which have provided an important platform for solving problems and exploring the potential in economic and trade cooperation for both sides. They also play an important role in developing a healthy and stable economic and trade relationship between China and the Caribbean region. At present, 13 bilateral joint economic and trade committees have been established between China and the Caribbean region.

In respect of these dialogue mechanisms, it is worth mentioning that the multilateral dialogue mechanism of China-Caribbean Economic and Trade Cooperation Forum set up in 2004, which is to be held by China and the Caribbean countries in turn, on a 4-year basis, aims to facilitate economic and trade communication and cooperation, and achieve mutual development. They also aim to promote contact and exchange, and enlarge the content and extent of Sino-Caribbean cooperation in economics and trade to fulfill the target of achieving mutual benefits and a win-win result. Thus, in February 2005, the first

China-Caribbean Economic and Trade Cooperation Forum was held in Kingston, Jamaica, where Zeng Qinghong, the then Chinese Vice President, made his keynote speech at the opening ceremony and attended some related activities. This event served to reaffirm China's policy of strengthening the Sino-Caribbean cooperation acknowledged by most Caribbean countries. In the forum, the representatives of China and 11 Caribbean countries signed the Action Programme for Economic and Trade Cooperation, which maps out the key fields where cooperation would be strengthened in the future including trade, investment, agriculture, fishery, tourism, transportation, finance, and human resource development. The first successful forum laid an important milestone in the history of the Sino-Caribbean economic and trade cooperation.

As ongoing evidence of the cooperation and mutual development between China and the Caribbean region, the 2nd China-Caribbean Economic and Trade Cooperation Forum was held on 7th September 2007 in Xiamen, China. Wu Yi, then a member of the Central Politburo and Vice Premier of the State Council, made her speech at the opening ceremony, stating that deepening the Sino-Caribbean friendship and enlarging the mutual cooperation conform to the people's desire and the fundamental and long-term interests of both sides, and China is willing to strengthen the economic and trade cooperation with the Caribbean countries for mutual development (http://news.sina.com.cn/c/2007-09-08/084612532621s.shtml —accessed on Dec 20, 2010).

Wu Yi also pointed out in her speech, that the Chinese government highly values the friendly relationship with the Caribbean countries, regarding it as an important part of China's relations with developing countries. As such China intends to deepen this cooperation with the countries of the Caribbean region based on the principle of equality and mutual benefit, and to normalize the diplomatic relations with a few countries in the Caribbean region, which still have not established formal diplomatic relations with China. In order to boost substantial cooperation within the fields of trade, investment, agriculture, fishery, tourism, transportation, finance, human resources development etc., China put forward the following six measures:

1. To improve trade conditions and promote a balanced development of trade.
2. To provide financial support and motivate investment and

cooperation, China would provide a concessional loan of RMB ¥4 billion in the next 3 years to encourage more Chinese enterprises to invest in the Caribbean.

3. To enlarge training scale and enhance workers' capacity, China has promised to provide a total of 2000 training positions for the workers from the Caribbean countries within the next 3 years.
4. To expand the technical exchange and deepen the cooperation in the agricultural and fishery sectors.
5. To implement the travel treaty to boost the cooperation in tourism.
6. To facilitate people's exchange to promote mutual understanding. In mid-September 2010, the 3rd China-Caribbean Economic and Trade Cooperation Forum, hosted by the Chinese Foreign Ministry, Commerce Department and CCPIT (China Council for the Promotion of International Trade), had been held in the city of Port of Spain, the capital of Trinidad and Tobago.

Currently the Sino-Caribbean relationship is kept in such a good esteem that more and more high-level visits are being arranged, exchange in economy and trade is being strengthened, and the Sino-Caribbean relationship is being consolidated with the deepening cooperation in economy and bilateral trade. Most countries in the Caribbean region are friendly to China. While maintaining their economic and trade relationship with the US and European countries which are their traditional target markets, the Caribbean countries are now urgently focusing on developing economic and trade relationship with Asian countries, especially with China. They do so with the aim of achieving the diversification of relationships in economy and trade and enlarging the amount and extent of bilateral trade and investment. With the growing economic strength of both sides, a new mutually beneficial situation of integrated development is likely to emerge between China and the Caribbean countries and in the process consistently enhance the economic and trade relationship of both sides.

The Problems and Obstacles in Economic and Trade Relations between China and the Caribbean Region

Over the past decade, China-Caribbean trade and economic relations have witnessed significant developments; however, this progress has been distinctively incremental, along with some problems and barriers that still need to be overcome, notably:

1. Overseas investments of Chinese companies show a lack of awareness of having international operations strategy and an effective strategic plan on a long-term basis. According to the enterprise business strategy, the overseas market development is a systematic project, and needs the awareness of international operations strategy and effective strategic design. But many Chinese companies do not devise overall strategic plans to develop the overseas market when they are entering the Caribbean region. In the field of trading, many companies have been frustrated by the volatile market there because of their short-term business plans, which often result in reduced commodity prices and the loss of profits, and sometimes even lead to anti-dumping duties being imposed by the importing countries. Indirect investment, blind investment, unclear investment purposes, underestimated changes and risks are the main reasons accounting for their failure in markets in the Caribbean region.
2. China's foreign investment regulations, policies and management system have much room for improvement. The Chinese government and its financial sector have shown insufficient support to the overseas development of Chinese enterprises. China's foreign investment legislation has lagged behind, unable to adapt to the needs of its overseas investment. For the divided investment management sectors, the overseas investment projects have to be approved by many departments concerned after going through complicated procedures. There are also loopholes in the management of funds for overseas investment, resulting in the lack of supervision and management regarding the use of funds. In addition, there exists financing difficulty as well as lack of strong banking and financial services support. So far, the development of China's financial sectors in the Caribbean market is still not mature, lacking in long-term development plans of harnessing the Caribbean market. The financial services network covering the whole Caribbean region is yet to be established.
3. The differences between China and Caribbean countries pose some difficulty in the development of the bilateral

economic and trade relations. There are great differences in values, people's ways of thinking, corporate cultures, management methods and so on between China and Caribbean countries. But very few Chinese companies going to invest in the Caribbean region have been fully aware of the differences and thus have not made enough effort to overcome those differences before their "going out." In addition, the investment environment in the Caribbean region is far from familiar to Chinese enterprises, which often results in great difficulties and unnecessary losses.

4. China's import and export commodity structure is not balanced or diversified. Currently, although the manufactured goods exported from China to the Caribbean region are increasing, there are still very few high value-added types of products, most of the exports still belong to the middle and low commodity goods, while the imported commodities are primary products and resources. It is very important for Chinese enterprises to improve their grade of commodity, increase the technical level and added value, optimize the export structure to reduce costs, enhance economic efficiency and expand the range of export commodities. Balancing bilateral trade and injecting new vitality to Sino-Caribbean trade often lies in expansion of the scope of imported goods and the optimization of the export commodity structure.
5. There are still huge trade imbalances between China and Latin America and the Caribbean. Trade imbalance is one of the important causes for trade frictions (see Figure 4.3). In some countries governments are often subject to pressures from their relevant industries, and as such they take the long-term trade deficit very seriously and may make irrational responses. For example, in April 1993 the Mexican Government launched anti-dumping investigations against ten main categories of products from China, including over 4000 tariff codes, and levied provisional anti-dumping duties ranging from 16 per cent to 1105 per cent in order to protect their sensitive sectors. Anti-dumping is in line with international practices, and there are some trade-related provisions in many market economies. Anti-dumping and countervailing duties are recognized by the WTO as measures to protect sensitive industries. It would follow that all the countries can use

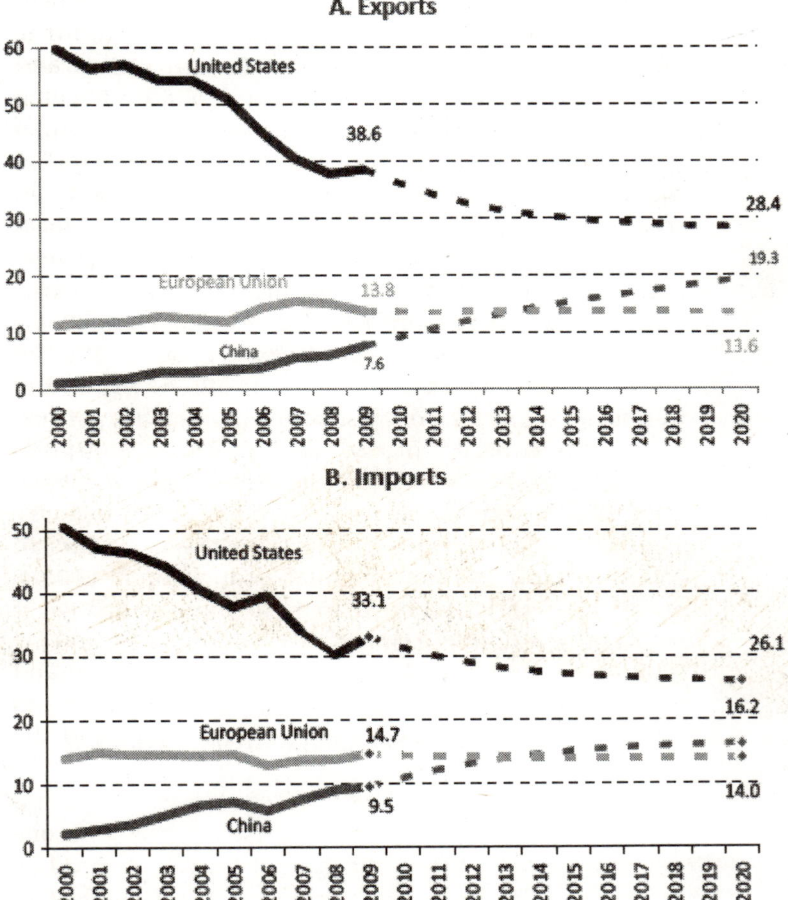

Figure 4.3: Latin America and the Caribbean (16 Countries)[2]: Share of the Main Destinations in Total Exports, 2000-2020 (percentage)

Source: Economic Commission for Latin America and the Caribbean (ECLAC), on the basis of information from the United Nations Commodity Trade Database (COMTRADE) and national sources.

them. But Mexico has made more anti-dumping investigations of Chinese goods than any other countries in the Latin American region and the world and undertook a large-scale anti-dumping measure with a wide range of imposed antidumping duties, which is seldom seen in the history of international trade.

6. There is some competition in trade among China and the Caribbean countries. Compared with China's exports to the Caribbean region, the imports of China from Caribbean countries is still in a very low level (see Figure 4.4). The commodity structure of Caribbean countries is similar with China's export structure, but the competitiveness of their products is far below that of China's commodities, so their trade deficit with China is increasing. Chinese products and Caribbean countries' products compete with each other not only in Caribbean markets, but also in the third country market—the USA. In fact, China has become the largest trading partner for the US, which is also the traditional and main market for most Latin American and Caribbean countries. For these countries, China is a strong competitor in the U.S. market. Therefore, the countries in this region often take anti-dumping and other protectionist measures to impose restrictions on Chinese exports. Though the exports from China to these Caribbean countries account for a very small proportion of China's exports, the market potential in these countries is huge; if they frequently adopt anti-dumping measures against Chinese imports, it will make a very negative impact on the healthy and sustainable development of the trade relations between China and the Caribbean region.

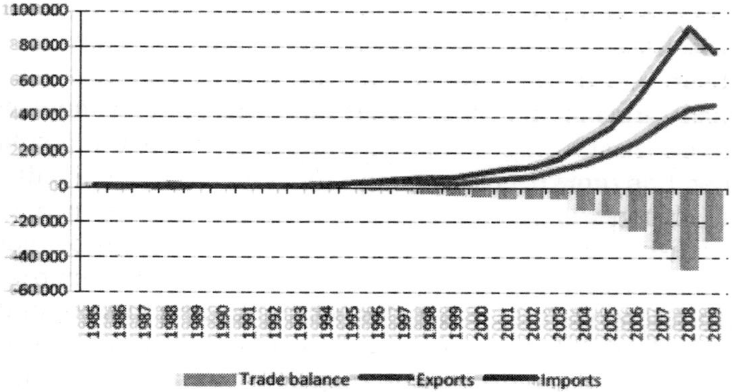

Figure 4.4: Latin America and the Caribbean: Exports, Imports and Trade Balance with China (US$ million)

Source: Economic Commission for Latin America and the Caribbean (ECLAC), on the basis of information from the United Nations Commodity Trade Database (COMTRADE).

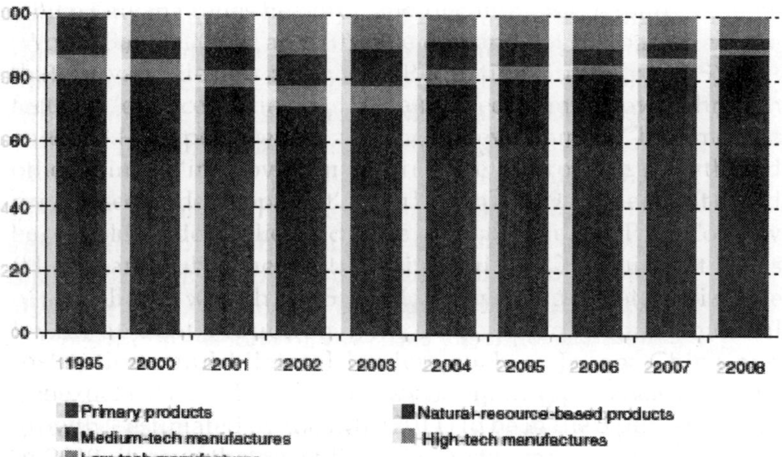

Figure 4.5: Latin America and the Caribbean: Exports to China, by Technological Content, 1995-2008 (Percentage)

Source: Economic Commission for Latin America and the Caribbean (ECLAC), on the basis of information from the United Nations Commodity Trade Database (COMTRADE)

Suggestions on Solving the Problems between China and the Caribbean

In order to secure the healthy development of economic and trade cooperation between China and the Caribbean region, the following suggestions are put forward:

1. Transition of the simple trade export policy to a combination of economic aid, trade and mutually beneficial economic cooperation. Due to the rapid economic integration process facilitated by the organizations such as CARICOM (Caribbean Community), Mercosur (Common Market of the South), CACM (Central American Common Market), most exchanges of goods in Latin America and the Caribbean region are now duty-free, and the duty-free policy will eventually be put into effect. The price advantage of Chinese products is offset to a large extent when the local products enjoy preferential tariffs. In addition, there are a considerable number of countries also implementing trade protectionism against China's products to varying degrees and the trend of anti-dumping action is increasing. Under

such circumstances, China's export trade in Caribbean countries becomes tougher. China should provide Caribbean countries with economic aid and have mutually beneficial cooperation with Caribbean countries in the form of joint ventures, cooperative projects and BOT (build—operate—transfer).[3]

2. There needs to be an expansion of investment in the fields of mining, forestry, animal husbandry, and infrastructure construction in the Caribbean region in a proactive and orderly pace. After years of exploration and research, China has found its own way to choose the investment fields in Latin America and the Caribbean. The Chinese government should support its enterprises to invest and explore the resources in Latin America and the Caribbean region under the consideration of their national "privatization" process and related policies. The major management authorities need to coordinate the fields and designate the companies to take charge of specific areas; those who have already been designated should make joint efforts to take an advantageous position in the markets of the Caribbean region.
3. Establishing the Chinese enterprises' own chamber of commerce to enhance and coordinate the relations with foreign countries. China has established approximately 200 state-owned enterprises in more than 20 Latin American and Caribbean countries. All these overseas enterprises have been very beneficial and have achieved a lot in developing bilateral trade. However, price-cutting competition is still widespread in these countries. China should try to establish its own enterprises' chambers of commerce according to the local conditions in different countries against the anti-dumping charges on Chinese products. The Chinese chambers of commerce's responsibilities should include coordination of export prices and responding to anti-dumping charges.
4. Expanding the market by improving the level of warehousing and distribution to meet both the needs of regional economic grouping and integration and of small-batch orders. It is necessary to continue to expand warehousing distribution. Additionally, it is important to upgrade the high-scale operation of promoting mechanical and electrical products and to solve the problems in after-

sales services and accessory supply so that we can expand the market there by gradually producing, selling and providing after-sale services locally in the Caribbean region.

5. Expanding the cargo trade and service trade. China and Caribbean countries are both in a period of strategic transition. In such a strategic transition period, both sides should foster a closer strategic partnership to their mutual benefits. Given that the proportion of foreign trade between the two sides is very small, the possibility of further expansion still exists. Although China and the Caribbean countries are both in their infancy in service trade and mutual investment, the situation is encouraging, because both sides have great potential for trade and economic cooperation.

Future Cooperation

The bilateral cooperation between China and the Caribbean region has a promising future. Since adopting the Reform and Opening-Up policies, China has achieved great progress in economic cooperation with the Caribbean countries; however there still exists a huge gap toward the ultimate aim of fully exerting both sides' potential and economic demand. The advantages in resources, technology and human resources of both sides are far from being fully utilized. The content of the Sino-Caribbean cooperation needs to be enriched, the cooperating relationship should be deepened, and the cooperating forms ought to be diversified. As noted earlier, it has been more than 30 years since China's adoption of the Reform and Opening-Up policies. Through independent research and innovation based on the absorption of imported technology and technological transformation of traditional technology, China has itself established a complete and high-level technological industrial system which has given birth to a large amount of mature industrial technologies and achievements in scientific research; some have even reached international standards. China's improved processing and export capacity has a great attraction to the Caribbean countries.

At the same time, it must be said that the Caribbean region also has its own unique advantages. Regional economic organizations in the region have developed rapidly, resulting in the convenience in goods and capital flows. Some countries in the region do benefit from the preferential tariffs and quota in European and American markets. However, constrained by the production capacity and level, the overall industrial base in the

Caribbean region is still so weak that a lot of manufactured products, especially those high technology and high value-added mechanical and electrical products, still mainly rely on the importation from Europe and the United States, for which the development of Sino-Caribbean cooperation has a great potential. Both sides can benefit from such cooperation, one that can yield a win-win result.

Conclusion

At the reception for the 50th anniversary celebration of the establishment of diplomatic relations between the People's Republic of China and the Latin American and Caribbean countries on 12th October 2010, Yang Jiechi, the Chinese Foreign Minister, noted that the establishment of diplomatic relations on an ambassadorial level between China and Cuba some 50 years ago opened the door for China to establish diplomatic relations with the countries in Latin America and the Caribbean. In the last 50 years, Sino-Latin American and Caribbean relations have withstood the test of various vicissitudes and made so considerable a progress that the mutual political trust has been deepened, the beneficial cooperation has grown, and mutual understanding has increased. The Chinese government attaches great importance to the relationships between China and Latin America and the Caribbean region. China and the countries of Latin America and the Caribbean region are in such a developing phase that both sides have similar tasks and extensive common benefits in achieving their own sustainable development, promoting a multipolar world and cooperation to meet global challenges. So both sides should join their hands more closely to propel a new progress through a comprehensive cooperation plan on the basis of equality and mutual benefit.

Velez Guillermo, Head of Latin America and Caribbean diplomatic missions and Ambassador of Colombia in China, has praised the friendly cooperation between China and Latin America and Caribbean countries over the last 50 years. He also made positive comments on China's successful experience in the international financial crisis and in its elimination of poverty initiatives. He further added that the countries of Latin America and the Caribbean highly value their relationship with China, in the firm belief that the Sino-Latin America and Caribbean relationship would continue to head in the direction of friendly political relationships and an active pragmatic cooperation between both sides (Xinhua Net 2010).

At present, the relationship between China and the Caribbean region has been developing rapidly, with further reinforcement through both official visits and increasing trade. Most Caribbean countries (which had previously concentrated mainly on the American and European markets) are gradually beginning to attach importance to developing economic and trading relationships with the countries in Asia, especially China, to enlarge their bilateral trade and investment while keeping the traditional economic and trading relationship with American and European countries. Due to the friendly political relationship and the desire to develop their respective economies, it is believed that a neo-situation of integrated development, mutual benefit and reciprocity could be set up by joint efforts on the part of China and the Caribbean countries.

Notes

1. Beginning first with Cuba on September 28, 1960, then with Guyana on June 27, 1972, Jamaica on November 21, 1972, Trinidad and Tobago on June 20, 1974, Suriname on May 28, 1976, Barbados on May 30, 1977 and Antigua and Barbuda on January 1, 1983, all in succession during the early 1970s to early 1980s. China subsequently established diplomatic relations with Bahamas in 1997, Dominica in 2004 and Costa Rica in 2007.
2. The 16 countries are Argentina, Bolivarian Republic of Venezuela, Brazil, Chile, Colombia, Costa Rica, Ecuador, El Salvador, Guatemala, Honduras, Mexico, Panama, Paraguay, Peru, Plurinational State of Bolivia and Uruguay.
   Estimates and projections based on GDP growth rates for the years 2000-2009 in Asia-Pacific, China, the European Union, Latin America and the Caribbean, the United States and the rest of the world. The growth rate of trade is expected to converge with the economies' long-term growth rate.
3. Build-operate-transfer (BOT) is a form of project financing, wherein a private entity receives a concession from the private or public sector to finance, design, construct, and operate a facility stated in the concession contract. This enables the project proponent to recover its investment, operating and maintenance expenses in the project. Traditionally, such projects provide for the infrastructure to be transferred to the government at the end of the concession period.

5

The Emerging Economies and Caribbean Development

The Case of Guyana's Megaprojects

Kalowatie Deonandan

Long overshadowed on the world stage by its Southern neighbours in Latin America, the Caribbean is now emerging as a global player in the 21st century. Emblematic of this new role was Trinidad and Tobago's hosting of the Fifth Summit of the Americas in 2009. Courted by resource hungry emerging economic giants—India, China and Brazil—for its natural bounties (gold, diamond, copper, bauxite, petroleum, timber and steel, amongst other assets), the region has not been shy in welcoming their attention. In fact, plagued by a plethora of social and economic ills and forced by the directives of international financial institutions (IFIs) such as the World Bank and the International Monetary Fund (IMF), many Caribbean states have been aggressively pursuing investments from these new economic behemoths to deal with their many challenges (though not neglecting their pursuit of long established global players from Europe, Canada, and the United States). Overwhelmingly, the strategy has been to liberalize the economies of the region and to restructure national legislation to establish conditions hospitable to foreign investors.

Some success has been observed over the past two decades as the emerging economies have significantly increased their presence in the Caribbean. However, they are concentrated in specific types of industries, in the resource sector (logging, mining, oil and gas), or in infrastructural development (roads, bridges, airports, hydroelectricity facilities). These are predominantly large scale projects and of the type encouraged by the IFIs for underdeveloped states. The rationale is that megaprojects help to accelerate development due to their capacity to enable sophisticated technology transfer, create sizeable employment, and build extensive infrastructure networks. For their cooperation with IFI directives, poor states such as those in the Caribbean then become eligible for financial assistance in the form of grants, loans and debt cancellation.

Drawing primarily from the example of Guyana, this chapter argues that while Foreign Direct Investment (FDI) from the emerging economies do indeed bring significant benefits to the Caribbean, the nature and terms of these investments often have a deleterious effect on good governance, the economy, the environment, and human rights. In the end, they undermine to a significant degree the very development they are expected to promote. In defence of this claim two lines of analysis will be pursued. Firstly, the chapter argues that the development model currently in effect in Guyana has been implemented at the behest of the IFIs, is based on the logic of neoliberalism, but is rationalized by the government under the auspices of a progressive philosophy. While the analysis deals primarily with the administration of President Bharrat Jagdeo and his People's Progressive Party (PPP), it places Jagdeo's ideological orientation and policy prescriptions within a historical context, seeing it as a continuation of the duality pursued by previous administrations, including that of Presidents Forbes Burnham and Cheddi Jagan.

Secondly, it contends that the investments in megaprojects have a detrimental impact on Guyanese development. They undermine good governance and subordinate the country's fragile democracy by perpetuating a pattern of lack of transparency and accountability in governmental decision-making; they bring limited economic benefits to the state; they harm the environment; and they violate human rights, especially those of the country's indigenous populations (and in so doing exacerbate social conflicts in a country already scarred by racial divisions). It should be pointed out that while logging and hydroelectricity are the projects which are foci of this analysis, Guyana's major exports are metals (bauxite, gold and diamond) and agricultural products (sugar and rice). However, the logging and hydroelectricity sectors are privileged in this study as these are the industries in which the emerging economies have a presence and also because they offer excellent case studies of the new model of development which emphasizes megaprojects.

This chapter is organized into six sections. The first is the introduction which lays out the thesis. The second briefly outlines the model of development being pursued and how it differs from previous strategies. The third provides an overview of challenges facing Guyana and the Caribbean that have led to the region's turn to the emerging economies and to megaprojects. The fourth focuses on the case study and traces the trajectory of Guyana's development ideology from socialism to neoliberalism. The fifth describes the developmental projects in logging and hydroelectricity undertaken in Guyana, assesses the role of the emerging economies in these, and analyzes the contributions of the projects to the country's development. The sixth and final section offers some concluding remarks on projections into the future.

The Development Model

Caribbean development path has been marked by a series of experimentation with "isms." Guyana's "cooperative socialism," Jamaica's "democratic socialism," Trinidad and Tobago's "state capitalism" (Conway 1997) are but a few. In the current times characterized by globalization and socioeconomic problems such as poverty and burdensome debt, it is not unreasonable to say that Caribbean states are all firmly aligned on the path of the newest "ism," neoliberalism (see Scholte 2005 and Robinson 1996 and 1999 for a discussion of neoliberalism and globalization). At their core, neoliberal programmes aim to liberalize, privatize and deregulate national economies to render them more accessible to global capital, and the national state and local elites are the local agents for the implementation of this agenda.

Aside from transnational enterprises, the more powerful agents of the neoliberal globalization are the IFIs. Through structural adjustment packages and poverty reduction strategies, IFIs compel debt ridden developing states such as those in the Caribbean to lay the foundations for transnational capital's easy access to their economies. This should not be surprising since the goal of these institutions of neoliberalism is to optimize the conditions for foreign capital's easy penetration of global markets. However, their policy prescriptions bring with them a cornucopia of problems for developing states as they frequently undermine/ compromise environmental standards, labour conditions, tax regulations, and human rights. The development model for the Caribbean in the current phase of globalization, as with Africa and Latin America, is premised on a shift away from an accumulation process based on agro-export production of traditional crops such as sugar, rice and bananas to one which emphasizes investments in services exploitation of natural resources and the construction of mega projects. As Robinson noted for the Latin American context, and the same holds true for the Caribbean, the domestic market is not the target of this development model; rather, the aim is to cater to the requirements of transnational capital (Robinson 1999, 117) which now includes the emerging economies, all of which are seeking access to the kinds of resources present in many Caribbean economies.

This hunt for resources in the Caribbean is not new, and for Guyana it is as old as the 16th century with Sir Walter Raleigh's search for El Dorado. Within the last two decades, however, with global demand for resources rising, driven by the rise in new economic actors, there has been a concomitant increase in the pace of investments in this sector around the globe. Caribbean states, eager to profit from this growing demand and to lure foreign investors to their shores have tried to carve out a niche for themselves. Accordingly they have been vigorously marketing their natural assets such as their timber, gold, diamonds, bauxite, and petroleum and have been restructuring their economies to facilitate the process. Of course, the emphasis on some of these products is not new. But now they are accorded even greater importance as sources of economic growth and thus are being produced on a larger scale in keeping with the demands of the global economy, and are being sold to new markets—the newly emerging economies. In this vein, the requirements of corporations continue to be the drive-wheel for the strategies and policies of developing states.

What is new and interesting in the current development phase is the framework within which many developing states, particularly those adhering to a progressive philosophy, have anchored their objectives. While their policies are market friendly and neoliberal in orientation, they have promoted them within a rubric of progressivism. As Marrero noted: "Extractive activities and the export of raw materials continue as before, but are now justified with a progressive discourse" (Marrero 2011). This is evidenced by Guyana's late socialist President Cheddi Jagan's advocacy of a programme of National Democracy while he advanced economic liberalization, and his successor Bharrat Jagdeo's environmental activism in defence of Guyana's pristine rainforest while he promoted large scale logging. Of course, Jagan and Jagdeo are not alone. Other leaders in Latin America such as Morales in Bolivia, Correa in Ecuador, and Chavez in Venezuela, all of whom claim to espouse some version of socialism or progressivism, are all opting for a similar strategy even though it has brought them into conflict with their electoral base (see for example Kuecker 2007).

The Caribbean: Issues and Challenges

Having briefly examined above the theoretical bases for the developmental strategies being pursued, we now turn to surveying the many challenges facing the Caribbean that provide the impetus for these strategies. There are many: its declining economy; its loss of competitiveness in tourism and in its traditional exports; the rise of crime and corruption; and the ongoing problems of debt, poverty and marginalization. In its 15 country report, *A Time to Choose: Caribbean Development in the 21st Century*, the World Bank (2005, xviii) provided a comprehensive survey of the region's economies and their problems. It noted that GDP per capita for a median country in the region grew at an average rate of 2.8 per cent per year during 1961-2002 and was expected to reach 2.3 per cent for 2001-2010. However, by 2009, the global economic crisis resulted in regional GDP declining by 3 per cent, and it was expected to grow only marginally in 2010 (IMF 2010, 34).

Contributing to this situation was the general decline in the agricultural sector. While still very important, agriculture has been experiencing a downward spiral due to the demise of the preferential trading agreements with the European Union (EU) for traditional crops such as bananas and sugar. As the World Bank (2005) noted though, even when these preferential arrangements were in place this sector was still not competitive, with them being phased out the problem is now even more pronounced. Replacing the preferential accommodations have been trade liberalization arrangements such as the Economic Partnership Agreements between the Caribbean Community and the Dominican Republic (CARIFORUM) and the EU, and other arrangements still in their nascent stages.

Declining foreign investments is another challenge to the region. As the World Bank (2005, 47) observed, the Caribbean possesses relatively few competitive sectors attractive to foreign investors and while it has "performed well by international standards" given its size and endowments, FDI has been on the decline. As measured by the United Nations Conference on Trade and Development's (UNCTAD) Foreign Direct Investment (FDI)[1] index, FDI fell from 2.8 in 1980-84 to 1.9 in 2000-02 (cited in World Bank 2005, 47).

Even in sectors in which the region has a comparative advantage, such as tourism, and for which most of the Caribbean island economies are dependent, there has been a decline. The Bank's (2005, 102) data reveal that CARICOM's[2] market share in terms of tourists arriving to the region declined from 0.93 per cent in 1990 to 0.7 per cent in 2002. Detrimental to the tourist industry and efforts to attract foreign investments are the other problems plaguing the region—corruption, drug trafficking, and high crime rates.

When it comes to the issue of corruption, Guyana for example was ranked 116 of 178 countries in the Transparency International's Corruption Perception Index (2010), giving it one of the lowest rankings in the region. Put another way, it scored 2.7 out of 10 (the higher the number the lesser the corruption), a slight increase over the previous year when it scored 2.6. Certainly some scholars have expressed skepticism about the way Transparency International makes its determination, but the index is nevertheless used to depict how a particular jurisdiction may be viewed through international lens. Exacerbating the corruption problem is the trade in illicit drugs. The UN *World Drug Report 2009* stated that the Caribbean serves as a conduit for 20 per cent of the illegal drugs destined for the United States market (cited in Frederick 2010). Crime and gang violence has also been on the increase. By 2007, it was calculated that the region's murder rate stood at "30 per 100,000 population...higher than any other region of the world" (quoted in Frederick 2010).

Aggravating the situation are the very high debt burdens that Caribbean states carry (see IMF 2011 for individual country data). Between 1997-2003, the region experienced an increase in its total public debt to GDP ratio from 67 per cent to 96 per cent (World Bank 2005, 31). Guyana's debt at that time was a staggering 179 per cent of GDP while Trinidad and Tobago's was 54 per cent (World Bank 2005, 31). Soon after, Guyana's debt climbed even further, reaching 183 per cent of GDP in 2005 (Scott-Joseph, Melville, Kendall and Harris 2006) but falling back to 120 per cent in 2007 (CIA Factbook 2011) due to assistance received under the Heavily Indebted Poor Country (HIPC) debt cancellation initiative. The global financial crisis however has reversed this decline as the debt has once again been rising (*Stabroek News* 2011; World Bank 2009, 7).

Underpinning the above problems is the rampant poverty across the region. In 2003, poverty rates in the region ranged from 12 per cent to 35 per cent with Guyana at the highest end with 35 per cent. Haiti is an exceptional case with 76 per cent (World Bank 2005, 5). By 2006, Guyana's poverty rate had climbed to 36.1 per cent with those in extreme poverty comprising 18.6 per cent (World Bank 2009, ii), making Guyana the third poorest country in the Western hemisphere behind Haiti and Nicaragua (World Bank 2009, 1).

Given the scope and urgency of these problems, Caribbean states have been eager to find ways and means of coping. One strategy, prevalent amongst poor states globally, is the adoption of structural adjustment measures designed by IFIs. These programmes demand, amongst other conditions, that the region establish conditions welcoming of foreign investment especially in those sectors in which it boasts a comparative advantage (namely the resource sector and services) in order to receive international assistance. In compliance, Caribbean economies have targeted the emerging economies as new sources of FDI and have implemented structural changes to make for an environment hospitable to them.

However, while these investors have brought with them several advantages, their concentration in specific sectors and their focus on megaprojects have aggravated many pre-existing problems and have even added new ones. Before analyzing these problems as they relate to Guyana, I first present a brief discussion of the ideology and practice of the country's political leadership historically in order to demonstrate the dichotomy between their philosophies and their policies.

Overview of the Guyanese Developmental Path: From Co-operative Socialism to Neoliberalism

Guyana's development strategy for the 21st century has been to follow in the path of many of its Caribbean neighbours and emphasize foreign investment as a core objective. Although this strategy is not new it has an added urgency as the nation's traditional exports in sugar, rice and other agricultural products are in decline. What is new, however, is that the Guyanese government is now trying to court capital from the rising economies of India, China and Brazil to its shores, to add to older players from Canada, the US, Europe and Asia. The enticement offered is the country's rich natural resources—ironic given that the government is concomitantly carving out for itself an image as guardian of the environment and winning awards in the process. This paradox too is not new as Guyana's leadership historically has been trapped in contradictions, sometimes of their own making but more often due to the many challenges confronting an underdeveloped and very poor nation.

The PNC—From Cooperative Socialism to Neoliberalism

In this section these contradictions are examined. An overview of the development strategies pursued by previous administrations is provided in order to demonstrate that while they advocated a left leaning ideology, be it socialism or national democracy, in fact the policies they implemented were in the end, accommodating of transnational capital often to the detriment of the nation's interest. These contradictions became especially evident after the fall of the Soviet Union and the end of alternative sources of aid or markets.

Guyana won its independence from Britain in 1966 in the wake of a tumultuous struggle between two of its iconic leaders, Forbes Burnham of the People's National Congress (PNC) and Cheddi Jagan of the People's Progressive Party, both of whom proclaimed adherence to some version of socialism. Once allies, the two became bitter opponents, divided by ambition and the machinations of imperial powers, Great Britain and the United States (Rabe 2005). Their split was also emblematic of the deep racial divisions that had been festering in the country between the two dominant ethnic groups, Afro- and Indo- Guyanese, and which continues to be a major political challenge. Burnham, an Afro Guyanese, drew his support from that ethnic group, while Jagan, an Indo-Guyanese, likewise was supported by his racial group who were in the majority. In the end, Burnham was deemed the lesser evil by the colonial administrators, his version of socialism more palatable, and so independence was granted under his leadership. He ruled Guyana until his death in 1985 (though his party remained in power until 1992) through electoral fraud, corruption, and exclusion. Thus, freedom from colonial rule did not bring democratic freedom for the country and its citizens.

In 1970, a few years after independence, Burnham declared Guyana to be a Cooperative Republic and "cooperative socialism" the guiding "ism" of his administration. What this meant in practice was a programme of nationalization of the dominant sectors of the economy, including bauxite and sugar. For regime critics, this was really a form of state capitalism. It was accumulation by the state to feed the interests of the expanding bureaucracy, one dominated by PNC loyalists. By the time of Burnham's death in 1985, the economy had contracted significantly with all important indicators in decline. GDP by 1998 was 68 per cent of 1976 level, external debt had climbed beyond 600 per cent of GDP, and debt arrears were mounting, reaching to over four times exports (cited in Gafar 1996, 43). Faced with this daunting economic crisis, Burnham's successor Desmond Hoyte was compelled to accede to an IMF and World Bank Economic Recovery Programme (ERP) in 1988.

As is the general thrust of all standard adjustment packages, the ERP entailed the liberalization of exchange rates and price controls, privatization of national enterprises, downsizing of the public sector and restructuring of banking and other legislation to foster conditions appealing to foreign investors. In keeping with this new direction, the Hoyte government also announced an end to nationalization and began a process of privatization. Between 1989-92 over a dozen state owned entities were privatized. At the behest of the IMF, the Guyana Natural Resources Agency was set up to promote investments in mining and logging (Colchester 1997b, 43). Importantly too for the purpose of analysis here, the Mining Act was revised to make it easier for large-scale mining operation to gain licenses and concessions. This liberalization of the legislation coincided with rising gold prices and set the stage for the construction of the Omai mine, the largest gold mine in South America. Formally known as Omai Gold Mines Limited (OGML), it was owned jointly by Canadian mining interest Cambior Inc. and US Golden Star Resources. The latter had begun prospecting in 1984, but received its very generous exploitation license in 1989; the mine became operational under the PPP in 1993 (Colchester 1997b).

In addition to mining, the logging sector was also opened up to foreign investors. According to Colchester (1997b, 47), Guyana is one of the tropics most "forested" country and has a loggable area the size of England and Wales combined. First to take advantage of the liberalization of this sector was the Barama Company Limited, the largest timber operation in the country and now wholly owned by Malaysian based Samling Global. It was granted a 25-year contract in 1991, automatically renewable for another 25-years, to log 1,690,000 hectares (almost 8 per cent of the national territory) in the northwestern part of the country (Toni, 1997). The company also won a five year tax holiday (from a slew of taxes such as income tax, corporate tax, withholding tax) and this too was automatically renewable for a further five years (Toni, 1997). Royalty payments, already extremely low, were fixed in Guyana dollars for the first 20 years (Colchester 1997b, 40) with the benefits to the company multiplying many times over as the Guyana dollar has been on a steady downward slide. Subsequent transnational investments in the logging sectors followed a similar trend, with the country gaining few benefits in the long run. With the ERP then, Guyana began its move from socialism to neoliberalism though still labeling itself a cooperative socialist republic.

The PPP—From Socialism—National Democracy—Neoliberalism

This process of opening up the country to mining and logging has been deepening even under subsequent administrations, namely the PPP, which also considered itself a socialist party, though one that believed in the electoral process. The PPP's electoral victory under its longtime leader and declared Marxist Cheddi Jagan came in 1992 when Jagan and his socialism were no longer perceived as a threat to global capitalism. The Cold War had ended, communism had been defeated, and the era of democratic transition had begun. Jagan's call for free and fair elections then could not be denied by the Western powers, especially Washington, when the latter was advocating this for the former communist states.

Once in office, however, Jagan found his socialist ideals were no match for the country's economic woes. Intense debt, poverty, unemployment and declining export earnings forced the former Marxist to modify and temper his ideological stance to one of "national democracy" (Jagan, 1997). He found the need to accommodate the demands of the market, more specifically, to attract FDI and to secure international financial assistance. This philosophical leaning towards a pragmatic stance was to be more pro-capitalist and favourable towards foreign investment, but, according to Jagan, not at the cost of labour or the environment (Jagan 2007). In other words, it was to allow for more economic pluralism.

While Jagan was massaging his early socialist leanings at the domestic level to accommodate market forces, he was still projecting himself as a champion of the poor at the global level as seen in his call for a New Global Order, which he believed possible with the end of the Cold War. The New Global Order was a development strategy to assist the global South, and policy prescriptions included debt relief or forgiveness,[3] a Regional Development Fund (parallel to the New Deal), the creation of a Corps of Development specialists to assist the South, the restructuring of the IMF and the World Bank, and a general emphasis on human development (Deonandan 2007, 318).

Despite its progressive stance, the PPP in practice followed in the footsteps of the PNC and pursued a traditional, market oriented development path, adhering to adjustment programmes and implementing policies to attract foreign investors primarily to its rich natural resource sector. Mining concessions, for example, increased tremendously under Jagan and the PPP. In 1995, the Guyana Geology and Mines Commission (GGMC) reported that it had granted 20 large scale mining licenses in total; however, in the first six to seven months of the following year, it had granted another 50 (cited in Colchester 1997b, 47). Most of these licenses were for gold mining, the leading source of the country's foreign currency earnings (Colchester 2010). While most of Guyana's gold mining industry is dominated by small and medium scale operations, there has been a significant increase in concessions for large scale mining. Aside from the massive Canadian-owned Omai mine which went into production under the PPP, there are at least another dozen large scale concessions (Colchester and LaRose, 2010; 14-15), though none of these are yet in the production phase. However, while Omai was responsible for 70 per cent of the country's gold production during its operations (1993-2005), and while it paid the requisite 5 per cent royalties (OMGL 2005; McLean 2005; Ramessar 2003), analyses of its economic contributions reveal that the country benefitted little from its presence in terms of taxes, employment and other gains (Ramessar 2003). Despite this situation, and despite the fact that it was responsible for one of the worst cyanide spill in 1995, the Jagdeo government has been in negotiations with Cambior for further explorations. Any new concessions granted to the company would be under a new contract which would renew the company's decade-long tax free status.

Concessions to other investors are also likely similarly generous. However, because the terms of these contracts are not publicly disclosed, and because they are one-off negotiations as Guyana has no formal mining regime under which contracts are negotiated, it is difficult to gather concrete knowledge of the terms.

Aside from mining, logging concessions, mostly to Asian Timber giants, also witnessed a significant increase under Jagan's PPP, this despite the very limited revenue the country was receiving from Barama due to the latter's very generous contract (Greenpeace 1997). Joining the Barama company were Demerara Timbers owned by Prime Group of Malaysia, which received a concession of 552,000 hectares, thus making it the country's second largest logging company at the time (Global Timber 2011), and Malaysian-owned UNAMCO (Universal Amalgamated Communal Industries Limited) which was granted a concession 345,000 hectares (FPP, 1998). Although the investment terms for the Barama company had been leaked to the public, the contracts under which subsequent concessions were granted to others remained undisclosed though one may speculate that they were not unlike that of Barama. Interestingly too in 1993, just one year after his assuming office, Barama funded Jagan's tour to several Asian capitals including China and Japan to solicit foreign investments for Guyana (Colchester 1997b, 50).

For critics of the logging industry, during the Jagan period Guyana gained little economically for parceling out its forests to foreign investors. As Colchester (1997a; 113-114) reported:

> A study carried out for the World Bank in late 1995 showed that loggers were getting their timber in Guyana extraordinarily cheaply; royalties, taxes, and forest fees being paid by loggers in Guyana were some of the lowest in the tropics, less than a tenth of those paid in African and Asian countries. Moreover, since 1988 fees had been falling in real terms. Royalties' rates were at 30 per cent of their former value, while customs duties and acreage fees had fallen by more than ninety per cent in the past decade. On top of this, foreign companies enjoyed generous tax breaks and other incentives creating conditions of unfair competition (for local producers).

Observing economic developments under the PPP, one commentator lamented that Jagan's project had become neoliberalism, or "structural adjustment with a human face" (cited in Deonandan 2007, 290).

The PPP-Socialism-National Democracy-Environmentalism-Neoliberalism

The promotion of neoliberalism under the auspices of a progressive discourse has continued under Jagan's successor Bharrat Jagdeo.[4] As Guyana's first 21st century president, he has not only maintained Jagan's platform of national democracy (this continues to be the party's official platform), but has also embraced the newest progressive "ism" in vogue, environmentalism, and carving out his own legacy in the process. His environmental advocacy is not surprising. Guyana is a nation blessed with an abundance of natural assets; it is rich in resources such as bauxite and gold, and over 80 per cent of its territory is covered by forests (World Bank, 2009, 1) due to its location at the centre of the Guiana Shields—a mighty and largely pristine tropical forest shared with Brazil, French Guyana, Suriname and Venezuela. His defence of the country' s dense and carbon-rich forests is exemplified by his widely publicized Low Carbon Development Strategy (LCDS) which won him the prestigious United Nations Environmental Programme (UNEP) "Champions of the Earth" Award in 2010, the highest environmental honour given by the UN. The award came with a US$40,000 prize which the President gifted to Guyana's indigenous communities.

The LCDS emerged as part of an agreement between the governments of Guyana and Norway whereby the latter agreed to pay the former up to $43 million annually for five years, to 2015, to reduce carbon emissions from deforestation (Palmer and Bulkan 2011), and it is also part of Guyana's Reduced Emissions from Deforestation and Degradation (REDD) Readiness Preparation Plan (R-PP), encouraged and funded by the World Bank.

President Jagdeo's credibility on environmental protection as well as that of his party's declared progressivism have been challenged by the economic policies implemented. Faced with an economy in deep distress, the President signed a new IMF restructuring package in 1997 to combat the country's rising deficit, debt, and unemployment. Aggravating this situation is Guyana's vulnerability to the current global economic crisis which led to a contraction of the developed economies and in turn has made for weaker commodity exports for Guyana, lower remittances (on which Guyana relies heavily), and declining foreign investments (World Bank 2009, ii and 10). The demands of the package were that Guyana design a Poverty Reduction Strategy (PRS) that focused "on accelerating and sustaining economic growth through enhanced competitiveness and social development" by, amongst other things, "improving infrastructure to promote growth and private sector development" (World Bank 2009, ii), before it could be eligible for debt relief under the Heavily Indebted Poor Country (HIPC), and subsequently the Enhanced HIPC. Significant levels of compliance with the PRS enabled Guyana to negotiate sizeable levels of debt reduction with both international financial institutions and bilateral lenders such as Japan, China and Venezuela. And, while the country has been experiencing "robust growth," estimated by the IMF (2011) to be in the 3 per cent range in 2010, it nevertheless still carries a staggering debt load. One important aspect of the country's compliance with the IMF terms was its acceleration of the economic liberalization policies begun under Hoyte to attract foreign investors. Aside from massive privatization of state owned enterprises, the reforms also included changes to the financial system, the budget process, the civil service and the structures of governance and tax administration. With these policy alterations Guyana became a country considered extremely open (with openness measured in terms of trade-to-GDP) to FDI. According to the World Bank (2005, 65), Guyana's openness which is rated at 204 per cent, far surpasses that expected (130 per cent) for a country of its size. Within Guyana, the effects of this liberalization are most evident in the resource sector to which logging and mining are being courted with generous concessions such as tax holidays, full profit repatriation, and lenient legislation.

Megaproject Development and their Impacts—Logging and Hydroelectricity

Taking advantage of the growing resource hunger amongst emerging economies, and in keeping with the policies of his predecessors, President Jagdeo continued the strategy of marketing Guyana's greatest assets, its natural resources, by granting huge concessions to foreign logging and mining companies. He also added investments in hydroelectricity to the mix. Ironically, his liberalizing and privatizing strategies were directed primarily at that sector he wanted to protect for the future with his LDCS, the environment. Furthermore, the impact of the investments in the natural resource sector is undermining the very goals the IMF and Guyana are seeking to promote, that is economic growth and development. As indicated by the World Bank Report (cited in Colchester 1997a), the country has gained little economically from investments in large scale logging.

It should be noted too that President Jagdeo also aggressively promoted large scale mining concessions (gold is Guyana's leading source of export earnings; bauxite and diamonds are also critical sources of income). According to Colchester (2010, 13), permits for large scale reconnaissance and explorations in mining now cover almost two-thirds of the northern part of the country. While mining is a central component of the government's investment strategy, as noted earlier, the focus here is on logging and hydroelectricity as these are two of the sectors in which the newly emerging economies are presently involved. However, it is worth stating that the mining sector too is plagued with many of the same challenges as that of logging and hydropower.

Logging

Expanding on his predecessors' focus on this sector, Jagdeo was actively encouraging the rising Asian economies India and China to this industry. Investors from these two countries now join the list of already well-established logging companies such as the aforementioned Barama, Demerara Timbers, and UNAMCO.

Dominant amongst Chinese investors are Jaling Forest Industries and Garner Forest Industries, both owned by China Timber Resources, each with concessions of 164,800 hectares and 92,737 hectares respectively (Global Timber, 2011). Another company, Sherwood Forrest, which received a 167,066 hectare concession in 2007, has as one of the company's principal Chinese investor Chu Hong Bo (*Stabroek News*, August 9, 2010a). India too is a major player in the sector. Actually, its presence dwarfs that of China. Vaitarna Holdings Private Inc. (VHPI), a subsidiary of Coffee Day Limited of India (a coffee shop chain) acquired a significant interest in Guyana's logging industry through a local subsidiary, Dark Forest Company. Dark Forest in turn acquired the 391,853 hectares (*The Daily Herald*, April 10, 2011) holdings of American timber giant Simon and Shock International which had been issued its permit in 2008 (*Stabroek News* January 8, 2008a). The permit was suspended in 2009 apparently due to the company's failure to comply with the terms of the agreement to construct a large sawmill in Linden prior to commencing logging (Global Timber 2011). VHPI also acquired the 345,961 hectares formerly belonging to Caribbean Resources Limited (*The Daily Herald,* April 10, 2011) which had its license rescinded in 2010, also for noncompliance. While with this deal VHPI controls much less than half the holdings of Barama (the latter's concession totals 1.6 million hectares or 3,953,686 acres), the deal is nevertheless quite significant as it is considered one of the largest of its kind in the country (*The Daily Herald,* April 10, 2011) and it gives VHPI the title of the country's second largest logger, bumping Demerara Timbers from that position. As of 2005, over half of Guyana's log exports were destined for China and India (Global Timber 2007); with the recent VHPI agreement this figure is expected to increase dramatically.

While the growing investments from the emerging economies of China and India are signs that Guyana is having some success in its FDI strategies, there are many challenges that come with their presence. For supporters, they represent a boon to the economy in terms of jobs, taxes, infrastructures and technological know-how. For critics, they undermine good governance and democracy, bring little economic gains, destroy the environment, and in the process aggravate social tensions, especially with indigenous communities.

Implications for Governance and Democracy

One of the central problems facing developing states like Guyana is that they lack institutional capacity in critical areas. Yet, the types of development being promoted, namely investments in large scale project, demand that the state be able to regulate and oversee these in order to gain maximum benefits from them and to ensure that national standards are not being violated. Guyana however, as a poor and underdeveloped country lacks strong governance structures, and in this case it translates into weak oversight capacity in the resource sector.

To begin, there was no Minister of the Environment under the Jagdeo administration. On the one hand, this is particularly surprising given President Jagdeo's LCDS to "leverage the preservation of the country's vast rainforests to raise capital to develop economic and social infrastructure" (World Bank 2009, 7). The absence of this portfolio means there was no advocate before

Parliament or the people for one of Guyana's greatest assets, its forests. As well, the President had a great deal of influence in the awarding of concessions. For example, when it came to issues such as "landlording" whereby the original recipient of the concession was legally prohibited from "outsourcing" the task, the President had override authority over this restriction. The motivation behind this legislation was to prevent companies that lack the necessary capabilities and that have not undergone the requisite scrutiny (for example through submitting the mandatory Environmental and Social Impact Assessment—ESIA) from participating in the industry and damaging the environment. The extent to which Presidential overrides are based on detailed knowledge of the new "landlord" remains debatable especially given the scarcity of resources and personnel necessary to inform his decision. On the other hand, some might argue that the absence of a Minister of the Environment stemmed from no clearly evident consciousness among the national populace about saving the environment, as they may be more preoccupied with challenges posed by crime and economic hardships.

A further issue with respect to the strength of national institutions relates to the decision-making structure of the logging regime. Concessions are granted by a small group within the Forestry Commission. The Commission, however, is not under the auspices of any Ministry, but under the Guyana Natural Resource Agency, which in turn is under the oversight of the Office of the President. As Colchester (1997b, 49) explained, this was part of the structural adjustment strategy and was meant to accelerate the process of FDI in the logging sector, and thus speed up development. In other words, reducing the bureaucratic channels that could deter investors was paramount. Its effects, however, are that it opens the process of granting concessions and permits to elitism and favouritism as there are only a few people in the upper echelons of power with the ability to make decisions and award contracts. There are also no guarantees that the requisite standards and procedures are adhered to, especially as much of the details of such concessions are not publicly disclosed. Furthermore, it leads to neglect and possible abuse as there are not enough personnel to supervise developments.

The frailty of national institutions are also evident in the oversight of the concessions. Caribbean Resources Limited for example was awarded its logging permit in 1989, and this was renewed every year despite the fact that the company was not in compliance with the terms of its contract. It was not until 2010 that the lease was repossessed by the state. This problem is likely related to the fact that Guyana is a poor state lacking in vital resources. As such, there is a limited amount of resources available to expend on personnel to oversee the industry. The focus, as *per* the demands of structural adjustment measures, is on attracting investments to the industry and the country, and not to impose barriers through greater bureaucracy.

Logging is not the only sector in which the weaknesses of state institutions are evident. The mining regime too is beset with similar woes. While mining is a crucial area of economic activity, representing over 10 per cent of GDP according to 2005 data (ECLAC 2010, 221), the country does not have an officially appointed Minister of Mines; this portfolio is held by the Prime Minister who plays a dual role. He, however, has no official staff serving him in this capacity. Rather, the regulation of the industry is done by the Geology and Mines Commission (GGMC) which is strikingly under-resourced. One report noted that while the country has over 10,000 mines (of varying sizes), there are only 11 mine officers (as of 2005) providing oversight: "The mines officers are overwhelmed by the mountain of administrative duties...cowed by the formidable bureaucratic hurdles...and defeated by the immensity of the territory...." (International Human Rights Clinic 2007, 32-34). These observations were confirmed by a GGMC lead engineer at the Omai site (currently under government supervision) (Ramdas 2010).

Another governance issue deals with the manner in which many of the concessions are awarded. Critics charge that the process is not always transparent, that contracts were granted without public tender and as such are illegal, unless authorized by the President. India's Dark Forest which gained the rights to the holdings of Simon and Shock International and that of Caribbean Resources has had the legality of its contract questioned by industry critics such as Bulkan (2011). The government denied the process was secretive and dismissed criticisms as being politically motivated, implying the company was Indian and hence black politicians were attacking the concessions transfer, when they did not question the original grant to the American company Simon and Shock (*Kaieteur News*, April 13, 2011).

A related governance issue draws attention to the question of whether the Forestry Commission is granting concessions to appropriately qualified enterprises. According to Guyanese law, it is illegal for contracts to be awarded to companies that lack the necessary logging capabilities. The terms of the *Forest Act*, Article 6 (Government of Guyana, 1998), stipulate that in order to receive logging rights, a company must first demonstrate that it has the financial and technical wherewithal (for example, to undertake a valid Environmental Impact Assessment and then follow through with efficient explorations and harvesting). Based on this criterion, questions have been raised regarding the qualifications of India's Dark Forest. It is known to be an affiliate of a coffee enterprise, Coffee Day, which in turn is interested in lumber as part of its furniture business (Global Timber 2011). The concerns expressed relate to whether a company whose expertise in the coffee business can meet the necessary criteria of the Forests Act when it comes to logging. Lack of public pronouncements from the government on the matter has only fed the suspicions of critics that the process has not been above board. As Bulkan (2011) notes, "No evidence has been given in the public domain that this coffee retailer has any competence in or experience of conducting natural resource inventories, preparing environmental and social impact assessments, or preparing a forest management plan."

Part of the problem here relates to issues of governance and accountability. A great deal of decision making is centralized in the office of the President (World Bank 2009). Consequently, there seems to be little interest or need, especially for a majority government, to respond to its critics. Furthermore, the government may suspect that this is not an issue with which the nation as a whole is preoccupied. For the majority in this, one of the poorest countries in the hemisphere, investments mean jobs. Social impact assessments, resource inventories and forest management plans are not necessarily matters of immediate concern for them (the Coffee Day controversy and issues of the company's qualifications are similar, as we shall see below, to the situation surrounding the company building the load bearing road to the Amalia Falls hydro facility).

Problems of governance and oversight arise also with respect to illegal logging, a major plague to the industry worldwide. In testimony before the US House of Representatives, the President of the US office of the London-based Environmental Investigation Agency (EIA), Allan Thornton (2005, 2), estimated that more than half of all the logging done in vulnerable regions (Africa, Latin America, and the Caribbean) is illegal. In a Chatham House report, Brack, Marijnissen and Ozinga (2002, 12) explain what makes for illegality in the industry and note that it exists across the supply chain:

> Illegal logging takes place when timber is harvested, transported, bought or sold in violation of national laws. The harvesting procedure itself may be illegal, ...[and can involve the use of] corrupt means to gain access to forests, extraction without permission or from a protected area, the cutting of protected species or the extraction of timber in excess of agreed limits. Illegalities may also occur during transport, such as illegal processing and export, misdeclaration to customs, and the avoidance of taxes and other charges.

Amongst the major consumers of illegal tropical timber, according to the EIA (2001, 4), are the US, the EU, Japan and now China. In the EU, the UK is particularly culpable with as much as 60 per cent of its timber imports being illegal, while in Asia Japan's illegal timber consumption is estimated to be in the 50 per cent range (EIA 2001, 4). China represents a more recent threat, and one that is rapidly growing. It is now the world's largest importer of timber products and the volume of its imports have been steadily increasing (Thornton 2005). Industry watchers, however, charge that a "substantial" portion of these log imports are illegal (EIA 2001, 5), including those from Guyana. Global Timber (2007b) estimated that almost 60 per cent of Guyanese timber to China consists of illegally harvested logs. With its poor oversight capacity and its lack of personnel and resources to police the forest sector, it is unlikely that Guyana will be able to alter this situation any time soon. And as Chinese companies gain a stronger foothold in the industry, the problem is likely to multiply to the detriment of Guyana's economy and environment.

As a poor underdeveloped economy Guyana cannot deal with the problem of illegal logging on its own. The initiatives must come from the consumer nations whose hunger is feeding the industry. Part of the hope for change lies in the adoption of international agreements such as the Voluntary Action Plan for Forest Law Enforcement, Governance and Trade (FLEGT) by consumer countries. FLEGT is a bilateral arrangement between EU consumer states and the timber producing countries to implement a licensing scheme for legal timber. Such agreements, while they are a positive step, nevertheless are woefully slow to be established and difficult to realize in practice as they are voluntary and not compulsory.

Implications for the Economy

Despite the many problems associated with the types of FDI entering Guyana, foreign investment nevertheless remains a crucial component of the government's development strategy. Importantly, this is not surprising as foreign investment promises to bring jobs which are desperately needed in poor states like Guyana that are burdened with high unemployment and poverty rates. In addition, it allows for backward and forward linkages that benefit the economy as a whole, contribute to infrastructural development, and add to the state coffers through taxes and royalties. However, the evidence from the logging sector demonstrates that these promises are not always borne out in practice.

Despite the claims of logging companies that they will be involved in processing and value-added activities in Guyana, critics charge that they are actually exporting most of their logs unprocessed to Asia (Bulkan 2011). Regarding the recent concessions to VHPI's Dark Forest, a report in the *Times of India* (cited in *The Daily Herald,* April 10, 2011) suggests that the company plans to send the logs to the Coffee Day Group's furniture plant in Chikmagalur. In essence, value added to the product will be done in India, not Guyana. When questioned, the Guyana government was adamant that VHPI will indeed set up processing plants and undertake other value-added activities in the country and that the above report "is only partially representative of the real facts" (*Kaieteur News* April 13, 2011). Furthermore, the government pointed out that according to the 2009 National Log Export Policy it is not illegal for companies to export unprocessed logs; rather the policy relies on an increase in the export commission charged as a deterrent (cited in *The Daily Herald* April 10, 2011).

Another economic argument in favour of FDI and megaprojects is the benefits the companies bring to state coffers and hence to the development of the state in general. However, as was pointed out earlier, logging companies (as well as those in mining) receive generous tax holidays (exemptions from import taxes, consumption taxes, export duties, etc.) as well as other financial concessions. The result can be little, if any gains, for the host state—as was determined to be the case for Guyana with Barama's investments. Critics have alleged that the Guyanese people have actually subsidized Barama for the past few decades at the same time the company's records show that it has been operating at a loss (Global Timber 2011). Yet, despite Barama's questionable contributions to the Guyanese economy, it was anticipated that President Jagdeo will renew the company's contract for another 10 years before he leaves office in 2011.

Aside from the losses due to subsidies in the form of tax concessions and other benefits, there are also allegations that Guyana is losing out when it comes to the price it is receiving for its forest products, and this relates to the issue already discussed above, that of illegal timber sales. The country is not alone; this is a situation faced by timber producers across the globe—Burma, Brazil, Cameroon, Indonesia, and Thailand to name a few (EIA 2001). Referring to Guyana specifically, the International Tropical Timber Organization (ITTO) stated that "the unit prices for [the country's] log exports are remarkably small relative to unit prices for equivalent products exported from other producer countries. The difference might well be attributable to transfer pricing fraud" (cited in Global Timber 2007a). Furthermore, it has been alleged by Global Timber (2007a), one of the few watchdog agencies that have provided data on this issue with respect to Guyana, that since both India and China are major importers of Guyana's logs, over 50 per cent, these countries are likely complicit in the process, though it provides no explicit evidence for this claim. Revenues lost from this artificially low transfer pricing has been placed in the millions, an estimated US$10 million in 2005 or 2 per cent of the country's export earnings for that year (Global Timber 2007a).

Tensions with Amerindian Communities

Logging concessions (like mining and hydro facilities) have come to represent sources of social tension. In a country already scarred by racial strife due to the historical conflicts between Afro- and Indo-Guyanese, megaprojects could aggravate an already simmering conflict with another group, the indigenous Amerindian population whose lands and livelihoods are at risk by these development strategies. Amerindians constitute 9.2 per cent of Guyana's population (World Bank 2009, 2) and make their living through subsistence fishing, farming, hunting and small scale artisanal mining. These communities suffer from a 78 per cent poverty rate (World Bank 2009, 2) where the national average is 36 per cent as noted earlier, and lack access to proper health and education facilities. Very importantly, they live in the remote hinterland where logging and mining are occurring and where the hydroelectric facilities and related infrastructures are being constructed.

One of the most contentious issues between the Amerindians and the government of Guyana relates to land rights. Historically, land demarcation and the assignation of titles have been vague and ill defined, and Amerindian groups have long been involved in ongoing struggles with the government over this. While some groups have been successful in settling their land disputes with the government, and while the latter has made some efforts to improve relations with the Amerindian communities (such as President Jagdeo donating his UNEP award to them), land tenure remains one of the most volatile issues in the relationship between the two sides. Concessions to mining and logging enterprises have only aggravated this conflict and undermined efforts at a long-term solution. According to the Amerindians, logging and mining permits are being awarded often with disregard for land claims or even in disregard of titles which have already been granted. As they declared: "After reviewing recent maps of mining concessions and exploration permits issued by the GGMC, we are alarmed that many of these concessions directly impact on our traditional lands (titled and untitled)" (Public Statement 2010). Part of this conflict relates to the tensions surrounding who controls surface versus subsurface rights.

Furthermore, Amerindian communities allege that their human rights are being violated at another level, that they are not being consulted regarding developments on their territory as required by international standards such as the 1966 UN Convention on the Elimination of all Forms of Racial Discrimination to which Guyana is a signatory, and by national codes. In particular, they argue that their right to Free and Prior Informed Consent (FPIC) is being violated as they do not receive adequate or timely information, nor are they consulted about developments with respect to logging, mining, and infrastructure construction on their territory which could seriously harm their livelihoods.

Troubling to Amerindian communities are the environmental damages occurring as a result of the mega projects, as these represent serious threats to their livelihoods. According to David James (cited in *Stabroek News*, May 28, 2008b), former President of the Amerindian People's Association (APA) and the organization's legal adviser, mining and logging companies have been exploiting the country's forest in an "unsustainable" and "unsound" manner by overharvesting of timber, polluting the waterways and destroying hunting grounds and he blames the government for not making the contracts more stringent (cited in *Stabroek News*, May 28, 2008b). Adding credence to James' claims are recent steps taken by the Norwegian government. In August 2010, it announced the removal of Samling Global, owner of logging giant Barama, from the portfolio of the Government Pension Fund Global (GPFG). The decision was based on the Norwegian "Council on Ethics assessment that [Samling is] contributing to or [is itself] responsible for grossly unethical activity...[T]he company's forest operations in the rainforests of Sarawak and Guyana contribute to illegal logging and severe environmental damage" (quoted in *Guyana Chronicle*, August 27, 2010). The Guyana government has denied this assertion stating that it "has found little evidence to substantiate such a position" (quoted in *Guyana Chronicle*, August 27, 2010); in response, no doubt from official pressure from Guyana, Norway retracted its criticisms of Samling (*Guyana Chronicle*, August 27, 2010) but did not reinstate the company in its GPFG.

Despite the problems with the logging sector, President Jagdeo continued marketing Guyana's natural resources. His contribution to the mix of FDI (mining and logging had begun prior to his taking office) is opening the economy to investments in a new type of mega project, hydroelectricity, which is still in its nascent stages. Yet this too threatens to bring and has brought many of the same challenges as the logging industry.

Hydroelectricity and Guyanese Development

Known as the "land of many waters" due to its many mighty rivers and waterfalls, Guyana is considered to have enormous capabilities for hydroelectricity generation. Its potential however remained untapped until now due in large part to the vast sums of capital required to set up such projects initially. The recently inaugurated giant Amaila Falls Hydroelectric Project (AFHEP), made possible with Chinese investments, opens up a completely new sector for FDI. While the project promises significant benefits, it is also not without costs.

The giant 154-megawatt hydroelectric power plant is being built deep in the Amazon rainforest on the Kuribrong River by

US-based Sithe Global Power. Considered the largest infrastructure investment in the country's history, it will be financially supported by loans from China and the International Development Bank (IDB). The lion's share of the financing, about US$500 million, is anticipated from the China Development Bank and the China Railway First Group (Palmer and Bulkan 2011) which signed a framework of Agreement with the Guyana Power and Light Company and Sithe Global in July 15, 2010. For its part, the government of Guyana committed to spend up to US$60 million earned from its Low Carbon Development Strategy (LCDS) to the purchase of equity in Amaila (Palmer and Bulkan 2011).

One of the primary aims of AFHEP is to provide the country with cheaper electricity (*Stabroek News* September 29, 2010d), and make electricity generation more reliable and available. In comparison with its South American neighbours, Guyana has "the lowest or nearly the lowest electric power *per capita*, and the least reliable and most expensive power tariffs....[as well as an] antiquated and poorly maintained [system]" (Palmer and Bulkan 2011). Improving the electricity infrastructure, then, will go a long way to enhancing the country's infrastructure and hence contribute to the developments necessary to attract foreign investments. In addition, Amaila Falls will restructure the country's energy matrix by reducing reliance on non-renewable fossil fuels to renewable resources (IDB 2010) and as such is very much in keeping with the LCDS. Jagdeo in turn referred to it as the "flagship" of the LCDS (Goodland 2010, 2). However, Amaila is not without drawbacks and some of these are reminiscent of the issues in the logging sector.

Firstly, there is concern that the project might in fact be more oriented to supplying refineries abroad, in particular Brazil, and also cater to Brazil's electricity needs and not that of Guyana. Secondly, there are transparency problems in terms of how contracts for related infrastructures were awarded—echoes of problems in the logging sector as seen with India's Dark Forest's concession. Access to the hydro facility requires the construction of a new load bearing road, which has already begun. However, there are questions regarding how the road construction contract was awarded and whether the company that won the US$15 million bid, Synergy Resources, is actually qualified to undertake the work (see for example Ram 2009). Firstly, according to national news reports there is no evidence of Synergy ever having built a road (*Stabroek News* August 17, 2010c). World expert on environmental impact assessment, Robert Goodland (2010), has alleged that Synergy "failed every valid eligibility test but was still selected out of five bidders," and the circumstances under which it was selected were not clear. Both the Guyana government and Synergy have denied the charges with the latter claiming that it has road building experiences in the US (*Stabroek News* August 17, 2010) and that it has been involved in the building of over 70 per cent of the world's dams (Stabroek News April 11, 2010). Secondly, there has been a lack of clear information regarding the ESIA. The road will pass through prime ecosystems in the Pakaraima Mountains, an area inhabited by Amerindian communities and understandably, these groups are concerned about the impact of this and the AFHEP on their livelihoods. Thus far, however, the details of how they will be affected remain unclear as the government appears to be sending contradictory messages. There is ambiguity as to whether communities will be displaced, whether the road will indeed pass through specific villages, whether road construction will mean jobs for Amerindians, and so on (see Goodland 2010 for a discussion). This too, like the logging concessions, is leading to escalating tensions between the government and the hinterland communities.

Finally, Amaila Falls and the accompanying load bearing road will inevitably alter and even destroy the natural environment in which they are located. For his critics, the AFHEP brings into question President Jagdeo's environmental advocacy via his much vaunted LCDS as they fear it will destroy thousands of acres of forest. Admittedly Guyana is a poor state in need of investments and infrastructure, but Amaila for them represents an inappropriate developmental strategy for the country (see Goodland 2010).

While megaprojects are not in themselves problematic, the question can be asked whether they are the best strategy for small underdeveloped states with weak institutional capacity. In Guatemala, for example, where such large scale hydro and mining projects are planned or underway, and where massive resistance has been mounted in response, especially by the affected indigenous communities (Yagenova and García 2009), critics assert that they are not opposed to the production of metals or electricity, they just question whether small scale is not more appropriate to the context given the environmental damage, population displacement, and employment losses that are associated with large scale operations. They support a model based on mini hydro plants which exist in many areas, in particular Cuba where it has helped to stem the flow of out migration from rural areas by providing employment and expanding the availability of local electricity supply (Inforpress July 15, 2005).

Adding to concerns in Guyana is the suspicion that Amaila will not be the only project of its kind and hence the problems will multiply. Goodland predicts that Amaila is "the first stage in a planned cascade of possibly three stages of dams... each larger than the last. One may even include diversion of an entire river..." (Goodland cited in *Development Today*, 2010). He may not be incorrect. An even more mammoth project is in the negotiation phase. The Russian Aluminum corporation, RUSAL, has been in talks with the government of Guyana and Brazil's state-owned hydro company, Eletrobras, to construct a massive 3000MW dam on a tributary of the middle Mazaruni River (Colchester 2010, 13). For RUSAL, the dam will provide a source of cheap electricity for its planned open-cast bauxite mine near the Patamona Amerindian community, while Brazil gains a "reliable supply of electricity [for its] northern State of Roraima (Colchester 2010, 13).

Conclusion

It seems Guyana has come full circle from the period of colonial rule. Under the period of British colonialism, Guyana's interests were subordinated to that of the imperialist powers and their multinationals. With the transition to democracy under the PPP, the country has come full circle, as foreign companies are again being welcomed to the major sectors of the economy. And, as with the colonial era, such investments have brought few tangible benefits to the state, but they have served well the interests of the company and the home state.

However, there are some differences between the FDI of the past and those of the current neoliberal era in which host states pass legislation and establish conditions conducive to foreign investors. Firstly, the present strategy is one being imposed not by old imperial powers directly, but their institutions, the IFIs, as part of their push to open national markets to transnational capital (most of which are in the developed North but now face competition from emerging markets). Host states, almost all of which are poor, underdeveloped, debt-ridden and in the South, have few options but to comply. Secondly, the investments promoted are in megaprojects with the rationalization that these will accelerate developments by transferring updated technology, create greater employment opportunities, and build much-needed infrastructure such as roads and ports. Thirdly, the area being opened for investments is the natural resource sector. While this is not completely new in the case of Guyana, the sector is receiving greater emphasis as seen in the cases of logging and hydroelectricity, and large scale mining is now being promoted (over small and medium scale operations). Finally, in the current period, the major investors are not just companies of the old colonial regimes of Britain or the United States, rather they are from the new "imperial" economies, the emerging economic giants—China, India and Brazil.

The courtship of these new economic powerhouses and the focus on megaprojects are Guyana's and the Caribbean's 21st century response to deal with their deep economic problems. The strategy, however, does not always bring the anticipated gains. In fact, as this chapter has suggested with respect to Guyana, it has proven the opposite as seen in the country's natural resource sector. Nevertheless, all indications are that the government will continue to adhere to this developmental path and will continue to articulate and rationalize it within the framework of a philosophy of progress. To be fair, it has few options given the many constraints under which it is operating, especially when it comes to debt, poverty and unemployment and the current global downturn.

Notes

1. "The numerator of the FDI Performance Index is the ratio o f a country's FDI inflows as a proportion of world inflows, while the denominator is the ratio of a country's GDP as a proportion o f global GDP. A ratio greater than one indicates proportionately higher FDI as compared to GDP." (Explained in footnote 60 of the World Bank's *A Time to Choose*, p. 47.)
2. CARICOM, originally known as the Caribbean Community and Common Market, now the Caribbean community is an organization of 15 member states and 5 associate states.
3. While seemingly idealistic initially, since Jagan's death, debt cancellation has very much become part of the development strategies of the IFIs, as seen in the HIPC for example.
4. Bharrat Jagdeo did not follow Cheddi Jagan directly. In the interim was Jagan's wife Janet who won the Presidency but retired for health reasons.

6

Primacy of Politics in Development and Poverty Reduction in the Caribbean*

Priti Singh

Introduction

Regardless of size, almost all the countries in the developing world have undergone structural reforms and policy transformations in recent years, and in different degrees towards what is currently described as the "shared governance" approach. There is no gainsaying that these reforms have hardly made any substantial impact or difference at the socio-economic level, most important of all in the area of poverty reduction. In most of these countries, including in some of the countries of the Caribbean, poverty remains as endemic a developmental challenge as before. Needless to say our understanding of the relationships between development and poverty reduction has undergone considerable change over time, and has been influenced by .prevailing ideological predispositions and intellectual disciplines. Moreover, the issues related to development and poverty are now understood as being multidimensional. The spectrum of prevailing views and the variety of definitions on who is "poor" and who is not and

---

* This chapter is a revised version of a paper presented at the first Meeting of the Caribbean Development Round Table held by the Economic Commission for Latin America and the Caribbean (ECLAC) in Port of Spain, Trinidad and Tobago on 13 September 2011.

why some regions/countries remain perpetually underdeveloped problematize any analysis on the development-poverty nexus.

Existing literature on poverty is not only rich but also varied, providing new and ground-breaking meanings attributed to poverty on the basis of which it has now become imperative to craft and fine-tune innovative policy initiatives to engineer poverty reduction alongside development generation. In light of these considerations, this chapter aims to unravel, to the extent possible, the linkages between development and poverty reduction initiatives in the Caribbean, and to underline the centrality of political processes—both internal and external—in shaping the outcomes. The first part of the chapter will attempt to establish some basic conceptual principles for analyzing the links between development and poverty. This undertaking involves, first, reviewing the various definitions of poverty and then outlining the ways in which each specific link between development and poverty reduction is assessed. It will also focus on how policy packages are designed and dispensed in the Caribbean region. The second part of the chapter attempts to critique the ongoing policy/academic debate on the question of foregrounding politics in the development-poverty reduction paradigm through two global initiatives: United Nations' Millennium Development Goals (MDGs) and the international financial institutions—International Monetary Fund and the World Bank—(IFIs) sponsored Poverty Reduction Strategy Papers (PRSPs). The third and final section of the chapter offers recommendations on what is to be done by the donor countries and aid agencies to evolve strategies which effectively situate politics in the development-poverty nexus and which will pave the way for sustainable and inclusive development.

Conceptual Framework

The definition of poverty in academic and policy discourses on international development has undergone considerable changes in recent decades. At least three broad strands could be delineated. First is the prosaic money-metric approach. According to this approach, poverty is defined by the official donors in a relatively simple quantitative way that is largely based on the concept of low income per capita or low consumption per capita computed through Living Standard Measurement Surveys (LSMS). Second is the approach of the United Nations aid agencies that actively promoted the concept of human development as an alternative based on Amartya Sen's seminal ideas on the different forms of entitlement that could lead to the realization of capabilities. Briefly stated, Sen's understanding of the status of being poor extends beyond income levels to include income-associated conditions such as health and education and what he calls "unfreedoms," like tyranny or bad treatment by the state and exclusion from participation in decisions, particularly those directly affecting the poor themselves. In turn, his idea of development is a process of expanding the real freedom that people enjoy—in other words, "the removal of major sources of unfreedom" (Sen 1999, 3). These would include poor economic opportunities, systematic deprivation, neglect of public facilities, and intolerance or over-activity of oppressive states. The third approach is largely based on the perspectives of the NGOs and academics who emphasize vulnerability as a core element in defining poverty. Over time, the meaning of vulnerability and associated human insecurity has been further expanded to include not only the economic shocks such as the current global financial crisis (GFC), but also natural disasters such as global warming, tsunami, and others. Many states (small and island states in particular) in different regions are frequently affected by inclement climatic and other natural events/disasters which impact adversely on certain segments of the population, and on the economy as a whole. Given the reliance of these small states on a narrow, less diversified endowment base, the impact of natural or ecological disasters on any of the economic sectors in these countries become extensive, resulting in the impoverishment of large sections of people who are dependent on the meager resources available in these regions. As the world faces up to the prospect of global warming and climate change, efforts to satisfy the criteria of efficiency and fairness as a global solution are reaching an impasse. The global search for solutions for equitable growth, income equality and environmental degradation is becoming difficult (Dookeran 2008, 24-28). Thus any approach to development and poverty alleviation must recognize and acknowledge the nature of aspirations for development (Singh 2009).

Over the last decade there has been a perceptible movement towards convergence of these different and sometimes overlapping approaches, which has brought to fore a multidimensional definition of poverty that encompasses three core elements, namely: lack of opportunity, insecurity and vulnerability, and powerlessness. Poverty is thus treated as deprivation of basic capabilities. So understood, the capabilities approach both changes the measurement criterion in poverty assessments and significantly alters policy options/choices to poverty alleviation as it directs attention to the need to strengthen the capabilities of individuals and households to participate in the initiatives aimed at improving their own welfare. It may be added here that even the capabilities approach is beset with built-in limitations because capability cannot be measured simply by taking into account the economic criterion. It needs to take into consideration the political and social context as well.

4Poverty Reduction in the Caribbean: An Overview

The Caribbean Development Bank (CDB) has poverty reduction programmes with funds allocated for the same (such as Basic Needs Trust Funds). There are measures of poverty, such as the Basic Needs Index (BNI) or the Human Development Index (HDI) which attach significance to non-monetary measures of poverty like the need for basic infrastructure and access to education. These programmes have provisions for participation of communities in identifying problem areas, designing a project around it, project implementation and project governance. They include social and physical infrastructure such as health centres, water supply systems, and roads to help enhance capabilities of communities (Bourne 2005). Various projects have been approved by the CDB. Some of these include reconstruction work in St. Lucia in March 2011 to overcome the impact of hurricane Tomas, student loan facility to upgrade the technical, vocational and professional skills at the tertiary level in Jamaica in 2010, low income housing programme in Barbados in 2010, and rural enterprise development in Grenada in 2010.[1]

For the Caribbean countries, data on poverty is collected on the basis of country poverty assessments (CPAs) sponsored by the CDB.[2] These CPAs generally involve four basic components:

- A review of available reports and statistics;
- A sample household survey (the Survey of Living Conditions-SLC) on household expenditure and incomes and employment information;
- A series of Participatory Poverty Assessments (PPAs) in communities and vulnerable groups; and

- Identification of programmes on poverty reduction and institutional analysis of entities involved (Caribbean Development Bank 2003, i)

Country Poverty Assessments are useful for designing programmes because there are limitations to general measures meant to reduce poverty. For instance, countries such as Anguilla which have a basic infrastructure and high life expectancy along with high school level enrollment would not be considered to be in need of any assistance irrespective of their vulnerability and lack of opportunity.

However, CPAs help design programmes based on country-specific income with well-being seen as a necessary part of poverty (CDB 2002, 6). Most of the national poverty reduction strategies have been formulated on the basis of these CPAs. At the same time, there are some deviations/variations in countries such as Jamaica which conducted surveys of living conditions patterned on the World Bank's model since 1989. The Inter-American Development Bank (IADB) too has sponsored poverty assessments in some of the countries of the region. The measurement of poverty in these surveys is focused on an identified poverty line and individuals/households that are below it; on the income of those in poverty below the poverty line; or the distribution of income among the poor.

In respect of dealing with poverty (i.e. intervention), the stakeholders are required to develop three interrelated capacities. They are: to be well-informed about the causes, magnitude and impact of poverty in individual societies, to be knowledgeable about global and regional practices and policy experiments in anti-poverty strategies, and to be skilled and trained in managing anti-poverty campaigns and programme interventions (Pathak, Subba Rao *et al.* 2005).

From the prevailing current practices of poverty reduction programmes in the Caribbean, it may be surmised that policy strategies are by and large factored on raising and mobilizing resources and redirecting them to identified segments of the society. Indeed, specific policy interventions would vary from country to country. For instance, in Central America El Salvador has recently implemented a programme—the *Red Solidaria,* which takes the form of conditional cash transfers aimed at breaking intergenerational poverty. Against this kind of innovation, job-creating strategies are being pursued elsewhere in the adjacent countries of the region (For details on *Red Solidaria,* see Britto 2007; Soares and Britto 2007).[3]

Despite the nature and content of specific measures, what is basic to this policy regime is a state committed to structural adjustment, leading to a free market economy that adopts a developmental strategy with emphasis on growth. Then reduction of poverty under this dispensation is simply a matter of "steering enough of the right resources to the right places and the right people" (Leftwich 2008, 3).

Challenges

After two decades of neo-liberal orthodoxies which informed policy in all the major multilateral financial institutions and the donor countries as well as the aid-receiving countries (though somewhat on the decline in very recent years), it is now acknowledged that there is nothing axiomatic in the neo-liberal postulations and, therefore, they are to be either dismissed as "econo-centric" fallacies or to be drastically fine-tuned to meet the specific challenges of the poor in the developing societies. Even the assumption that the democratic processes in the less developed countries would be further bolstered and consolidated under the neo-liberal orthodoxies is now being seriously questioned and replaced by the assertion that indeed it is democracy which is a necessary pre-requisite/pre-condition for the successful implementation and consummation of neo-liberal economic policy and not the other way around. Against these revised theoretical underpinnings and new perspectives has surfaced yet another approach that emphasizes the primacy of bringing politics back into the development discourse. Leftwich has argued that policy-researchers and policy-makers need to focus on the politics or, more correctly, the political processes—both internal and external, and their interaction—in shaping the goals and capacity of state institutions and their developmental outcomes including poverty reduction. The logic, Leftwich points out, is that given the dominance of economists in most aid agencies and development research institutions, far too little attention is paid to understanding the diverse political contexts, processes and practices. It is the political processes that frame developmental outcomes, whether positive or pathological, and thus determine poverty reduction outcomes (Leftwich 2008, 5).

More robust advocates go further to argue that development

and poverty reduction—policy goals that are mutually re-enforcing and admittedly consistent—are not to be deemed as "technical processes"; instead they are "quintessentially political" (Leftwich 2008, 5) and underpin the intrinsic elements of what is delineated as the "politics" of poverty reduction.

Suffice it to say, the emerging consensus now is that sustained progress on these two trajectories—development and poverty reduction—depends substantially on the infusion of politics into both. After all, what is politics if it is not a process (or a cluster of processes) of cooperation, conflict and negotiation between interest groups/elite which alone, in the final analysis, influence decisions about how resources are produced, distributed and used (Leftwich 2008, 6). The nexus through which different interest groups/elite struggle, negotiate, and agree yields what is called "the rules of rule," of which some are enshrined as formal and even embedded in the constitution and others which are less rigorous remain informal yet allowing the interest groups to play legitimate "games" within through public contestations/debates, group movements and claims-making (e.g. *Lok Pal* movement in India).[4] Better players in such informal contestations—meaning reasonably more responsible interest groups—over time would evolve appropriate and effective devices/practices, whether on issues relating to poverty reduction or on general social welfare. More importantly, the better the players—i.e., more responsive the elite groups— the better would be the game—that is, better strategies and more effective delivery mechanisms would be the outcomes.

Current Strategies for Situating Politics in Development-Poverty Agenda

Going by the volume of recent academic outpouring it is evident that the foregrounding of politics in the development-poverty debate is admittedly welcome to all those engaged in the exercise of policy-making and policy-research on poverty reduction. There appears even an emerging general consensus suggesting that it is only in politics that explanations for varying developmental performances of national societies are found as much as it is from such empirical evidence and developmental experiences that one can seek the much-needed correctives to distortions and lapses in economic development policies and processes.

However, a closer look reveals a different picture. The so-called consensus is neither solid nor substantial. The surfacing schism, though seemingly subdued and understated, is indeed extensive and wide-ranging. Almost all of the differences invariably revolve around the terms and circumstances under which politics is now being sought to be inserted in the development discourse as well as in the policies devised and dispensed by the international financial institutions (IFIs), the donor countries, and the aid recipient countries.

Furthermore, the upsurge of interest in inserting politics within international development policy framework at this juncture, it may be noted, has occurred just about the same time when the poverty agenda is being catapulted to the forefront by multilateral global organizations, IFIs and some donor countries. This coincidence, according to some observers, is not a mere happenstance. In their view, when the "one-size-fits-all" approach of the externally imposed (through IFIs) neo-liberal structural adjustment policy failed "to deliver" in low income countries (LICs) and especially in small "island" economies such as those in the Caribbean, apparently a "post-Washington consensus" had emerged seeking to resurrect the neo-liberal policy regime by centre-staging politics and poverty in its policy framework. To them, the post-Washington consensus, whereby the neo-liberal hegemony has been subtly but "significantly re-morphed by new institutionalist thinking" into something that might be called "inclusive liberalism," is defined in terms of its dual focus on Good Governance and Poverty Reduction (Craig and Porter 2006).

Seen from this perspective, the United Nations-sponsored Millennium Development Goals (MDGs) of 2000 is nothing but a strategic ploy to undergird poverty agenda. The MDGs primarily seek to improve social and economic conditions in the world's poorest countries with an increased set of "good" governance reform prescriptions, through which adherent governments have committed to halve poverty and hunger by 2015. It was envisioned that in the realization of these goals it would be possible to achieve opportunity, security and empowerment for all the poor.[5] Be that as it may, MDG by most accounts has so far achieved trifle little. Some of the enumerated goals have not even been considered by the respective governmental departments/agencies, and many others have not taken off ground. For a programme of such ambitious goals, and being implemented in the midst of a looming global financial crisis (GFC) and uncertain international political climate, how the MDG is likely to trigger a genuine grass-roots bottom-up political process remains elusive, if not an open question.

The other poverty related multilateral policy initiative viz. the IFIs' sponsored Poverty Reduction Strategy Papers (PRSPs)—the "other poverty-related game in town" (Hickey 2008, 355)—does not seem to fare any better in putting politics in the development discourse. It may be recalled, around the same time when MDG was declared, the IFIs for their part announced the introduction of PRSPs as a means of securing comprehensive development again like MDG with emphasis on poverty reduction. The PRSPs, it is claimed, is a path-breaking developmental framework because of its credentials to deal frontally with poverty rather than focusing on the narrowly identified economic objectives of the yester years' structural policy regime. Together, the PRSPs, it is further claimed, seeks to bring strategic planning back into the development agenda. Of its other merits, it is often said that Poverty Related Strategic Papers are not only structured specifically around each of the enlisted countries but, more importantly, are need-based and circumstances-specific in view of the fact that each of the countries would have a national plan devised by their own government in consultation with the civil society and "owned by these actors rather than donors" (Hickey 2008, 354).

The PRSP for Dominica aimed at poverty reduction through the promotion of economic growth and job creation. This was deemed essential to provide employment opportunities for all Dominicans and to generate government revenues that can be used to target residual poverty and identified social problems. In addition, basic health and education would help development of the skills and lead to a sustainable and fulfilling life. According to Country Poverty Assessment reports, in spite of many of the programmes being implemented, they were not fully addressing the demand (IMF 2006, 26). Additionally, it has also been pointed out that the Poverty Reduction strategy attempts to transform Dominica from a public-sector-led to a private-sector-led growth economy. Dominica is not internationally competitive, nor does the PRSP seem to have helped it overcome its lack of diversity (IMF 2006, 104). However, it is envisaged that the PRSP process put in place by the government can, along with civil society organizations, improve efforts aimed at poverty reduction. On the whole PRSPs have been claimed as successful because they are adaptable to the specific circumstance or situation of a given country.

Notwithstanding the distinct merits attributed to PRSPs, critics are of the view that this policy framework is nothing but "a new face" of old-style structural adjustment and stabilization policy regime. A recent evaluation report on PRSPs published by the prestigious Brooks World Poverty Institute (Marshall and Walters 2011, 26) disagreed with the critics stating that there is little indication that PRSPs represent "merely the latest form of IFI-sponsored structural adjustment." Nonetheless the report admits that PRSPs "place (too) much emphasis on macroeconomic stability"—the most important policy plank of neo-liberalism. The report goes further to suggest that since higher levels of poverty reduction is by and large determined by enhanced growth outcomes, the PRSPs bias is in favour of growth alone and not on equitable distribution. The report candidly states that there is presently "a lack of a pro-poor orientation within PRSP arrangements relative to any strong notion of pro-poor growth" (Marshall and Walters 2011, 26). It is arguable that this finding runs counter to both the spirit and operational claims of the PRSPs initiative, so much so, many of the pro-poor policies to which the Low Income Countries (LICs) are most committed do not figure in the PRSPs. According to critics, it even casts doubts and misgivings on the "ownership" claim—the idea that these project designs are discussed and drafted by the participant governments and not by the IFIs or any other external agencies (Marshall and Walters 2011, 26).

Whether the PRSPs are pro-poor or not, most LICs opted for the approach because of its professed participatory framework involving the concerned people in designing anti-poverty and pro-poor strategies. However, PRSPs in reality adopt a consultative process that neither gives citizen groups the space nor scope to effect real change or to get policy-makers to deliver on agreed-upon goals. Many groups that participate in the process typically feel that real decisions on important policies lie elsewhere. Participation is often limited to NGOs without the active involvement of associations of informal and formal workers, farmers or artisans, whose livelihoods are directly affected by development policies. Research in many countries shows that important issues are often left out of discussions. According to testimonies, the macroeconomic framework of PRSPs, which is largely based on the IMF's Poverty Reduction and Growth Facility is negotiated strictly between governments and the IMF, an area "ring-fenced" for other interest groups to have any say (Bangura 2011; Leftwich 2008; Marshall and Walters 2011).

While the philosophy of PRSPs apparently extol the virtues of putting politics back in the development paradigm, in its operational dynamics, politics is permitted only to the extent that it can be managed and controlled by the IFIs, suggesting thereby a different type of "disciplining" of the political processes by the aid agencies. Here one finds a striking parallel between the PRSPs and the earlier "good governance agenda" of the IFIs which was also credited for effectively bringing politics back in the development paradigm until it was discovered that the role assigned to the state in the good governance agenda was very restricted, decentralized and "framed as a manager of development rather than a historic site of struggle over what development might mean to different societal interests" (Hickey 2008, 351).

Recommendations for the Way Forward

Basic to any recommendation for the way forward is the recognition that development and poverty reduction are policy goals that reinforce each other and are consistent. Neither of them is to be deemed as a "technical" process that could be engineered "top-down" with modern managerial skills and organizational structure.

A second component is the recognition that in the developing world the state under the pressure of the neo-liberal economic reforms has become lean, mean and, in some instances, has even become anti-poor. Not only has the state been downsized with the attendant expansion of the role of the private sector, but the paucity of resources has led the state to withdraw many of its traditional welfare schemes and initiatives including poverty reduction.

At this juncture therefore, to devise a growth strategy that is at the same time employment-generating, poverty-alleviating and devoid of any pressures—external or internal—the state at all levels has to be actively involved in the ways in which the markets are structured and the way markets deliver goods and services. It then calls for the formation of a state with its constituent institutions to be capable, accountable and responsive to the different segments of its citizenry. This is the so called CAR framework developed by British government's Department for International Development (DFID) (Moore and Teskey 2006).[6]

Given that such state-building is not a simple "top-down" constitutional exercise, the stake-holders—the donor countries and aid agencies—need to invest in and develop analytical frameworks (like DFID's Country Governance Analyses) on the political dynamics. This endeavour encompasses the formal and informal institutional arrangements where policies take shape.

It needs hardly any emphasis that basic to development and poverty reduction is the nexus of power relations in any polity. The complex and intricate ways by which the power relations evolve/change, in turn, determine which actors are in a position to define policies and influence development processes and outcomes. Policies need to be coordinated. To achieve this task, the influence network approach to state capacity with its egalitarian network of relations and interdependent state and social actors seems to be feasible (Moore and Teskey 2006, 6). It is democracy that provides the political space for contestation which may even seem to be extra-constitutional but may become constitutional over a period of time. While democratic institutions are significant, more important is democracy itself. The key is to let it flourish even while strategizing to overcome poverty.

Strategies that seek to bring about changes in poverty outcomes must therefore consider ways to sift/shift and calibrate the balance of power. Group organization, contestation, and claims-making are important in generating such shifts and ensuring that governments respond more effectively and meaningfully to social needs.

Notes

1. A list of the approved projects are available from the website of the Caribbean Development Bank. Accessed January 10, 2012. http://www.caribank.org/titanweb/cdb/webcms.nsf/AllDoc/C55DE8EAF022350C042573A70057BA59?OpenDocument.
2. For a list of the country poverty assessment reports, see website of Caribbean Development Bank, Accessed January 10, 2012. http://www.caribank.org/titanweb/cdb/webcms.nsf/75f7ba2c7557 c2e50425745900719b7a!OpenView.
3. *Red Solidaria* adopted in El Salvador is a conditional cash transfer (CCT) scheme, paid to the mother of the family, in return for fulfilment of "co-responsibilities" such as sending primary school-aged children to school, taking preventive health and nutrition measures (e.g., immunization, child growth monitoring, etc.). Thus it is not simply a cash transfer but also gives permanent training to families in relation to health, nutrition, hygiene, child labor, violence, etc. Small scale productive projects and micro-credit programmes are carried out to support poor agricultural producers and increase their productivity.

4. One such legitimate game played in India is the Jan Lokpal movement, an informal anti-corruption movement that gained currency and legitimacy with civil society playing a massive role. The huge debate that resulted in India has led to a Lokpal Bill being passed, calling for a civic body to have powers to intervene in matters of the state. While the process is still in its formative stages, the fact that discussions are on is indicative of the success of the informal movement.
5. In September 2000, 189 states and members of the United Nations, of which 147 were represented by Heads of State or Government, made a new global commitment to development. The Millennium Declaration is the political manifestation of that commitment. The objectives were known as the Millennium Development Goals and were broken down into eight goals. The first seven Goals embody commitments to be fulfilled primarily by developing countries as they gradually achieve the capacity to provide universal access to minimum levels of well-being. Goal eight is to "develop a global partnership for development."
6. The development of the CAR framework was intended to give political scientists a common vocabulary for discussing governance issues. Capability refers to organisational attributes and to the ability to get things done; accountability refers to having a set of institutionalised relationships with answerability and sanction; and responsiveness means to identify and then meet the needs or wants of the people who will benefit from pro-poor growth.

7

Caribbean Embassies

Bridging the Gap between the Caribbean Diaspora and the Home Country as Part of an Initiative to Stimulate Growth and Development in the Region

Samantha C. Joseph, Martin Franklin and *Roger Hosein*

The Caribbean was created from a migratory flow of people; evidence of this goes as far back to the rediscovery of the Caribbean in 1492 (United Nations 2002). Over the last fifty years the Caribbean region has lost over five million people to the metropolitan countries, with places such as Guyana, Suriname, Jamaica and St. Lucia experiencing the greatest percentage levels of emigration with regard to total population (United Nations 2005). Table 7.1 below outlines the stock of international migrants for select geographical areas. It is evident from the data that the stock of international migrants from the Caribbean increased from 1990 to 2005 but declined significantly in 2010; the latter being a result of the global financial crisis. This global financial crisis led to unfavourable economic conditions (inclusive of high levels of unemployment) in the metropolitan countries. This trend of increasing migration from the region has resulted in the Caribbean having a large diaspora located predominantly in the United States of America[1].

There are many factors that can explain migration from the Caribbean. Migration in the Caribbean has been justified by a search for a better life outside the region due to poor economic conditions in the region. Other push factors which contribute to Caribbean migration are "deteriorating economic and social conditions, high unemployment particularly for younger people

Table 7.1: International Migrants Stock (millions) for Selected Geographical Areas 1990–2005

Geographical Area	*1990*	*1995*	*2000*	*2005*	*% population 2005*	*2010^e*
World	155.52	165.97	178.5	195.25	3.0	213.94
More Developed Regions	83.35	94.12	104.43	117.19	9.6	127.71
Less Developed Regions	73.16	71.85	74.06	78.06	1.5	86.23
Africa	15.97	17.92	17.06	17.74	1.9	19.26
Asia	50.88	48.77	51.92	55.13	1.4	61.32
Europe excluding UK	45.68	50.53	52.85	58.56	8.7	63.57
UK	3.72	4.19	4.79	5.84	9.7	6.45
Oceania	4.37	4.73	5.02	5.52	16.4	6.01
USA	23.25	28.52	34.81	39.27	13.0	42.81
Canada	4.50	5.05	5.36	6.30	19.5	7.20
Latin America	5.96	4.96	5.08	5.36	1.0	5.89
Caribbean	0.23	0.26	0.28	0.31	2.0	0.34

Source: United Nations Population Division: World Migrant Stock. The 2008 revision database.[1]

Note: e—implies estimated

1. Accessed on http://esa.un.org/migration/index.asp?panel=, 1. September 23, 2010

and little hope for improvements" (United Nations 2002, 10). The term "diaspora" is defined by Sheffer (1986, 3) as "Ethnic minority groups of migrant origins, residing and acting in host countries but maintaining strong sentimental and material links with their countries of origin or their homeland." Cohen (2008) noted that there are five types of diasporas, namely, refugee/victim, colonial, labour/service, trade and cultural/hybrid, and categorized the Caribbean as a cultural diaspora.

In this chapter we attempt to examine the various avenues through which the Caribbean diaspora can make a greater contribution to growth and development in the Caribbean region, and to investigate the potential of Caribbean embassies to facilitate the contributions of the diaspora to the home country given their strategic relationship with the members of the Caribbean diaspora. In particular, we argue that the Caribbean diaspora is capable of transforming the Caribbean through an increase in the knowledge-based segment and pool of skills within the Caribbean region. More specifically, the Caribbean diaspora can facilitate the creation of a more competitive workforce, entrepreneurship, investments and trade between the home country and itself as well as strengthening networks and joint collaboration between the home and host countries. However, in order for this to materialize, Caribbean governments must recognize the importance of their respective embassies and consular offices as key institutions in harnessing the resources of the Caribbean diaspora.

In order to gain deeper insight on the areas of development that need the attention of the diaspora, a socio-economic profiling of the Caribbean was undertaken based on available comparative data for specific years. This profiling highlights some of the challenges of the region as well as some areas for improvement. Accordingly, the remainder of the chapter is organized as follows: Section one presents the socio-economic profile of the Caribbean region; section two highlights the various avenues through which the diaspora can impact growth and development in the Caribbean region; section three focuses on Caribbean embassies as facilitators between the Caribbean diaspora and the Caribbean region and best practices in such facilitation. Section four presents the empirical analysis and section five, the final section, highlights the conclusion and policy recommendations.

Socio–Economic Profile of the Caribbean

The countries of the Caribbean region are grouped into different classifications such as Most Developed Countries (MDCs)[3] and Least Developed Countries (LDCs).[4] These countries have suffered tremendously from external shocks over the years due to the high level of vulnerability and risk in the region. Life expectancy rates have been on the increase for most Caribbean countries; these range from 66.5 to 77 for the MDCs and 71.4 to 76 for LDCs in 2007 as shown in Table 7.2. There has been much emphasis on reducing the infant mortality rate. Available data for 2007 in Table 7.2 show Haiti as having the highest rate at 67.1 per 1000 live births and Trinidad and Tobago, Guyana, and Jamaica also having relatively high rates of 31.1, 30.8 and 26.1 respectively.

With regard to education, the region's education policies have emphasized the need to ensure significant levels of access to structured education programmes by all. Despite this emphasis, 1.3 million people in the region were not served by any educational programme in 2007 (UNDP 2007). Table 7.2 illustrates that in 2007, Antigua and Barbuda had the highest adult literacy rate of 99 per cent followed by Trinidad and Tobago (98.7 per cent) and St. Kitts and Nevis (97.8 per cent). Haiti is an exception; its adult literacy rate for 2007 was at 62.1. Barbados ranked 37 in the Human Development Index for 2007 followed by Antigua and Barbuda (47); Haiti ranked 149 as shown in Table 7.2 below.

With respect to technology diffusion and creation, Table 7.3 below illustrates growth in telephone mainlines, cellular subscribers and internet users per 1000 persons over the period 1990 to 2005. It is quite evident that usage in the above technologies increased in all Caribbean countries over that period, with Jamaica leading the way with 1,017 cellular subscribers per 1000 population, followed by Barbados (765) and St. Kitts and Nevis (663). Jamaica, Barbados, Dominica and St. Lucia, in that order, had the top four incidences of internet usage per 1000 population in 2005. It is evident from the table that in the 1990s when there was a strong wave of migration from the Caribbean, the level of technology diffusion was very low in the region.

From an economic standpoint, the Caribbean region has a very high import bill resulting in trade deficits for most of the Caribbean countries. There is also a high level of intra regional trade among Caribbean countries, with Trinidad and Tobago enjoying the dominant share (CARICOM 2009). In 2006 Real GDP for the region

Table 7.2: Human Development Indicators for Selected Caribbean Countries for the Year 2007

Countries	*GDP Per Capita (PPP $US)*	*Life Expectancy at Birth*	*Infant Mortality per 1000 Births*	*Adult Literacy Rate*	*Gross Enrolment Ratio*	*HDI Rank*
Antigua and Barbuda	18,691	na	11.6	99.0	na	47
Bahamas	20,253	73.2	9.4	na	71.8	52
Barbados	17,956	77.0	10.4	na	92.9	37
Belize	6,734	76.0	17.1	75.1	78.3	93
Dominica	7,893	na	9.2	88.0	78.5	73
Grenada	7,344	75.3	13.4	96.0	73.1	74
Guyana	2,782	66.5	30.8	na	83.9	114
Haiti	1,155	61.0	67.1	62.1	na	149
Jamaica	6,079	71.7	26.1	86.0	78.1	100
St. Kitts and Nevis	14,481	na	14.2	97.8	73.1	62
St. Lucia	9,786	73.6	17.5	94.8	77.2	69
St. Vincent and the Grenadines	7,691	71.4	12.6	88.1	68.9	91
Suriname	7,813	68.8	25.5	90.4	74.3	97
Trinidad and Tobago	23,507	69.2	31.1	98.7	61.1	64
Caribbean	10,591	71.3	na	88.8	75.7	80.8

Source: World Bank Development Indicators 2011 and USAID Development Statistics for Latin America and the Caribbean 2007.

Table 7.3: Technology Diffusion and Creation in the Caribbean 1990-2005

Country	*Telephone Mainlines per 1000 population*		*Cellular Subscribers per 1000 population*		*Internet Users per 1000 population*	
	1990	*2005*	*1990*	*2005*	*1990*	*2005*
Antigua and Barbuda	252	467	0	663	0	29
Bahamas, The	274	439	8	584	0	319
Barbados	281	500	0	765	0	361
Belize	92	114	0	319	0	130
Dominica	161	293	0	585	0	339
Grenada	162	309	2	410	0	182
Guyana	22	147	0	375	0	213
Jamaica	44	129	0	1017	0	404
St. Kitts and Nevis	231	532	0	213	na	na
St. Lucia	127	na	0	573	0	339
St. Vincent and the Grenadines	129	189	0	593	0	84
Suriname	91	180	0	518	0	71
Trinidad and Tobago	136	248	0	613	0	123

Source: UN Human Development Report, 2007.

averaged $97,382.3 million, of which $71,198.4 million was from the MDCs. Moreover, growth in GDP for CARICOM averaged 7.3 per cent for the period 2002 to 2006 (CARICOM 2009).

The rapidly changing globalised environment has resulted in a reduction in the demand for labour, thus producing high levels of unemployment, reduced labour income, and increased poverty (Downes 2006). Even though the Caribbean has benefited from economic growth and now has fairly high human development indicators, the economies of the region have not succeeded in drastically reducing unemployment rates. Table 7.4 shows that with the exception of 2007 and 2008, the majority of countries had unemployment rates in excess of 10 per cent annually. The World Bank (2009) attributes the unemployment rates in 2008 to a mismatch between declining agricultural opportunities and the inability of the remaining sectors to absorb these workers. The International Labour Organization (2009) reports the average unemployment rate for all CARICOM countries (with the exception of Haiti) as rising to 10 per cent in 2009.

With regard to poverty as measured by the ability to finance a basic consumption basket of food and non-food items—for example, education, housing and transportation—Haiti and Suriname were at the high end of the spectrum of poverty incidence in 2006 with an estimated 65 per cent and 63 per cent respectively of their population living below the poverty line. Belize, Dominica, Grenada, Guyana, St. Kitts and Nevis, and St. Vincent and the Grenadines are in the 30 per cent to 40 per cent range. Anguilla, British Virgin Islands, St. Lucia, Trinidad and Tobago, and the Turks and Caicos fall between 20 per cent and 29 per cent. Barbados had a poverty rate of 14 per cent in 1997 while Jamaica had a rate of approximately 20 per cent in 2002 (Bourne 2005).

Caribbean people usually migrate in search of a better standard of living, educational opportunities and better employment opportunities, but such migration can have adverse impacts on the region's education resources. Table 7.5 below shows that a large share of the region's educated human resource has migrated. This brain drain makes development of the region difficult.

The Caribbean Diaspora and its Potential to Impact Growth and Development

The concept of diasporas and their contributions to the home country is not new; it has been around from the period of the slave

Table 7.4: Unemployment Rates in Selected Caribbean Economies for Various Years

Country	*1991*	*1995*	*1998*	*2001*	*2002*	*2003*	*2004*	*2005*	*2006*	*2007*	*2008*
Bahamas	12.3	10.9	7.8	6.9	9.1	10.8	10.2	10.2	7.6	7.9	12.1
Barbados	17.3	19.6	11.8	9.9	10.3	11.0	9.6	9.1	8.73	7.4	8.1
Belize	na	12.5	14.3	9.1	10.0	12.9	11.6	11.0	9.4	8.5	8.2
Grenada	13.7	17.0	15.2	11.5	11.5	11.5	15.0	18.5	Na	na	na
Jamaica	15.4	16.2	15.5	15.0	14.2	11.4	11.7	11.2	10.4	9.9	10.6
St. Lucia	na	16.3	21.6	18.9	24.6	21.0	22.3	18.7	15.7	14.0	15.7
Suriname	na	8.4	10.6	14.0	10.0	7.0	8.0	11.0	Na	10.7	9.3
Trinidad and Tobago	15.9	14.7	12.6	10.8	10.4	10.5	8.4	8.0	6.2	5.6	2.5

Sources: Downes (2006) for period 1991-2002; Caribbean Development Bank Social Economic Indicators Report 2006 for the period 2003-2006; International Labour Office Labour Review 2009 for 2007-2008.

Table 7.5: Migration by Education Level in Selected Caribbean Countries 1990-2000

Country	*Primary Level*		*Secondary Level*		*Tertiary Level*	
	1990	*2000*	*1990*	*2000*	*1990*	*2000*
Antigua and Barbuda	7.0	6.0	31.7	35.9	65.3	70.9
Grenada	7.5	9.9	61.1	69.5	68.8	66.7
Guyana	10.9	13.7	30.6	34.1	89.2	85.9
Jamaica	11.0	8.3	28.9	30.0	84.1	82.5
St. Kitts and Nevis	10.8	10.3	21.4	37.1	89.9	71.8
Suriname	15.7	17.5	54	43.9	92.0	89.9
T & T	5.7	6.1	19.3	20.6	77.2	78.4

Source: Docquier and Marfouk (2004).

trade more than three hundred years ago. Williams (1944) in his book *Capitalism and Slavery* conducted an economic study of the slave trade and noted that its profits provided one of the main streams of accumulation of capital in England which in turn financed the Industrial Revolution. The Caribbean diaspora community in the United States is the largest subset of the Caribbean diaspora internationally and possesses an inherent potential to contribute to Caribbean development (Nurse 2004).

The Caribbean diaspora has been contributing to the Caribbean region through diaspora transfers; these take the form of cash and non-cash remittances, and social remittances. Cash remittances are "a percentage of household income from foreign economies arising mainly from the temporary or permanent movement of people to those economies" (International Monetary Fund 2009). Cash remittances are being increasingly recognized internationally as an important source of development capital. In the Caribbean, Haiti, Guyana and Jamaica are the largest recipients of remittances comprising a significant share of their GDP, while in The Organisation of Eastern Caribbean States (OECS),[5] Grenada, St. Kitts and Nevis, and St. Vincent and the Grenadines are the largest recipients.

Table 7.6 depicts the flow of remittances to the English speaking Caribbean and Haiti for the period 1995-2008. It is evident from the table that remittances to all the selected Caribbean countries have been increasing over the time period, reaching a maximum in 2008.

The Caribbean is also known for the receipt of non-cash remittances also known as 'remittances in kind' or barrels from the diaspora. These include household items, medical and educational supplies, foodstuff such as maize-meal, sugar, salt and cooking oil, supplies for resale, consumer goods such as bicycles, radios, sofas, agricultural inputs and building materials which are usually packaged by the migrant and sent to the home country (Maphosa 2005). The region can also benefit from social remittances. Levitt (1998, 926-948) defines social remittances as "ideas, behaviours, identities and social capital that flow from receiving to sending country communities." The Caribbean diaspora also contributes to the region through diaspora investments that include human capital investments and financial investments such as diaspora bonds, insurance, savings and real sector investments. USAID (2008, 2) noted that diaspora bonds are:

> ...typically issued by a country to raise debt capital to finance development projects. India and Israel have been very successful in issuing a series of these bonds that were aimed to mobilize resources to support public-sector projects. Also, local banks in Mexico, Brazil, Kazakhstan, and Ghana have been able to raise long term capital from the international markets by collateralizing their future flows of remittances (remittance-backed securities).

The issuance of bonds to the diaspora by the home country is one way for the home country to tap into the diaspora's accumulated wealth. These bonds are redeemed upon maturity and serve as a good source of foreign exchange into the home country (Kethar and Ratha 2007). Notably, diaspora bonds are not yet widely used as an instrument for growth and development in developing economies because most countries have yet to recognize the large flow of funds that diaspora bonds can make available to their economies. The Caribbean diaspora can also make real sector investments which can take the form of foreign direct investments, trade in nostalgic goods, and entrepreneurial investments (Ionescu 2006).

Home Town Associations (HTAs) usually begin as informal groups that seek out people with similar nationality to establish ties and bonds as well as a support framework (Somerville, Durana and Terrazas 2008, 5). Over time these groups develop into formal associations that extend their support not only to co-nationals in the host country but also to households of family, friends and communities in the home country (Somerville, Durana and

Table 7.6: Remittance Flows (US$ million) for Selected Caribbean Countries, 1995-2008

Years	Antigua and Barbuda	Barbados	Dominica	Guyana	Haiti	Grenada	Belize	Jamaica	St. Kitts and Nevis	St. Lucia	St. Vincent and the Grenadines	T&T
1995	3	53	3	2	109	18	14	653	2	2	2	32
1996	3	60	3	15	152	20	17	714	2	2	2	28
1997	6	69	2	15	256	20	23	730	3	2	2	30
1998	12	76	3	15	327	20	23	758	4	3	3	45
1999	12	87	3	20	422	21	21	790	4	3	3	54
2000	10	102	3	27	578	22	22	892	4	3	3	38
2001	16	118	4	[illegible]	624	22	30	1058	4	2	3	41
2002	6	109	4	51	676	23	29	1261	3	2	4	79
2003	9	113	4	99	811	23	34	1399	3	2	3.4	87
2004	21	109	23	153	932	72	35	1623	31	29	26	87
2005	22	140	25	201	985	52	46	1784	34	30	27	92
2006	23	140	25	218	1063	54	66	1946	36	30	30	91
2007	24	140	26	278	1222	55	75	2144	37	31	31	109
2008	26	168	30	278	1300	64	78	2220	37	31	31	109

Source: World Development Indicators (2009).

Terrazas 2008). HTAs and other voluntary groups within the diaspora can play an important role in impacting the home country's social, economic, political and cultural structures (Latapi and Janssen 2006). This impact can take the form of educational and health programs, charitable donations, community beautification/enhancement as well as the building of infrastructure for the local community (Fagen *et al.* 2009).

Many people migrate from the Caribbean region to metropolitan countries such as the United States of America, Canada and the United Kingdom and as such become part of the Caribbean diaspora. Figure 7.1 showcases Diaspora Transfers, Direct Diaspora Investments (DDI) and the contributions of Home Town Associations as three different avenues through which the diaspora can impact growth and development in the Caribbean region.

It is normal for the diaspora to interface frequently with its respective embassies for consular services. Accordingly, Figure 7.1 above points to the respective embassies utilizing their unique relationship with the diaspora to facilitate transfers, DDI, and the contributions of Home Town Associations to the home country.

Given the socio-economic conditions of the Caribbean, opportunities exist for the diaspora to play a key role in stimulating or contributing to the development of the region. There is still the need for technical vocational programmes in the Caribbean. Notwithstanding the fairly high literacy rate by international standards, functional literacy must be enhanced. The diaspora can help in satisfying the need for vocational programmes through financial support, the provision of equipment to support these programmes as well as the provision of short term lecturers. The members of the diaspora can also support online learning and distant education programs.[6]

There is also the need in the region to enhance the delivery of health care at the community level, thereby reducing the excessive demands made on general hospitals located in the urban areas.

Furthermore, the diaspora can play a key role in helping to develop these community health centers as well as providing some training in the skills and expertise required, given that a large share of the region's nurses and doctors have migrated.

Small business development and entrepreneurship are perceived as tools for stimulating economic growth and development in the Caribbean. The region has failed to adequately educate its people on the importance of entrepreneurship.

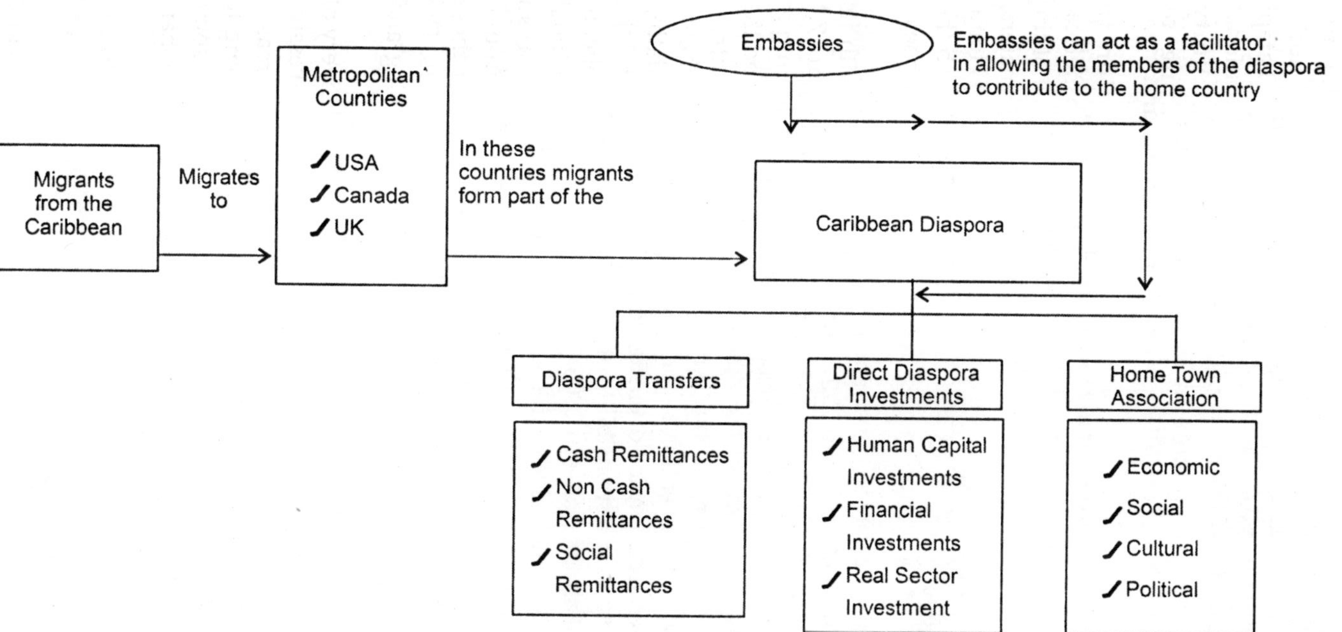

Figure 7.1: Avenues through Which the Caribbean Diaspora can Make a Greater Contribution to the Development of the Region

Source: Authors' Design.

Currently, there is only one tertiary institution in the region which offers a bachelors degree in entrepreneurship. Opportunities exist for the diaspora to create small and medium business enterprises within the Caribbean. Members of the diaspora can be the strategic agents for the investments in small and medium business enterprises such as consultancy firms, restaurants and retail companies.

Realistically, in order for the members of the diaspora to make a significant contribution to the development of their respective economies, there is a need for a facilitator.

Embassies: Bridging the Gap between the Diaspora and the Home Country

In recent times, Caribbean governments have increased the number of their embassies and consular/expatriate offices in all of the metropolitan countries. These offices have the goal of better serving expatriates, increasing communication channels, and dealing with the issues and concerns of the diaspora (Ionescu 2006, 36). The embassies and expatriate/consular offices in recent times have begun to pay more attention to the "feeling of belonging" and to the non-material dimension of engaging with diasporas in addition to discharging their responsibility of dealing with consular matters and national affairs (Ionescu 2006, 36).

An embassy inclusive of the building in which it is housed is a permanent diplomatic mission; it is much larger than a consulate. Embassies are an important component of foreign relations, given that they serve as a bridge between the visiting and host countries. An embassy's main responsibility is to represent the home country in the host country and to address major diplomatic issues including ensuring the legal rights of migrants abroad. The highest official at the embassy is the ambassador who is the chief diplomat and acts on behalf of the home country's government (Briney 2010). Embassies can be effective in facilitating resolution of tariff issues, trade disputes and political tensions among countries before they escalate. Embassies and consular/expatriate offices abroad are responsible for issues relating to the economy, specific industrial sectors, governance and politics, history and culture, the people and society, travel and leisure, technical support as well as diplomatic relations of the home country.

Different countries assign other duties from three broad categories to their embassies. The first category involves offering advice and assistance to nationals abroad and issuing visas and passports. The second category involves providing individual assistance to migrants with various needs which include the hospitalization of a migrant, assistance to migrants who are either detained, missing, or deceased, as well as assistance to the next of kin in the home country. The third category concerns crisis management issues of migrants in the host country (Heijmans and Melissen 2006).

Embassies and consular offices may also be responsible for the commercial and economic interests of the home country. Accordingly, they may be charged with the responsibility of setting up meetings in which groups of people in the home and host countries come together to explore arrangements and partnerships which will extend economic cooperation and stimulate growth in the respective home country (Heijmans and Melissen 2006).

Cultural exchange is another important role of embassies and consular offices. They are responsible for bridging exchanges in the culture through different initiatives such as jointly hosted cultural events, cultural fairs and celebrating national holidays. Such interactions involve cooperative projects in the arts, music, humanities and social studies, science, performing arts, food, and design (United States Department of State Cultural Heritage Center 2010). The degree to which these institutions carry out these roles depends on the strength of their respective government as well as their diplomatic relations with the host country (Brand 2006).

Embassies as Facilitators: Best Practices

Many countries have recognized the importance of their diaspora and have come to the realization that in order for them to successfully tap into the resources of their diaspora, they must have a facilitator who can bridge the gap between themselves and their diaspora in the home country. This facilitator is no other than their respective embassies and consular offices.

Ireland is one such country that has recognized the importance of embassies and consulate offices in their economic recovery. In 2007, the Ministry of Foreign Affairs in Ireland developed a new strategy to target the Irish diaspora for development purposes. By 2009, over one million people worldwide claimed Irish decent (Ancien, Boyle and Kitchin 2009). Ireland has approximately fifty-six embassies and eight consulates around the world; they regularly offer a full range of diplomatic and consular services to their citizens resident abroad. The Department of Foreign Affairs of Ireland has been mandated to coordinate engagements with the diaspora for the development of Ireland (Ancien, Boyle and Kitchin 2009).

In a similar manner, African governments are intensifying outreach to their diaspora. Increasingly, they have been using their embassies and consular offices abroad in outreach efforts to bridge the gap between the diaspora and the home country. In Ghana, the members of the High Commission are working closely with the diaspora to form links, networks and partnerships to aid development in Ghana as one of the main priorities. The same actions are being undertaken by the Embassies of Burundi, South Africa, and Rwanda (Grey 2006). The primary aim of these efforts is to get the African diaspora involved in contributing to the national development of Africa. Concrete measures undertaken and facilitated by these consular offices include, but are not limited to, the establishment of investment funds through which members of the African diaspora channel their capital into productive investments as well as data collection initiatives that establish a databank of the skills and expertise of the members of the African diaspora (Grey 2006).

Ethiopia is also establishing relations with its diaspora by assigning new roles and responsibilities to its missions and consular offices abroad. These include community outreach programmes and constituency building organized so as to impact growth and development. It is also formulating units within the embassies to deal specifically with diaspora issues. New units are being established within its embassies to provide accurate information on the Ethiopian diaspora; organize research on the diaspora; inform the diaspora about the various privileges and opportunities that are available to them for contributing to the development of Ethiopia (Belai 2007).

In the Caribbean, embassies collectively form part of an important government institution under the direction of the Ministry of Foreign Affairs; as such, these form part of an institutional framework which needs to be built and further developed across the region. It is therefore important that the respective stakeholders in the Caribbean region assign to their embassies and consular offices the responsibility and role of facilitator between the Caribbean diaspora and their home country. It is in this light that an empirical study was undertaken by the authors to examine the potential of Caribbean embassies to serve as facilitators between the diaspora and the home country and act as a bridge between the two. The study is summarized in the next section.

Empirical Analysis

Methodology

This empirical study is an attempt at evaluating the potential of Caribbean embassies to serve as facilitators between the Caribbean diaspora and the home country, thereby allowing members of the Caribbean diaspora to make a greater contribution to the development of their home country through economic transfers, direct diaspora investment, and Home Town Associations. This study also assesses the role of these embassies in diaspora relations with the home country, the obstacles that these embassies encounter as well as the relationship and support from the government in the home country.

The methodology adopted was a sample survey which was conducted amongst twenty four (24) Caribbean embassies drawn from Jamaica, Guyana, Trinidad and Tobago, Barbados, St. Lucia, St. Vincent and the Grenadines, Dominica, and Antigua and Barbuda and that are located in the USA, Canada and the United Kingdom. Purposive sampling was employed so as to ensure representation from the top recipients of remittances in the CARICOM as well as the countries with the larger migration rates. The research instrument employed was a structured questionnaire which was executed on the Ambassador or High Commissioner of each embassy within the sample. The questionnaire solicited primary data on the willingness of embassies to act as facilitators between the diaspora and the home country.

Analysis of Results

Respondents from the twenty four (24) embassies interviewed in the survey were asked how frequently they met with the members of their respective diaspora. The results indicated that the embassies met with the members of the diaspora on a regular basis at the Home Town Associations monthly meetings. In addition, all the respondents confirmed that embassy representatives attended all the social functions organized by the various diaspora associations. All the embassies also reported having regular face to face contact with the members of the diaspora whenever the latter accessed consular services such as the renewal of their passports. The data therefore supports the fact that the embassies are in regular contact with the members of their diaspora.

With regard to the availability of programmes within the embassy for facilitating members of the diaspora who wish to contribute to the home country, 95 per cent of the embassies surveyed admitted to not having the responsibility for coordinating such programs; the Guyanese Embassy was the lone exception.

The Guyanese Embassy in Ottawa, Canada indicated that it organized programmes such as "School Net Guyana," in which the Embassy of Guyana works with members of the Guyanese diaspora to computerize all the high schools in Guyana, and another programme in which professionals such as medical doctors travel to Guyana annually to perform surgeries at no cost in local hospitals. However, with respect to the other Caribbean countries represented in the sample, the embassies reported no programmes that facilitate such contributions by members of their diaspora to the home country. The data suggest that it is necessary for the other Caribbean embassies to learn from the experiences of the Guyanese embassies and create programmes which encourage members of the Caribbean diaspora to contribute to the development of their home country.

All twenty-four (24) embassies in the sample reported that members of their diaspora approached them on a regular basis to indicate their interest in making a contribution to the home country. Such contributions can take the form of sending supplies to the home country or giving charitable support to various organizations in the home country. In the case of the latter however, there appears to be no available programme in the home country or the embassies to facilitate the movement of these supplies from the host country to the home country. One respondent cited as an example the offer of new beds to the Embassy and Consulate of a Caribbean country for use in the hospitals in the home country consequent on the closure of a large hospital in Canada. Although the Embassy applied to the relevant ministries in the home country to pay for the shipment of these beds, no decision was taken. Consequently, the Embassy lost these beds to non-Caribbean countries that were more proactive in receiving and transporting diaspora contributions.

The Jamaican Embassy representative stated that the members of the Jamaican diaspora visited their embassy to access information on investment opportunities available in Jamaica's tourism and ICT sectors. All the sampled embassies also admitted to encouraging the migrants from their home country to buy local Caribbean goods. Local goods are promoted through newsletters, the embassy's webpage and small business ventures which sell local goods in the host country. All the embassies admitted that they do not offer any help to members of the diaspora with regard to importing local goods from the Caribbean.

When questioned about the various investment initiatives offered by the government and stakeholders in the home country, 95 per cent of the sampled embassies claimed that no investment initiatives had been offered by the respective Caribbean countries to the diaspora; yet again, the Guyanese Embassy was the notable exception (see Figure 7.2 below). The Guyanese government and various stakeholders have made investment packages available to the members of the Guyanese diaspora for investment in agriculture, real estate, restaurants and supermarkets. The Guyanese Embassy in Canada also reported that there had been an increase in small business investments in Guyana by members of the diaspora since the onset of the global financial crisis.

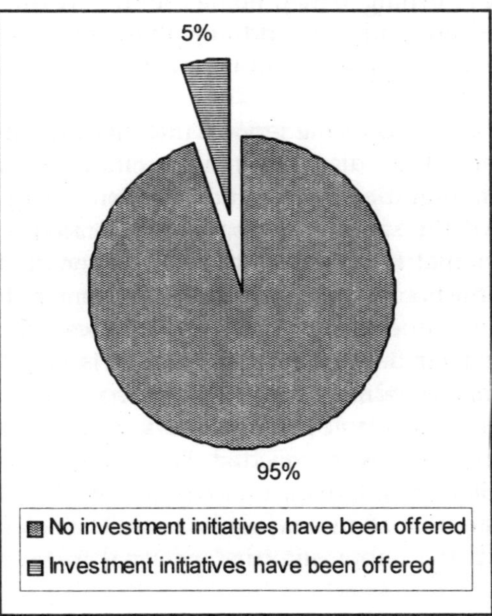

Figure 7.2: Offers of Investment Initiatives to the Diaspora by Stakeholders in the Home Country

The Jamaican Embassies, on the other hand, highlighted the fact that the Jamaican government had been discussing the idea of diaspora bonds for the past few years. Unfortunately, to date, nothing has been implemented with regard to these bonds. The data suggest that the Guyanese government has recognized the value of their diaspora and made an effort to tap into their resources by targeting them with investment opportunities.

All the sampled embassies noted that they communicated with the members of their diaspora about issues and events taking place in the home country on a regular basis. This communication is done via newsletters, flyers, meetings, or through the embassy's general website.

When asked about existing programmes for facilitating the return of migrants to the home country, all the embassies indicated that there exist no specific programmes which facilitate this process; available information relate to what the migrant can bring back to the home country and products in which they can invest on their return to the home country. This information is available on the embassies' websites and members of the diaspora who are considering returning to their home country are directed to these websites for information. In addition, there is no programme that smoothly allows the migrants to assimilate into the society on their return.

The embassies listed the services that they provide to migrants and members of the diaspora; these include consular services, passports, immigration issues, trade, tourism relations as well as advising. All the sampled embassies indicated an interest in programmes that facilitate the transfer of knowledge from the migrants to the home country. Many (60 per cent) of the embassies are now in the process of creating skill and knowledge banks of members of their diaspora grouping. This is very important in that it allows the country to be aware of the variety of skills and expertise that are available in the diaspora grouping and to identify particular expertise when needed. For example, if a particular ministry in St. Lucia is looking for a consultant or a technical expert in a particular discipline, it may access its skill bank for the diaspora and identify a suitably qualified national instead of hiring a foreigner.

Ironically, 90 per cent of the sampled embassies indicated that the greatest hindrance to members of the diaspora contributing to the home country is the lack of support from the government in the home country. This finding was especially evident for Trinidad and Tobago. Moreover, these embassy representatives indicated that their governments had not established any programme for partnering with the diaspora through the embassies. However, steps in this direction are being initiated by Guyana, Jamaica, Dominica and St. Lucia. Interestingly, all sampled embassies held the view that the members of the diaspora lacked the necessary information on how they can contribute to the development of their home country as well as incentives for contributing to the home country.

The Barbadian embassies located in the USA, Canada and the UK in the sample noted that the problem does not only resonate with the government and the embassies but with the members of the Barbadian diaspora themselves. They noted that Barbadians living abroad lacked a sense of identity and belonging with regard to the Caribbean. In particular, when these citizens migrated to the metropolitan countries, they no longer considered themselves as "Bajans" or Caribbean people but assimilated themselves into the host country's culture. This situation could serve as a potential hindrance to contributing to their home country.

Conclusion and Recommendations

This chapter has identified the various avenues in which the Caribbean diaspora can significantly impact growth and development in the Caribbean. It also makes the point that there is the need for a bridge/facilitator between the home country and the Caribbean diaspora in matters related to the involvement of the diaspora in the development of the region. It drew attention to the importance of embassies and consular offices of Caribbean countries in the context of mobilizing the resources of the diaspora to stimulate growth and development. The authors argue that embassies and consular offices of Caribbean countries should serve as the bridge and facilitator between the home country and the Caribbean diaspora, but this will require that the government authorities give a new mandate to their respective embassies, one that encompasses diaspora affairs.

In most cases, embassies and consular offices are overburdened with other consular issues and are unable to address diaspora affairs adequately and effectively because of the lack of personnel and capacity. In this regard, a new unit or department should be set up within the embassy or consular offices which will deal exclusively with diaspora issues. Moreover, the functions of the new unit should include the promotion of relationships between the home country and the diaspora, building economic relations with the diaspora, educational and cultural outreach, investment and trade relations, knowledge transfer as well as the management of information on the diaspora. The respective governments should explore efficient ways of funding the related increase in the staff at the embassies.

Furthermore, the governments need to make it mandatory for their respective embassies and consular offices to create and maintain a data bank with reliable information on the geographic location, skills, education and background of its overseas nationals. These embassies need to promote the registration of members of the Caribbean diaspora with their offices in order to keep track of their location as well as to be able to draw on the wealth of knowledge and resources of the members of the diaspora. The availability of such data on the Caribbean diaspora and its groupings will allow the home country to network and collaborate with the diaspora as well as implement programmes that meet identified local development needs with respect to health, education, poverty alleviation, infrastructure and telecommunication, among others. Such data should be regularly updated by the embassies. Embassies may share summaries of their databases on the diaspora with the CARICOM Secretariat provided that privacy of the members of the diaspora is protected.

It needs be said as well that the governments of the Caribbean through their embassies and consular offices should facilitate and provide more opportunities for trade, investment, skill and knowledge transfers to the members of the Caribbean diaspora. The various stakeholders, inclusive of the government, the private sector (including financial institutions) and the embassies, need to establish a forum whereby they can meet and flesh out the implementation plan of various programmes aimed at encouraging the members of the Caribbean diaspora to invest in the home country. The delegates from the embassies and consular offices will be in a better position to initiate dialogue with the diaspora after participating in the forum. Preliminary consultations should be conducted amongst the various stakeholders before the actual forum to inform the selection of a shortlist of initiatives which will form part of the forum's agenda. Such dialogue should result in collaboration with the diaspora in areas such as education, knowledge and skill transfers, and cultural programs.

There is also the need for the embassies to fill the information gap[7] by providing current information about the home country to members of the diaspora. This task will require that the embassies get current information on the economy, government initiatives, private sector initiatives as well as significant events in the home country. Such information will help the members of the diaspora to identify the various ways that they can make a contribution to their country of origin.

In summary, the Caribbean has a wealth of resources located in the Caribbean diaspora that can be leveraged for the development of the region. This can be made possible through an institutional mandate of the respective embassies to serve as a bridge between the home country and the Caribbean diaspora. Such a mandate will ensure that the Caribbean diaspora is included in the region's development plan. Respective governments should therefore promote the necessary institutional change for ensuring that the assets in the Caribbean diaspora play a positive role in the mission of their embassies and consular offices. In this regard, governments ought to implement the necessary relevant policies to assist their embassies and consular offices in successfully making the change. In this way, development of the Caribbean region may be on an accelerated path.

Notes

1. 80 per cent of the Caribbean diaspora reside in the USA (Nurse 2004).
2. Accessed on http://esa.un.org/migration/index.asp?panel=1 — September 23, 2010.
3. Barbados, Guyana, Jamaica, Suriname and Trinidad & Tobago.
4. Belize, Antigua and Barbuda, Dominica, Grenada, Montserrat, St. Kitts and Nevis, St. Lucia, St. Vincent and the Grenadines, The British Virgin Islands and Anguilla.
5. The Organisation of Eastern Caribbean States (OECS) is a sub-regional grouping within the Caribbean which consists of the following countries: Antigua and Barbuda, Dominica, Grenada, Montserrat, St. Kitts and Nevis, St. Lucia, St. Vincent and the Grenadines, The British Virgin Islands and Anguilla. The OECS is governed by The Authority (Heads of Government) comprising the Prime Ministers/Chief Ministers from all of the Member States. Supporting the Authority is: the Foreign Affairs Committee, the Defence and Security Committee, the Economic

Affairs Committee (which oversees the operations of the East Caribbean Common Market) and a Central Secretariat.

6. A study conducted by the authors of this chapter found that the members of the diaspora displayed keen enthusiasm in wanting to contribute to the development of the region by facilitating online programmes to help members of the home country.
7. A study conducted by the authors on members of the Caribbean diaspora indicated that there exists an information gap where the members of the diaspora were not aware of the needs of the home country. This lack of information prevents the members of the diaspora from making a significant contribution to the home country.

8

The Push and Pull Factors of Migration

Why Jamaican Professionals are Leaving Jamaica*

Natasha C. Parkins

This chapter focuses on how Jamaicans have mitigated against the threats to human security through migration. Peoples of the Caribbean in general, and Jamaicans in particular, have always been a migratory people. However, over the last 30 years, the emigration rates have been rapid, with alarming rates in particular of highly skilled individuals. In the case of Jamaica, there are four major factors which influence this phenomenon: crime and violence, occupation and skill mismatch, lack of economic opportunities, and the lack of social opportunities. While the general state of crime was not the sole factor that propelled respondents' migration choice, it was found to be the most influential factor. This chapter begins with an outline of the concept of human security. A brief overview of Caribbean migration is provided, followed by an analysis of why Jamaican professionals emigrate, which by proxy, depletes Jamaica, a developing country, of its highly skilled labour force.

The Concept of Human Security

Alkire (2003) posits that the notion of human security is not a novel one. According to her, threats of famine, war drought, flood and

* The author would like to thank the editors of the *American Review of Political Economy* (ARPE) for kindly permitting the publication of this chapter which initially appeared in the journal 8:2 (December 2010): 6-24 as "Push and Pull Factors of Migration."

plagues have existed from time immemorial. What has changed considerably is the nature of threats people face today and the ability to counteract these threats. But what exactly is human security all about? The United Nations Development Programme's (UNDP) Human Development Report (HDR) of 1994 crafted by the former Pakistani Finance Minister, Mahbub ul Haq, sought to address the concept of human security.

According to the Report, "the concept of security has for too long been interpreted narrowly: as security of territory from external aggression, or as protection of national interests in foreign policy or as global security from the threat of a nuclear holocaust" (22). Human security seeks to address the everyday concerns of ordinary citizens whose immediate threat may not necessarily be the same as the state they live in. Threats include but are not limited to disease, hunger, employment or lack thereof, crime and violence, and environmental hazards. These phenomena are considered threatening as they are more worrisome for individuals as opposed to nuclear warfare. The Report claims that in the final analysis, "human security is a child who did not die, a disease that did not spread, a job that was not cut, an ethnic tension that did not explode in violence, a dissident who was not silenced" (22).

The concept of human security has been problematic as it has been defined in various terms by different people. However, the UNDP's Human DevelopmentReport is explicit with its definition. It postulates that human security has two main aspects: "It means, first, safety from such chronic threats [such] as hunger, disease and repression. And second, it means protection from sudden and hurtful disruptions in the patterns of daily life—whether in homes, in jobs or in communities" (23). Given these various all encompassing definitions, it is not surprising that the notion of human security has faced criticisms. Jolly and Basu Ray (2006) posit that many international relations practitioners and academics, such as MacFarlane and Foong-Khong (2006), Ayoob (1997), Paris (2001) and Foong-Khong (2001) have expressed reservations about human security. Their doubts focus on five main points:

- Human security, they argue, merely involves renaming many problems that have already been recognized in other contexts and that already have perfectly good names.
- Human security lacks definite scope, therefore anything and everything could be considered a risk to security. This makes the task of policy formulation nearly impossible.

- Human security, when broadened to include issues like climate change, terrorism and threats from disease, complicates the international machinery for reaching decisions or taking action on the threats identified.
- Human security risks engaging the military in issues best tackled through non-military means.
- Human security under the United Nations risks raising hopes.

At the heart of the concept of human security are two components: freedom from fear and freedom from want. The basic concept of human security focuses on four essential characteristics. It is a universal concern which has no boundaries as regards ethnicity, economic status or gender. Human security components are interdependent in that all nations are likely to get involved when there is a security threat to another nation. Haiti's devastating earthquake in January 2010 is an example, as there was an almost immediate response from surrounding countries and those in the distance, in addition to various international agencies. Threats to human security are easier to mitigate through early prevention. Thus mitigating the threat of HIV/AIDs through social marketing and mass education campaigns may do more to stem the spread of the disease as opposed to acquiring drugs to treat the actual disease. Finally, human security is people-centred in that it is concerned with how people live and breathe in their societies. It speaks to the empowerment of people by taking a position that persons should be able to have opportunities to meet their most essential needs and to earn their own living. So understood, human security means that people can exercise their choices safely and freely today without fear of having their opportunities totally lost tomorrow. The Table 8.1 summarises the various categories of human security.

In the Caribbean context, Griffith (2002) has argued that the Caribbean's security has never been solely about protection from military threats. For him, it has been all encompassing and defined as the "protection and preservation of a people's freedom from external military attack and coercion, from internal subversion, and from the erosion of cherished political, economic, and social values" (2). Harriott (2010, 3) believes that the primary source of insecurity in the Caribbean is social violence, followed by natural disasters. As far as social violence is concerned, Harriott posits that this stems from predatory and drug crimes and interpersonal

Table 8.1: Summary of Human Security Categories

Human Security Category	*Summary*
Economic	Requires a guaranteed basic income either from being productive or a social safety net as poverty has negative implications for human security.
Food	This speaks to having physical and economic access to basic food at all times.
Health	People are vulnerable to various diseases whether or not they have the economic means to mitigate this threat. Access to clean water and air, for example, help to mitigate threats to health.
Environmental	Bajpai (2000, 15) notes that the integrity of land, air and water are crucial for environmental security.
Personal	Threat to a person's physical being by the state, other states and various groups with the propensity to inflict harm on others.
Community	This refers to cultural dignity and to inter-community peace within which an individual lives and grows.
Political	Protection from human rights violations.

Source: Adapted from United Nations Development Programme (UNDP). *Human Development Report 1994—New Dimensions of Human Security*. New York: Oxford University Press, 1994.

conflicts. Natural disasters are construed as forms of insecurity as citizens may feel insecure due to the lack of preparation for any eventuality, especially unpredictable disasters such as earthquakes. For Harriott, citizen insecurity depletes the Caribbean region of human capital, especially highly skilled labour, through migration. This insecurity, he claims, stems not just from crime and violence but also from a lack of opportunities in the home country and (perception of) better opportunities abroad. This variable will be elaborated further in this chapter. This has serious implications for regional and state development. In the case of Jamaica, it has some negative implications for gaining developed country status by 2030, as envisioned by its national development plan "Vision 2030."

Caribbean Migration

Migration has been a part of the Caribbean landscape for centuries, beginning with forced migration of slaves in the 17th, 18th and 19th centuries. Thus, one must distinguish between voluntary and involuntary migration. However, over the last century there has been an increase in voluntary migration, primarily for economic reasons. This historical account serves to expose the reader to the fact that Caribbean peoples have drifted towards economic opportunities as very few existed for them in their countries of origin. These opportunities afforded early migrants the chance to mitigate the threats to their economic security, which has implications for safeguarding the other forms of human security.

According to Marshall (1987, 15), "the history of the Caribbean can be seen as a succession of waves of migration." This claim is buttressed by Nurse (2004, 7), who claims that migration is "one of the defining features of the history of Latin America and the Caribbean (LAC)" and Thomas-Hope (2002, 1.2.1) who posits that "migration has become deeply embedded in the psyche of Caribbean peoples over the past century and a half." Marshall points out that one common feature of migration in the Caribbean region is that, historically, its movements and flows are in response to the global and regional economic climate. Marshall traces migration trends by illustrating the various waves the region has experienced. For her, Caribbean populations were formed almost wholly as a result of migration. Marshall states that in the post-Emancipation period, there were four waves or phases of migration. The first wave occurred from 1835 to 1885 and was mainly inter-territorial movement. She cites the various opportunities within the Caribbean region which encouraged migration. "In 1835 opportunities for migration existed mainly in the territories of Trinidad and Tobago and British Guiana" (17). This was a result of the plantation owners' inability to retain their 'slaves' in the post-Emancipation period and the great demand for labour to meet the demand for sugar.

The second wave from 1885 to 1920 was the movement to Panama and Belize which received only Jamaicans in the first phase. According to Marshall, this period of movement resulted in a net loss of about 130,000 people in the English-speaking Caribbean. She goes on to say that while the first-phase of migration movements were mainly to other British colonies in the Caribbean, the second-phase movements were directed to "foreign" territories such as Cuba and the Dominican Republic to work on the expanding sugar plantations, and to Central America to work on the banana plantations and railroads. From 1920-1940 there was very little out-migration and movements were mainly comprised of forced repatriation and voluntary return migration.

According to Marshall, "the present phase, begun in 1940, is dominated by movement to the metropolitan countries of the United Kingdom and North America" (16). This tradition has continued, however, and Caribbean people are no longer solely dependent on the traditional receiving countries (United States, Canada, and United Kingdom) for economic security. In fact, there has been movement into other territories such as the United Arab Emirates and countries in the Far East and Africa.

Migration of Jamaican Professionals

The Problem

Beine, Docquier and Schiff (2008, 4) state that the Caribbean region has the highest small-state brain drain with a rate of approximately seventy-five per cent (74.9%). According to them, "as far as small states are concerned, three out of every four skilled Caribbean live outside their country of origin" (4).

Docquier and Marfouk (2005, 23) list Jamaica as the third highest source country of skilled emigrants with a rate of about eighty five per cent (85.1%). Jamaica has the twelfth highest emigration rate in the world—but ranked among the twentieth least attractive countries in the world for immigrants (United Nations Development Programme, 2009). It is therefore not surprising that many persons are concerned about brain drain in Jamaica. Migration has often been seen as a "cash cow" in the sense that most Caribbean economies like Jamaica rely heavily on remittances. Jamaica has the fifth highest per capita remittance in the world (UNDP 2009). The Planning Institute of Jamaica (PIOJ) (2008) state that while remittance, a bi-product of migration, is now the leading source of foreign currency for Jamaica, which in turn impacts positively on welfare and poverty reduction, there is still great concern for some of the social and economic consequences. These include family life, the labour market and population growth and structure. Remittances, therefore, should not be the main focus of any discourse on migration.

According to Skeldon (2005) "Human capital is considered to be of central importance to development and the ultimate reduction, even eradication of poverty. Thus, any loss of the skilled through migration may be prejudicial to the achievement of development goals and any discussion of the movement of the skilled is inextricably bound up with what is generally referred to as the "brain drain," a debate that has been ongoing for over four decades" (5). Schmid (2006) claims that while some countries prefer the remittances over human capital, they are still unable to provide the necessary social services for their populations. Professionals are needed for sustainable development and therefore the constant depletion of same will only exacerbate the harm to the origin countries further.

It is important to keep a larger proportion of critical professional personnel in Jamaica to increase the chances of achieving developed country status, certainly by 2030. However policies must be guided by objective migration studies. The Human Development Index (HDI) evaluates human development based on the following criteria: living a long and healthy life (measured by life expectancy), being educated (measured by adult literacy and enrolment at the primary, secondary and tertiary level) and having a decent standard of living (measured by purchasing power parity, PPP, income), among others. According to the 2009 Human Development Report, Jamaica has an adult literacy rate of eighty-six per cent (86.0%) and is ranked 100 out of 182 countries. This pales in comparison to highly developed countries such the United Kingdom, Canada and even Barbados in the region, with rates of ninety-nine to one hundred per cent (99-100%). While a Jamaican's life expectancy at birth is approximately seventy two years (71.7), there is almost ten per cent (9.9%) chance of not surviving to age forty. Jamaica also has a homicide rate of 62 per 100,000 persons. According to the United Nations Office on Drugs and Crime (2007), countries with low levels of education are prone to high homicide rates, thus helping to explain why Barbados is the most developed country in the region. Education not only prepares persons to participate in the labour market but also teaches people life skills and how to cope in mainstream society. Given the critical importance of education and training and the fact that not everyone in Jamaica is privileged to achieve this position, the migration of the educated must be of paramount concern.

In essence, Jamaica is training workers for the global market without serious consideration of ways to retain a significant proportion of critical professional and technical persons. Degazon-Johnson (2007) claims that over the last few years she has not been convinced that enough attention has been dedicated to the migration of the highly skilled from the region. She warns: "we must also not forget that when that qualified doctor, nurse or teacher migrates, they take with them (i) the capital outlay that went into their education from primary school through university (ii) the future taxes which their income would have generated (iii) the skills which could make a great difference to health, education and welfare of many people in their country" (4-5). The burden on middle class households cover only about a fifth of the cost of secondary and tertiary education. Thus, the Jamaican taxpayer is not only subsidizing the education of people from higher than average income families and who will have higher than average incomes once they graduate, but who will not even pay taxes on those incomes, nor provide any benefits to the community in terms of teaching/nursing. Nevertheless, migration can be a rewarding experience for a developing country like Jamaica, once it is managed.

The PIOJ (2005, 12) gives a synopsis of Jamaica's migration trends since the 1970s. According to the PIOJ, between 1970 and 2003, almost three quarters of a million (745,289) persons immigrated to the United States, Canada and the United Kingdom. On average, this amounted to twenty-one thousand, nine hundred and twenty persons (21,920) per annum. "The largest number of migrants was recorded in 1980-1989 (252,659 persons), followed by 1990-1999 with 220,498 persons." The Table 8.2 summarises emigration rates between 1970 and 2003.

Table 8.2: Total Number of Jamaican Emigrant Stock (1970-2003)

Country	*Total number of Migrants (1970-2003)*
United States of America	588,066
Canada	134,676
United Kingdom	22,547
Grand Total of Migrants	745,289

Source: The Labour Market Information Newsletter of Jamaica. Jamaica: Pear Tree Press, 2005.

There is no indication that the situation is stabilizing. The most staggering statistics were obtained from the PIOJ's (January 2007, 4) issue of *The Labour Market Information Newsletter of Jamaica*. The data outline that the total stock of Jamaican tertiary graduates is three hundred and eighty thousand, two hundred and twenty six (380,226) for the period 2001-2005. Of this total, almost sixty per cent (59.5%) were trained in Jamaica, implying tremendous national subsidy. Even more critical is the fact that less than a quarter (23.4%) of Jamaica's tertiary educated stock remains in Jamaica (see Table 8.3).

Table 8.3: Stock of Jamaican Tertiary Graduates (2001-2005)

Tertiary Graduates trained in Jamaica	*Tertiary Graduates Trained Abroad*	*Tertiary Graduates Overseas at Time of Study*	*Tertiary Graduates in Jamaica at Time of Study*	*Total amount of Tertiary Graduates*
226, 147 59.5%	154, 079 40.5%	291, 166 76.6%	89, 060 23.4%	380, 226 100%

Source: An Assessment of the Emigration of Highly Skilled Workers from Jamaica. *The Labour Market Information Newsletter of Jamaica,* No. 54, Planning Institute of Jamaica, 2007.

These data motivated this writer to embark on a study on the migration of Jamaican professionals in 2009. The study is the first of this nature as Caribbean migration studies have traditionally collapsed all labour types into a singular category, that of "migrants."

Explored Theories of Migration

Several theories were examined and it was found that earlier theories focused mainly on economic reasons. One such popular theory examined is the Neo-classical Economic Theory, which Massey *et al.*(1993, 433) claim is "probably the oldest and best-known theory of international migration." These theories suggest that people migrate based on whether or not there is available work in their immediate surroundings. Other macro theories include Wallerstein's (1974) World Systems Theory, which posit that migration is mainly a means of mobilising cheap labour for capital which perpetuates uneven development and the exploitation of poor peoples in order to make rich countries richer, and Piore's (1979) dual labour market theory which claims that international migration is caused by a permanent demand for immigrant labour that is inherent to the economic structure of developed nations. Micro-theories suggest that "individual rational actors decide to migrate because a cost-benefit calculation leads them to expect a positive net return, usually monetary, from movement" (Massey *et al.* 1993, 434). These theories suggest that people move to geographical spaces where they can be most productive, based on their skills. From the micro-economic lens, it is evident that there is consensus that persons weigh personal factors to arrive at the migration decision. Micro-theories include

Lee's (1966, 50) who posited that there are four major factors which affect the decision to migrate: namely factors associated with the area of origin, factors associated with the area of destination, intervening obstacles, and personal factors.

A number of scholars have recognized the limitations of pure economics as an explanation for migration. Castles and Miller (1998) argue that such theories are not grounded in empiricism and are flawed as they are essentially individualistic and ahistorical in nature. They claim: "It emphasises the individual decision to migrate, based on rational comparison of the relative costs and benefits of remaining in the area of origin or moving to various alternative destinations" (20). Theories such as those discussed above do not offer explanations for migration due to political warfare, social violence or other forms of forced migration. In fact, these theories posit that "constraining factors, such as government restrictions on emigration or immigration, are mainly dealt with as distortions of the rational market, which should be moved" (20-21).

Economic factors as explanations for migration were welcomed frames for this study but they cannot be treated as complete, as the social realities of the respondents studied are far more complex. For the purpose of this chapter, Migration Systems Theory is applied, as it gives a holistic view on the individual's decision to migrate or not. This theory emerged on account of preceding theories failing to adequately explain why migrants move from one country to another, but instead giving snippets of myriad reasons. Migration Systems Theory, advanced by Kritz and Zlotnik (1992) and expounded by others such as Castles and Miller (1998), is increasingly used in comparative research. According to Castles and Miller "this theory emphasises international relations, political economy, collective action and institutional factors" (23). They posit that a migration system comprises two or more countries exchanging migrants with each other. The tendency is to analyse regional migration.

This theory concerns itself with examining all the linkages between migration territories. Fawcett and Arnold (1987, 24) identify these linkages as the "state-to-state relations and comparisons, mass culture connections and family and social networks." Castles and Miller (1998) further discuss this theory, claiming that migratory movements occur "from the existence of prior links between sending and receiving countries based on colonisation, political influence, trade, investment and cultural ties." They claim that this theory posits that any migratory movement is a result of macro structures such as the political economy of the world market, interstate relationships and laws interacting with micro structures such as beliefs and networks.

The Push/Pull Factors of Migration

The International Organization for Migration's World Migration Report (2008, 52) claims that the definition of a skilled migrant is unclear, however the typical indicators of such an individual is usually their occupational or educational status. For the purpose of this study, both occupational status and educational attainment were used to define the Jamaican skilled migrant, with the exception that the individual is an adult who has completed at least a formal three-year college education. The reason why a three-year college education is the criterion used to define the highly skilled Jamaican migrant is because generally it takes no less than thirty-six (36) months to complete a ninety (90) credit degree programme at most accredited universities in Jamaica.

Martin and Zürcher (2008) argue that the decision to relocate to another country can be grouped loosely into two categories, economic and non-economic. However, for the purpose of analysis, the factors which actually propel a migrant to make that final move might best be divided into three categories: Demand-pull, Supply-push, networks/other (See Table 8.4).

Table 8.4: Factors which Affect Migration

Type of Migrant	*Demand-Pull*	*Supply-Push*	*Network/Other*
Economic	Labour Recruitment	Unemployment or Underemployment issues such as low wages	Jobs and wage information flow
Non-Economic	Family Unification (husbands and wives join spouses, children join parents)	Fleeing war and/or civil unrest	Communications; transportation; assistance organizations; desire for new experience

Source: Philip Martin and Gottfried Zürcher. "Managing Migration: The Global Challenge." *Population Bulletin,* 63 (1) (2008): 4.

Lowell and Findlay (2001, 3) claim that not only has the demand for skilled labour in developed countries increased, but pull factors such as "better wages and employment conditions, better information, recruitment and cheaper transportation" have encouraged skilled migrants to seek jobs and opportunities in developed countries. With limited social and economic opportunities available to most persons in Jamaica, the lure of the lifestyle in developed countries is difficult to stave off. Nurse (2004, 108) argues that "economic decline, widening inequality, increasing poverty social displacement, crime and political crisis have been the main drivers of emigration." He claims that there is a widening income gap between the Latin American and Caribbean region and North America. North American conditions are far more favourable as they offer higher wages and better working conditions; these are two important pull factors. Countries that are a part of the Organization for Economic Cooperation and Development (OECD) see the need to lure people into their economies, due to their ageing populations and population decline. According to Nurse (2004, 108), "replacement migration is necessary to maintain current population and working population levels to in part finance the looming deficit in the social security system and pension schemes." The shortage of certain skills, such as health and education sectors, is also another reason why OECD countries recruit from the region. These skills cannot be transferred or relocated to the low-wage developing regions.

The major push factors influencing migration include, but are not limited to, general crime and violence, an unstable economy which in turn affects an individual's social and economic opportunities and career advancement. In the case of Jamaica, The World Bank's study, "The Road to Sustained Growth in Jamaica" (2004, 2) suggests that poor unemployment opportunities and sluggish economic growth have contributed to Jamaican emigration. This coupled with the ease and availability of information about opportunities outside of Jamaica play a vital role in the migration decision-making process. Thomas-Hope (2002) provides supportive evidence through her analysis of various advertisements published in the Jamaica Gleaner between 2000 and 2001. She claims that during this period, recruiters from various agencies in the United Kingdom, the United States, and Canada advertised various recruitment fairs, which offer better working conditions and salary scales than what obtains in Jamaica. In Thomas-Hope's (2002) study, crime and violence factored highly into making the ultimate migration decision. These persons believed that if nothing was done to curb the crime and violence their lives would not be harmonious in Jamaica.

According to the United Nations Office on Drugs and Crime (2007), the Caribbean region has the highest murder rate in the world, with a rate of 30 murders for every 100,000 persons. The report further elaborates that from 1998-2000, Jamaica's average homicide rate was close to thirty four per cent (33.8%) per 100,000 citizens. According to the National Intelligence Bureau of the Jamaica Constabulary Force (2009), there has been a steady increase from 33 per 100,000 persons to the current rate in 2008, of 61 per 100,000 persons. The World Bank's study, "The Road to Sustained Growth in Jamaica" (2004, 31) implies that the high levels of crime in Jamaica make the country unattractive to external investors. According to the report, "crime has a negative effect on the development of human capital, creates incentives for migration, introduces inefficiencies into the economy, undermines the work ethic, and diverts resources from investment to crime management." In addition, the report laments the effect of crime and violence on business interests by claiming that they were detrimental to operating costs. The report claims that crime also helps to erode the development of both human and social capital which in turn affects growth. "The crime situation in Jamaica seems to be an important reason for migration, since the fear of crime significantly reduces the quality of life. Crime and violence have also been blamed for slowing down the rate of return of migrants back to Jamaica" (The Road to Sustained Growth in Jamaica 2004, 116).

The mismatch between an individual's skill set and suitable occupation serves as a supply/push factor for emigration. Quinn and Rubb (2005) believe that migration occurs when the individual cannot find the appropriate job which matches with his/her skill. They argue that the "education-occupation" factor plays an important role in the individual's decision to immigrate to another country. Quinn and Rubb (2005, 164) posit that this and other findings have implications for governmental policy on education. In their view, policy makers should focus on increasing educational levels and employment opportunities simultaneously as this could lead to mass migration of persons with higher levels of education compared to the rest of the population. Anderson's (1997) study *Youth Unemployment in Jamaica* gives insight to the skill/employment mismatch in Jamaica. Her examination of Jamaica's labour force between 1972 and 1995 showed that the attainment of secondary education was not enough to guarantee work. For her, the labour market could not absorb young workers and hence the possibility would exist that on average, the unemployed have higher education levels than those employed. Even in 2008, the employment trends have held strain. The absolute unemployment figure for 2008 stood at one hundred and thirty seven thousand and three hundred persons (137,300). This number represents a 10.6 per cent increase from 2007. In addition, the youth unemployment rate increased by about two percentage points, from 23.7 per cent in 2007 to 25.9 per cent in 2008. Such data imply there is bound to be a high propensity to migrate to places where there are opportunities, especially amongst the highly educated.

Another migration influence is the fact that globalisation has shrunk the world. While there is no one agreed-upon definition for globalisation, Potter *et al.* (2004, 127) argue that there are three defining features of globalisation. Firstly, the world is shrinking in terms of time and distance. Secondly, communications such as cable and satellite television have improved and thirdly, "the ascendancy of global corporations and global marketing activities is resulting in standardised products and television programmes throughout the world..." Added to this is the ease of transportation. No longer does one have to wait on the traditional post office to deliver a letter or the media to deliver global news. The internet provides delivery of these services in real time. With the ease of and access to information, the potential migrant has information on jobs, housing, lifestyle and various opportunities, at his/her fingertips. Persons are able to cross the Atlantic Ocean in six to ten hours and from Jamaica to most North American cities within two to four hours. This ease facilitates many Jamaicans who enjoy a "trans-national" lifestyle where they can commute between their new country and Jamaica.

Having reviewed some of the prevailing literature on migration, there is now a greater appreciation for the decision to emigrate from Jamaica. For the most part, it seems that while there has been more access to education overall, educated persons have either become marginalised from the job market or not adequately compensated. In addition, varying factors such as an unstable economy, and high violence rate are helping to push skilled workers through the door and highly developed countries are on the other end opening that door, with welcoming arms.

Methodology and Sampling

This study was a comparative snapshot study assessing the migration decision-making process of professional Jamaicans. It was comparative in nature as there were four groups (persons who are not migrating, persons who are thinking of migrating, persons who are in the process of migrating and persons who have already migrated) being assessed and compared with each other. This study was taken within a specific period and so provides a snapshot of feelings, expressions and thoughts within a particular time frame (15th May-14th July, 2009). The interviews were conducted only once and no follow-up arrangements were made. The research employed a mixed instrument to achieve standardization (quantitative) and depth (qualitative) concurrently. The instrument comprised two parts. The first part was quantitative in nature as it sought to ascertain particular demographic details about each respondent. These details include but are not limited to the respondent's age, sex, education level, area of training, current occupation, work experience, parents' and grandparents' academic achievement, and childhood neighbourhoods. The second part had standardized open-ended questions, designed to allow respondents to provide rich data, described by Geertz (1973) as thick description. This approach is necessary given the fact that the study is inevitably exploratory, since there is not sufficient material on the matter in Jamaica to have carried out a quantitative study.

Non-probability sampling was employed in this study, as there is no known registry of persons who have indicated their emigration or immigration status, and therefore the full population is not known. In addition, one's emigration/immigration status is a personal and private matter and so in order to gather this kind of data, non-probability sampling techniques were most appropriate. Three non-probability sampling methods were employed in collecting data: snowballing, purposive and convenience. This study comprised thirty two (32) females and eight (8) males making a total of forty. The figures 8.1-8.3 illustrate the respondents' age, highest level of education and years of work experience.

These data indicate that the respondents were persons in the prime of their working life and careers as the majority were between 26 and 45 years old. In addition, the majority of these respondents held at least a masters degree and the majority had ten or more years of working experience. After comparing

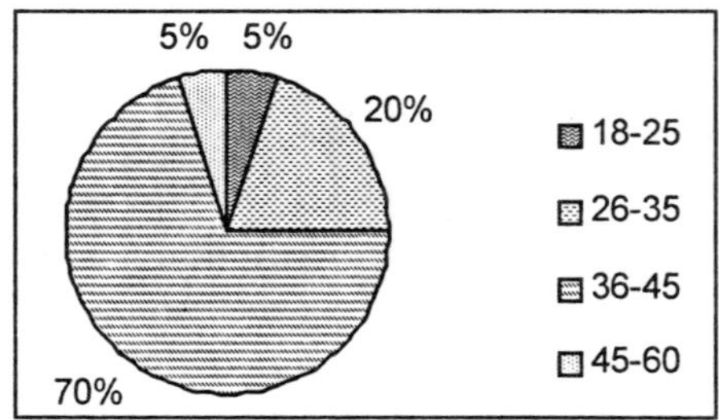

Figure 8.1: Respondents' Age Group

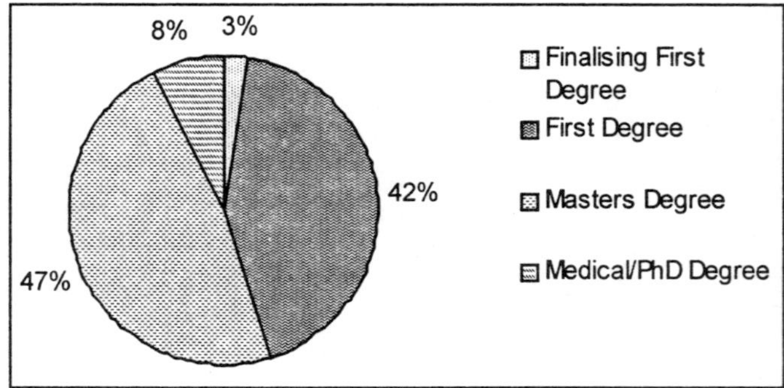

Figure 8.2: Respondents' Highest Level of Education

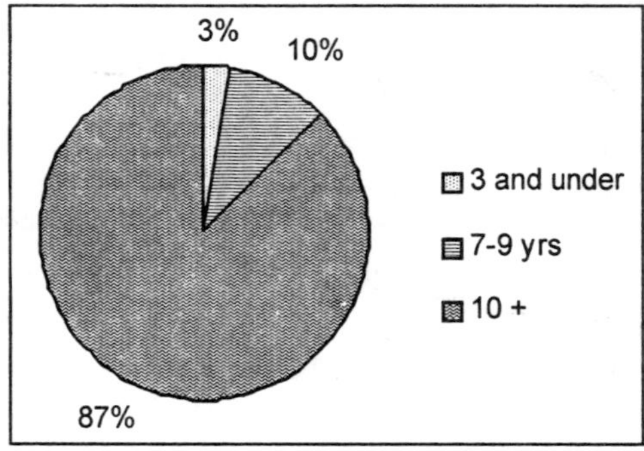

Figure 8.3: Respondents' Work Experience (years)

respondents' highest education level to that of their parents and grandparents, it was concluded that the majority of respondents came from a background with middle class parents even though they had more education than their parents and grandparents. The remainder can therefore be described as "straddlers" from working class origins seeking upward social mobility. However, when the three test groups were separated (persons who are thinking of migrating, persons who are in the process of migrating and persons who have already migrated) there was no change in the education distribution of same. This can only lead one to believe that the Jamaican professional migrant is from the "straddler" class with humble beginnings and higher levels of education than their parents and grandparents.

Key Findings

To reiterate, this study's main purpose was to unearth the various reasons why some Jamaican professionals are emigrating from Jamaica. During the interview process, four distinct themes emerged: Crime and violence/general societal indiscipline and lawlessness, the issue of occupation-skill matching, lack of economic opportunities, and the lack of social opportunities. The rising crime rate with the accompanying lawlessness and general societal disorder was the main factor which influenced emigration from Jamaica. This was followed by the inability to find suitable career/ job opportunities, lack of social opportunities and lack of economic opportunities. The Table 8.5 illustrate the main reasons why each group has based their decisions to migrate or not to migrate.

Table 8.5: Snapshot of Key Findings

	Primary Factor	*Secondary Factor*	*Tertiary Factor*
Already Migrated	Crime and violence. 100% not returning due to the current trends	Occupation/Sk ill Mismatch	Perception of better Economic and Social Opportunities Overseas
Thinking of migrating	Crime and Violence. Has caused 70% of the respondents to begin the thinking process	Occupation/ Skill Mismatch	Perception of better Economic and Social Opportunities Overseas
In the process of migrating	Crime and violence has played a major role in the decision-making process with 70% not willing to return on a permanent basis	Occupation/ Skill Mismatch	Perception of better Economic and Social Opportunities Overseas
Not migrating	Skill is compatible with current occupation status. 90% said to be employed in their field of study	Economic Stability	Happy with overall lifestyle and value current family and social life in

Crime and violence were the most discussed issues as they were of major concern. The literature has shown that there is a domino effect which stems from both crime and violence, which in turn has implications for available economic and social opportunities. Most respondents recognised that if crime and violence are not contained then Jamaica would find itself in a seriously bad situation, that of being unable to create and/or provide opportunities for the general population. However, persons with no intention to migrate acknowledged that crime and violence is not just a local phenomenon, but a global one. Therefore, it was not enough to influence them to migrate. It was evident that the respondents who have already migrated, thinking of migrating or are in the process of same share similar views on the factors which influenced their decision to migrate. It is clear that crime and violence, followed by occupation and skill mismatch weighed in heavily on the decision making process. Ten out of ten respondents indicated that the crime and violence seemed to be "closing in" on them and was a deterrent to even giving thought at this time to one day returning to Jamaica permanently. All ten of the respondents who are in the process of migrating said that crime and violence had become excessive enough for them to begin the process. Seven out of these ten respondents did not believe that they would return to Jamaica in the near future on a permanent basis. For the respondents who are thinking of migrating, the daily trauma of unsolved killings and murders was enough to get them to start the thinking process.

The issue of occupational matching and professional development were burning issues. For persons who have already migrated, the lack of the ideal job opportunities has heavily influenced the decision to migrate. For those who are in the process or thinking of migrating, the feelings are similar. On the one hand, some of the respondents said that they did not feel as if their job was helping them to develop personally and/or professionally. On the other hand, those who have chosen not to migrate indicated that they were happy in their careers in Jamaica. Interestingly, all respondents in this category, with the exception of one person, stated that they were employed in their area of training and expertise. This information would suggest that it is the combination of two push factors: crime and violence and skill and occupation matching which influence most potential migrants' decision making process. The respondents who have already migrated believed that they had made the right decision when they migrated as they found satisfying jobs in a relatively short period. Persons who are in the process of migrating believe that even though they are blindly going into a new environment that the chances of finding a suitable career path overseas were greater than if they continued to reside in Jamaica. Respondents who are thinking of migration shared similar views and believed that they were wasting their time in Jamaica. When the fields of study were compared to actual occupation for this group, seven out of ten persons were not working in their field. In addition to this, it was clear that they were underemployed.

The lack of economic and social opportunities were major issues which surfaced across the board. To those who have already migrated, those who are in the process of migrating, and those who are thinking about migrating, the lack of social and/or economic opportunities in Jamaica heavily influenced their position in emigration. Some of the respondents expressed frustration about not being able to acquire certain basic assets. However, those respondents who have no intentions of migrating felt that they were quite happy in Jamaica. Respondents who have already migrated believed that they were able to move ahead economically. Most spoke of owning their own homes abroad which was not possible for them in Jamaica. They believe that the available health care, education, and recreational activities are superior to what Jamaica has to offer them. Those who are in the process of migrating perceived attaining the same sort of lifestyle would obtain once they relocated and found suitable employment. The respondents who are thinking of migrating also felt this way. Most believed that life in Jamaica overall is too hard and when they compare perceived lifestyles with current lifestyles migration is a viable option.

Generally speaking, those who are thinking of, or in the process of migration believe that since their finances are not healthy, it is unlikely that they will be able to afford social services such as good health and education opportunities. Overseas respondents shared similar views while persons who have no intentions to migrate reported that they are satisfied with social life in Jamaica. The Table 8.5 provides the reader with a synopsis of the sentiments shared by interviewees. The persons who are not migrating expressed that the main reason why emigrating from Jamaica does not appeal to them is because of their career status. Respondents either believed that where they were with their careers currently allowed for comfortable lifestyles and good quality of life, or perceived that they would not find a similar or better career path abroad. When the fields of study were compared to the actual area of employment, nine out of ten of these respondents have experienced a "best-fit" with their skill-occupation match. This has positive implications for their economic and social outcomes. The majority expressed that their lifestyle in Jamaica had met their expectations. There were several tertiary factors expressed, such as the climate change in most developed countries and familial arrangements in Jamaica as some respondents shared that their extended family was part of their support system. In addition most respondents had compared social life abroad vicariously through others and believed that their social life in Jamaica was more enjoyable. As regards the crime and violence situation in Jamaica, the majority of persons in this group expressed that they had never been a victim of same and that crime happens everywhere. However, one striking feature about this group is that the majority of these persons said that if they experienced any direct impact from crime, whether to their person or family members, they too could become a potential migrant.

Migration Trends of This Study

This researcher identified several prominent trends during the course of this study. Among them is the fact that Canada is the country of migration choice mainly because its current immigration policies welcome highly skilled migrants. Individuals with children are most likely to migrate as they want a better life for their children and individuals are willing to go into new environments to get away from here [Jamaica]. It was found that males in this study are least likely to migrate. The face of the Jamaican migrant in this study is one from the "stradler" class with more education than their parents and grandparents. Of great concern is that the current crime situation can drive those in the "not migrating" category easily into any of the other three categories. The majority of respondents who are thinking of, in the process of or already migrated, has no intention of sending remittances and the majority of respondents who are thinking of, in the process of or already migrated, has no intention of returning to Jamaica in the near future.

Migration Implications for Jamaica

For many Jamaicans, emigration is considered to be a blessing as this means increased chances of better economic and social opportunities. However, the implications for Jamaica must be considered.

Highly skilled persons are the bedrock of most developed societies. This is why there appears to be a global hunt on for talent. Kapur and McHale (2005, 1) argue that outflows of highly skilled migrants help trap countries in poverty. Apart from the skill set that the migrants take with them, there are costs associated with acquiring the same. While some persons may have benefited from private preparatory education, most, if not all, have attained secondary education in Jamaica. The cost of this is financed by the taxpayers of Jamaica. In addition, tertiary education is heavily subsidised by taxpayers up to eighty per cent. This means that the migrant and/or the potential migrant has benefited from at least six to twelve years of education at the expense of the public purse, only to be using it to the benefit of more advanced and/or developed countries without any bonded repayment to Jamaica. In addition to the loss of the positive externalities generated by highly skilled workers in a developing economy, skilled migration can reduce the capacity to deliver key services that are important for economic and social development.

The flight of highly educated individuals also has implications for future investment which, in turn, has serious implications for social and economic opportunities for the general populace. If it is suggested that there is a high correlation between high levels of education and low levels of crime, then it could be inferred that with the migration of highly skilled professionals, the threat of escalating violence is imminent. This has severe implications for foreign and local investment as the costs associated with crime and violence, in some cases, outweigh the benefits of doing business in Jamaica. With the decline of industries, the economy risks the chance of becoming sluggish or stagnant which in turn affects the volume of basic goods and services available to the general population. In essence, high levels of emigration can help to create a vicious cycle of violence and poverty and creates a 'lose-lose' scenario for Jamaica. Migration also has implications for family structures and, as Ritchie Dawson (2007, 3) has stated, one of the drawbacks of migration is the "costs to family and society including family break-up and loss of particular social groups such as university graduates."

While migration has some negative implications for Jamaica, there are some positive outcomes. Remittances have rivalled bauxite and tourism to be a major income earner for the Jamaican economy. The Human Development Index (2009) states that in 2007, remittances to Jamaica amounted to US$2,144 million dollars. The report further states that average remittances per person was US$790 compared to the rest of Latin America and the Caribbean, whose average remittances per person was US$114. In fact migration is often associated with remittances and perhaps this is why there has been a deafening silence on the matter. However, one must be cautious when praising the notion of remittances. The core question is whether or not remittances are worth all the negatives associated with such heavy emigration as is experienced in Jamaica.

Lowell (2001, 19) argues that "highly skilled or not, most international migrants send money home to their family. There is a sizable literature on the impact of remittances but some ambiguity about whether or not remittances boost economic development." He goes on to elaborate that "there is a long-standing tendency to dismiss the value of remittances because the bulk of research demonstrates that they tend not to be spent on productive investments. Most remittances are spent either on basics like food or medicine, or on consumption goods such as televisions or clothing. While basic expenditures may help poor households, the purchase of consumption goods, it has been argued, stimulates imports and not domestic manufacturing. Critics charge that the manner in which remittances are spent does little to boost domestic production, employment, or exports" (Lowell 2001, 19).

Schmid (2006, 3) argues that "whereas some governments seem to favour the exodus of their skilled in exchange for desired remittances to boost their economies, many countries suffer tremendous constraints in their capacities to provide equal, qualitative and affordable social services to their populations." She goes on to explain that more studies need to be conducted on the pattern of remittances: "Regardless of the efforts already undertaken, more research is needed to gain insight into the flow of resources to better understand the flow of remittances. It cannot be assumed that all migrants remit to the same extent. While male migrants with dependants back home generally remit more and more regularly, young professional women with neither children nor spouse most probably will remit much less" (Schmid 2006, 6).

Another positive implication of migration is that of 'brain gain' or return migration. This involves the migrant gaining experience and knowledge from First World countries to be later used in the country of origin. According to Hunger (2002, 1), "The basic idea of the "brain gain" hypothesis is that intellectual and technical elites from the Third World who emigrated to an industrialized country represent a potential resource for the socioeconomic development of their home country."

Conclusion

In concluding, this study highlighted the consequences for a state when it cannot provide sufficient human security. In addition, Jamaica has not done enough to create an environment where its most productive citizens can equip themselves sufficiently to be able to mitigate the threats to human security. One of the end results is the migration to other states which are perceived to have the capacity to offer more security than the migrant's homeland. Of great concern to this writer, is the question of how persons who are not privileged to own as much social capital, such as higher education and reliable sources of income as those who are highly skilled, cope in the absence of such assets.

Caribbean migration in general and Jamaican migration in particular require more in-depth research and analysis to gain insight into the dynamics and dimensions of migration. The potential for further research exists in areas such as taking a closer look at the ethnic and social backgrounds of migratory Jamaican professionals as well as their remittance patterns. Other areas which require further research are their social relationships and the ease or difficulty in adjusting to life in the host country. There is great need to explore the lifestyles of these migrants in their host country, as well as their contributions to their host country, as not enough empirical data exists in this area.

9

Indian Migration to the Caribbean

Reflections on the Formation of Ethnic Identity

Satya R. Pattnayak

In the long history of people's movements across national borders, Indian migration overseas has few rivals in scope and magnitude. Previously, it was thought that only about 20 million Indians had settled across the globe in the past two hundred years. But that, we are now told, was a gross understatement of the real number. Many historians, using new archival data, have recently argued that between 1846 and 1940 about 48 to 52 million people from India and China settled overseas, mainly in South-east Asia, Indian Ocean rim, South Pacific, and in the Caribbean (McKeown 2004; Markovitz 1999; and Markovitz 1966). About 60 per cent of these were from India; the rest were Chinese. This magnitude of migration compares quite favourably with that of European migration to the Americas during the same time period, which accounted for about 55 million to 58 million people. In a global sense, then, Indian migration overseas was a major world cultural phenomenon, not an aberration or accident (Nugent 1919; Hoerder 2002). If the later numbers are indeed true, it is all the more important to study the processes of ethnic identity formation among the members of the Indian Diaspora overseas.

A modest attempt is made in this chapter to better understand the dynamics of diasporic ethnic identity of Indians as it applies to three settlement societies of Suriname, Guyana, and Trinidad in the new world. Politically, it is necessary to examine the Indian world diaspora as many of its current and past members have indeed become world leaders in their own right. For example, the names of Cheddi Jagan of Guyana and Basdeo Pandey of Trinidad and Tobago, both former chief executives of their respective countries, come to mind (Jagan 1994). Not only do their fellow ethnics of Indian origin enrich the societies in which their forefathers had chosen to settle but the success stories overseas by people of Indian origin look only good on the source country: India. This is quite an important fact as India is in the process of carving out a place for itself as a major power in today's world. Keeping in mind the world historical significance of the past overseas migration of Indians and the current increasing influence of India on the world stage, it is important to examine in a comparative context the dynamics of Indian ethnicity and identity formations in the Caribbean. I begin this examination by raising the question as to whether theories matter.

Do Theories Matter?

Theories do matter but they need a constant dose of new information from comparative settings to be polished and improved upon. Social science theories that attempt to study ethnic dynamics in diasporic settings prove to be inadequate, particularly so in the current era of globalization. For example, the *cultural persistence* thesis posits that cultural forces persist over time unabated despite changes in material conditions in the settling societies (Smith 1961). Such simplified argument can probably justify the continuation of certain ritualistic aspects of the sender society but it fails to take into account the syncretism that develops over time as settlers come into contact with a vastly different set of economic, political, and social forces.

The *cultural adaptation* theory, by comparison, is more appropriate in explaining the reactive ability of humans to changing circumstances in an alien society. Very Spencerian in orientation, this approach perhaps better explains the survival oriented behaviours of settlers (Taylor 1996). However, much evidence supports the argument that immigrants not only adapt to changed circumstances, they also over time innovate to better negotiate their existence in the new societies. In this regard, the cultural adaptation approach only partially explains the changed aspects of the diasporic societies populated by Indians in the Caribbean.

It is much easier to find support for the *structural-functional* paradigm anywhere, as most social facts exist because they do perform a set of social functions (Merton 1973). But other than being quite general in nature, structural functionalism does not grant us any additional insight into foretelling the negotiated identities that are much more symbolic than material in nature.

In a similar vein, one could critique the theories that have been borrowed from the immigrant experiences of the United States. Two theories that stand out in this regard are: assimilationist and pluralist (Thomas and Znaniecki 1996; Portes and Rumbaut 1996; and Portes and Rumbaut 2002). For example, based on a series of studies of European immigrants to the US, sociologists have argued that cultural legacies of the various national origin groups are likely to progressively diminish and ultimately disappear as later generations increasingly acculturate into the dominant cultural forms prevalent in the host society. But in the context of the Caribbean societies, one can find this particular thesis as a gross oversimplification. For one, the assimilationist approaches do not take into account the saliency of certain hybrid cultural traits that may exist as time progresses. All traits do not have to disappear. Even in the United States, the Pennsylvania Amish, known for their adamant resistance to the use of modern technology, have begun to develop selected levels of syncretism of existence in which they have incorporated several new technical skills from the larger society in order to harness more capital and resources for the material benefit of the members themselves.

The other much maligned theory, again borrowed from the studies in the US, is pluralist theory (Abramson 1973; Greeley 1974). Pluralist theory has elements common with the cultural persistence approach mentioned earlier. Generally, proponents of the pluralist approaches are of the opinion that, notwithstanding the changes in the major areas of society, such as the labour market, patterns of interaction between groups in informal settings and increased opportunities, cultural heritage of immigrant groups have persisted in the US, in particular since the late 1960s. It would be fair to disagree with the above variants of studies, as both have tended to ignore the dynamic nature of "ethnic identity" in the processes of societal transformation.

Because of major inadequacies in the theoretical approaches to the ethnic experiments in Caribbean societies, a *comparative political economy* approach is advocated here (Skocpol 1979). Within this approach, cultural patterns and ethnic identity based behaviours are influenced by economic-labour market conditions, state policy, and state role in societal transformation, and the nature of the individual and group based negotiations in arriving at a certain identity formation. The *comparative political economy approach*, then, does not believe in the constant salience of background cultural forces independent of the economic, political, and symbolic forces of negotiation. The study of group behaviours across countries and by sector, region, and class within a country can only be explored more productively through a comparative study of the aggregate and individual/group behavioural manifestations across ethnic group formations.

In addition, we are strongly in favour of creating typologies of group identity formations and other behavioural manifestations. If a few important characteristics of the economy, state policy, and data on group resources can be adequately captured, then, it is possible to create global as well as regional typologies. For example, ethnic identity formation in civilizational societies, such as Mexico, Peru, and the Mayan areas of Central America, are likely to vary in terms of the patterns of adaptation among ethnic groups than in purely settlement societies, such as the US, Canada, and the Caribbean (Portes and Rumbaut 2002). The distinction between the two types of societies is important as they are indeed characterized by significantly different but important forms of economic, political, and cultural forces. In addition, the sheer number of the group, the areas in which the members settle, whether or not the group is able to create a vibrant ethnic economy and enclave, state policy toward specific group migration and movements, and the general public reaction to the group's arrival and survival in the new setting are important variables (Portes and Rumbaut 1996). It really is much more complex than just simply characterizing the identity formation of Indians in the Diaspora as just persisting, adapting, assimilating, or stagnant.

It is argued here that ethnic identity is a dynamic concept, and its manifestations are complex and segmented. For example, any number of identities may be discovered in the intersection of the economic, political, and social forces in facilitating or impeding such interaction. This complexity of the processes and the interplay of the various factors ultimately contribute to the specific kind of ethnic identity formation in the three countries under observation here: Suriname, Guyana, and Trinidad and Tobago.

In order to develop a comparative political economy of the Indian ethnic identity formation in the Caribbean, the rest of this chapter is organized into four sections. The first section describes the broad parameters of life in the Caribbean. In the second section, the Surinamese experience is parsed in light its own historical and institutional evolution. A similar exercise is undertaken in the third section for Guyana and the fourth section for Trinidad and Tobago. Finally, in the last section, a set of general concluding remarks are developed about the Indian identity formation in the Caribbean.

Population and Human Development

In the total population, those pertaining to Indian origin constitute about 41 per cent in Trinidad and Tobago, 46 per cent in Suriname, and 51 per cent in Guyana (Census publications from the Governments of Trinidad and Tobago, Guyana and Suriname). Although they live in the same general geographic vicinity, their lives could not be more different in terms of how long on average they are expected to live. In Trinidad and Tobago, the average is 74 years of life expectancy; in Suriname, it is shorter by three years at 71; in Guyana, however, they have the shortest life expectancy at 63. Three out of every four Trinidadian and Surinamese live in urban areas, while only 36.3 per cent of Guyanese live in urban areas. The basically urban living in Trinidad and Suriname and primarily rural existence in Guyana should figure prominently in the construction of a certain type of ethnic identity in these countries.

In the areas of adult literacy, all three countries have at least 94 per cent literacy, meaning that many of their population age fifteen and over is capable of basic reading and writing. But this comparable overall literacy has not translated into similar levels of affluence across the three countries. It could not be more contrasting: For example, as per the early 21st century data, the highest per capita Gross Domestic Product is registered in Trinidad and Tobago at almost 8,900 US dollars, compared to about 3,900 dollars in Guyana, and 3,800 dollars in Suriname. On the basis of the overall Human Development Index, the one constructed by the United Nations, Trinidad and Tobago comes out way ahead at .805, Suriname at .756, and Guyana with the lowest score of the group at .708. In comparison, the scores for the US and Canada in the same Hemisphere are .939 and .940 respectively. India has a score of .577 (United Nations 2002). Relative affluence breeds a sense of ethnic identity that is qualitatively different in poorer settings. In comparatively poorer settings, such as in Guyana, ethnic identity may be construed as a reaction to behaviours of other groups, including the state.

The general level of poverty as measured by the United Nations also varies across the three nations. For example, in Guyana in early 2000s, 43.2 per cent of the population lived below the poverty level. In Suriname, during the same time period comparable data were not available but in Trinidad and Tobago it was 21 per cent. If, however, we take a different poverty related indicator into account, a pattern emerges. For example, the probability at birth of not surviving to age 40 for the cohort born during 1995-2000 was only 4.1 per cent in Trinidad and Tobago, 7.4 per cent in Suriname but 15.4 per cent in Guyana (United Nations 2002). A general pattern, then, emerges among these three countries. Trinidad and Tobago has demonstrated a much higher level of affluence and lowest poverty; Guyana has the lowest level of affluence and highest poverty; Suriname stands in between at an intermediate level of existence, closer perhaps to Guyana than to Trinidad and Tobago.

Trinidad and Tobago faces a potential population replacement problem. For example, its total fertility rate stands at 3.4 per cent during 1970-75 but by 1995-2000, this rate has plunged to 1.6, dangerously under the 2 per cent reproduction rate (United Nations 1990-2005). If the rate continues to be low, the government may contemplate instituting more relaxed immigration policy. With the new Caribbean initiative on exchange and money, this would be a possibility, as people from other islands are likely to settle more in Trinidad and Tobago than the other way around. This particular trend has implications for the future demographic and political capital of the Indian community. Indian groups are likely to oppose an active implementation of this free border policy among the Caribbean nations unless it is also open to the inflow of people from Guyana and Suriname.

Suriname's total fertility rate during 1970-75 was registered at 5.3 per cent but since it has declined. During 1995-2000, this rate stood at 2.2 per cent. In the case of Guyana, the total fertility rate has declined from 4.9 per cent during 1970-75 to 2.4 per cent during 1995-2000 (United Nations 2002). Comparatively, therefore, Guyana has still the highest fertility rate of the three with Trinidad registering the lowest fertility rate, and Suriname fits in-between.

Of course, total fertility rate only tells a partial story. The under-five mortality rate per 1,000 live births demonstrates a different pattern. For example, in Guyana this mortality rate stood at 74 in 2000, down from 101 in 1970. It is still one of the highest in Latin America, second worst only after Haiti. In Suriname, the infant mortality rate has declined by more than half in thirty years; from 68 in 1970 to 33 in 2000. In the case of Trinidad and Tobago, the under-five mortality rate is 20 per 1000 in 2000, down from 57 in 1970 (United Nations 2002). In general, higher infant mortality rates indicate a dimension of development not captured by other indicators; they attest to the extent to which healthy conditions exist in society.

Ethnically divided societies, if characterized by extreme inequalities may become seedbed of violence and societal disruption, particularly so if the state is perceived to be in the hands of one of the contending ethnic groups. The share of the richest 10 per cent of total income in Trinidad and Tobago amounted to 29.9 per cent whereas the poorest 30 per cent accounted for 7.6 per cent of total income. In Guyana, on the other hand, the richest 10 per cent in the population accounted for 32 per cent of total income or consumption whereas the poorest 30 per cent controlled 8.7 per cent (United Nations 2002). This is interesting. Since Trinidad has a higher level of development, one would expect the distribution of income to reflect a little more egalitarian pattern. Apparently, such is not the case, as the distance between the rich and the poor in Guyana is actually less than it is in Trinidad. In a general climate of relative affluence if such inequalities persist and because Indians are generally more affluent than the Afro-Trinidadians, this could heighten the inter-ethnic tensions. The data on Suriname are not available for these years.

It is interesting to note that the Gini index for both Trinidad and Tobago and Guyana are almost the same, despite radical differences in the level of development and the role of government in society. That brings forth a critical point. Gini as an indicator of inequalities in a transforming society may prove to be inadequate in capturing the real processes of state-society dynamics.

In ethnically polarized societies, the ratio of military to civilian personnel could be critically important in lessening inter-ethnic tensions. In Trinidad in 2000, only 2.3 military personnel were available per 1000 civilian population; in Suriname this figure was 5.0, and in Guyana there were 2.5 military personnel for every 1000 civilians (United Nations 2002). These data certainly confirm that the coercive capacity of the Surinamese state was the highest of the three, followed by Guyana, and then followed by Trinidad.

Inter-ethnic tensions can be exacerbated by low levels of empowerment for women. If political participation in the legislature can be held as an important indicator of empowerment, then, in Trinidad and Tobago, according to the Human Development Report, 21 per cent of the national parliament seats were held by women, compared to 17.6 per cent in Suriname, and 20 per cent in Guyana. Women as a per cent of the professional and technical work force constituted 53 per cent in 2000 in Trinidad and Tobago, compared with 51 per cent in Suriname. The Guyanese data were not available. Female participation as a proportion of the formal labour force constituted 44 per cent in Trinidad and Tobago in 2000, compared to 36 per cent in Suriname, and 41 per cent in Guyana (United Nations 2002). Female participation rates across ethnic boundaries may indicate a general level of modernizing trends than anything else with its indirect effect on the use of broader ethnic labels for political purposes. Keeping these macro parameters of social and economic indicators in mind, we shall now proceed to understand the comparative processes of Indian ethnic identity formation in Suriname, Guyana, and Trinidad and Tobago.

The Surinamese Model

The preponderance of the Dutch colonial influence sets this case apart from Guyana and Trinidad and Tobago. The historical evolution of the Indian immigration to Suriname is unique in at least three respects. First, despite the fact that Suriname was a Dutch Colony, the British retained the right to inspect the conditions of Indian indentured labour both on the water and on land. In addition, the Dutch state was intensely involved much more than the British government in either Guyana or Trinidad, from the very beginning in subsidizing labour and putting together the framework of labour control. Third, the presence of the Javanese labourers from the Dutch colony of Indonesia gave Suriname a much different blend of ethnic alliance formation and politics (Hoefte 1998). In the case of Suriname, then, in addition to those of African ancestry, the society was also characterized by labourers from India and Indonesia, a fact that would play an important role in the evolution of identity negotiation and formation.

The percentage of Muslims in the Surinamese population is much larger than both Guyana and Trinidad. Estimates, as per the census data of 2004, have put the share of Muslims in the total Surinamese population at 13 per cent, down from 20 per cent in the 1980 (Chickrie 2011, 97). The identity formation among Muslims is somewhat different from the Hindus although both derive from the Indian subcontinent. Yet, the general argument of reactive ethnicity would be valid in the case of Muslims in general as they fought for recognition in an adverse climate of forced conversion efforts by some Hindu Organizations.

Furthermore, struggles to gain political representation in the state administration in post-independence Suriname formed a major part of the struggle for recognition. Surinamese Muslims, although increasingly smaller in number in the total population, do enjoy multiple recognition as a separate ethno-religious community from entities as varied as the Organization of Islamic Conference to the Government of Indonesia (Chickrie 2011). Such national and international recognition of their existence as a separate ethno-religious community probably contributed to their sense of identity more strongly than the Hindus in Suriname. For this reason alone, in a general sense, the arguments developed in this chapter would still apply, but less stringently, to the Muslim community in Suriname.

But many conditions on the ground in Suriname were probably the worst of all three. The mortality rates of Indian labourers were higher than Guyana and Trinidad. Similarly, Census data show that the repatriation rate in Suriname, indicating the percentage of labourers returning to India upon completion of their contracts, was also the lowest. By the early 20th century, the numbers of Indians and the Javanese were roughly equal, hence facilitating a pattern of coalition building and negotiating with the state and other ethnic groups in the country, in particular the Afro-Surinamese (Wengen 1975).

The case of Suriname is characterized by a greater number of inter-ethnic marriages. Part of these marital patterns was a function of imbalance in the number of males and females in the various age groups. The imbalance was also seen in Guyana and Trinidad but the cultural proximity of the Javanese certainly contributed to a greater incidence of inter-marriages, unlike in the other two cases. Much inter-marriage across caste also took place (Speckmann 1967). However, in official documents very few inter-ethnic marriages have been recorded, partly because most Indian marriages were not officially recognized as official marriages, hence the contradiction, at least on paper, persists.

Although in general the economic situations in the British colonies were comparatively better than in Suriname, Indian labourers accumulated greater amounts of savings, as they were paid higher wages than the Javanese.

The political formations in Suriname with a multiparty system under the tutelage of the Dutch took on a less violent course than in Guyana. The distinctions between the Indians who toiled in the countryside and the Creoles and the Africans who were more urban centered created its own contradiction. However, the political processes generated by the National Party of Suriname in the beginning played an important role in moderating racial and ethnic antagonism. The Party from the very beginning of its inception made a serious attempt to cultivate a broad based ethnic support. In addition, the early years of politicking saw both the Javanese and Indians forming one political party, although they later split. But the more conciliatory beginnings of the Hindustani-Javanese Central Council (HJCC) championed a pan-ethnic position on instrumental issues, such as jobs, housing, wages, and discrimination (Traa 1974). These overarching political parties in Suriname put it on a different course than what we see for Guyana and, to a lesser extent, Trinidad.

In the beginning, of course, Indian ethnic identity was mainly the function of the background factors associated with the 19th century social and cultural conditions in the subcontinent along with its necessary regional variations. These were manifested in the village patterns of interaction, rituals, ceremonies, and political and economic behaviours. Subsequently, however, an overarching identity took shape as some old caste distinctions gradually disappeared under the new set of conditions in the New World. The main distinction between the *Pundit/Pandit* and the rest of the community, however, persist over time, though in diluted forms. In particular, the growing influence of the Arya Samaj promoted an overarching national identity and ethnic consciousness, which generally superseded the parochial regional and caste identities. The rather egalitarian message of the Arya Samaj was popular among those born in Suriname; it was a novel attempt to find ways in which the modernizing traits of individualism and technology can be reconciled with the older hierarchical Brahminical version of a Hindu society. Similar such efforts were also seen in Guyana and Trinidad, but in Suriname it had produced the maximum effect (Stipriaan 1993).

The Surinamese Indian ethnic identity as a pan-Indian ethnic identity cannot be understood in isolation from other similar movements taking place in the country. In particular, the activities of the Christian missionaries of the Moravian and the Catholic Churches are important. The missionaries generally found Indians, in particular Hindus, easier to proselytize and convert, much easier than Muslims and the Javanese. But the point here is that because of these efforts a reactive as well as a reformist ethnicity came into play among Indians, which over time contributed towards the creation of a pan-ethnic identity. Similar such developments also happened in Guyana and Trinidad, although in a diminished form.

Some of the ethnic political organizations, like Bharat Uday (BU), did not pursue confrontational positions in the incipient years with the colonial authorities, quite unlike the British colonies. But since the 1930s, in the wake of the Great Depression, years of ethnic labour militancy championed by organizations such as the Suriname General Labourers' Organization, although culminated in riots, also contributed to an economic definition of reactive ethnicity. Resistance to unchecked colonial power is a human tendency, even under the most desperate of circumstances, as much of the sociological literature on social movements indicates (Meyer *et al.* 2002).

The Surinamese Indian identity is also qualitatively different in many ways from that which exists in Guyana and Trinidad. In Suriname, the descendants have indeed managed to sustain some of their old linguistic traits, though in modified forms, which supports our contention that even under the most adverse of conditions humans can be innovative in developing synergetic or hybrid forms of languages. Notice also that Indians came with a variety of Indian languages to the New World. In this respect, the Dutch colonial policy that encouraged the persistence of ethnic languages played an important role. In comparison, no such linguistic traits have persisted in Trinidad. In Guyana, they exist only in scattered and splintered forms, not as organized as these have been in Suriname (Speckmann 1972). The British colonial policies have a lot to do with that. It is not a surprise, then, that at home a great many Surinamese Indians speak *Sarnami* but in public religious functions the use of Hindi is surprisingly widespread.

Overall, much like Guyana and Trinidad, the hardships under indenture probably contributed to the proliferation of religious and cultural expressions under the most adverse of circumstances. Indians used their languages as a protective shield against colonial authorities, and to build solidarity with their fellow ethnics. The Dutch policy of letting pluralist cultural traditions persist also played a role. In the case of Suriname, a major part of the Indian manifestation of ethnicity can be characterized as "reactive ethnicity." This reactive ethnicity can be characterized as an innovative form of ethnic identity formation as it is largely the function of both economic and political forces, in particular the role played by the Dutch state and, subsequently, the post-colonial state. This particular interpretation gives credence to the comparative political economy approach that we think is useful to help analyze these issues of ethnic identity.

The Guyanese Model

Guyana forms an interesting case in many respects as it developed its own patterns of ethnic dynamics. These, although bear some similarities, are quite unique to Guyana and much different from Suriname and Trinidad. But the uniqueness of Guyana can be explained historically as well in the evolution of the main political and administrative apparatus. For example, despite the fact that the British wrested political control from the Dutch early in the nineteenth century, much of the Dutch parliamentary structure already in place continued to influence the evolution of Guyanese politics until the first quarter of the twentieth century. The British did not abruptly change the patterns of politics and economy that were already in place. The Dutch practice of granting almost exclusive autonomy to the plantation owners continued under the British (Nath 1950).

This was quite evident under the Article of Capitulation under which the control of Guyana passed into the hands of the British from the Dutch. It stated... "The laws and the Usages of the Colony shall remain in force and be respected, the mode of taxation now in use be adhered to, and the inhabitants shall enjoy public exercise of their Religion..." (Scoble 1840: 41). This agreement was respected until a new Constitution was in place in 1928, so for over a hundred years the Dutch practices shaped Guyana (Swan 1957). This was quite unlike what happened in Trinidad, the other former British colony under study here. But it suffices to say that the Dutch Law was less feudal than the British, and it would set the tone for some specific developments in Guyana subsequently.

The Guyanese planter aristocracy, for example, had pretty much complete autonomy over the economic matters affecting their plantations. The Crown did not interfere, and the violent and aggressive antagonism between the ethnic groups in pre- and post-independent Guyana is probably a consequence of the utter disregard the Guyanese system permitted towards human dignity and rights. For example, even though the indenture contracts were initially for five years, no Indian labourer was allowed to leave Guyana until he/she had spent a total of ten years (Luckhoo 1921: 20-28). These extra years were probably used to re-indenture or abuse free labour by imposing other political and cultural restrictions on their movements.

The absence of standardized procedures (hardly ever implemented) addressing grievances fueled the resentment of the Indian labourers against the planter class. Of course, as the exploitation increased, the number of Indians being imported into Guyana increased. By 1915, Indians had already constituted about 52 per cent of the population, a number that had more or less stood constant since that time. This huge number played an enormous role in galvanizing ethnic sentiments, first, against the colonial authorities, and, subsequently, against the abuse of power by Forbes Burnham and his political party (Gibson 2003).

It is important to note that the active role played by the Guyanese state since 1928, in particular the enactment of the new constitution. Since that year, the colonial government became more active in the economic, social, and health matters of all inhabitants (Freeman 1946). This was not witnessed in Suriname, but was similar to Trinidad. The increase in state role in society, and the ethnic divisions between the Afro-Guyanese and the Indo-Guyanese were sustained by a collection of factors: economic, religious, cultural, and social.

In the economic sphere, the importation of indentured labour created immediate animosity between the freed African labour and the newly hired contract labour from India. It is true that such hiring depressed African wages, and probably created a buffer between the white aristocracy and the Indians. The "divide and conquer" rule of the British, which had so successfully been applied elsewhere, was in full display.

In religious matters, most Afro-Guyanese had already imitated the European ways of life. Because of the tragic history of slavery, they had virtually been stripped of the African mores and ways of conducting societal affairs. There was a clear schism between the religious preferences of the Afro-Guyanese, most of whom were Christians, and Indians, most of whom were Hindus (Erikson 1934).

In cultural matters, the differences in family composition, marital and settlement practices, and the use or lack thereof of family capital played a significant role in depicting a different identity. The Indians generally preferred extended family settlements, were tied to mostly agriculture, whereas the Africans were primarily urban based and favoured nuclear families over time (Beachy 1957).

In social matters, in the beginning Africans were more educated than the Indians. The fear of losing their cultural identity caused so few Indians to enroll in schools. A combination of urban settlement and greater access to education facilitated a greater number of positions in the army, police, and bureaucracy to go to the Africans whereas Indians mostly preferred agriculture, trade, and other forms of business enterprise. These stark differences played a major role in heightening the inter-ethnic rivalry and animosity in Guyana. This became more acute as Guyana as a whole is much less resourceful, quite unlike Trinidad and, to a lesser extent, Suriname.

Discrimination in matters of education played a role in Guyana. In the pre-independence years, most Indians did not go to school, as formal education was mostly European and Christian. None of the schools taught any of the Indian languages. Also, Indians feared the loss of their religion, culture, and other social practices considered dear to their community survival. As it is strongly correlated with education, involvement in voluntary associations was three times as large in the African communities as in Indian townships and villages (Luckhoo 1921; Bronkhurst 1888).

Needless to say, the role of the Guyanese state under Forbes Burnham in the post-independence period played a pivotal role in galvanizing ethnic politics in favour of one group or the other, and made it out to be a real zero sum game. The twenty-one-year rule of Forbes Burnham as leader of the People's National Congress (PNC) made Guyana ultimately look like a predator state, where resources were carted off for sectarian and private gains at the expense of the majority. Indians had comprised a numerical majority in Guyana. The role played by the Guyanese state in many ways facilitated the dominance of Afro-Guyanese in public sector employment. Indians were mostly active in agriculture and business ventures although since Burnham's death in 1985, the situation has considerably changed. The division among the Indians also helped Burnham to cement his position as the supreme leader. Guyanese politics resembled much like that of some Indian states like Jharkhand of the 2000s than it did of Trinidad. But since 1992, the largely Indo-Guyanese party, People's Progressive Party (PPP), came to power (Gafar 1998). Politics played a much more antagonistic role by this time in inter-ethnic relations than it did in Suriname or even Trinidad and Tobago.

The Guyanese Indian ethnicity and identity formation is much influenced by the peculiar clientelistic politics unleashed by Burnham, the lack of much economic growth and occupational diversity, and the role played by big powers at a critical period in its history. Had the United Kingdom and the United States not intervened to negate the continuation of Jagan (whom they deemed as a Communist threat) in power in the 1960s, Guyana would have taken a different road to development. Therefore, the Indo-Guyanese identity is much more a reaction to decades if not centuries of discrimination, subjugation, and exploitation, first by the colonial state and, subsequently by the post independent state controlled by the authoritarian dictatorship of Forbes Burnham.

The Trinidadian Model

The economic, political, cultural, and social differences just highlighted in regard to the Guyanese Indians and Guyanese Africans also applied to Trinidadian Indians and Trinidadian Africans. But Trinidad, although underwent the same pattern of colonialism as Guyana, developed several unique conditions of its own. First, the relative resourcefulness of its endowment, mostly in oil and natural gas, gave its inhabitants a higher level of affluence than its counterparts in Guyana and Suriname. Secondly, though both Guyana and Trinidad were British colonies, the differences in political mobilization and culture set Trinidad apart. In general, Trinidadian political parties showed smarter political leadership in their efforts to mobilize across ethnic lines. This applies to the leadership of both the Indo-Trinidadian and Afro-Trinidadian political parties. The increased importance of independents in the political-electoral competition also ranks it apart from Guyana and Suriname. Of course, the development of such political culture is probably highly correlated with the relative affluence of Trinidad, thanks to an abundance of oil and gas, quite unlike Guyana or Suriname.

The stewardship of Dr. Eric Williams, despite its limitations, was much more nationalist and all encompassing than the leadership of Burnham in Guyana. Many of the political maneuvers of the Indian political formations proposed communalist politics, largely as a function of the community's higher level of economic success than otherwise (Ryan 1972). But the communal politics platform of many Indian political formations gave Williams enough room to win over sufficient number of Indian votes to capture win electorally and this helped to sustain him in power for a considerable period of time.

It is important to note that the Guyanese and the Trinidadian roads to current inter-ethnic politics and democracy were erected in opposite style. While in Guyana it was the idealism of Jagan and the parochial and predatory politics of Burnham, in the case of Trinidad it was more the ideological nationalism of Williams and the parochial and communal politics of major Indian political formations and parties. Tensions were created and were really intense in both cases but they both got there through different combinations of forces. The case of Suriname in this respect is in a league of its own, as for most of the years since independence and, until recently, it had been under a series of authoritarian regimes.

Since the 1980s, however, the Trinidadian situation has improved considerably, and with the new discovery of major natural gas outlets and its prominence on the world market with liquefied natural gas (LNG), the inter-ethnic relations have become much more manageable. Although the vocal and active community leadership still scrutinizes the policy regime of the successive PNM administrations, a significant portion of the Indian community does not subscribe to the antagonistic characterization of the inter-ethnic politics (Singh 1974).

The greater economic affluence of the Indian community in Trinidad brings out other differences within the community that are much more salient. For example, the class and status differences between the very rich Indians and the mass of middle and lower class members are significant and there is limited interaction between these groups at best.[1]

In addition, the presence of a greater number of *Dooglas* in Trinidad, the name given to children of inter-ethnic marriages with non-Indian spouses, adds an interesting dynamic not so much present in Guyana or Suriname. This is because an overwhelming number of these mixed marriages are between Indian females and African males. In the case of Guyana, there are fewer inter-marriages, and in the case of Suriname a greater number of intermarriages have occurred between Indians and the Javanese, not with Africans. These marital dynamics play a role in instilling a stronger or weaker sense of Indian ethnic identity. The racial and ethnic composition of Trinidad is likely to change significantly as the number of interethnic marriages increase over time.

In contrast to the situation in Trinidad, the isolated existence of the Guyanese villages, having been scattered around a much larger country, has produced segmented existence. In the case of Trinidad, the smallness of the island has forced ethnic groups to live in close physical proximity. Overall, much greater interaction between Indians and Africans are observed in Trinidad; quite the contrary in Guyana; Suriname falls in between the two in terms of the degree of inter-ethnic interaction, in particular the relations between those of Indian origin and African origin.

The Comparative Political Economy of Ethnic Identity

An argument is developed here that inter-ethnic relations may be exacerbated in a certain direction if the labour market and political conditions are not favourable. To that end, in the first section, we presented the major structural differences among these countries in terms of the economic, occupational, and social landscape. It is noted that the total number of people with Indian ancestry registers currently at 51 per cent in Guyana, 46 per cent in Suriname, and 41 per cent in Trinidad and Tobago. Although this share does not tell us the percentage that is married to non-Indians, it is fair to say that Indians are sizeable in number in all three. If all else is constant, they should politically rule Guyana, could share power by reaching out to other population segments in Suriname, and play a critical role in determining who controls political power in Trinidad and Tobago. But as we have seen throughout history, number does not by itself explain everything about the power game. It is a function of several major variables, among which the role of the state (and who controls it!), the nature of the economy, extent of rival ethnic mobilization, the level of literacy, level of political and cultural organization, and the extent of factionalism within a community, and the importance big power rivalry, among others, have played their part in preventing Indian political organizations from capturing or consolidating power in all three cases (Kolff 1995).

The state role in the economic, political, and social development of the nation played a key part. The macro societal changes determined the evolution of ethnic identities as well. In all three cases, the history of survival guides the Indian community members to engage in cultural behaviours as if their physical existence is at stake. Of course, with development over time with the concurrent occupational diversity, this survival mentality is expected to change.

The salience of ethnicity in varied forms in Trinidad, Guyana, and Suriname brings forth several complex models of identity formation. In the case of Trinidad, assuming all else constant, it is the relative affluence that fuels the desire to practice cultural manifestations that designate them as distinct and different. In the case of Guyana, it is relative poverty, comparatively speaking, that facilitates a kind of reactive ethnic identity that has been nourished largely as a reaction to negative state policy. The case of Suriname in our estimation falls in between these two cases.

In concluding, it is argued here that although all three countries went through similar historical experiences of Indian indenture labour importation following the abolition of slavery by the European colonial regimes in the nineteenth century, the end product turned out to be different in each case. Although the politicization of the ethnic label primarily catering to ethnic group interests has played a major role in all three contexts, the outcomes have been quite different.

It is also argued that the ethnic dynamic is much more confrontational and violent in Guyana, largely due to a series of factors unique to Guyana. These include the persistence of the Dutch colonial institutions well into the 20th century, and the aggressive mobilization of ethnic politics under the aegis of a predatory state that betrayed the ideologically nationalist politics of the pre-independence period. The situation was also sustained by the absence of visible economic development and the lack of modernizing effects of limited industrialization that did not usher in an era of significant occupational diversification.

In the case of Trinidad, the level of affluence has preempted the violent aspects of ethnic polarization. Instead, in Trinidad, we see ethnically mobilized fights over access to major institutions of power and the potential consequences of any suggested or actual changes in state policies. Suriname squarely remains in between these cases as it is the most sub-continental in its formation of Indian ethnic identity yet with much more pan-ethnic orientation. The Surinamese variation indicates that it is inclusive of past caste, religious, and regional differences within the Indian group. In addition, the linguistic heritage is the most vibrant in Suriname. It exists in isolated and diluted forms in Guyana but it has disappeared almost completely in Trinidad, thanks to the modernizing influence of relative affluence.

Overall, then, it can safely be said that ethnic identity formation is indeed a complex process. This complexity can be better understood on the basis of a comparative political economy approach. But that should not give the impression that Indian ethnic communities are homogeneous in their formations; they are by no means that by any stretch of the imagination. The community members are divided by class, region, level of education, and occupation. These variables determine their level of participation in the labour market, which in turn influences a sense of self and identity. As occupational structure evolves with the passage of time and the rate of occupational mobility is experienced by a great majority of the Indian ethnic group members, their perception of themselves and as they are perceived by others undergo change accordingly. In addition, the role of the state and the politicization of ethnicity play critical roles in identity formation.

In the current phase of globalization, then, the old sense of what constitutes "Indian" no longer exists. If the extent of integration with the outside world is brought into the equation as an additional variable, then, the ethnic identity formation of Trinidad would be quite different from Suriname and Guyana, as each experiences a different level of globalization or, to use another expression, different degrees of self-examination with regard to what an "Indian" implies (Sen 2004). As globalization brings into the fore other notions of Indian experiences and identities from across the world diaspora, the Caribbean Indians, particularly those who are exposed to these multitudes of representations of Indian-ness in other settings, are likely to engage in much exploration of comparative Indian identity. Once again, comparative studies of ethnic identities would be much richer if they also examined the larger, macro processes of comparative political and economic conditions and how these affect individual negotiations of identity in various social settings.

As Indian community members accumulate greater resources in the three societies under mention here, some would probably find it advantageous to use such "Indian" label. But others would probably not use it as frequently as their relative advantage will be minimal, largely because of their poorer resource base. When leaders of organizations and political parties catering to the community's interest would use broader ethnic labels to mobilize votes and other support resources, class and other status differences would probably blur; but as soon as the elections are over these superficial unison would subside, and real status differences on the basis of income, occupation, labour market trends, education, region, and proximity to the city would probably play a much more important role in facilitating identities that may or may not be what traditionalists would call "Indian." Over time, then, many members of Indian origin are likely to remember India as part of the twilight of "fond memory" and not as a basis from which they would organize their political and social activism. This is likely to be true across the global Diaspora that claims some connection with India.

Notes

1. These impressions were gathered from a series of interviews with a cross-section of Trinidadians in the fall of 2004.

10

Bling, Brands and Hypersexuality

Globalization and Cultural Constructions of Caribbean Masculinities and Femininities*

Rhoda Reddock

In this chapter I reflect, perhaps a bit redundantly, on the impact of globalization on the shaping of Caribbean masculinities and femininities. I examine the ways in which the continuous negotiation between the local and the global takes place and the shifting identities and realities which emerge. At this time those of us in the Economic South are experiencing the full impact of the collapse but not the demise of the *neo-liberal* paradigm of capitalist globalization. It has come after a close to 20-year period where the forces of free trade and the free market 'market fundamentalism' were paramount. Yet we see little real challenge of its efficacy.

Globalization is a term that is not easily defined. Indeed, there is much debate as to exactly what globalisation is although it is a term that is in constant use (Bairner 2001, 8). As noted by Petras and Veltmeyer:

> Currently the term "globalization" enjoys immense popularity. It is a key word in not only the dominant

* Some sections of this paper were published previously in the article "Caribbean Masculinities and Femininities: The Impact on Globalisation and Cultural Representations," in Barbara Bailey and Elsa Leo-Rhynie (eds.) *Gender in the 21st Century: Caribbean Perspectives, Visions and Possibilities*, Kingston: Ian Randle Publishers, 2004.

> theoretical and political discourse, but also in everyday language. As both a description of widespread, epoch-defining developments and a prescription for action, it has achieved a virtual hegemony and so is presented with an air of inevitability that disarms the imagination and prevents thoughts of and action towards a systemic alternative...(Petras and Veltmeyer 2001, 8).

In other words many accept neo-liberal globalization as inevitable and simply seek to adapt to it.

But what really is globalization? In its simplest sense, it is usually taken to refer to a *process*, rather than a fixed situation. Some argue that it should really be seen as two processes: one *structural*—related to the fast pace of developments in information and communications technology, which make communication much more instant and global and the other—*ideological* or *political* and related to the hegemony of neo-liberal economic ideology of the unfettered free market, free trade and the individual pursuit of wealth as the only economic and political alternative. Although these two processes are currently tied together, the question is, does this necessarily have to be this way? Globalization's power as noted by Thomas Klak (1998,20), is highly ideological. It is advanced by its advocates as the only way to achieve economic prosperity and political democracy. The term 'globalization' or more accurately global economic restructuring, has become an ideological tool with which to justify a range of economic interventions many of which were introduced to the region through structural adjustment programmes. They include the removal of trade barriers, the removal of subsidies and protections to local industry and agriculture, cutbacks in social spending—e.g., on social services, health and education—and the opening up of local markets to international investments, trade and communications media often to the detriment of local industry and agriculture. The assumption here is that the resulting increase in global trade would be beneficial to all groups and all countries willing to take up the challenge.

Bringing both of these aspects together, it is generally acknowledged that globalization entails the increasing 'free' flow of people, finance, services, products, technology, images and ideas across national borders. If such a definition is accepted, then it becomes evident that the Caribbean has been subject to such a process, or processes, for centuries, dating back to the era of slavery and later indentureship. This view is supported by no other source than the International Monetary Fund (IMF) itself, in a 2001 article which argues that globalization is a process dating back to the 19th Century. The article states:

> Globalization or internationalization, is not a new phenomenon. The period through the end of the 19th Century was also characterized by unprecedented economic growth and global integration. But globalization was interrupted in the first half of the 20th Century by a wave of protectionism and aggressive nationalism, which led to depression and world war. International economic and political integration was reversed, with severe consequences. Since 1945, democracy and capitalism have been embraced by an increasing number of countries—including since 1989, by most of the previously communist world. As a result, the past 50 years have been a period of growing economic and political freedom and rising prosperity. Global per capita income has more than tripled, and most of the world has experienced a major improvement in life expectancy (IMF 2001, 1).

Indeed, one can argue the current trend of globalization is an intensification and expansion of a process established several centuries ago (Robertson 1992, 1)—an assertion supported by Petras and Veltmeyer (2001) when they argue that globalization is simply the latest era of imperialism. The major difference however, as Robertson states, is that the current situation has stimulated a global consciousness, where people have a significantly heightened awareness of the experiences of others (1992, 183). This is largely due to the expansion of the communications media, in particular global television; information technology, in particular, Internet technology and other technologies for fast travel and transnational communication. Indeed, we can perceive the growth of global telecommunications with computer networks, satellite TV and the Internet as the technological infrastructure in the globalisation of finance, production, marketing and patterns of consumption (Demers 1999, 18).

The proliferation of new information technologies and electronic communications has played a vital role in interconnecting peoples' lives and establishing the so-called 'global village', a term coined by McLuhan in the 1960s. (And we cannot now conceive of living without these technologies). The notion of the "global village" is central to the ideology of globalization as it suggests that the world is "shrinking" in that countries and peoples are becoming more integrated, resulting in a blurring of territorial boundaries (Klak 1998, 5). Today it is theoretically possible for everyone in the world to be connected via electronic messaging systems such as the Internet. The free movement of people is another matter.

Much of this interconnectivity however is more apparent than real. While the Internet may aid the dissemination of information and knowledge, it too is working within specific boundaries, and is subject to economic and political control and hence is not objective, "the political freedom of the Internet, as it was first envisaged, today seems something of an illusion" (Harcourt 2003, 6). What we are experiencing more and more is the *economic* freedom of the internet, which provides the freedom to sell everything, everywhere to everyone with few standards or controls. Further concerns are centred on the notion that not everyone has equal access to the benefits of new communication technologies, which in turn, may result in greater disparities between members of the global community. Global media, new information technologies, and telecommunications have enabled many people in the world to become instantly connected to others and this has had positive and negative results. And yet, events in distant locations of the world are quite often more easily available on television in the Caribbean than information originating from the rural areas of the same Caribbean countries, or indeed capitals within the Caribbean itself (Dunn 1995, xii).

In spite of widespread international criticism, the process of global restructuring has continued and is now affecting almost every aspect of life. Local and national manufacturers, farmers, and even educational institutions now have to become "globally competitive" or perish. Little attention is being paid to the proverbial 'level playing field' which used to be important for more welfare-oriented liberalism. Companies and/or countries have to become competitive in spite of historical, natural resource, human resource, cultural or economic differences. Women and increasingly men, their bodies and their sexuality are even more so today perceived as commodities. Hence, the onslaught of neo-liberal global restructuring exacerbates inequalities at the national level, internationally, between differing states, at the social level, between men and women, and between the "haves" and "have-nots".

The case is often made of China and India as key beneficiaries of globalization from the Economic South as evidence that economic neo-liberalization can work for such societies and not only for those in the North. An article by Pankaj Mishra in the *International Herald Tribute* points to the impacts within China of the removal of the earlier social welfare programmes and the expansion of the market economy. He notes that the new "left" in China although small, has been advocating for a Chinese alternative to the neo-liberal market economy, "one that will guarantee the welfare of the country's 800 million peasants left behind by recent changes." He notes:

> The embrace of neoliberal market economy has meant the dismantling of welfare systems, a widening of income gap between rich and poor and deepening environmental crises not only in China but in the United States and other developed countries (Mishra *IHT*, October 2006, 2).

A point echoed by the 2005 *United Nations Human Development Report* for China in relation to the decline in availability of health care and services as well as India in relation to the pack of progress in poverty reduction (UNDP 2005).

It must be noted however that a large movement critiquing the orthodoxy and hegemony of globalization has emerged, often using the Internet as a tool of communication; and although it has forced governments of the South to be more forceful in trade negotiations, and bilateral agencies like the World Bank to set up social safety nets, it has so far been unable to seriously challenge its ideological control and influence. This movement, according to Girvan (2000, 68), "critiques the market-oriented, corporate-led globalisation" and advocates "alternative ways of managing national and international exchange." This movement he notes does not recommend a return to national autarchies, but rather it questions whether "global market liberalisation will work to the benefit of all" (Girvan 2000, 68).

Interestingly many of the activists in these anti-globalization movements come from the economic North although there are also activists from Asia, Africa and Latin America. The Caribbean in my opinion has been largely silent. There have been organizations and individuals involved. For example the West Indies Farmers Association (WINFA); while the Caribbean Association for Feminist Research and Action (CAFRA) and Development

Alternatives with Women for a New Era (DAWN) in the Caribbean have been working on an international Gender and Trade Project and Peggy Antrobus and Mariama Williams have been internationally outspoken on these issues. At a more general level however, the Caribbean voice in this global critique in my opinion has been has largely missing.

Globalization and the Caribbean

The Caribbean has often been described as the most historically globalized of all regions. Indeed many of the characteristics of globalization have been part of the historical experience of this region. This includes the movement for exploitation of cheap/ sometimes unwaged labour, the large scale movement of people and goods, the involvement of transnational trading and manufacturing companies and the negative effects of surviving in a brutally competitive capitalist economic context. In the words of Thomas Klak:

> Since emerging global linkages come as no news to the people of the Caribbean, which historically is perhaps the most globalized of world regions. Since the 1500s, the Caribbean has been controlled by outside powers, based economically on imported labour, cleared to create monocrop landscapes...and reliant on the import of virtually everything else needed to sustain local populations (Klak 1998, 6).

Today, the region is facing new manifestations of this phenomenon. The destruction of the main agro-based plantation and peasant production systems (established during earlier periods of economic globalization) with the removal of protective mechanisms such as the European Union quotas for preferential markets has had major impacts on the smaller Caribbean countries. Interestingly these preferences were negotiated as reparations in some way for the extreme exploitation and dehumanisation of colonialism generally and the slave and post-slave era from which Europe gained so much. The current context acknowledges no such debt and calls on all countries to operate as if they are beginning from the same starting point and urges them to aim for the same conclusion.

This has been especially devastating in the banana-producing countries such as Jamaica, Dominica, St. Lucia, St. Vincent and the Grenadines, and Grenada where the removal of preferential quotas to the European Union has all but devastated the banana export industry. But even in oil and gas rich Trinidad and Tobago, the sugar industry, livelihood for over 30,000 people, has suffered a similar fate. The theoretical argument is that the liberalisation of national markets and hence the free flow of goods, services and information, will benefit everyone equally. It is interesting that while Caribbean countries along with others in the Economic South are feeling the negative effects of this removal of protection for agricultural commodities, the United States and the European Union continue to protect their agricultural producers with large subsidies, often to the tune of $1 billion per day (Watkins 2003, 6). As stated in an editorial of the *International Herald Tribune:*

> Poor and developing nations have long—and rightly—complained that while the richest countries want open markets for their manufactured goods, they rig the game when it comes to agricultural products. Now it appears that the United States and Europe are beginning to get the message. Their trade negotiators have agreed to *try* to reduce their farm subsidies and other barriers to agricultural imports. ... As this page has been reporting in recent weeks, poor nations buy into the mantra of globalization and free trade orthodoxy, only to find their farm products locked out of the developed nation's markets by high tariffs, or competing hopelessly against subsidized European and American goods, which sell below cost (IHT, 6).

As we all know this continues to be a stumbling block in international trade negotiations.

Globalization, Communication and Gender Ideologies

Although globalization is often viewed as an economic process, every process, be it economic or not, impacts greatly upon other aspects of human experience. Hence, globalization involves a myriad of cultural, social, political, psychological as well as economic effects. Speaking at a debate on 'UNESCO in a Globalising World', it was stated by the Chairperson of the

Executive Board that "those who see globalisation as a purely economic process are wrong. Firstly, no human phenomenon of such scope can be limited to the sole production and consumption of goods and services and because even the smallest economic transaction occurs against a backdrop of beliefs and is conditioned by its socio-political context" (UNESCO Press, 2000). So, how indeed have people been affected by the forces of globalization? In the remainder of this chapter, I focus on one aspect of this—its impact on the shaping of gender ideologies in this region.

As noted in an earlier publication (Reddock, 2004), Gender ideologies can be defined as culturally specific identities, norms, and symbols associated with social constructions of masculinity and femininity. In other words they refer to, for example, notions of appropriate behaviours, attitudes, mannerisms, etc., for women and men; for relations between women and men; and among women and men. Gender ideologies are not fixed, although some aspects can be extremely pervasive and difficult to change. They vary from society to society and from one era to another and are dynamic and constantly being negotiated and re-negotiated due to changes taking place in society at various levels.

Colonial and neo-colonial cultural domination and contemporary globalization, have resulted in increased homogenisation of gender ideologies, although there is still a great deal of diversity. The communications media has played a significant role in informing our sense of acceptable and unacceptable gender roles, and gender identities, particularly through the display of sexual and gendered images. Feminist scholarship have been e pecially interested in the politics of representation and in challenging the ways in which media of all forms construct images and messages related to women, men and gender relations and constantly re-construct and re-organise these messages.

Scholars on globalization argue that the control over these representations lies in the hands of the global (read US) communications industry. It is interesting, therefore, that even those national communications media involved in the representation and communication of ideas draw their inspiration, their formats and their design from the Economic North, in particular the United States. Local creativity in this case lies mainly in adaptation and adoption.

But not only has the world become a market for US communication products, as a result of this it has also become a consumer of US products for which the communications media are a successful marketing mechanism. This has undoubtedly led to a homogenisation in tastes and consumption habits. Yet the most crucial question remains: "Are societies such as the Caribbean passive recipients of the output of the global North or are they engaged both in contributing to a global culture as well as in the re-interpretation and selective assimilation of received information or entertainment?" (Dunn 1995, xiii).

This is a legitimate question and indeed, the Caribbean influence on the cultures of the North cannot be denied. Trinidad and Tobago–type carnivals now exist in 36 overseas locations while Jamaica, I would argue, more than any other country on earth, has intervened culturally on a world stage in a way that no other country other than the US has at this time and I shall come back to this later. Cultural studies scholars also point to the skilful ways in which Caribbean artists and entertainers have "glocalized" foreign cultural products—that is, adapted the global to the local and vice versa (Saunders 2003). Yet Caribbean artistes signed to a US music label often have to adapt their style to the labels marketing requirements. Patricia Saunders notes that:

> The inequity between Caribbean artists and markets and North American record producers and labels that assume the primary audience for all music is first and foremost American, demands a certain uniformity in the production of goods (in this case music and lyrics) (Saunders 2003, 110).

And while she argues that there is much resistance to this, the case of the afrocentric, Bobo Shanti artiste Sizzla is instructive. Described by Saunders as a 'conscious vibes artiste' "whose work reflect(s) the ethical, moral and religious discourses" (Saunders 2003, 96), the transformation in his image on signing with a US recording firm described by Gabrielle Hosein below is even more disturbing:

> First, the transition began with him singing songs about sex, pussy and wining. The first set of lyrics, noticeable on Trinidad radio, was his hit about giving it to fat punane. In a song with US based, Trinidadian-born hip hop entertainer Foxy Brown, his lyrics were "Come wine for me, give it to me girl, come wine for me, I'm here to rock your world". His latest video, featured on MTV Tempo, shows him in a

> jacket, since in the urban US, with a crowd of dancing Black people around him. This is a far cry from an earlier video in full African-imagined regalia standing by a river with a 'rod of correction' in his hand. In later shots in this latest version of public identity, he is shaking a fanned-out handful of money in one hand while singing, counting money on a table while a brown-skinned woman in short shorts dances next to the table, his face mere feet from her hips.

She concludes:

> [The change from] Sizzla the voice of consciousness to sizzla the pimp may be the result of his desires to hit bigger markets and access bigger profits, his signing to a US label or simply the gender politics he was holding back all along (Hosein 2006).

Therefore while much of Caribbean popular culture—calypso, soca, dancehall, etc, involves a negotiation between the demands of the Caribbean audiences and the hegemonic interest of the US market including US based Caribbean communities, what we witness is more than simply a hybridization of forms and content. We are witnessing the clear reflection of the new market fundamentalist ideology that is—if it sells it is worth it, and of course "Sex, i.e., women's hyper-sexualized bodies, sells." Hence the extreme hyper-sexualization of Caribbean music videos and local music channels such as MTV Tempo, CVM Plus and Synergy in a style similar to that in US music videos and music programmes on BET and MTV.

At the same time Saunders acknowledges a thriving black market of recordings aimed primarily at a Caribbean market, of material that is not interesting for US recording companies. It is important to note however that globalization of Caribbean culture is not possible on its own terms, but only through the route of the USA or to a lesser extent the United Kingdom. Bob Marley was a Jamaican performer for many years, but unknown elsewhere. His international and Caribbean recognition came with his success in North America and Britain. Those in the know also observe that to make his work internationally acceptable certain adjustments in sound had to be made. Most Caribbean superstars who 'make it' globally such as Vincentian Kevin Little have to do this in order to gain the endorsement of the US entertainment establishment, sometimes even to be accepted in the Caribbean region itself. The question remains however, which countries or which corporations should direct and control the directions of this hybridization process? And should the pattern where ideas and information flow from the North to the South continue?

Globalization, Gender Ideologies and Caribbean Femininities

The economic and cultural changes mentioned above have coincided with the challenge to patriarchal norms and attitudes by the women's movement and increasingly by individual women in Caribbean societies. While some women, mainly middle class women in some parts of the region have been able to use the increased opportunities for education, to access senior positions, especially in the public sector, with the decline in agriculture and manufacturing, for the majority of poor women local economic opportunities have significantly declined. The main solution proposed by the neo-liberalists has been micro-enterprise or small business development, which by definition is a competitive activity in which some succeed and others do not. Additionally, such enterprise needs a consumer base willing and able to patronise their business activities. Vincentian women, for example, have been trading in agricultural products and running small businesses for decades, so this is really nothing new but even these are compromised by global competition. Today many of the options available for women and sometimes accepted by their governments to address this situation either explicitly or inadvertently, e.g. tourism and casino development, involve the use of their bodies and their sexuality. As noted by Kamala Kempadoo:

> Not only has the erosion of older economic bases for Caribbean peoples and the proliferation of survival strategies that involve some form of sexual labour become important to many women and men, but today Caribbean colonial and postcolonial states are increasingly incorporating sexuality into their national strategies for competing in the globalized economy. There is a growing world population that desires and demands, and has the possibility to command, new leisure and pleasure activities that involve sex, and that makes its presence felt in the Caribbean (Kempadoo 2004, 3).

At the same time the increased visibility of women in urban and white-collar employment and in public life, as well as their predominance in institutions of higher education is seen as a threat to men, at a time when men's employment is becoming less secure. Women's jobs are not any more secure but their identity is less defined by employment and they tend to adjust better to changes within it. This has created a context for increased violence against women, as men perceive a loss of control over women and a loss of traditional markers of masculine gender identity. This sense of impotence brings into sharp focus men's feelings of reduced economic security and challenges the legitimacy of their presumed identity as 'provider' and head of household. This has resulted in serious tensions in gender relations, increased violence against women and other men, and more recently, a backlash against the women's movement. Unfortunately, in many places women's legitimate struggles for equity and equal opportunity are perceived as a foreign imposition like globalization and as a result consciously rejected (Saunders 2003).

Globalization and Bodies

The use of women's bodies in the marketing of products is not really new, however the highly sexualized images of young women and young girls in particular have had serious impacts on young women's understanding of themselves, undermining many of the gains of the women's movement in relation to women's perception of themselves. The analysis of ideologies and representations around bodies has become increasingly important with the emergence of the fields of Gender Studies and Cultural Studies. These new approaches build on earlier work, examining the different meanings attached to bodies and the importance placed on bodies as mechanisms for representations and communicating information about one self and one's group(s). Scholars note the different meanings and power ascribed to "black" bodies and "white" bodies, "female" bodies and "male" bodies, black female bodies and white male bodies as well as transgendered bodies, disabled bodies etc. Bodily innovation therefore has been a means through which people have sought to alter the meanings and power relations represented by their bodies and therefore appearance has always been important for groups perceived as subordinate.

Bodies, and how we dress them, mould them, and use them (perform them) therefore become mechanisms for 'passing', for improving status, for justifying access to certain social and economic resources and for communicating belonging in important groupings or status categories such as class, ethnicity, religion and most importantly gender. Not surprisingly therefore bodies become a useful site for the manipulation of marketing techniques to encourage higher rates of consumption. This is particularly important for groups who begin from the deep down insecure feeling that they are inadequate, incomplete and deficient. As noted by Caroline Allen:

> 'Aesthetic innovation' ...is used, particularly in advertising and fashion, playing on desires and fears and offering constantly changing ideas for the re-fashioning of self. ...In the historical situation of Western white, male, heterosexual hegemony, the bodies and emotions of 'others' become major objects of knowledge, control and thus are particularly subject to disciplinary regimes. At the same time the capitalist dynamic requires that gendered identities are constantly in flux and modifiable 'there is always the promise of improvement' (Allen 1998, 286).

Bodily innovation has been particularly important for groups which feel themselves subordinate. These include women and men of colour as well as women of all ethnicities. A review of the Women, Girls and Media web-site provides some critical insight into the portrayals of women in popular programmes aimed at young women and young men 11-18. It found the following:

- "MTV the favourite TV of girls 11-19, regularly includes girls and women in the traditional role of sex object, as seen in features on the network (think *Spring Break)* and many music videos. Girls and women who are serious musicians (excluding singers) are rarely featured. Programmes and videos show boys/men as sex objects much less frequently (MTV Programming; and *Media Use in America,* 2000, Mediascope).
- A study shows that when men are shown in the background of a video, they are most often fully clothed. But when women are in the background, approximately half the time they are dressed in ways that expose or focus on their breasts and rear ends (ChildrenNow, *Boys to Men: Media Messages About Masculinity,* 1999).

This should not be surprising as a study from the mid-1990's shows that 90 per cent of the top 100 music videos shown on MTV were directed by men (Sut Jhally, *Dreamworlds 2*, Media Education Foundation, 1995).

- A study of video games found that the few female characters in those games are often highly sexualized—wearing tight revealing clothing and having unrealistically large breasts and distorted small waists (Girls and Gaming, Children Now; 2000).
- Video games and other media sometimes use prostitutes as characters that are targets for the male hero. In a game from the *Duke Nukem* series, prostitutes are forced to strip and are then killed. In the number one selling video game for 2001, *Grand Auto Theft III*, the player can clobber a prostitute with a baseball bat with a new game technique that allows the player to feel he or she is really doing this. In other popular media, prostitutes and strippers are often included to add scenes of female breasts and rear-ends on camera. These offer viewers images of women and female sexuality associated with exchanging sex for money, and associating sex with violence.
- In advertising, women's bodies are used sexually to sell products more often than men's. A 1997 advertising study showed that white women in roughly 62 per cent of ads were "scantily clad," in bikinis, underwear, etc, while the same was true for 53 per cent of black women. For men, the figure was only 25 per cent. Women were also represented in stances of powerlessness more often, and black women were likely to be featured in animal prints, in predatory poses *(Racial and Gender Biases in Magazine Advertising*, S. Plous and D. Neptune, 1997, *Psychology of Women Quarterly*).

A related phenomenon is that of the globalization of the beauty contest industry and I notice that St. Vincent and the Grenadines has also become involved in national, regional and international beauty contests.

Globalized Notions of Beauty—The Beauty Contest Industry

Beauty is one of those factors closely associated with femininity in most parts of the world. While it is supposed to be culturally specific in that each culture and society can define what is beautiful in its eyes, through the globalizing impact—first of European colonialism and now of United States media and popular culture, Euro-American notions of beauty have become hegemonic throughout the world. There is no greater representation of this than the Beauty Contest, in many ways an extension of the continuous competition against each other that women are supposed to engage in to secure a desirable male spouse.

The modern beauty contest has its origins in the United States early in the 20th century. According to Kathy Peiss, they "evolved from modest May Day celebrations" into the Miss America pageant by 1921 (Peiss 1998, 190). Concurrent with the development of the beauty pageant, was the evolution of the cosmetics industry with headquarters in Paris and the United States. By the end of the 20th Century, beauty contests had become an important part of popular culture internationally. US and British franchises ran international pageants such as the Miss Universe and Miss World competitions but lesser international, regional and group-specific competitions such as Miss International, Miss India Overseas and Miss Big and Beautiful also emerged as beauty contests became a successful area for commerce and business.

US and British beauty pageants set hegemonic standards of beauty based on Euro-American preferences. These were of course light skin colour, straight hair, near-European phenotype, slim size (except for special competitions for larger women like Miss Big and Beautiful) and the Euro-American ideologies of girlhood and femininity. Hence by the early 21st Century, contestants or delegates as they are now called at international pageants, are supposed to be young, very slim, unmarried and childless and referred to as "the girls". These ideals, already powerful through the wide reach of United States and British cinema and television, by becoming international, drew women from every quarter of the globe into its sphere of influence.

In the article "The Ugliness of Beauty Contests: The Miss India's these days do not look very 'Indian'," the author highlights the concern among some that beauty standards all over the world are becoming aligned with what are deemed to be 'Western' ideal. For example, the Indian winner of Miss Universe 2002 was criticized for not resembling an Indian at all. In fact, the article argued: "rather than touting the Indian woman as the ideal beauty, these beauty pageants reward women who fit the Western standard of ideal beauty in height, weight, features and complexion" (Khan

2002). The author likens the trend to a form of neo-colonialism, in which the Western notion of beauty becomes thoroughly globalized at the expense of local concepts of beauty, and cultural values:

> Beauty contests have permeated the social fabric of Indian culture to such an extent as to be called an obsession. The ideals of beauty include fair skin and 'Caucasian features'. Promoting such standards may have a seriously detrimental affect upon those who cannot meet the homogenized criteria, this is a viewpoint echoed by many (Khan 2002).

In response to this viewpoint, others argue that the contests are simultaneously universal and local and provide an avenue through which ideals about gender roles and norms, and notions of femininity, can be conveyed (Ballerino *et al.* 1996, 3). Beauty, they suggest, is heavily linked to ideas of culture and power, and there remains a wide variation cross-culturally in what is deemed beautiful (Ballerino *et al.* 1996, 6).

Beauty Contests—The Caribbean Experience

In the Caribbean, issues of colour, phenotype, hair and body shape have always been important to the beauty contest experience. During the early part of the 20th Century at least until the Black power revolts of the 1970s, women with strong African features were never involved. Colour, race and phenotype continued to be important influences for most of the 20th Century. This hegemony of Euro-American ideals of beauty and femininity was much more highly developed in the USA and was a powerful influence on the nearby Caribbean. Whereas in the earlier years, there was some ambivalence towards these contests based on notions of morality and female modesty, by the 1960s and 1970s Caribbean women became the first women of colour to win international beauty contests.[3] In today's context, it has become difficult even for women's movement activists to be critical of beauty contests.[1]

Issues of power are inherent in arguments over subjective qualities such as beauty. There is contention between local ideas of beauty and international ideas. The two do not sit neatly together. Judging local representations of beauty on a large scale is bound to give rise to disagreement, and hierarchy is asserted in these cases (Wilk 1996, 229). In the end, "The continuing lesson is that the local is subordinated to the national, and the national to the global" (Wilk 1996, 230).

Among the global impacts of the increasing consumerism and westernization of world cultural expression and the excesses of the media imagery has been the emergence of sites of cultural resistance even in the Economic North. This is often reflected in a refocusing inward to elemental religious or ethnic identities resulting in new forms of xenophobia, religious intolerance, heightened ethnic tensions and new racisms. One of the most important of these has been the heightening of religious fundamentalism of all kinds and indeed a competition among these fundamentalisms which have negative impacts at global and local levels especially for women's rights and autonomy. Peggy Antrobus has argued that the growth of religious fundamentalisms—Christian, Muslim and Hindu—are all related to neo-liberal global restructuring. For example, religious bodies become spaces where the poor, especially women can go for food and sustenance in periods of economic deprivation; religion also becomes a site for ethnic and cultural identification against the homogenising impact of globalization, while for young women in many societies the alternatives presented are between covering themselves completely through, for example, Islamic veiling or representing themselves in the hypersexualised way characteristic of the 'video hos' of US music videos. The gendered performance of piety therefore becomes an alternative to the gendered performance of hypersexuality.

Gender Ideologies and Globalized Black Masculinities

In a recent television interview social anthropologist and men's studies scholar Barry Chevannes expressed his frustration at the negative impacts of neo-liberalism on male youth in the Caribbean region. He could have been referring to a number of factors including the influence of globalized images and musical representations of male violence in particular black male violence; the proliferation of small arms and light weapons through the globalized drug trade and arms trade; the generalization of conspicuous consumption such as "brands" and "bling" as markers of social status and bases of "respect" and a "get rich quick or die trying" mentality, which is directly linked to the consumerist imperatives mentioned before. In an openly homophobic popular cultural context, there is also an increased pressure on young males to demonstrate their heterosexuality by having visible access to young women as a representation of their status and gender identity. These patterns and trends are transferred throughout the world by US media and influence Black communities and masculinities throughout the world from Latin America to continental Africa.

In their essay "Globalization, Migration and the Shaping of Masculinity in Belize," Linda Matthei and David Smith, examine a problem common to the Caribbean region through the specific case of the Garifuna people of Belize. The essay explores the phenomenon of male children left in the region by migrating parents, especially mothers who leave to work illegally in the United States as domestics, an issue of great concern within the Caribbean, in this case migration to Los Angeles. One of the reasons leading to this concern has been the link made between this and youth criminality especially of male youth.

Matthei and Smith examine the phenomenon of male gang violence in Los Angeles and its impact on this community, identifying a phenomenon that they call the globalization of Belizean[2] space. They observe:

> Unlike Los Angeles, where gang violence has abated somewhat, the violence in Belize continues. During a holiday weekend in 1999, for instance, three men were killed and two wounded in seemingly trivial disputes over a bottle of stout and a stolen bicycle....Between August 1998 and July 1999 there were fifty-six homicides in Belize, thirteen of these were believed to be drug and gang related, and guns were the murder weapons in twenty-two of the murders...By US standards the figures seem infinitesimal, yet given Belize's small population they represent a crime rate almost three times the United States—and this tiny nation is ill-equipped to deal with it (Matthei and Smith 2004, 268).

Matthei and Smith argue that this unwelcome transformation taking place in Belize is the result of the following: particular patterns of labour migration to the United States; the increasing shaping of youthful identities by forces which transcend family and locality; and among young males in particular, identities profoundly affected by a complex array of transnational linkages created through migration, markets and global media. "Belizean masculine identity formation," they conclude, "occurs at the intersection of complex local and global forces" (Matthei and Smith 2004, 269).

This so-called "globalization" as in other parts of the region and possibly other parts of the world, I have argued elsewhere, may more correctly be seen as a process of "americanization" or "USization" (Reddock 2004). Matthei and Smith note the identification with United States icons such as T-shirts, baseball caps, and so on with sports logos of US basketball teams. The generalization of US cable TV and the continuous interaction through electronic and other communication systems highlight the extent of the influence on this predominantly rural Central American community. They trace the transnationalised processes through which patterns of urban U.S. masculine ideology influence Garifuna youth who migrate to Los Angeles and those who are left at home with relatives. One of these is the 'gangsta' ideology current in Los Angeles and transported to the Garifuna town of Stann Creek.

Although focussing on Belize, this chapter speaks to a reality throughout the region and by extension the world, one that is beginning to receive greater attention. The increasing violence in Caribbean societies the result of numerous factors including the sharp and continuing decline in traditional agro-based production; increasing income disparities between the haves and the have-nots, the increased availability of small arms and light weapons that has accompanied the drug trade and local involvement in transnational militarist adventures facilitated by recruitment by the United States and British militaries in Third World societies. Some also point to the impact of the violent entertainment characteristic of globalised US media and video and internet games, which are particularly attractive to young men. Matthei and Smith (2004) illustrate clearly the ways in which constructs of masculinity and femininity cannot be understood today outside of the framework of past and present capitalist globalizations and United States economic, cultural and geo-political dominance.

According to Judith Large, in the stricken economic and political contexts of most poor communities of the Economic South, contemporary masculine youth cultures create cycles of violence as goals in themselves, where through a lack of viable alternatives, young men become conscripts (Large 1997, 270). A globalized US media in such contexts becomes an important conduit of new images of masculine glory and representations of forceful triumphant identities, replacing more indigenous and home-grown versions. This influence is increasing and the degrees of violence intensifying. For example, Large speaks of the global influence of US Rambo movies and of the Rambo character in the 1980s and its influence on military forces in Southern Africa (1997:26), while more recently scholars refer to the spread of gangsta genres in Jamaica and other parts of the Caribbean. Already in the 1980s, Laurie Gunst in writing about Jamaican "badmen " who later went on to form the posses in the US identified this connection with the heroes of the silver screen (Gunst 1986, xxii).

> The gunmen infused their cruelty with a certain cinematic style, a cool detachment from the agony they inflicted. Most of these paladins had come of age in the 1950s and 1960s, when Hollywood churned out countless westerns and Jamaicans began a long love affair with the legendary bandits of the silver screen...I discovered the power of the myth as I came to know the gunmen and sufferers of Kingston. We shared an affinity with the Wild West, and this carried us across many a cultural bridge. There were the veteran outlaws who were brought to tears by 'Ghost Riders in The Sky.' There was the tense afternoon in a shantytown near Kingston where I had gone to meet a ranking named 'Billy the Kid' who was very reluctant to talk to me until someone mentioned that I'd only recently come to Jamaica from Wyoming.
>
> "Whoy," Billy breathed in a reverent whisper." I know 'bout that place!. Nuff-nuff bad-mon come from out there! Hole-in-the Wall, Butch Cassidy an' the Sundance Kid..." (Gunst 1986, xxii)

Buvunic and Morrison (2000) observed that "if it bleeds it leads is a shorthand description for the media's tendency to sensationalize episodes of violence, whether or not they are particularly newsworthy or even characteristic of underlying trends" (Buvunic and Morrison 2000, 58). Between the 1980s and 1990s, a period characterised by the shift to economic neo-liberalism they note that the world average of homicides rose from 5.82 for every 100,000 persons in 1980-1984 to 8.86 per 100,000 during 1990-1994 (Buvunic and Morrison 2000, 58-59). But the rates for the Economic South or Third World are even more alarming. They point to the growing feelings of personal insecurity felt by us all in these times. They note that the homicide rates were 40 per 100,000 in sub-Saharan Africa; 23 per 100,000 for Latin America with the Drug capital Cali, Colombia having rate of 91 per 100,000 (Buvunic and Morrison 2000, 59).

In pointing to factors contributing to these trends these authors identify the following:

- The fight-back of the have-nots—they argue that the perception by some that they are worse off than others is a powerful instigator of violence. After a short period in the 1970s when income disparities had declined, they note these rose again in the 1980s and definitely in the 1990s in Latin America and elsewhere. The decline in social services attendant on structural adjustment—that early phase of economic neo-liberalism—also contributed to reduction in access to pre-natal care and early childhood support which could have affected the mental health of a new generation leading to increased deprivation and violence.
- Tuning In and Lashing Out—the "global" media also plays its part in highlighting the economic disparities. Consumers in the economic South become closely aware of the consumer items which they do not own and this increases demand as well as feelings of deprivation. One solution to this is to import it; a second to migrate in order to earn enough to buy it; and a third, to commit a violent offence to gain access to it.

But there is another factor which must be brought into the equation: that is the constructions of notions of manhood and womanhood and how these interact in the changing context of globalizing economic neo-liberalism. In many contexts masculinities are associated with violence, violence as protection, defence or as a mechanism for gaining and preserving power. As noted by WINAD (2005), although violence is not strictly a practice of men, it is linked to masculine identity. With economic restructuring the economic possibilities for women decline yet the consumption demands increase not only for food, shelter, and essentials for family and children but also for a wider range of consumer items. For women in low-income contexts the choices are either migration or a relationship with a male partner or child father who is economically viable. Further, violence is often a response to perceived threats to a person's dignity, which is closely associated with men's masculine identity (Fergusson, Hearn, *et al.*, 2004: 21-22). Caribbean men's gender identity often includes both the need to be 'respected' as a man and the ability to use money to access women and/or to economically support them.

For countries of the African diaspora and people of colour everywhere, the influence has been particularly strong as transmissions of commercialized US Black culture through television, music videos and the recording industry generally has a significant influence on diasporic populations the world over including Africa, a responsibility not often recognised by the artistes themselves in their quest for economic success and certainly not the concern of the corporations. In his book *Manufacturing Powerlessness in the Black Diaspora,* Charles Green (2001) links the urbanizing effects of global capitalism to the environment of failure and despair characterizing Black youth, in particular male youth in the African Diaspora who cannot be reached by local education and other programmes. He notes that:

> In the global information age, the roles of television and the advertising industry are pivotal for the creation of innovators. Increasingly, desperate youth throughout the Diaspora are enticed by an infinite array of ubiquitous consumer products displayed on every entertainment medium with the subliminal message that to not possess these things is to be an outcast.

Jacklyn Cock (2001) in her essay on gun violence and masculinity in South Africa, examines the bloody legacy of apartheid and its continuing influence on masculinities in South Africa. Cock introduces the notion of "militarised citizenship" to delineate the ways in which the right to bear arms becomes a mark of full manhood, and full citizenship in the new South Africa in ways possibly similar to the United States. This militarized form of citizenship, she notes, has its roots in the apartheid era when political citizenship implied compulsory military service for white males. Black males (and females) in being denied full citizenship could not serve in the armed forces or bear arms. This denial of the right to bear arms became a representation of the denial of manhood and citizenship to African men, the result being a militarized citizenship and a militarized masculinism.

But in South Africa as well, the impact of neo-liberal economic policies accepted by the post-apartheid government compounds an already difficult situation. Cock notes that:

> In contemporary South Africa widespread poverty and a high unemployment rate have contributed to the commoditisation of violence as increasing numbers of citizens have come to rely on criminal violence of various kinds as a means of livelihood (Cock 2001, 44).

Violence, therefore, becomes a way of survival as well as of seeking socio-economic redress in a society which continues to reflect grave economic disparities.

Conclusions

In carrying out the research on this theme, one of the things that struck me was that the only icons of music, performance, ideology and culture that have been able to challenge or at least exist alongside US global cultural icons have been those from Jamaica. Although as I mentioned earlier, these are also being co-opted into the market mainstream yet, this represent a welcome respite from an overriding norm. Although we may be critical of some of the messages of Jamaican popular culture such as its homophobic and sexist stance, it would be important to isolate those characteristics that make Jamaican culture so attractive to many on a global scale. The literature suggests there may be a kind of grassroots globalization around the resistance tradition of Rastafarianism which has been incorporated into reggae and in some ways transferred to dancehall. In many ways Rastafari reflects an alternative cultural and spiritual resistance to the excesses of capitalism and consumption as reflected in economic neo-liberalism. This has accounted for its spread throughout the world among persons of African descent as well as others in many parts of the world. As Black Stalin[3] said years ago, in observing the spread of Rastafari internationally in his calypso Caribbean Man—"...[there] must be something the Rastas know that the politicians don't know."

In presenting the scenarios that I have above I would be remiss if I failed to mention the efforts which are already taking place in the region to address this situation. Additionally it would also be important for me to mention some of the things which I believe ought to be done. In the area of the economy, Caribbean leaders need to take the people into their confidence, explaining the global context and developing collectively with them alternative (but healthy) resistance strategies to address this situation. In so doing the Caribbean could learn a lot from other countries of the Economic South that are seeking creative alternatives in a difficult global situation. Breaking traditional and colonial patterns of trade and communication is another strategy to be explored. The possibilities of trading directly with countries in Africa, Asia and Latin America needs to be explored more effectively as well as the exchange of communication products—television programming, music, educational exchanges, etc.—to break the North to South pattern that has dominated for so long. In South Africa, for example, the label "proudly South African" identifies locally produced products to the consumer and in spite of the imperatives of a globalized market, citizens and visitors alike are encouraged to be conscious consumers.

Already within the region, after an overwhelming dosage of US dominated programming, we are seeing the emergence once more of Caribbean television channels with a focus on local content. This is an excellent development although those pioneers involved will let you know that it is still an extremely difficult challenge. For one thing, some of the local stations have so patterned their content, style and format along the mainstream lines that many of the negatives associated with them prevail. Many of these new cable channels transmit the same globalizing messages of 'brands' 'bling' and hypersexuality and present no new alternatives for Caribbean people, in particular Caribbean youth. Those pioneering companies that seek to be different, such as Gayelle in Trinidad and Tobago, have to compete with the fast moving, sexual and violent content to which Caribbean populations have grown accustomed. They often lack the financial resources to do so adequately and resort to paid religious programming mainly from the United States. This influence is increasing and the degrees of violence intensifying. Here again we can benefit from South-South linkages to develop truly international cable programming including channels from a wider range of countries with well developed television and film programming such as South Africa or Cuba. Regionally, the development of a regional Caribbean cable channel featuring Caribbean film—documentaries, sitcoms, soap operas, features as well as news and current affairs is long overdue.

Broadcast policies also need to be developed and introduced on issues of local content; grading of material, and agreed on standards in relation to the media content. Local media development would also open up new employment opportunities for Caribbean artists, musicians, performers, actors, directors, film-makers, designers, screen writers etc., to use their craft within the region and not have to have our shores to be viable. As small states the only way this can be feasible is if it can be achieved at a regional level and efforts in this direction, hopefully, are already in process.

Notes

1. These included—Carole Joan Crawford—Miss Jamaica/Miss World, 1963; Jennifer Hosten- Miss Grenada/Miss World, 1970; Janelle Commissiong—Miss Trinidad and Tobago/Miss Universe, 1977, Cindy Breakespeare—Miss Jamaica/Ms World,1976, Giselle La Ronde—Miss Trinidad and Tobago/Miss World, 1986, Lisa Hana, Miss Jamaica/Miss World, 1993 and most recently Wendy Fitzwilliam—Miss Trinidad and Tobago/ Miss Universe, 1998.
2. Belize's population at the time of writing was 293,000, Matthei and Smith, p. 267.
3. Black Stalin, a leading Trinidad and Tobago Calypsonian. *Calypso* is a popular song usually commenting on some social issue or development.

Interviews

Joannah Bharose, journalist 14, April 2003.
Lutalo Massimba (Brother Resistance), performance poet, 24, March 2003.

11

Olympics, Athletics and Building Social Cohesion in the CARICOM

Roger Hosein, Jeetendra Khadan and *Nicholas Paul*

The Caribbean region is very passionate about sporting activities such as cricket, football and athletics. In the Caribbean sport is a unifying factor, as is captured in the rally cry and unofficial "national anthem" of the West Indies cricket team: "Rally Round the West Indies." West Indies cricket continues to play a significant role in deepening the integration efforts in CARICOM. When the West Indies cricket team is victorious in a game the celebration and the feeling of West Indian pride transcends all barriers. The region has also done well in both football and athletics at the international level with Trinidad and Tobago having qualified for the 2006 FIFA World Cup Finals in Germany. A number of Caribbean players also play for international football clubs. The region also accounts for a number of high profile athletes in the field of athletics.

As it stands, social conditions in some segments of the region have been deteriorating. For example, the murder rate in Trinidad and Tobago increased from 93 murders in 1999 to 509 murders in 2009, an increase by 447.3 per cent. Most alarming is that the murder rate in the capital city of Port of Spain rivals those in Johannesburg and Baghdad (Townsend 2010). This chapter argues that sport can help to reduce crime levels in Caribbean society especially in crime prone economies like Trinidad and Tobago, Jamaica, and Guyana, by providing at-risk youths with positive alternatives through sporting programs. Cameron and Mac Dougall (2000, 1) note that: "... sport and physical activity can reduce crime by providing accessible, appropriate activities in a supportive social context."[1] Furthermore, sport programmes facilitate the diversion of energies away from negative activities such as aggression and self-destruction and simultaneously assist the individual in building up their skills and values base to avoid conflict and discord in the community (United Nations Children Fund 2007).

In this regard, sport can promote a number of important developments for a small developing region like the CARICOM. Sport can help in strengthening community involvement, engagement, identity and pride. Some researchers such as Delaney and Keaney (2005, 33) have also noted that "sport could be a useful tool for building up community networks and relationships." Sporting activities provide opportunities for social interaction, often with alternative peer groups, which can create awareness of differences and break down barriers for individuals and communities (Larkin 2008). Sport can also smooth the process of establishing relationships in communities by "building a sense of shared identity and fellowship among groups that might otherwise be inclined to treat each other with distrust, hostility or violence" (Sport for Development and Peace International Working Group 2008, 207). The development of sporting activities and programmes across the sport spectrum also encourages teamwork and cooperation in communities; this then has the ability to promote the strongest of social bonds among the participants (Joseph 2009). The formation of strong ties in communities can then facilitate a more effective approach to dealing with other social problems that may exist at the community level. Former Secretary-General Kofi Annan (2002) noted that, "Sport can play a role in improving the lives of individuals, not only individuals, I might add, but whole communities. I am convinced that the time is right to build on that understanding, to encourage governments, development agencies and communities to think how sport can be included more systematically in the plans to help children, particularly those living in the midst of poverty, disease and conflict."

Sport can also contribute to building the capacity of a community. The involvement of local people as volunteers in decision-making and management of local sporting activities, events, teams and facilities, can make local sporting opportunities more sustainable and relevant to local needs. Additionally, sporting activities can contribute to stability in communities as it imparts "core values such as cooperation and respect...and it brings individuals and communities together, bridging cultural or ethnic divides" (United Nations Inter-Agency Task Force 2003, 2). Through participation in activities such as sport volunteering, individuals can develop greater self-esteem and transferable skills, and communities may develop a sense of empowerment or ownership.[2] This can give individuals or communities the confidence to then tackle wider local issues. Moreover, sport can facilitate positive changes and develop various aspects of community life by bringing together the various segments in the community. Levermore and Beacom (2009, 1-16) remarked that,

> The expansion of sport as an actor for social change...is partially a result of the recognition that the orthodox policies of 'development' have failed to deliver their objectives. Such policies emphasize the economic rather than the social environment, yet have often been unsuccessful in enhancing the standards of living as absolute poverty remains endemic in many parts of the world... Sport can contribute to the development process, particularly where traditional development approaches have difficulty in engaging with communities.

This chapter focuses on one aspect of sport as relates to the Caribbean—the Olympic Games and relevant generalizations are thereafter made. The Olympic Games since ancient times were held in South Western Greece at 4 year intervals.[3] These games ran for about 1,100 years until Emperor Theodosia of Rome brought them to an end on the basis that they were pagan (the games ended in 393 AD). Pierre de Coubertin started a revival process of the games in 1892 with a formal start taking place in 1896. These games have survived until today despite various wars, boycotts and all out political struggles.[4] In 2008, 204 nations sent 11,028 athletes to the Olympic Games in Beijing.[5] Today winning a medal at the games is a source of significant national pride as it "represents the pinnacle of achievement...not just for one individual, but for an entire sponsoring nation, just as an Olympic victory did thousands of years ago"(Papoutsy 2004, para. 10).

The rest of this chapter unfolds as follows: section 1 outlines the concept of comparative advantage and specialization as it relates to sport. Section 2 assesses the comparative advantage status in three key sporting areas namely cycling, swimming and athletics. Section 3 takes a closer look at Jamaica s recent success in athletics and section 4 explores the use of sport as a catalyst for Caribbean integration. The chapter then concludes.

Revealed Comparative Advantage and Specialization

Many scholars have reviewed the factors that influence the medal outcome of an economy in sport, (see Tcha and Pershin 2003; Bernard and Busse 2004; Bian 2005). With relevance to this chapter, Hosein, Khadan and Paul estimate a linearized Cobb Douglas production function base.[6]

These researchers found the size of a country in terms of its population, income per capita, its political structure and its host/ home nation advantage and literacy levels were important variables favourably influencing the medal outcomes for a country. Table 11.1 provides these regressors with their associated estimated coefficients.

Table 11.1: Regression Estimates of Various Models

Regressors	*Coefficients*
ln population	0.085
ln GDPPC	0.896
ln medal04	0.701
ln literacy	0.195[a]
Host	0.298
Communism	0.196
R sq. adj.	0.833
DW	2.09

a: Every variable in the model was significant at the 5 per cent or less level (only the literacy variable was significant at the 15 per cent level).

The notion of comparative advantage has its origins in the theory of international trade. Developed by David Ricardo in 1817, the theory of comparative advantage asserts that a nation should specialize in the production of goods and services in which its factor endowments allows it a margin of superiority. That is, if a nation benefits from a lower opportunity cost of production in a particular good, then that country should devote its resources to the production and export of that good. Ricardo (1817) illustrated this notion through the following example:

> Two men can make shoes and hats and one is superior to the other in both employment; but in making he can only exceed his competitor by one-fifth, or 20 per cent, and in

> making shoes he can only exceed his competitor by one third or 33 ⅓ per cent. Will it not be for interest that the superior man should employ himself exclusively in making shoes, and the inferior man in making hats? (Ricardo 1817, 136).

Balassa (1965,116-117) in an evaluation of the factors that determine the comparative advantage of an economy noted that: "Comparative advantage appears to be the outcome of a number of factors, some measurable, others not, some easily pinned down, others less so. One wonders, therefore, whether more could not be gained if instead of enunciating general principles and trying to apply these to explain actual trade flows, one took the observed pattern of trade as a point of departure." On this basis, Balassa promoted the line of enquiry focusing on post-trade equilibrium rather than pre-trade equilibrium.[7] Concerning post-trade equilibrium, Balassa claims that it: "reflects relative costs as well as differences in non price factors." (p. 103).

Thus, just as some economies may have a comparative advantage in the production of crude oil, other economies may have a comparative advantage in terms of sporting events. Certainly Brazil seems to have a comparative advantage in football and Australia in cricket (Brazil won the Football World Cup a record five times while Australia won the Cricket World Cup a record four times). This recognition of the similarity between success in sports and success in international trade has opened up a vast tool kit for economists to analyze outcomes in sport (see Appendix 2 for technical details associated with the model employed in this study).

Revealed Comparative Advantage in Cycling, Swimming and Athletics

Table 11.2 shows those countries with a comparative advantage in cycling at the Beijing Olympics (see Appendix 1 for Table 11.2). The following generalizations can be made from Table 11.2. These countries are generally large economies both in terms of GDP and population (a large population is treated here as in excess of 5 million people) with 10 of the 13 economies with a revealed comparative advantage (RCA) greater than one having a Human Development Index (HDI) score above 0.9 and all having a Gender Development Index (GDI) above 0.85.[8] Using the ratio of high technology exports as a percentage of total exports as a reflection of the capital intensity of a country, the cycling results infer that most of the countries that have a revealed comparative advantage score in cycling above one are also fairly capital abundant.[9]

In swimming, a similar pattern emerges in that all of the economies with RCAs above one are large economies in terms of population (except Norway and Slovenia) and most are large in terms of GDP. Again these countries have high HDI and high GDI score (see Appendix 1 for Table 11.3). Excluding Zimbabwe, Slovenia and Tunisia these are also generally capital intensive economies.

In athletics, however, a different picture emerges. In particular, 12 out of the 32 countries have small populations and only nine of these economies have HDIs above 0.9 (9 have HDI scores below 0.8). Three CARICOM economies (Bahamas, Jamaica and Trinidad and Tobago) have a revealed comparative advantage score in athletics above one. The majority of these economies are not relatively capital intensive as reflected in low ratio of high technology exports as a percentage of total exports as compared to say cycling and swimming (see Appendix 1 for Table 11.4).

On the basis of the data in Tables 11.2, 11.3 and 11.4 one can tentatively conclude that even countries with low capital intensity and relatively poor with small population endowments can enjoy a comparative advantage in athletics. Conversely, countries that enjoy a comparative advantage in swimming and cycling have a relatively higher capital intensity as compared to countries that have a comparative advantage in athletics (see Appendix 1 for Table 11.5).

Having RCA in one Olympic year could be due to random chance and so our argument assumes that an economy has comparative advantage in a particular sporting area if its RCA scores were above one in the last four Olympic Games. Table 11.6 provides the relevant list of countries that follow this pattern regarding athletics.

Two CARICOM economies, the Bahamas and Jamaica feature in this Table; even more, the Bahamas and Jamaica have the highest RCA scores listed in Table 11.6 (note also that in 1996, 2000 and 2008 RCA scores for Trinidad and Tobago in athletics were above one).[10] For Barbados, in 2000 its RCA score was also above one in athletics. Because of the overall stronger showing of Jamaica in Table 11.7, the next section provides some guidelines as to why Jamaica did so well in athletics.

Table 11.6: RCA Score in Athletics for States with RCA Scores Above One for 4 Consecutive Years

	1996	2000	2004	2008
Bahamas	6.38	6.92	6.73	6.79
Belarus	1.70	2.04	1.35	2.50
Czech Republic	1.74	1.73	1.68	1.13
Ethiopia	6.38	6.92	6.73	6.79
Jamaica	6.38	6.92	6.73	6.79
Kenya	6.38	6.92	6.73	6.79
Morocco	6.38	5.54	6.73	6.79
Nigeria	4.25	4.62	6.73	3.40
Norway	1.82	1.38	1.12	1.36
Portugal	3.19	3.46	4.49	3.40
South Africa	2.55	4.15	2.24	6.79
United States	1.45	1.07	1.65	1.42

Table 11.7a: Medal Count in Athletics for Bahamas

	Athletics	*Total*	*Athletics medals as % of total medals*
1992	1	1	100
1996	1	1	100
2000	2	2	100
2004	2	2	100
2008	2	2	100

Table 11.7b: Medal Count in Athletics for Jamaica, Post Independence

	Athletics	*Total*	*Athletics medals as % of total medals*
1968	1	1	100
1972	1	1	100
1976	2	2	100
1980	2	2	100
1984	3	3	100
1988	2	2	100
1992	4	4	100
1996	6	6	100
2000	7	7	100
2004	5	5	100
2008	11	11	100

A Closer Look at Athletics in Jamaica

An outline of the medals won in athletics by Jamaica and other CARICOM economies for the time period 1968-2008 is provided in Table 11.8 (see Appendix 1 for Table 11.8). Observe that whilst in 1968 and 1972 the amount of medals won by CARICOM economies tallied one (1) per year, by 2008 this had climbed to fifteen (15). This is a sharp increase.

As concerns Jamaica specifically, in 2006 (4th November), Count Jacques Rogge, President of the IOC, noted that "Jamaica had a good system to prepare athletes." The successes of Jamaican athletes in track and field have been attributed to a variety of factors. For example, Irving and Charlton (2009) identified some of these factors as genetics, environmental and nutritional. Franklyn noted that the success in Jamaica's track and field can be credited to:

> The Boys and Girls Inter-Secondary Schools Track and Field Championship ("Champs") and other annual competitive athletic meets; organized track clubs and performance centres; a legion of volunteers; a proliferation of trained coaches; the general assertiveness of Jamaicans; increased provision of sport facilities; increased private sector sponsorship; and enthusiastic popular support (Franklyn 2010, 34).

In the Beijing Olympics, Jamaica won 11 medals (distributed as 6 gold, 3 silver and 2 bronze), and was the most successful country of its size (measured in terms of population). According to Franklyn (2010, 33), Jamaica's success at the 2008 Beijing Olympics and the 2009 World Championships allowed it to overtake the USA to become the "sprint capital of the world." Since 1948, Jamaica has won 53 medals (13 gold, 24 silver and 16 bronze). In the 1952 Olympics, Jamaican athletes won 2 gold and 3 silver medals which placed the country 13th in the medal count Table, some 5 places higher than the United Kingdom which won 1 gold, 2 silver and 8 bronze medals. Table 11.9 shows the RCA scores of Jamaica in the time interval 1968 to 2008.

Jamaica has a system of management and administration in its sporting activities that is almost 100 years old. The sporting system in Jamaica is unique and, as Robinson (2007) recently stated, is a model for the world. Jamaica's athletic regime is properly organized at all tiers of the primary, secondary and adult training

Table 11.9: RCA Score of Jamaica Athletics

1968	4.9
1972	5.5
1976	5.5
1980	5.5
1984	5.5
1988	5.8
1992	6.2
1996	6.4
2000	6.9
2004	6.7
2008	6.8

programs. Jamaica's athletics sporting model looks like a pyramid structure, as illustrated in Figure 11.1.

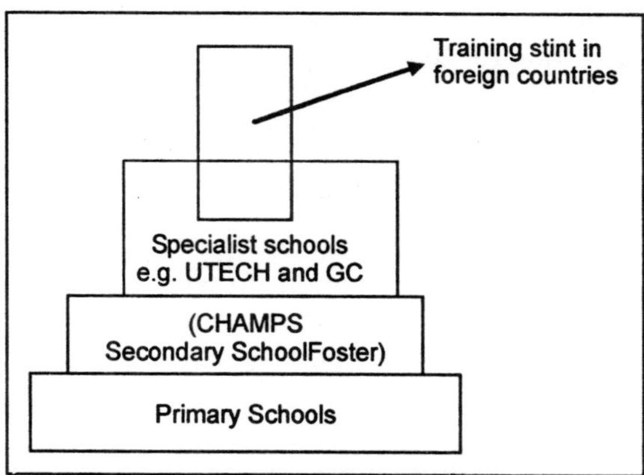

Figure 11.1: Pyramid Structure of Athletics Training Program in Jamaica

At the base of this system is the Inter Scholastic Championship, (popularly called CHAMPS). At the level of each school there are qualified coaches. The CHAMPS started in 1910 and has helped to produce a vast miscellany of world class athletes starting with Norman Manley. The CHAMPS system has been extended just from a handful of schools to virtually all secondary schools in Jamaica. Robinson (2007) argues that "even though Jamaica has tremendous athleticism, it is the system that has evolved since 1910 that underpins and explains Jamaica's high performance in athletics at the international level (quoted in Percival 2009, para. 2)."

Local sporting facilities have served the Jamaican people well. When Jamaicans (and other CARICOM nationals) go abroad for training, they are sometimes exposed to a culture shock, i.e., they have to cope with a feeling of alienation (Lowrie 2008). For example, the dietary pattern is different and athletes run the risk of suffering from a lack of nutrition. Athletes in most sporting disciplines are also exposed to this culture shock. For example, in a recent interview with Ian Cheeseman of the British Broadcasting Company (BBC), Dwight Yorke admitted that he experienced a huge "culture shock" on his arrival to play football in England for the first time. Yorke noted that "the food, the people, the weather, the clothing, everything was totally different to what I was used to" (Cheeseman 2009, para. 17).[11] Sometimes athletes are promised incentive packages but on arrival these are not fully delivered and they often have to work while studying (Lowrie 2008). Coaches at the institutions visited by these athletes push students to excel in those programmes that are of benefit to the institutions. Running for one's home country may cease to be the priority for some of these athletes (Lowrie 2008). Acclimatizing can sometimes be a challenge for foreign athletes as well. At the post secondary school level the Jamaicans have excellent facilities each at the UTECH and the GC Foster College. UTECH programs[12] started with former world record holder Dennis Johnson and his ideas in the late 1960s to develop a competitive US style College Athletic programme in Jamaica to provide a service similar to what he received in San Jose University, USA.[13] Johnson felt too many athletes left Jamaica to go abroad and never came back home, some of whom were very successful. Examples include Donovan Bailey of Jamaica and Linford Christie of the United Kingdom.

The GC Foster institution was opened on 11 September1980. The main objective of this school is to train specialist teachers in both physical education and in sports. This College is the only one of its kind in the English Speaking Caribbean. In a recent commentary Ventley Brown, the overseer of the College's program, noted: "... if you look at 99 per cent of the performances at Boys and Girls Champs, all the big coaches are G.C. Foster graduates..." (Foster 2008, para. 25).

CARICOM Integration: Social Cohesiveness and Sports

On the 1st May 1968, 12 countries of the English speaking Caribbean entered into agreement to create CARIFTA (Caribbean

Free Trade Area). The CARIFTA agreement, however, did not significantly boost the manufacturing export performance of Caribbean countries, especially for the larger member states such as Jamaica and Trinidad and Tobago. This failure encouraged a greater call for more pronounced integration.

By 1973, the integration of the economies of the Caribbean geosphere became more of a reality with the signing of the Treaty of Chaguaramas—the objective of which was CARICOM (Caribbean Common Market). The initial signatories were Barbados, Jamaica, Guyana, and Trinidad and Tobago. Other territories joined and by the 4th July 1983 the Bahamas became the thirteenth Member State of the Community. The British Virgin Islands and the Turks and Caicos Islands became associated members of CARICOM in July 1991. Several other members of the Commonwealth Caribbean and some Latin American countries now enjoy observer status in CARICOM. In July 1995, Suriname became the fourteenth member of CARICOM.

Several institutions have been established within CARICOM which carry regional significance. They are the Organization of Eastern Caribbean States (OECS), the Caribbean Court of Justice (CCJ) and the University of the West Indies (UWI). Although these institutions have made significant contributions to regional development there remains many issues that need to be addressed. One such gap is in the area of sports. Sport is arguably the most popular form of leisure activity in the world, and people old and young, boys and girls, men and women participate in various forms as coaches, players, spectators etc.

The benefits of participating in sporting activities transcend into other aspects of social life by improving communication skills, decision-making skills and overall discipline. It also improves the work ethic of individuals to become more goal oriented and enables them to learn from their mistakes by managing success and failure (United Nations Inter-Agency Task Force on Sport for Development and Peace 2003). Annan (2002)[14] also noted that "....when young people participate in sports or have access to physical education, they can build up their health and self esteem, use their talents to the fullest, learn the ideals of team work and tolerance and be drawn away from the dangers of drugs and crime." This is critical for as Figure 11.2 shows, the Caribbean has a high crime rate reflected in a high international homicide rate per year per 100,000 inhabitants as compared to Singapore and

Mauritius (see Appendix 1 for Figure 11.2). Improved social cohesion in the Caribbean region can help to ease this situation.

Daniel Tarschys, former Secretary General of the Council of Europe, stated that:

> ....the hidden face of sport is also the tens of thousands of enthusiasts who find, in their football, rowing, athletics and rock climbing clubs, a place for meeting and exchange, but, above all, the training ground for community life. In this microcosm, people learn to take responsibility, to follow rules, to accept one another, to look for consensus, to take on democracy. Seen from this angle, sport is, par excellence, the ideal school for democracy (quoted in Carmichael 2008, 2).

The use of sport as a tool to suppress drug abuse and criminal activity has been successfully utilized by many agencies and governments. For example, the United Nations Office on Drugs and Crime (2007) in collaboration with the Qatar National Olympic committee through the launch of the Global Sport Fund in 2007 has been able to engage at-risk youths from different parts of the world. Sheikh Saud bin Abdulrahman al-Thani, Secretary General of the Qatar Olympic Committee, noted that "the Sport Fund targets young people at the age when the temptation to experiment with illegal drugs is high. The main purpose is to promote sports activity among young people and to prevent drug use and crime worldwide" (United Nations Office on Drugs and Crime 2007, para. 7).

Hawkins (1998) noted that in Kansas City, Missouri the implementation of an evening and midnight basketball programme have significantly reduced the crime rate among African American youth. Another successful initiative is the Northern Fly-In Sports Camps in Winnipeg, Manitoba, Canada. The focus of this sports camp is on building teamwork, character and self-esteem among young offenders and potential young offenders. The programme experienced exceptional success and resulted in crime reductions from 20 per cent to 78 per cent in eight communities, in comparison to the years the programme was not offered (Winther and Currie 1987). Sport England (1999, 18) also noted that Bristol City Council has been utilizing sport as a "central policy vehicle in its programmes to overcome exclusion and to regenerate the poorest areas of the city." One such initiative in Bristol, England known as the "Voice of Southmead" reported phenomenal results in reducing problems such as drug abuse and criminal activity. The statistics reveal a 15 per cent decline in crime for the period October 1997 to January 1998 in comparison with the same period from 12 months earlier. The decrease in juvenile crime was even more impressive, with a 43 per cent reduction for the same period. There are several other studies that concur with the suggestion that sporting programmes can do much to modify youth behaviour in a positive way. The substantive statements by some of these studies are presented in Table 11.10.

Table 11.10: Empirical Evidence on Sport Programs

Researcher	*Substantive statement supporting sport programs.*
(Howell 1995).	Organized sport can prevent youth crime by developing capable, mature and responsible youth.
(Jamieson and Wolter 1998).	Community sport networks involving local sport groups and non-traditional stakeholders such as the police, social service agencies and local businesses seem to be the most effective at reducing youth crime.
(King *et al.* 1998).	Young offenders in organized sport programmes have demonstrated significant increases in ratings in perceived competence in sport skills and increased self-esteem.
(Diana 2000).	An investment into sport for at-risk youth would significantly reduce incarceration costs, minimize personal harm to youth and adults, and maximize social development among young people.
(Gatz *et al.* 2002).	The organized sport programmes that are successful at reducing youth crime appear to develop feelings of competence, connectedness and empowerment among youth.
(Sheehan *et al.* 2002).	Organized sport programmes that engage at-risk youth by empowering them and providing opportunities for positive peer mentoring will foster reductions in youth crime.
(Saskatchewan 2003).	Organized sport programmes for youth that develop social skills, mentoring opportunities with adult role models, cognitive skills, and increase feelings of self-confidence and self-esteem provide an antidote to antisocial behaviour.
(Jamieson and Ross 2007).	Organized sport programmes can, however, contribute to reducing youth crime by giving young people a positive identity, feelings of empowerment and by helping youth acquire leadership, teamwork and self-governance skills under adult supervision.

Source: Carmichael (2008).

The prevalence of HIV/AIDS infections in the Caribbean is among the highest in the world, ranking second only to Sub-Saharan Africa (UNAIDS and World Health Organization 2009). Sporting activities and programmes can provide an effective method of reaching out to young people that may have been alienated and discriminated against by creating an atmosphere of support and camaraderie in the community (United Nations Children Fund 2007). Sporting programmes can also be utilized to influence participant's behaviour. Many sporting programmes have been used to curb the spread of HIV/AIDS and modify the behaviour of young people. For example, Football for Life in Honduras is one such programme that protects young people from sexual exploitation and child labour. This is done through a volunteer programme where older adolescents are used as role models to inform younger football players about the risks associated with HIV/AIDS.

Ogi (2005, para. 1)[15] noted that: "With sport, children and young adults have the opportunities to make mistakes and learn the worth of essential values that will help them throughout their lives. Sport is more than just entertainment and fun. Sport teaches lessons of social behaviour and integration, it builds character, it helps with self-esteem and it fosters respect for others. Through sport, young people can actively prepare themselves for their professional life."

For many ordinary CARICOM nationals sport provides an escape valve from many of the pressures of society. Sport helps to promote a sense of belonging, reducing the need to take illicit drugs and such types of deviant behaviour (Cameron and MacDougall 2000). The use of illicit drugs in the Caribbean is becoming more prevalent and in many Caribbean countries there is a high prevalence in the use of cannabis (World Drug Report 2010). For example, in Trinidad and Tobago the prevalence of cannabis use among the general population increased from 3.7 per cent in 2002 to 4.7 per cent in 2006 and in the Bahamas from 4.7 per cent in 2003 to 5.5 per cent in 2008 (World Drug Report 2010). Sporting programmes can be of use to reverse this trend as they provide a structured environment for young people to learn appropriate social skills, enhance self esteem, and promote opportunities for social advancement.

The World Drug Report (2009, 8) noted that the problem (of crime) "can only be solved by addressing the problem of slums and dereliction in our cities, through renewal of infrastructures and investment in people—especially by assisting the youth, who are vulnerable to drugs and crime, with education, jobs and sport."

Sport is important as it can help young people to become more involved in their communities. Physical activity promotes more positive social health amongst young people. Sport also helps to develop the moral character of young people. The simple explanation here is that moral behaviour can be partly achieved through the teamwork that generally occurs with sport and physical activity in a collective fashion (Bredemeier and Shields 2006).

Sport helps to create a diversion for at-risk youths from at-risk youths. Sporting programmes can also discourage anti-social behaviour and promote a greater sense of self esteem and discipline among the youth, which can develop important social skills to keep them away from drugs, violence, or criminal activity (United Nations Inter-Agency Task Force on Sport for Development and Peace 2003). Moreover, sports help to promote an improved element of interest by young people in schooling as measured by pupil attendance (Hartman, 2008, 5). Information from the same source also reveal that there exists a strong and positive correlation between students participation in sport and their academic success, that is, "students who participate in high school sports tend, on average or in general, to perform better academically than their non-athletic peers."

A greater sense of social cohesiveness in the region can be achieved by harnessing the positive externalities on offer from sport. The authors suggest that a good place to start is with the replication of the Jamaican CHAMPS system into other secondary schools throughout the region. A replication of the GC Foster and UTECH setting in at least two other member states, possibly Guyana and Trinidad and Tobago because of their larger population base, may significantly help to improve region wide outcomes. Critically, there will be the need for a greater degree of functional cooperation by member states in athletics, probably including more intra CARICOM competition. One possible starting point opportunity here is for CARICOM to engage successful regional athletes to have a motorcade after each Olympic Games in the various CARICOM member states to provide motivational support to aspiring athletes.

Another intervention can be based on that used by the Liverpool Football Club of England. The Liverpool Football Club, one of the richest in the world, uses its star players to visit schools with high levels of truancy to talk to students about the importance of attending school (Cameron and MacDougall 2000).

There is now the urgent need for the formation of a specific arm within CARICOM to deal with the development of sport in general and athletics in particular in the region as a whole. The St. Vincent and the Grenadines National Olympic Committee (SVGNOC) proposed the formation of a CARICOM Sports Commission (SVGNOC 2008). According to the SVGNOC (2008, para. 42), the formation of such an institution should establish the guidelines to "place sport prominently in the matrix of regional development and to craft programmes for enhancing the sports tourism thrust that is only currently espoused by a select few." The only real form of unification in sport at the regional level is exemplified through the West Indies cricket team; however, some quarters of the West Indies cricket team is considered to be in a state of disarray. For example, Girvan (2007, 22) has noted that the "one symbol of sporting integration we have, WI Cricket, is in a complete shambles." Thus, a much more tangible, well structured institution should be introduced to perform such an undertaking. The SVGNOC advocated that the CARICOM Sports Commission should be modeled in a similar vein as the Caribbean Tourism Organization so that it "can and should facilitate a harmonized approach to regional wellness, active lifestyles for all and genuine regional integration in the best interest of all of us" (SVGNOC 2008, para. 47).

The implementation of any sporting programme specific to athletics in the region should be grounded in the framework of the Jamaican athletics model at various levels of the school system. The Jamaican athletics model as mentioned before is almost 100 years old and can provide a vast pool of technical knowledge and experience for other territories in the region. Key to the success of such a programme in the region may reside in the extent to which Jamaica's wealth of experience and knowledge in producing world class athletes is utilized by other CARICOM members. The relevant personnel such as coaches, trainers and administrative staff from various territories in the region should be exposed to the various components of the Jamaican system so as to achieve a comprehensive understanding of the factors that influence and contribute to successful athletes.

Conclusion

The central point of this chapter is that sport in the Caribbean has a cohesive property and if harnessed appropriately could be utilized to deal with some of the challenges that exist in the Caribbean region. This study is not suggesting that socially cohesive societies are without problems. Rather, it makes the point that building greater regional social cohesiveness through sport can help the CARICOM people work closer together when either crisis or opportunity strikes. Greater social cohesiveness within CARICOM is critical to generate regional confidence and patience in the Caribbean Single Market and Economy (CSME) process. Building a more socially cohesive CARICOM society working through sport can facilitate CARICOM nationals having more confidence in the CSME process and help to build more meaningful economic outcomes. Sport helps to build human development and as Soubbotina and Sheram (2000, 8) noted: "To be sustainable, economic growth must be constantly nourished by the fruits of human development...conversely; slow human development can put an end to fast economic growth."

The study also identifies that Jamaica has a good system of sport management in athletics and a greater degree of sport cohesion can be built in the CARICOM by replicating the Jamaican UTECH experience within the ambits of say a Caribbean Sports Commission. The region stands to gain from this opportunity and the Heads of Government should pay serious attention to it, given social conditions in the region. Furthermore, to achieve these additional benefits sport must not be a leisurely option only. It must be taught like English and Mathematics as a subject to help build functionally participative individuals.[16] Just as English and Mathematics are subjects that help economic agents to better participate in a globalizing world characterized by skills-based technical change, so too can physical education programmes help to make economic agents more physically active and arguably better able to participate in the faster paced economic environment motivated by globalization.

Indeed, a closer look at sport integration with focus on athletics in CARICOM can provide a fertile ground not only for the development of sport but also to strengthen the integration movement. Regional sporting organizations such as the West Indies cricket team has had tremendous influence on promoting solidarity and social cohesion in CARICOM, however in recent times the performance of the West Indies cricket team leaves much to be desired, and so a wider programme built around sport in general with some emphasis in athletics may now become necessary.

Appendix 1
Tables and Graphs

Table 11.2: RCA Scores in Cycling and Various Socio Economic Properties of Relevant Economies, 2008

	RCA cycling	*Population (2008 est)*	*GDP, PPP (current international $ million)-2008*	*GDI Score (2007)*	*HDI Score (2007)*	*High-technology exports (% of manufactured exports) 2008*
Switzerland	11.83	7,647,675	324,376.69	0.946	0.960	23
Sweden	7.10	9,219,637	340,769.81	0.956	0.963	16
Latvia	5.91	2,266,094	37,065.40	0.865	0.866	7
Great Britain	5.28	60,943,912	2,178,205.07	0.943	0.947	19
New Zealand	3.94	4,268,900	116,371.05	0.943	0.950	9
Spain	3.94	45,555,716	1,442,935.68	0.949	0.955	5[b]
Argentina	2.96	39,882,980	570,846.32	0.862	0.866	9
France	2.66	62,277,432	2,121,724.12	0.956	0.961	20
Denmark	2.53	5,493,621	202,414.92	0.947	0.955	16
Poland	1.77	38,125,759	658,611.40	0.877	0.880	5
Germany	1.30	82,110,097	2,904,556.83	0.939	0.947	14
Italy	1.27	59,832,179	1,871,708.68	0.945	0.951	7
Netherlands	1.11	16,445,593	673,634.23	0.954	0.964	22

Source: World Development Indicators, Human Development Report 2009 and own calculations.
[b] 2007.

Table 11.3: RCA Scores in Swimming and Various Socioeconomic Properties of Relevant Economies, 2008

	RCA in swimming	*Population (2008 est)*	*GDP, PPP (current international $ million)—2008*	*GDI Score (2007)*	*HDI Score (2007)*	*High-technology exports (% of manufactured exports) 2008*
Tunisia	9.21	10,327,800.00	82,163.54	0.752	0.769	4.88
Zimbabwe	9.21	12,462,879.00	2311.62[c]	n.a.	n.a.	3.1[d]
Australia	4.01	21,431,800.00	831,219.79	0.966	0.970	11.81
Austria	3.07	8,336,926.00	316,070.09	0.930	0.955	10.93
Serbia	3.07	7,350,221.00	77,574.44	n.a.	0.826	n.a.
Hungary	2.76	10,038,188.00	198,645.81	0.879	0.879	24.15
United States	2.60	304,060,000.00	14,093,309.95	0.942	0.956	27.12
Japan	1.84	127,704,000.00	4,358,471.93	0.945	0.960	17.87
Norway	1.84	4,768,212.00	279,962.24	0.961	0.971	19.88
Slovenia	1.84	2,021,316.00	56,325.01	0.927	0.929	6.10
France	1.38	62,277,432.00	2,121,724.12	0.956	0.961	20.24
Denmark	1.32	5,493,621.00	202,414.92	0.947	0.955	15.57
Brazil	1.23	191,971,506.00	1,978,138.97	0.810	0.813	11.97
Great Britain	1.18	60,943,912	2,178,205.07	0.943	0.947	19
Netherlands	1.15	16,445,593.00	673,634.23	0.954	0.964	22.21

Source: World Development Indicators, Human Development Report 2009 and Own Calculations.
c: 2005, d: 2007.

Table 11.4: RCA Scores in Athletics and Various Socioeconomic Attributes of Relevant Economies, 2008

	RCA athletics	*Population (2008 est)*	*GDP, PPP (current international $ million)- 2008*	*GDI Score (2007)*	*HDI Score (2007)*	*High-technology exports (% of manufactured exports), 2008)*
(1)	(2)	(3)	(4)	(5)	(6)	(7)
Bahamas	6.79	337668	n.a.	n.a.	0.856	0.39[e]
Bahrain	6.79	775585	27,067.18	0.895	0.895	0.05[f]
Belgium	6.79	10708433	377,346.41	0.948	0.953	8.12
Cameroon	6.79	19088385	41,892.10	0.515	0.523	2.71[g]
Ecuador	6.79	13481424	108,044.39	n.a.	0.806	4.55
Ethiopia	6.79	80713434	70,121.54	0.403	0.414	5.94
Jamaica	6.79	2687200	20,735.60	0.762	0.766	0.43
Kenya	6.79	38765312	60,115.64	0.538	0.541	4.59
Morocco	6.79	31605616	136,859.20	0.625	0.654	8.81[h]
Panama	6.79	3398823	42,478.69	0.838	0.84	0.03
South Africa	6.79	48687000	492,530.65	0.68	0.683	5.22
Sudan	6.79	41347723	89,101.22	0.516	0.531	0.1
Trinidad and Tobago	6.79	1333388	33,565.93	0.833	0.837	0.77
Estonia	3.4	1340675	27,686.43	0.882	0.883	10.5
Nigeria	3.4	151212254	317,410.97	0.499	0.511	0.32
Portugal	3.4	10622413	247,014.99	0.907	0.909	8.38
Belarus	2.5	9680850	118,863.87	0.824	0.826	2.35
Latvia	2.26	2266094	37,065.40	0.865	0.866	7.14
Finland	1.7	5313399	192,316.36	0.954	0.959	21.23
Greece	1.7	11237094	329,876.69	0.936	0.942	9.96

(Contd.)

(1)	(2)	(3)	(4)	(5)	(6)	(7)
Turkey	1.7	73914260	991,715.15	0.788	0.806	1.74
Russia	1.7	141950000	2,260,202.41	0.816	0.817	6.52
New Zealand	1.51	4268900	116,371.05	0.943	0.95	9.27
Cuba	1.42	11204735	n.a.	0.844	0.863	35.33[i]
United States	1.42	304060000	14,093,309.95	0.942	0.956	27.12
Lithuania	1.36	3358115	59,617.36	0.869	0.87	11.42
Norway	1.36	4768212	279,962.24	0.961	0.971	19.88
Poland	1.36	38125759	658,611.40	0.877	0.88	5.24
Slovenia	1.36	2021316	56,325.01	0.927	0.929	6.1
Croatia	1.36	4434000	78,319.06	0.869	0.871	9.14
Ukraine	1.26	46258200	336,611.83	0.793	0.796	3.22
Czech Republic	1.13	10424336	256,889.89	0.9	0.903	14.26

Source: World Development Indicators, Human Development Report 2009 and own calculations.

f, h, i: 2007, e, g: 2006.

Table 11.5: The Relationship between RCA in Swimming, Cycling, Athletics and GDI Score, HDI Score and the Degree of Capital Intensity for the Relevant Economies

	Average RCA (2008)	*Average GDI (2007)*	*Average HDI (2007)*	*Average High-technology exports (% of manufac-tured exports) (2008)*
Swimming	3.0	0.9	0.9	15.3
Cycling	4.0	0.9	0.9	13.9
Athletics	3.9	0.8	0.8	7.8

Source: Table 11.2, 11.3 and 11.4.

Table 11.8: CARICOM Medals Won in Athletics

	Jamaica	*Barbados*	*Bahamas*	*Trinidad and Tobago*	*Medal count*
1968	Men's 100 m				1
1972	Men's 100 m				1
1976	Men's 100 m Men's 200 m			Men's 100 m	3
1980	Men's 200 m Women's 200 m				2
1984	Men's 4x100m Relay Women's 100 m Women's 200 m				3
1988	Women's 200 m Men's 4×400m Relay				2
1992	Women's 100 m Women's 200 m Men's 400 m Hurdles		Men's Triple Jump		5
1996	Women's 400 m Hurdles Women's 100 m Women's 200 m Men's Long Jump Women's 4x100 m Relay Men's 4x400 m Relay		Women's 4×100 m relay	Men's 100 m Men's 200 m	9

(Contd.)

	Jamaica	Barbados	Bahamas	Trinidad and Tobago	Medal count
2000	Women's 400 m Women's 400 m Hurdles Women's 4x100 m Relay Men's 400 m Women's 100 m Men's 4x400 m Relay	Men's 100 m	Women's 4x100 m relay Women's 200 m	Men's 100 m Men's 200 m	12
2004	Women's 200 m Men's 400 m Hurdles Women's 100 m Women's 4x400 m Relay		Women's 400 m Women's 200 m		7
2008	Men's 100 m Men's 200 m Men's 4 x 100m Relay Women's 100 m Women's 200 m Women's 4 x 400m Relay Women's 400 m Women's 400 m hurdles		Men's 4x100 m relay Men's triple jump	Men's 100 m Men's 4 x 100 m relay	15

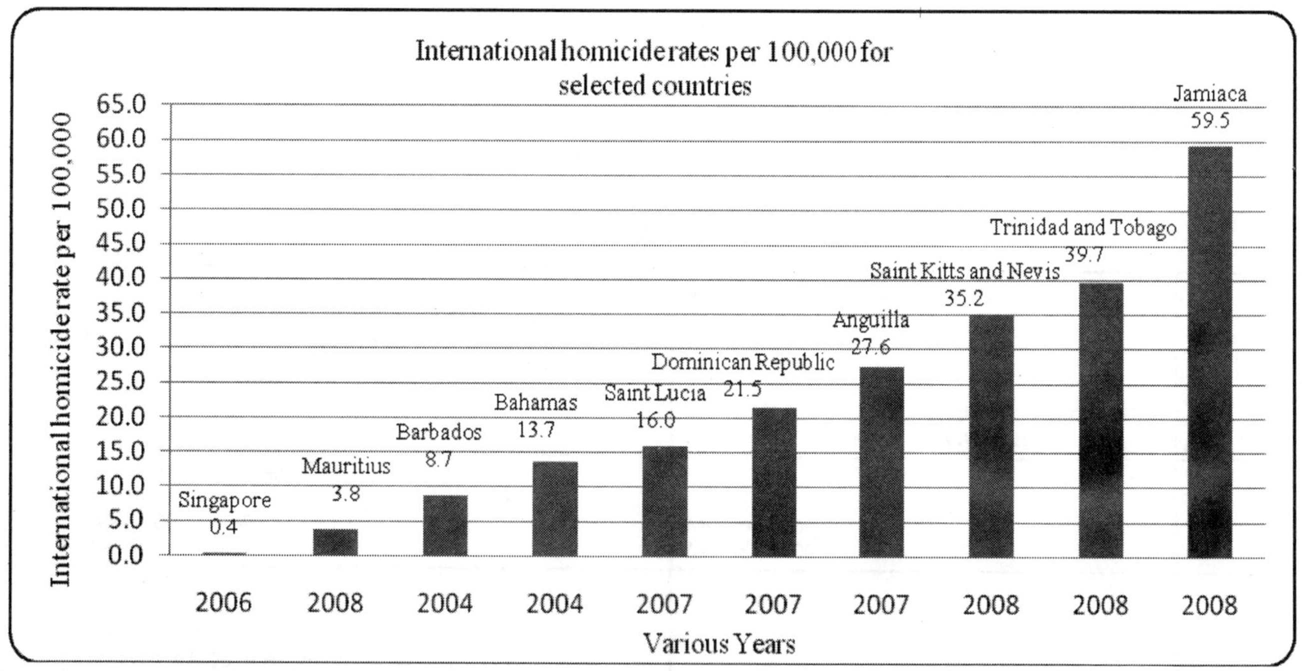

Figure 11.2: Intentional Homicide Rate per year per 100,000 Inhabitants, 2008

Source: United Nations Office on Drugs and Crime (2010).

Appendix 2

Technical Notes

The Balassa index as utilized by Tscha and Pershin (2003) adapted for our purposes can be represented as illustrated in the formulation below:

$$R_{ij} = \frac{M_{ij}/M_i}{T_j/T}$$

where

M_i : amount of medals won by country i,
M_{ij} : Country's i medal in sports j,
T_j : the number of medals won in sport j,
T : total number of medals won at the Olympics.

The numerator M_{ij}/M_i shows the amount of medals in say athletics that country i wins as a proportion of the total amount of medals won by country i.

The Balassa index (BI) has a theoretical range from 0 to infinity and is based on post-trade and not on pre-trade data. This range of the index can be divided into two substantive groups:

$0<RCA<1$ – comparative advantage class,
$1<RCA<\text{infinity}$ – comparative disadvantage class.

Hinloopen and Marrewijk (2001) further divided Balassa's revealed comparative advantage index into four categories, (see Table below).

RCA classifications		
Class a	0 < RCA < 1	Industries with a comparative disadvantage
Class b	1< RCA < 2	Industries with weak comparative advantage
Class c	2 < RCA < 4	Medium comparative advantage
Class d	4 < RCA	Strong comparative advantage

Appendix 3

Athlete	Nation	Sport	Years	Sex	Gold	Silver	Bronze	Total
Phelps, Michael	United States	Swimming	2004-2008	M	14	0	2	16
Latynina, Larissa	Soviet Union	Gymnastics	1956-1964	F	9	5	4	18
Nurmi, Paavo	Finland	Athletics	1920-1928	M	9	3	0	12
Spitz, Mark	United States	Swimming	1968-1972	M	9	1	1	11
Lewis, Carl	United States	Athletics	1984-1996	M	9	1	0	10
Fischer, Birgit	Germany	Canoeing	1980-2004	F	8	4	0	12
Kato, Sawao	Japan	Gymnastics	1968-1976	M	8	3	1	12
Thompson, Jenny	United States	Swimming	1992-2004	F	8	3	1	12
Biondi, Matt	United States	Swimming	1984-1992	M	8	2	1	11
Ewry, Ray	United States	Athletics	1900-1908	M	8	0	0	8
Andrianov, Nikolay	Soviet Union	Gymnastics	1972-1980	M	7	5	3	15
Shakhlin, Boris	Soviet Union	Gymnastics	1956-1964	M	7	4	2	13
Čáslavská, Věra	Czechoslovakia	Gymnastics	1960-1968	F	7	4	0	11
Chukarin, Viktor	Soviet Union	Gymnastics	1952-1956	M	7	3	1	11
Gerevich, Aladár	Hungary	Fencing	1932-1960	M	7	1	2	10
Mangiarotti, Edoardo	Italy	Fencing	1936-1960	M	6	5	2	13
Van Innis, Hubert	Belgium	Archery	1900-1920	M	6	3	0	9
Nakayama, Akinori	Japan	Gymnastics	1968-1972	M	6	2	2	10
Fredriksson, Gert	Sweden	Canoeing	1948-1960	M	6	1	1	8
Scherbo, Vitaly	Belarus	Gymnastics	1992-1996	M	6	0	4	10

Notes

1. 2005 was declared as the International Year of Sports and physical education. In this year the international community unanimously agreed on the role of sports as a peace keeping factor (Kvalsund 2006).
2. As early as 1952, Jamaica was placed 13th amongst the medal winners in the Helsinki Olympics ranking them above their colonizer, Great Britain. In 1950, the WI beat England for the first time in test cricket and these events would have helped the region's sense of belief in their quest for independence.
3. According to a China Daily report (6 September 2008) the Beijing Olympics attracted over 4.7 billion TV viewers. For the 2007 World Cup Cricket tournament, however, the number of television viewers was estimated to be about 2.2 billion as compared to the Football World Cup which drew the attention of 715.1m viewers. This establishes the international reach of the Olympics tournament.
4. In 1976 Nazi Germany made the games a point of national focus. The Cold War also affected the games with the USA boycotting the games in 1980 and other Communist nations boycotting the games in 1984.
5. The winter games are not considered in this study because it draws on a smaller set of countries with less intense competition.
6. The model these authors used is outlined as:

$$1n \;\; M_t = \alpha_0 + \alpha_1 \;\; 1npop_t \; + \; \alpha_2 \;\; 1ngdppc_t + \\ \alpha_3 \;\; 1nmedal04_t + \alpha_4 \;\; \ln literacy_t + \\ \alpha_5 Host + \alpha_6 C_t + e_t$$

   Where: ln Mt = Log of the medal count, lnpopt = Log of the population, lngdppct = Log of the GDP per capita, ln medal04t = medal count in 2004, lnliteracyt = Log of Literacy, Host = Host country, Ct = Communism, et is a disturbance term and á0 is a constant term.
7. Greenaway and Milner (1993) noted that these indirect methods obviously needed to make assumptions about the relationship between observable and unobservable variables.
8. The Human Development Index (HDI) is a measure for a country's achievement in three basic areas of human development: health, knowledge and standard of living. All countries included in the HDI are classified into one of three clusters of achievement in human development: high human development (with an HDI of 0.800 or above), medium human development (HDI of 0.500–0.799) and low human development (HDI of less than 0.500). On the other hand, the Gender-related Development Index (GDI) measures the same areas as the HDI but focuses more on the inequality in achievement between women and men.

9. A revealed comparative advantage score above one indicates that the country has a comparative advantage while a score below one indicates the country has a comparative disadvantage in the respective sporting discipline (see Appendix 2).
10. Barbados also had an RCA score above one in 2008.
11. Dwight Yorke is a former Trinidad and Tobago national footballer, and also played for Aston Villa, Manchester United, Blackburn Rovers, Birmingham City, Sydney FC and Sunderland.
12. This programme started off under the branding of College of Arts, Science and Technology (CAST). In 1995 CAST was transformed into UTECH and was joined by Steven Francis with his Maximum Velocity Performance Club (MVP). The partnership between UTECH and MVP is strategic. MVP provides coaching to UTECH students and UTECH provides MVP with facilities. The following is a list of outstanding MVP athletes that train at UTECH and were successful in Beijing:
    - Melanie Walker: Olympic 400m hurdles gold medal.
    - Micheal Frater: Olympic 4 x 100m gold medalist.
    - Usain Bolt: triple gold medalist and triple world record holder (also a past student of UTECH).

    Other outstanding UTECH athletes in Beijing were:

    - Asafa Powel: Olympic 4 x 100m gold medalist and former world record-holder for men's 100m.
    - Nesta Carter: Olympic 4x100 gold medalist and UTECH sportsman of the year 2007/08.
    - Shelly Ann Fraser: Olympic 100m gold medalist.
    - Sherone Simpson: Olympic silver medalist for women 100m.
    - Sherick Williams: Olympic 400m silver medalist.
    - Markino Buckley: Olympic finalist in men's 100m hurdles.

    UTECH/MVP athletes comprised more than one fifth (1/5) of Jamaica's Olympic contingent at the games.
13. Johnson, a brilliant sprinter himself, had just returned to his homeland after obtaining a physical education degree from the University of San Jose.
14. Former UN secretary general—noted at the Olympic Aid Roundtable Forum.
15. Adolf Ogi, Special Adviser to the UN Secretary-General on Sport for Development and Peace, former President of Switzerland.
16. Schools in the CARICOM offer physical education programmes with varying degrees of seriousness, with the extent of the commitment dependent on human, financial and physical resources. At both the primary and secondary level the physical education programmes typically exclude an academic content. The addition of Physical Education to the list of CXC subjects means that now there is some flexibility to address the lack of academic content that characterized the physical education programs.

12

Social-Psychological Dimensions of Caribbean Family Life

Sustainable Human Development

Jaipaul L. Roopnarine and *Ambika Krishnakumar*

Improving the living conditions of families and children by attending to factors that enhance their social, psychological, physical, and cultural well-being inevitably translates into multilevel societal gains (Desai, Dubey, Joshi, Sen, Sharrif, and Vannenman 2010). For example, addressing poor parent-child relationships through early intervention programmes has been shown to translate into positive academic and social outcomes in children, placing them on a better developmental trajectory for school success while at the same time reducing potential expenditures tied to school failure and remediation (Engle *et al.* 2007; Wasik *et al.* in press). Yet the importance of family well being for the economic development of low- and middle-income (LAMI) countries is often ignored or underestimated. In this chapter, we build on previous discussions (Roopnarine in press; Roopnarine and Hossain in press; Roopnarine, Evans and Pant 2011) on the social-psychological functioning, cultural processes, and the socio-demographic characteristics of African Caribbean and Indo Caribbean families that have a direct bearing on human development in everyday contexts. After providing a brief account of the socio-historical experiences of African Caribbean and Indo Caribbean families, we focus on three interrelated aspects of family functioning that are deemed pressing for advancing the general welfare of the family in Caribbean countries: parent-child relationships, domestic violence, and mental health. By attending to these familial issues at the societal level, we believe that LAMI Caribbean countries have a greater chance of increasing sustainable social and economic development.

Socio-historical Factors

Researchers within psychological anthropology and cross-cultural psychology (e.g., Ogbu 1984; Greenfield 2000; Sinha 1997) have proposed that in order to fully understand the cultural basis of family relationships, it is necessary to take into account socio-historical experiences and indigenous practices. A continuing challenge for scholars of the Caribbean and Caribbean diasporas has been to determine the effects of socio-historical experiences in shaping patterns of family life. More specifically, debates continue on the enduring influences of slavery and poor economic conditions on current African Caribbean family social-structural organization and functioning patterns (e.g., Barrow 1998; Beckles 1998) and on the maintenance of religious, linguistic, and family practices from India among Indo Caribbeans through the indentureship (1837-1917) and post-indentureship periods (Deen 2005; Reddock 1994).

Divergent theses have been proffered on the influence of slavery on current patterns of social-structural arrangements, family functioning, and socialization practices in African Caribbean families. On the one hand, it is argued that mate-shifting, child-shifting, and low marriage rates witnessed in African Caribbean families today have their origins in the disintegrating effects of slavery on the structural arrangement of the traditional family based on marriage and extended networks (see Nsamenang 2010, for a discussion of African family systems). During slavery, males were marginalized from family life because the offspring born to slaves belonged to the master of the woman slave, and the relationship between parent and child was determined through the mother, disregarding paternal rights (Patterson 1988). It is presumed that this led to a preponderance of the matrifocal family structure, with extended female networks and strong intergenerationl social ties (Frazier 1966; Patterson, 1988; Smith, 1996). On the other hand, some (e.g., Higman 1973) believe instead that slave families were more varied in structural arrangements in a plantation system (e.g., Craton 1979; Higman 1973), reflecting African ancestral patterns of family organization. It is likely that current African Caribbean family social-structural organization and male-female roles are more influenced by difficult economic conditions and men's views about manhood than mainly by socio-historical experiences (Brown, *et al.*, 1997). Nevertheless, one consequence of persistent difficult social and economic circumstances was that marriage became less central to male-female relationships in African Caribbean families over time (Barrow 1998; Brunod and Cook-Darzens 2002).

Just as in slavery, the major goal of indentureship was to obtain cheap labour. Because most indentured servants were men (68%), there was a striking gender imbalance among East Indians in Caribbean countries. Women who came to the Caribbean left India under trying circumstances; most were abandoned by their husbands, unmarried pregnant women, or prostitutes (Reddock 1994). A marriage system was in place, including child marriages, during the indentureship period (Mohammed 1997). But the unfavourable gender ratio, deplorable living conditions in the barracks, and lack of legal recognition of Hindu and Muslim marriages in Guyana and Trinidad and Tobago all had deleterious effects on the social functioning of the traditional Indian family (Barrow, 1998). In a number of cases, competition for mates led to violence toward women, and infidelity and polyandry were not uncommon (Sharma, 1986). By the time indentureship drew to a close in 1917, there were semblances of the traditional East Indian family and this pattern continued as the gender imbalance narrowed considerably in subsequent decades. Ethnographic accounts of Indo Caribbean family life in the 1950s, 1960s, and 1990s suggest that Indo Caribbean family structural and social organization was largely patriarchal, wherein women assumed much of the domestic labour and men managed the affairs outside of the family (Jayawardena 1963; Rauf 1973; Roopnarine *et al.* 1997).

It would be difficult to ignore varying degrees of influence and the integration of ancestral practices in African Caribbean and Indo Caribbean family structural organization and social functioning as we know them today. In both groups of families, extended kinship networks and multiple caregivers are quite evident, and religious beliefs and practices (e.g., Hinduism, Orisha) bear resemblances, integrate, or replicate aspects of those in the ancestral cultures. Beyond these parallels, it is rather onerous to speak of cultural continuity. Yet, the disintegrating effects of slavery on family life cannot be discounted (Frazier 1966; Patterson 1988). Nor can the creolization process that has occurred over time whereby Indo Caribbean and African Caribbean families have made structural, social-cultural, and cognitive adjustments as a result of exposure to each other and other cultural groups in constructing a contemporary understanding of family organization and socialization patterns in different ecological niches. It is perhaps true, as has been argued elsewhere (Roopnarine in press), that a more credible case can be made for the maintenance of religious practices and marital patterns from the ancestral culture among Indo Caribbeans. But significant increases in marital dissolution, cohabiting couples, and nuclear family structures all allude to the changing social dynamics of the Indo Caribbean family (Nevadomsky 1980; Samuel & Wilson 2009)

Parent-Child Relationships

Across the developing world, there are stepped up efforts to sharpen parenting practices with the expectation of enhancing parent-child relationships and child development outcomes. This is a particularly salient issue for Caribbean countries given harsh parenting practices and shifting of parental figures. The trust and security children develop emanate from consistent, predictable, and warm parent-child encounters which set the stage for the development of healthy relationships with peers and later on romantic partners (Bosmans, Braet, *et al.* 2011; Brenning, Soenens, Braet, Bosmans 2011; Thornberry 2005). In other words, one's developmental history within one's own family is a good predictor of parenting practices and mental health (Dutton 2007). Equally important is the role of the father or father figure in the development of stable family relationships (see Lamb 2010).

There is a voluminous body of work, consisting of studies from different regions of the world (e.g., Finland, China, United States, and Canada) on the importance of sensitively-attuned parent-child relationships for the development of social and cognitive skills in children from infancy through the adolescent years (see Sorkhabi 2005 for a review). Both normative and intervention studies have pointed to the connections between authoritative, democratic modes of parenting (parental warmth and responsiveness, consistency, moderate levels of control, guidance through explanations, realistic expectations, etc.,) and social competence and cognitive skills in children (see Baumrind 1967 for definitions of parenting styles). For example, an authoritative parenting style is associated with higher academic achievement in European

American children (Chao 2001) and social competence in Chinese children (Chen *et al.* 2001). By contrast, an authoritarian parenting style (autocratic, high levels of control, low levels of warmth) is associated with negative language outcomes in preschool-aged children of English-speaking Caribbean immigrants residing in the New York City area of the United States, and high psychological control has been shown to contribute to behavioural difficulties in kindergarten-age Finnish children (Anoula & Nurmi 2005).

Of relevance here are the parenting styles of African Caribbean and Indo Caribbean families and their associations with childhood development. Both Indo Caribbean and African Caribbean families use an admixture of warmth and high levels of rule setting and controlling behaviours during parenting. Factor analysis performed on the responses provided on the Ghent Parental Behaviour Scale by a national representative sample of families (N=1504) in Trinidad and Tobago support the seemingly inconsistent pattern of parenting behaviours of Caribbean families: warmth, autonomy, material reward, harsh discipline, positive parenting, and ignoring behaviour (Roopnarine & Krishnakumar 2011). Further, cluster analyses conducted on data gathered on the parenting practices of low-income Indo Caribbean families in a rural area of Guyana (N=139) and a sample of families from different ethnic groups and socio-economic backgrounds in Trinidad (N=180) showed that parents displayed high levels of warmth along with high levels of behavioural control and moderate levels of harshness (Roopnarine & Krishnakumar 2010).

The high level of par :ntal nurturance displayed through warmth is ideal for enhancing intellectual and social skill development in children. At the same time, the prevalence of harsh parenting in the context of warmth is rather worrisome. Harsh discipline (hitting with an object, slapping, pulling etc.) and verbal insults and threats (e.g., "hardened" or stubborn in Trinidad and *A-betant* or troublesome in Dominica) are strongly embraced by Caribbean parents (Duburow 1999), and high levels of physical punishment have been recorded for adults in Barbados (Handwerker 1996), Guyana (Pant *et al.* 2007), and St. Kitts (Rohner *et al.* 2001). Within the Caribbean and in other cultural settings, physical punishment and harsh parenting in general are linked to internalizing (e.g., depression; withdrawn behaviour, somatic complaints) and externalizing behavioural problems (e.g., aggression, delinquency) (Achenbach 2004; Berlin *et al.* 2009; Davies, Harold, Goeke-Morey, Cummings 2002; Lansford *et al.*

2005; McLoyd *et al.* 2007; Rohner *et al.* 2001; Roopnarine and Krishnakumar 2010).

Adding to the complexity of Caribbean parenting practices is the impact of paternal instability on family socialization processes and on social and academic development in children. As has been described by social scientists (e.g., Anderson 2007; Brown *et al.* 1997; Smith 1996), mate-shifting is a common life-course practice among African Caribbean families. That is, men and women start having children in visiting unions, then move on to common-law unions before getting married. In the course of these mating relationships, men acquire several "baby mothers" and women several "baby fathers" (Anderson 2007; Brown *et al.* 1997; Chevannes 2001). There are two inherent problems with mate-shifting: many children have limited or no social contacts with fathers (Anderson 2007) and children may be hesitant to form close emotional bonds with temporary male or female caregivers who are expected to move on to other mating relationships or to find employment elsewhere in Caribbean countries or North America and Europe.

Although the practice of mate-shifting is normative in Caribbean countries, there are attendant psychological risks associated with paternal and maternal instability. These risks are compounded by meager economic resources and bleak prospects for employment. Evidence from a study conducted in Jamaica (Samms-Vaughan 2005) showed that preschool-aged children who lived with poor material resources and whose parents were in unskilled jobs had lower cognitive scores than their peers who lived under better economic circumstances. Among these families, there were significant associations between family functioning (cohesion and adaptability) and children's receptive vocabulary scores, and between paternal and maternal education and intellectual performance in children. As in some other cultural settings (e.g., US, see Roopnarine and Hossain in press), children in married households performed better academically and had better cognitive scores than children in non-legal unions. Mate-shifting by father figures was associated with internalizing behaviours in children, and children who had multiple father figures showed more withdrawn behaviours; children who lived with biological fathers and surrogate mothers also had academic and social difficulties (Samms-Vaughan 2005).

These findings underscore the importance of economic and social stability within Caribbean families as protective factors in fostering optimal childhood development. On the economic side, labour market fluctuations affected Caribbean men's satisfaction with their role as fathers and those from the lowest income levels were the most likely to have several baby mothers and more children, and to use violence during partner conflicts (Anderson 2007). Turning to family stability, cohesion and adaptation contributed to more favourable outcomes in children and so did sustained father presence. It appears that children who lived with multiple parental figures, be they maternal or paternal, seem to accrue greater psychological and academic risks and these risks become exacerbated as children progress from preschool to grade school (Samms-Vaughan 2005). In Caribbean countries where men struggle with gender mistrust and anoint traditional patriarchal roles, partner/spousal conflicts and violence within families can only add to the already heavy toll poor economic conditions and inadequate parenting exert on the mental health of individual family members. Next, we expand our focus on family-related concerns in our discussion of the chronic problems of child maltreatment and family violence in Caribbean countries.

Family Violence

In as much as families provide individual members with an enriching environment for fostering healthy development, they are sometimes confronted by abusive and oppressive interpersonal relationships. In particular, family violence that includes a range of coercive, neglectful, and emotionally manipulative behaviours perpetuated by members to exert power and control over others (Randle & Graham 2011) can engender feelings of social isolation, powerlessness, and humiliation. Research on the multiple expressions or dimensions of family violence has mostly focused on issues related to violence between heterosexual and same-sex partners living in intimate settings (Intimate Partner Violence), child maltreatment, and elder abuse. Needless to say, different forms of violence within Caribbean families have serious implications for individual mental health and physical safety.

Child Maltreatment

As stated earlier, both small-scale (Rohner, *et al.* 2001) and comparative country-wide studies (UNICEF-Multiple Indicator Cluster Survey) suggest there is strong cultural acceptance of physical punishment (giving "licks" to correct "wicked" and "hardened" children) and psychological aggression toward children (e.g., threats, insults, humiliation) as desirable methods of discipline in Caribbean countries (Samms-Vaughan 2005). As can be gleaned from Figure 12.1, most children across Caribbean countries have been exposed to at least one incident of violent discipline. Incidents of verbal, sexual, and emotional abuse, abandonment, and neglect vary across Caribbean countries (UN Secretary General's Report on Violence Against Children in the Caribbean: Regional Assessment 2006). Boys experience higher levels of physical abuse and are more likely to be abandoned (61.4% versus 38.6%) (Sargent and Harris 1992) than girls who are more likely to experience sexual abuse. Rates of sexual abuse were higher in Jamaica and Dominica, whereas neglect was higher in Grenada, Belize, and Barbados compared to other Caribbean countries.

Sadly, a significant number of children in the Caribbean not only witness violence in their families but are also victims of family, community, and school violence (Samms-Vaughan, 2011; Soyibo & Lee 2000). With high homicide rates in some parts of the Caribbean (e.g., Trinidad and Tobago, Jamaica, and Guyana), children are likely to know individuals who are victims of violence. Samms-Vaughan (2005) reported that 38.4 per cent of young

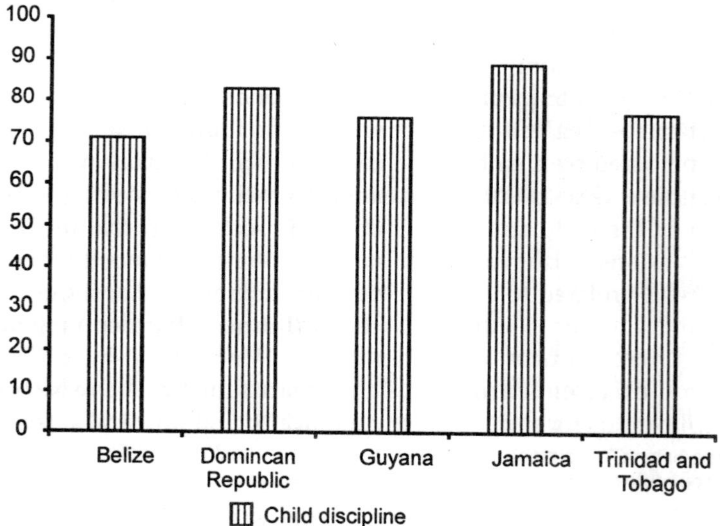

Source: http://www.childinfo.org

Figure 12.1: Percentage of children aged 2-14 who experience any form of violent discipline (2005-2008)

Jamaican children had seen a dead body, 24.5 per cent had seen someone shot, 70.4 per cent had seen someone beaten up, and 30.8 per cent witnessed adults hitting each other in their homes. About a third of the children in the sample were beaten up. Experiences with violence were similar for boys and girls. Children with more material resources witnessed fewer episodes of violence and had more positive experiences overall, but had more personal experiences with violence than those with fewer material resources. The latter may indicate a trend for Jamaican children who are better off economically to be bullied more than those with less material resources (Samms-Vaughan 2005).

Parental drug and alcohol use, parental migration, and limited knowledge about the nature and consequences of abuse and neglect are all possible reasons for the high levels of child maltreatment in the Caribbean. Often, different forms of maltreatment of children are considered a family matter and go largely unreported and untreated. In these situations, children become silent sufferers. The effects of child maltreatment are well established. Parental neglect, perhaps the most common form of maltreatment, is related to problems in interpersonal relationships, speech and language disorders, intellectual problems, and mental health (Arnold, 1997; Culp *et al.*, 1991; Eckenrode, Laird and Doris 1993; Edwards *et al.* 2003; Garno, *et al.* 2005; Kim-Cohen *et al.* 2006; Melancon and Gagne 2011), and the negative consequences of harsh/violent discipline on children's social competence and adjustment have been laid out (Gershoff 2003).

Intimate Partner Violence (IPV)

In view of the diverse nature of family arrangements in Caribbean countries, intimate partners include couples in married, common-law, dating, and visiting relationships. Former partners and ex-spouses are also considered as part of the intimate partner network. The frequency and severity of IPV rates are generally high throughout the Caribbean, and the proportion of women who experience violence varies across nations. For example, up to 30 per cent of women in the British Virgin Islands and Barbados and 15 per cent of women in Dominica experienced physical violence. Half the men in Jamaica report having abused their wives—a society in which a significant number of domestic violence cases result in murder. In a recent nationally representative study of 1504 parents in Trinidad and Tobago, it was discovered that IPV (various forms of physical, psychological, and verbal abuse) was mostly perpetuated by men on women (Narine 2011). And, it appears that protection orders have had limited effect in lowering the hazards of repeated abuse in the Caribbean. In Barbados, where protective order provisions were implemented in 1992, the rates of domestic violence are comparable to those in St. Kitts where there are no protective order provisions (Spooner 2009).

It has been postulated that historical, cultural, and ecological factors are tied to the high rates of IPV in the Caribbean. Among them are: (a) the colonial history of slavery, indentured labour, and harsh life on the plantations (not all Caribbean nations share this history); (b) the culture of drugs, drug related crimes and violence; (c) ethnic and political violence; (d) economic inequality and poverty; (e) patriarchal traditions and religious and cultural prescriptions regarding the roles of men and women; (f) undeveloped economies with poor or limited infrastructure; and (g) in and out migration. In many Caribbean countries there is a sanctioning and justification of IPV by women (including adolescent girls) particularly in Haiti and Guyana. Data collected by UNICEF through the Multiple Indicator Cluster Survey (MICS) programme indicate that women and adolescents (male and female) justify physical violence by men toward women. Women (15-49 years) and adolescents (15-19 years) believed it was justified for a spouse to hit or beat his wife under certain circumstances: (1) if she went out without telling him, (2) if she neglected the children, (3) if she argued with him, (4) if she refused to have sex with him, (5) if she burnt the food (see Figure 12.2).

Exposure to family violence in childhood (witnessing or experiencing) and subsequent violent behaviour enacted towards intimate partners has received mixed support in the research literature (Beckles 1996; Heyman and Slep 2002; Kalmusss 1984; Stith *et al.* 2000). Put differently, the modeling of violent behaviour across generations may be a contributing factor in IPV. But issues of unemployment, underemployment, and over-employment and power inequities in gendered-relations have all been linked to IPV. Women in both high and low end jobs are susceptible to IPV. Viewed within the context of intergenerational history of violence, acceptance of violence, and inequities in gender relations at home and in the society at large, women in minimum wage jobs (e.g., seasonal, unstable work in the domestic and informal sectors) are not in economically advantageous power-relations situation in their homes. Nor are women in high earning power professions/jobs.

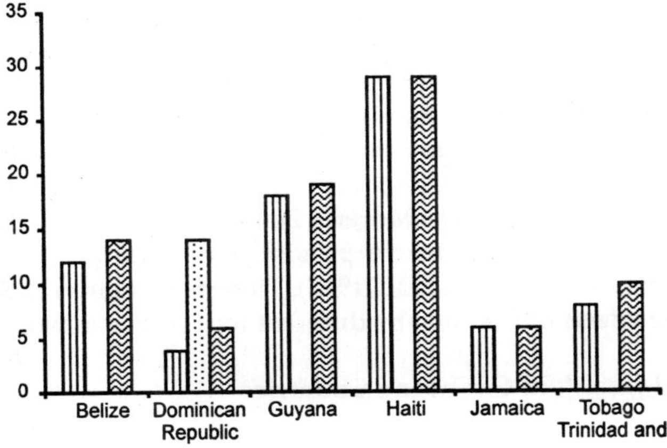

- Women's attitudes towards domestic violence(15-49 years)
- Male adolescents attitudes towards domestic violence (15-19years)
- Female adolescents attitudes towards domestic violence (15-19 years)

Source: http://www.childinfo.org

Figure 12.2: Percentage of Caribbeans who think that a husband/partner is justified in hitting or beating his wife/partner under certain circumstances (2002-2009)

Because there has been disproportionate research focus on the prevalence of IPV in different Caribbean countries, few investigations have focused on the multidimensional nature of IPV to include the co-occurrence of physical, verbal, sexual, emotional, psychological, and financial threats and behaviours in intimate relationships or the nature, causes, and outcomes of IPV (Centers for Diseases Control and Prevention 2009; World Health Organization 2002). There is a need to focus on the frequency, severity, and duration of IPV, on IPV perpetuated by women against men (in addition to male-perpetuated violence), and on the bi-directionality of IPV in couple relationships in different family structural configurations (see Randle & Graham, 2011). Despite the lack of outcome data, findings on IPV from other cultural settings can inform us about its potential impact on families in the Caribbean. The short and long-term negative effects of IPV/domestic violence on women's mental and physical health across ethnic/cultural groups are very clear (Bonomi *et al.* 2007; Mouton 2003). For instance, a World Health Organization (WHO) multi-site study (e.g., Brazil, Thailand, Peru, Japan, Ethiopia,

Serbia, Namibia, Samoa, Tanzania showed that women with a lifetime of experience with physical and sexual violence were more likely to report poor or very poor health and were more likely to report pain, problems with walking, memory loss, dizziness, and vaginal discharge, and to have thoughts of ending their lives or attempted on one or more occasions to do so (Ellsberg, Jansen, Heise, Watt, and Garcia-Moreno 2008). The effects of IPV on Australian women seem to persist over time (see Roberts, Lawrence, Roberts & Raphael 1998). There is no reason to believe that the effects of IPV are any different for Caribbean women.

Mental Health in Caribbean Countries

Mental health difficulties are multi-modal and encompass a wide range of issues at the societal (e.g., treatment facilities, trained personnel, attitudes toward the mentally ill, awareness of mental health difficulties in population), individual (e.g., coping and adaptation, developmental history, individual rights, response to medications and behavioural therapies), and intra-familial levels (e.g., social support, stressors, material resources, family history, advocacy). Because of the lack of adequate mental health services and policies (only 35% of Caribbean countries have a mental health policy), low expenditures for mental health services, inadequate numbers of trained personnel, and ignorance surrounding mental health disorders across Caribbean countries and territories, many individuals afflicted with mental and social disorders go untreated or are isolated at home and in health facilities (WHO-AIMS Report on Mental Health Systems in the Caribbean 2011). Moreover, prevalence studies of mental health disorders and symptoms in adults and children in Caribbean countries are rather rare. In this segment of the chapter, we piece together a synopsis of what is known about mental health within families in Caribbean countries from a few published studies and our own emerging work in this area.

Some Caribbean psychiatrists (Sharpe & Mohammed in press) have intimated that the prevalence of mental health disorders in Caribbean children is similar to those of children in other parts of the world. It is estimated that between 10 and 20 per cent of Caribbean children will need mental health services (Milburn, Sharpe, Samms-Vaughan 2005; see also Belfer & Rohde 2005 for a discussion of prevalence rates in Latin America and Caribbean). But greater behavioural difficulties (above 98th percentile) have been assessed in Jamaican children compared to children in the United States (Samms-Vaughan 2005). Jamaican parents reported more behaviour problems across individual syndromes (with the exception of anxiety/depression) on a modified version of the Child Behaviour Checklist (CBCL) for boys than girls. According to parental assessments, Jamaican children had more behavioural difficulties on all syndromes, with the exception of anxiety/ depression and thought disorder, than children in the United States. Teachers' reports indicated higher behaviour problem scores for girls in withdrawn behaviour, somatic complaints, and attention problems, and higher behaviour problem scores for boys in thought disorders, delinquency, and aggression.

Social difficulties in the early childhood years often stem from the disruption of attachment relationships due to mate-shifting, child-shifting, and migration, child abuse and neglect, violence in families, schools, and the community, poverty and neighborhood quality, malnutrition, parental substance abuse (high levels of alcohol use in some countries), and poor parenting skills and practices (Samms-Vaughan 2005; Sharpe & Mohammed in press). In low-income Caribbean families, parental education, family income, parenting support systems (e.g., multiple caregivers, church), and family stability (cohesion, adaptation) are primary protective factors in attenuating risks for mental health problems during early childhood and adolescence.

In an extensive survey of the mental health of 15,695 children (10-18 years; 78.5 per cent African Caribbean, 6.5 per cent East Indians) from 9 Caribbean countries (Antigua, Bahamas, Barbados, British Virgin Islands, Dominica, Grenada, Guyana, Jamaica, and St. Lucia), Halcon *et al.* (2003) found that 83.4 per cent of the respondents saw themselves as happy, whereas 16.6 per cent saw themselves as angry, sad, or irritable. Despite the high level of happiness, 15 per cent of children experienced severe distress. Roughly 16 per cent of the children indicated that they were physically abused, 10 per cent said they were sexually abused, 12.1 per cent had attempted suicide, and 10.5 per cent had been in a fight in which a weapon was used. Boys were far more likely to attempt suicide than girls. Of children who attempted suicide, 28.9 per cent had experienced both physical and sexual abuse. Other risk factors associated with attempting suicide were: parents' and friends' history of suicide and rage. Not surprisingly, rage contributed to involvement in violence. Connectedness to parents was a significant protective factor against attempting suicide, rage, and involvement in violence (Blum *et al.* 2003). In other work in Caribbean cultural communities, the quality of parent-child relationships was linked to better social and cognitive outcomes in children (Samms-Vaughan 2005; Roopnarine & Krishnakumar 2010).

Among adults, schizophrenia was the most prevalent disorder reported at outpatient clinics followed by mood disorders in sixteen Caribbean countries. Similarly, in general and mental health hospitals schizophrenia was again the most common diagnosis followed by substance abuse (WHO-AIMS Report on Mental Health Systems in the Caribbean 2011). Socioeconomic and gender differences have been noted in assessments of mental health functioning in some countries. Using the Brief Symptom Inventory (BSI), Samms-Vaughan (2005) found that Jamaican families with more material possessions scored higher on agoraphobia (fear of being outdoors) than those with fewer possessions and scored lower on hostility, somatic complaints, and mild depression, and Roopnarine and Krishnakumar (2011) reported that men experienced higher levels of anxiety and phobic anxiety and displayed less interpersonal sensitivity than women in Trinidad and Tobago. Assessments carried out on a multi-ethnic sample in Guyana revealed that a staggering 80 per cent of respondents indicated some dissatisfaction with their life circumstances. In spite of their dissatisfaction, 93 per cent of respondents had scores below the midpoint on the Center for Epidemiological Studies Depression Subscale (CES-D). However, Indo Guyanese were far more likely to be represented in the higher quartiles of depression (between the median and 75th percentile) than Afro-Guyanese or Guyanese from mixed-ethnic parentage. Level of educational attainment did influence mental health outcomes across all groups (Wilson, Wilson, & Johnson 2010).

It has repeatedly been demonstrated that parental mental health (e.g., depression) influences the quality of parenting and has direct and indirect effects on childhood adjustment and functioning in the technologically developed world (Treyvaud, *et al.* 2010). Attempts to systematically assess the relationships between mental health and parenting practices and childhood development in the Caribbean are only now beginning to take shape. Among Jamaican parents, somatic complaints, paranoia, hostility, minor depression, major depression, and agoraphobia were all significantly correlated with internalizing (coefficients range from .36 to .41) and externalizing behaviours (coefficients range from .29 to .36) in children. Life stress (e.g. parenting stress) was also significantly associated with internalizing and externalizing behaviours in children (Samms-Vaughan 2005). Similarly, parental mental health as measured by the BSI was correlated with parenting practices and with preschool-age children's cognitive and social functioning in a representative sample of families in Trinidad and Tobago (Roopnarine & Krishnakumar 2011).

This brief overview does not begin to capture the levels of complexity involved in addressing mental health issues in Caribbean countries. Poverty, neighborhood and household violence, parenting stress, life course events (e.g., divorce, death of a family member), level of social support, unstable living arrangements, and separation due to migration, among several other intrapersonal and interpersonal factors can influence individual mental health. The challenge for Caribbean countries is to build a viable mental health infrastructure that can meet the needs of families and children. From the small literature just reviewed, domestic violence/inter-partner violence, hostile/harsh parenting practices, and childhood difficulties would appear to need the most immediate attention.

Implications for Sustained Human Development

It has often been stated that the family is a strong pillar of society. Before Caribbean nations can more fully realize their economic, social, and intellectual potential, it is perhaps first necessary to rid themselves of the scourge of violence both within the home and in society at large, address optimal parenting, and improve the mental health delivery systems. We chose to discuss these three social and psychologically-based issues because of their far-reaching implications for individual and interpersonal functioning within the family and because they have carryover effects to employment situations and community relations. It is our contention that social, educational, and economic policies that are family- and child-centered with an emphasis on human dignity, social justice, human rights, and respect for different family configurations (see Dominelli 2007) can do much to enhance the development of human and social capital and, in turn, overall productivity in Caribbean societies. Accordingly, the following may assist in further shaping sustainable human development across Caribbean countries:

(a) Eradicating the harsh treatment of children through legislation and effective parenting programmes that are developmentally- and culturally-appropriate. Parenting programmes have demonstrated social and educational benefits to children and their caregivers (Roopnarine, 2005; Spijk, Rosemberg, & Janssens, 2008; Wasik *et al.*, in press) and have calculated cost-benefit to society in terms of better educational returns, less delinquency, and lower teenage pregnancy rates (Cunningham, Bremner, & Boyle 1995; Reynolds, Temple, Robertson, & Mann 2002; Wasik *et al.* in press).

(b) Because so many children are born in non-legal unions in Caribbean countries and children have multiple caregivers, it makes little sense to hold fathers against the two-parent norm in childrearing. As such, there is no single formula for responsible fatherhood. Father involvement initiatives in Caribbean countries should entail improving economic opportunities for men, the establishment of paternity (biologically declared father at birth or soon after), responsible fatherhood educational and parent training programmes that target young fathers, improving inter-partner relationships, and child support. These initiatives have been shown to strengthen relationships within families and improve the life chances of children (see O'Brien 2010 for a review).

(c) Address family violence head-on by improving knowledge and cooperation through partnerships with the legal and police systems, community agencies, and public health/healthcare systems to offer maximum protection and support to victims (including children) of domestic/ IPV; by conducting systematic public campaigns to increase awareness of violence among family members and their communities and to change internal working models about domestic violence/IPV (note the high endorsement of domestic violence within Caribbean families); and by improving treatment programmes for perpetrators.

(d) Promote awareness of mental health issues at the societal and family levels through public (e.g., Ministry of Health, Hospitals, Social Service Agencies, Churches) and private initiatives. The focus should be on early screening, diagnosis, and treatment (behavioural and cognitive therapies and medications). This relies on the availability of trained personnel at all levels of the mental health and health care systems (e.g., psychiatric nurses, home visiting nurses, social workers, counseling psychologists, drug counselors, psychiatrists) and access to outpatient and mental health facilities. It is quite disturbing that a primary modality for the treatment of mental illness in the Caribbean is isolation and restraint (WHO-AIMS Report 2011).

By steering resources toward families and children, Caribbean countries will not only be investing in human capital and developing a skilled and healthy workforce, they are essentially laying the foundation for individuals to invest in building solid families, communities, and social, cultural, intellectual, and economic institutions. This is sorely needed in Caribbean nations that have low educational attainment among the citizenry while facing soaring crime rates.

13

Forging a New Ontology of Familial Care in the Caribbean*

Linden Lewis

The time could not be more urgent than the present for establishing a new social contract between men and women. Changing global economic conditions, new political configurations, sustained challenges to patriarchy worldwide, increasing empowerment of women, and new patterns of public discourse have all combined to forge new social relations between men and women. A new social contract would suggest different terms and conditions of social intercourse. We must, in other words, find new ways of relating to each other. The old ways have outlived their usefulness. New challenges demand new patterns of behaviour, new arrangements for living and social reproduction, and new ways of thinking about the sharing of responsibilities and about caring for each other and families.

At this historical conjuncture, the Caribbean faces some very serious challenges. According to the annual report of the Caribbean Development Bank (CDB) for 2010, the economic conditions of the region are not the most encouraging. Despite some relief from the global economic crisis, the Caribbean area's main sources of

---

* An earlier version of this chapter was presented to the United Nations Division for the Advancement of Women Expert Group Meeting on "The equal sharing of responsibilities between women and men, including care-giving in the context of HIV/AIDS" Geneva, Switzerland, 6-9 October 2008. This paper was also presented to the international and interdisciplinary seminar, 'Masculinités en Développement, Université de Toulouse-Le Mirail, Thursday, May 20, 2011.

revenue have remained sluggish, especially so in sectors such as tourism, agriculture, employment and manufacturing. Available information indicates that the fallout from the global recession in terms of employment, wages and other aspects of the regional labour market has been severe (Caribbean Development Bank 2011, 9). Unemployment rates vary in the Caribbean, for example in St. Kitts and Nevis the rate is 5.1 per cent, while in Barbados it is 8.1 per cent. However while in Guyana unemployment is 11.8 per cent, and in Jamaica it is 11.4 per cent, in the Dominican Republic unemployment is 14.28 per cent, and in St. Vincent and the Grenadines unemployment is at a staggering level of 20.2 per cent (World Bank 2011). Added to these statistics is the fact that growth is only expected to be 1.9 per cent of Gross Domestic Product for 2011, and there is also a growing debt problem for most Caribbean countries.

Beyond these economic indicators is the playing out of the grim tragedy of the impact of HIV/AIDS in the region. For example, prevention programmes have not significantly halted the spread of the disease (UNAIDS 2010, IV). High infection levels have persisted in certain populations, such as in the case of sex workers: 4 per cent in the Dominican Republic, 9 per cent in Jamaica and 27 per cent in Guyana, according to UNAIDS Factsheet. Another group, which is vulnerable to a high incidence of HIV infection, is that of men who have sex with other men. In addition, infected drug users who share needles also transmit HIV/AIDS in the Caribbean. In Puerto Rico 40 per cent of new HIV cases in 2006 were the result of contaminated drug paraphernalia (UNAIDS Fact sheet: Caribbean, November 23, 2010, http://www.unaids.org/documents/20101123_FS_carib_em_en.pdf). As the UNAIDS Report of 2010 indicated, the majority of persons in these populations are not being reached through the current prevention efforts. This fact is part of a very disturbing trend in the region.

The urgency of the need for change cannot be overstated here. As is well known, change is always potentially a vexed question. Furthermore, apprehension about the nature and scope of change tends to add complexity as well as resistance to people's fears. Few would argue against the claim of the gendered nature of the business of provision of care in general. Providing care for the elderly, the young, the sick or the disabled, has long been a critical but neglected dimension of our understanding of the phenomenon of labour. Care is not normally part of the calculus of capital[1] and labour, except in those circumstances where it is rendered as a service outside of the domestic unit, and remunerated accordingly. Productive labour is that which is employed by capital. The labour of care is in this sense considered unproductive in a capitalist context and not valued highly. To emphasize the labour of care therefore is to disturb the relations between capital and labour, which operate differently within capitalism (Gulli 2010). Caring has largely been considered central to the activity of women, but given its marginal status within the process of the reproduction of labour, it has also been undervalued, unrecognized and often under-appreciated. As Makhijani (2004, 92) argues:

> The total discounting of non-monetized work, which is largely the work of women, is a major political as well as an economic problem. These inequalities are indicators of an undemocratic economic system in which the economically weak have no representation in the marketplace. That economic weakness translates into political weakness and often into effective deprivation of political representation.

The issues then of representation and democracy are all packaged with the practice of equal sharing of responsibility between men and women. "Caring labour is a particularly important kind of work because it has a direct effect on our emotional well-being" (Folbre 2001, xii).

It stands to reason that a call for equal sharing of responsibility between men and women presupposes an unequal distribution of power, privilege and valued resources, namely access to credit, to state apparatuses, to key decision making processes, and to opportunities for advancement. If many men are not as involved in assuming their share of responsibility for domestic chores, for caring of the sick and the elderly, or for child care, it would seem to suggest that men's social and economic positions, their control over valued resources, and their capacity to determine their own destinies and the destinies of others, play a significant part in whether or not they take any responsibility for sharing household tasks. In most societies, men's earning power, their political and social status, along with cultural understandings about appropriate roles, give them a degree of autonomy that affords them leverage over which responsibilities to undertake, which to ignore, and which confirm or, in their opinions, undermine their roles as men. Though clearly not all men possess this material base of power, even in its absence, it is not unusual for men to behave as though they do, or to have some expectation of entitlement about what responsibilities they would assume, and which they think are not part of their charge but that of their wives or women and girls in their families.

There are some other issues to be addressed with respect to this asymmetry of power between men and women. Promoting equal sharing of power cannot be realized until we develop a new understanding of power; this means establishing new modalities of power. We cannot expect to usher in a new dispensation of sharing of responsibilities without rethinking the ways power is exercised and experienced in social relationships in society. Within the current system, power for the most part is exercised as an agent of domination and oppression. To realize any type of change of this practice, power has to be unhinged from domination and subjection, and placed in a transformative trajectory that ultimately leads to its humanization. The question then arises as to whether this transformation of power is possible within the context of global capitalism, as we understand capitalism today, or whether we have to envision some alternative system that might be more compatible with such an objective. This issue then is a political question that can only be answered by reference to the specific social, economic and cultural contexts in which it is posed.

The importance of understanding power in this context, however, not only has implications for equal sharing of responsibility between men and women, but very significantly, it also reveals how men interact with, express respect for, or dominate other men of different classes, races, religions and sexual orientations. The point to note here is that deconstructing the way power is organized and practiced can also yield some insight into how men behave towards each other, which is a critical component of the social relationships between men and women, and by extension between boys and girls, especially since the examples of the adults inform the future behaviour of the youth of today. In order to change the unequal sharing of responsibilities, it is necessary to challenge the foundation of patriarchal power at all levels.

As mentioned before, not all men are in positions of power and privilege, but even those men with diminished capacity for fulfilling traditional male roles owing to unemployment or other obstacles may still benefit from the patriarchal dividend. There is some realization that despite all the onslaughts on patriarchy by women, feminists and progressive men, as an ideology it retains a remarkable resilience that continues to authorize certain types of male behaviour, which transcend race, class, and nationality. In short, we should not lose sight of the fact that a discussion about sharing responsibilities between men and women is a discourse on power, how roles are negotiated, and how cultural norms reinforce particular options that are mostly available to men in society. Failure to comprehend the dynamics of power in this discourse may result in an incomplete understanding of the complexity of the problem, and lead to ill-informed and unworkable solutions.

HIV/AIDS in the Caribbean

In a world plagued by the human suffering caused by HIV/AIDS, the needs of families, communities, and societies demand a re-thinking of the practice of care. In areas more devastated by this disease in such places as sub-Saharan Africa, Latin America and the Caribbean, there is greater urgency for this type of adjustment in people's consciousness about equal sharing of responsibility between women and men. AIDS has been described as a leading cause of death among people of ages 15-44 in the Caribbean. The region is second only to sub-Saharan Africa with a prevalence of approximately 1.0 per cent among adults. HIV prevalence rates refer to the number of people who are living with the HIV infection in a given year. For most countries this figure is less than 1 per cent, with the exception of countries in sub-Saharan Africa and the Caribbean. The UNAIDS Report notes that HIV prevalence is highest among men who have sex with men and among sex workers in the Caribbean (UNAIDS 2010a, 3). UNAIDS estimates that people living with HIV/AIDS in the region number approximately 270, 000 (UNAIDS 2010b). There are variations in the extent of the presence of the disease in the region, with Cuba having a low HIV prevalence of 0.1 per cent, while the Bahamas has the highest prevalence of 3.1 per cent. Women account for 50 per cent of the people in the Caribbean living with AIDS and young women have the highest prevalence.

In many of these countries the brunt of the provision of care falls on the shoulders of women, in many cases requiring grandmothers to begin new cycles of mothering and providing care for grandchildren who are left orphaned. UNAIDS estimates that there are some 140, 000 children orphaned as a result of this disease in the Caribbean. In some instances it is the oldest female child who assumes the responsibility for taking care of younger siblings, or parents in the throes of human decline. Rarely does a male adult child provide such responsibility for the care of others. This unequal burden cannot be allowed to continue. Caring has to be reconfigured from the conventions of gender practice and away from the popular consciousness which views such work as an outgrowth of some generic maternal instinct, and therefore the provenance of women exclusively. In short, public health policy must actively embrace a new ontology of caring. Women and girls provide an estimated 70 to 90 per cent of the care worldwide for people living with HIV/AIDS.

The situation of AIDS in Haiti deserves special mention here. Even before the devastating earthquake of January 2010, there were approximately 120, 000 people living with AIDS in Haiti. The adult prevalence of the disease was 1.9 per cent. The earthquake occurred in those areas in which there were some 68, 000 people living with AIDS. This was also the site where the facilities for supporting the national HIV/AIDS programme were located. The earthquake exacerbated an already bad situation, increasing the vulnerabilities of women and girls among the 1.3 million displaced people, who now occupy the 891 tents which were set up in the aftermath of the earthquake. According to Amnesty International, an NGO, The Commission of Women Victims for Victims, reported 250 cases of rape in the first 150 days after the earthquake in January 2010 (Amnesty International 2011). Gang rape of women and girls has become common in the camps of displaced people, and is facilitating the spread of HIV and AIDS. Given the devastation of the earthquake, there is now additional pressure on the delivery of care services to alleviate the suffering of those without access to anti-retroviral treatment.

A new ontology of caring presupposes that new questions about the ethical dimensions of the provision of care be asked. Why should one gender have to assume the bulk of the responsibility for providing care for those unable to do so themselves? Are there specific modalities of suffering that preclude male intervention in order to effect relief? Are men as agents of their own existence lacking in empathy? Is gender behaviour so rooted in tradition that it cannot be refashioned, even in the face of a pandemic? Added to these ethical questions is the negotiation of stigma that is attendant to people living with HIV/AIDS. Given the mode of transmission of this disease and the moral and cultural framework that often over-determine it, does the provision of care require more courage of men to become involved, or is it much easier for them to distance themselves from a process which already implicates them as perpetrators? Alternatively, are women, who have long had to navigate the terrain of one stigma or another, better equipped to defend themselves from these forms of discrimination? Whatever may be the answers, it is clear that stigma subverts the delivery of care. We might then ask: What can women teach men about coming to terms with stigma in the face of an urgent need to offer assistance? Perhaps seeking answers to these questions is a good place to start the process of initiating equality in the sharing of responsibility between men and women. If this recognition is in anyway valid and sound, then the process of socialization has to be recast so that men and boys may begin to feel invested in the process of providing care for others.

Having pointed to the unequal responsibility for caring with respect to HIV/AIDS, one must hasten to note that it does not mean that men are totally absent in providing some forms of care. There are some men and boys who are involved in providing care for people living with HIV/AIDS. Often, the contribution of men at this level is not recognized. The Report of the Expert Group Meeting on "The equal sharing of responsibilities between women and men, including care-giving in the context of HIV/AIDS" convened in Geneva, Switzerland 6-9 October 2008, was careful to note that some men play an important role as secondary care providers to women who assume primary responsibility for care (Division for the Advancement of Women 2008). They provide relief for the primary care providers, they contribute or sustain the household which people living with the disease occupy, and in some cases, as single parents, they become the primary care givers. As a result of stigma however, some men are less inclined to participate in providing care, because in so doing they are subject to the embarrassment about the disease, or are mocked by both men and women for the roles they are expected to undertake.

These contributions of men should not be minimized or devalued. Rather, there is a need to stress the issue of equality of effort. Men must now begin to see themselves as sharing in the provision of the essential care that is necessary for long-term illnesses of aging parents suffering from dementia and Alzheimer's disease, and for those battling the disease of HIV/AIDS, whose care demand major investments of time and supervision. Men must be socialized away from the idea that this is women's work. Men and boys must become more sensitized to the fact that when only some members of the family or community are expected to provide care, that the amount of time they have for other activities is severely restricted, and therefore their potential is limited by the weight of their responsibilities. These actions place certain groups, namely women and girls, at a disadvantage. Men must come to understand the ways in which the unequal burdens of these responsibilities circumscribe the full benefits of citizenship for women. There is a need then to promote the broadening of the understanding of the scope of caring among men. The public health efforts to educate people about this disease have to be redoubled, so that badly needed care is not jeopardized because of prejudice and inaccurate information.

A final comment about HIV/AIDS and the provision of care is in order here. As one commentator observed, the HIV/AIDS pandemic is a human rights crisis. If we recognize the human right to health, then by logical extension, the right to care is also included in that package of rights. The human cost to society of this disease is palpable. The economic, political, and demographic implications are also evident. Less clear are some of the more philosophical issues of the impact of HIV/AIDS. There is an urgent need to begin to assess the ethical dimensions of the disease. If the disease represents a human rights crisis, then the inadequacy of the provision of care for the 10 million persons worldwide, mentioned earlier, who are living with the pandemic, amounts to a violation of their human rights. There is considerable stigma and discrimination associated with HIV/AIDS in the Caribbean. Stigma undermines prevention and treatment of the disease. Moreover, stigma and discrimination lead to social exclusion, thus making it infinitely more difficult for 'at risk' persons and people living with HIV/AIDS to be organized in any effort to secure, or to advocate for, increase human rights. In most Caribbean countries, there are laws against buggery and other forms of homosexual behaviour. The criminalization of such practices means that there is no recourse in law for people who engage in such practices in the Caribbean. In addition, what is sometimes described as legalized stigma and discrimination (see UNAIDS Report 2010a, 13), also heavily penalize homosexual practices in various territories. UNAIDS in its report on the Caribbean, notes that one can be given a life sentence for practicing homosexual acts in Barbados and Guyana, while other penalties for similar acts range from 25 years in Trinidad and Tobago to 10 years in Belize, Dominica and St.

Lucia among other places (UNAIDS 2010, 14). The violation of some of the human rights of people living with the disease can be gleaned from the following observation:

> In some instances, mandatory HIV testing without consent occurs during recruitment for the protective services, entry into prison, applications for citizenship, health or life insurance, in clinical settings for particular conditions, and during pregnancy. The extent of pre-employment screening is not known despite the fact that it has been reported to be widespread (UNAIDS 2010a, 14).

The need to have more men and boys share in the responsibility of providing care for persons living with HIV/AIDS is one that should become a priority for women's groups and feminists, for human rights advocates and public health officials, and should be central to the establishment of public policy. To move the phenomenon of care to occupy a space within the discourse of human rights increases its level of importance in much the same way that an economic accounting of the value of care work was so clearly articulated in the Expert Group Meeting [EGM] Report. In addressing many of these issues, the EGM Report would have made a significant contribution to placing the idea of equal sharing of responsibilities and of care giving on the front burner of public policy where the matter cannot easily be ignored (Division for the Advancement of Women, United Nations 2008).

Re-socializing Men and Boys

Men and boys must begin to feel invested in the process of equal sharing of responsibility. Even though it is not often the case, there are occasions, particularly when the oldest child is male, that he has to assume the responsibility of doing chores that would not normally fall to a boy. Assuming such responsibility should not happen by chance however, it should be built into the way households socialize members about its social reproduction. The socialization of equal responsibility of caring must begin early in a similar fashion to the way we orient girls into a sense of social duty and responsibility, if not destiny. The reality is however, that the consistent increase in the incidence of HIV/AIDS in the Caribbean is occurring among women. It should come as no surprise therefore that the Caribbean has one of the highest rates of new cases of AIDS among women in the sub-regions of the Western Hemisphere (CARICOM 2002, 4). The urgency for transformation in the thinking about the provision of care and about equal sharing of responsibility between men and women is highlighted by this problem of new AIDS cases, which plague the region. If women are the chief victims of this disease, and it is upon their shoulders that are placed the burdens of care, then clearly others, namely men, must now step up to assume more of this responsibility. The point is, as human societies, we should not wait until such matters reach crisis proportions before acting.

We should hasten to signal an important note of caution here. Though in this chapter there are references to sub-Saharan Africa and the Caribbean, one should not associate the unequal responsibility of sharing between men and women as a peculiarity of the culture of so-called Third World countries or the Global South. The problem of placing the onus on women for providing care is global and should not be reduced to the behaviour of people in poor countries. Having stated this point, we should nevertheless also be careful to investigate the extent to which issues of race, ethnicity, religion and culture exercise an influence in determining how the roles of men and women are performed, the taboos which uphold gender conventions of behaviour and practice, and the challenges that such cultural markers pose for the idea of change.

The Obstacle of Gender-Based Violence

A real problem for bringing men and boys into the process of taking on equal responsibility for sharing and caring is the issue of violence. How do we reconcile the general upsurge of gender-based violence with a new ontology of caring? Some of this violence is related to the asymmetry of power that was mentioned earlier. Violence as a mechanism of control is not only a physical threat to women's security, but it also limits their options for realizing social progress. Violence then is anathema to the idea of equal sharing of responsibilities, and of the provision of care. There is a clear and understandable emphasis on the impact of violence on women in this EGM Report, as in other reports and analyses. Women after all are more likely than not to be the victims of violent attacks.

Violence against women has been on the increase globally, and the Caribbean is no exception. As EMG report of Division for the Advancement of Women, United Nations (2008, 12) observes:

> Violence against women is widespread on a global scale and is one serious consequence of systemic subordination of women and gender inequality. Violence against women is both a cause and consequence of unequal sharing of responsibilities between women and men. In population-based studies worldwide, 10 to over 50 per cent of women report physical assault by an intimate partner. In some countries the percentage of women reporting that their first sexual experience was forced is as high as 30 per cent. Women suffer violence for such seemingly 'mundane' reasons as disobedience, talking back, refusing sex or not having food ready on time. Many men see violence as the only way to resolve conflict and 'control' their partners. Physical violence, the threat of violence and the fear of abandonment are significant barriers for women to negotiate condom use, discuss fidelity with their partners, or leave a relationship that they perceive to be risky. Women who are known or suspected to be HIV positive are sometimes targeted with violence because of their status. A ten-country study on voluntary counseling and testing and disclosure, published by the World Health Organization in 2004, reported that the proportion of women reporting violence as a reaction to disclosure ranged from 3.5 per cent to 14.6 per cent.

The joint UN/World Bank report echoes the same concern when it concluded: "In sum, violence against women seems to be endemic in Caribbean countries—as it is in most countries around the world (UNODC and World Bank 2007, 13)." Violence, in its essence, inhibits the practice of caring, so addressing the issue of violence has to be central to a new ontology of familial care. It is unlikely that the notion of sharing responsibilities will have much appeal in a context in which there is physical, sexual and emotional abuse. Women as victims of violence is only one side of the coin; the other has to do with the tremendous violence that men mete out against each other on a daily basis, in the Caribbean and around the world. The violence that men inflict on each other is highly correlated with short-term hedonism, which valorizes the notion of 'dying like a man'—the idea that the pay-off between risk-taking and immediate gratification is worth the effort, and that life in a Hobbesian sense is poor, nasty, brutish and short.

The joint UN/World Bank report cited above also noted that many of the persons who initiate such violent actions, and those who fall prey to the same, "are young men of low social-economic status, with a low level of education and poor prospects for income generation, who have witnessed violence at close range (UNODC and World Bank 2007, 133)." We cannot assume therefore that the problem of promoting the idea of equal sharing of responsibility can take place outside of an economic and material context within which life is taking place. Violence in this sense then has to be analyzed in terms of power and economic deprivation. There are no quick fixes; change in this context has to be a comprehensive strategy, which in turn requires adjustment of both men and women to new modalities of interaction.

The violence that transpires between men cannot be overstated. It is not intended here to make simple comparisons about comparative victimhood. Rather, it is an attempt to create a broader understanding of the phenomenon of violence. If we are to break the cycle of violence as a mechanism of conflict resolution, we must work simultaneously to stop men from using violence to patrol the boundaries of women's sexuality for example, while intervening to stop men from maiming, assaulting and killing each other. Too much of this behaviour has become normalized, so much so that we have almost become anesthetized by the increasing number of prisons that are being erected all over the world to warehouse men because of one form or another of the violence of their behaviour. We need not detain ourselves here with any analysis of the prison system, which short of rehabilitating men, schools them in the ways of more sophisticated techniques of violence, and represents a challenge in the struggle against HIV/AIDS.

There are other forms of violence that should concern us as we tackle the notion of equal sharing of responsibilities and care giving. One such issue is the restriction of movement that is imposed on refugees and internally displaced individuals, and the suspension of their rights as human beings caught in situations of statelessness. This suffering is also a form of violence meted out on both men and women. People in some cases trade the violence of repression and persecution at home for the violence of the refugee camps. In the case of Haiti, people in effect are forced to trade the violence of poverty that existed before the earthquake for the pervasive violence of the tents. In this space, refugee women are even more vulnerable. Moreover, when in such contexts men undertake domestic roles not by choice but out of necessity, they feel dejected and angry. Violence against women and children is not an uncommon response in such situations.

Violence therefore must also be seen structurally in terms of the deprivation of rights. We must name and challenge the limiting of options of women as a form of structural violence, namely the violence that is independent of any individual action or that is physical in nature, but that which is systemic in origin and impact. The obstacles placed in the path of women that prevent them from participating in the political life of the country, that effectively restrict their access to decision making, and that circumscribe their involvement in public life, all constitute forms of violence. It is this totality of the concept of violence that should be borne in mind in terms of its impact on equal sharing of responsibility between men and women, and the provision of familial care.

Economic Crisis and Equal Sharing and Caring

No one could possibly imagine that change involving familial care occasioned by a new ontology as suggested above would be easy, but a new variable has emerged to complicate the issue. It is the current economic crisis. The full limitations of the neoliberal agenda, with its emphasis on deregulation, privatization, and rolling back of welfare provisions of the state, have come up against the contradictions of capitalism, posing new challenges for the accumulation of capital, which have led to the economic crisis that we are currently experiencing, particularly in the financial sector. As experience would have taught us, in a climate of fiscal instability, the delivery of welfare provisions is usually the first to be affected. Women tend to bear the brunt of all these adjustment measures. Though one could make a compelling case for the need for government and employers to create more family friendly policies, including generous maternity and paternity leave policies, flexible work arrangements and reduced working time, these are all alternative strategies that are contingent on more favourable economic conditions. We would be well served to be mindful of how easily alternative policies could be shelved as being too costly to be implemented at this time, or the extent to which they compete with other more immediate priorities such as jobs or housing. An awareness of the extent to which economic and political considerations could derail recommendations for ushering in a new social contract means that the struggle for change has to be an unrelenting one. Reallocation of resources is already on the way as is suggested by the following:

> Over the last decade, the region has received over US$1.3 billion for its HIV programmes; with current financial and economic crises, donor governments have less fiscal space, and as budgets tighten, external resources for HIV are likely to decline. Caribbean countries, many of which are classified as Upper Middle Income, are now less eligible for development assistance. Increasingly, and within the short-term, the financial cost of the region's HIV programmes is likely to be passed on to national governments (UNAIDS 2010a: iv).

Resource strapped economies such as those in the Caribbean are unlikely to go unaffected by these financial rigidities.

The need for establishing a new social contract between men and women has at its foundation a complex interplay of rethinking notions of social justice, reshaping democratic participation in society, and guaranteeing the right to the benefits of full citizenship for women and girls. Men and boys must be encouraged to become more involved in this process of change. Men can no longer be allowed to remain, for the most part, marginal to the process of familial care. The EGM Report then is an important policy document in this regard.

Change Agents

Among those agents charged with effecting change of the order suggested in this chapter, the role of the state cannot be over-emphasized. We must lobby to create a balance between a state of caring and a caring state. A state of caring refers to an environment that is conducive to the delivery of adequate care for those in need of it. A caring state is one which places the needs of its people at the center of its operations. It is a state which through its government uses its resources to ensure adequate treatment for the sick, elderly and the young, and which functions for the wellbeing of its least able citizens. Only those who are politically naive would assume the state to respond with such magnanimity. The state is a site of the most intense struggle where such demands are hammered out between the government and the people. It is this type of social pressure that has to be waged in order to push governments to provide resources for the welfare needs of its people. Not only should one expect the state to finance the provision of appropriate care, but to invest in training of caregivers to render their services efficiently and effectively. The following examples should demonstrate the point at hand.

Patients suffering from HIV/AIDS and other devastating diseases tend to suffer from severe bouts of depression, where they sometimes express little point in continuing a life lived in suffering. These occasions are stressful not only for the sick but also for the caregiver. In these circumstances the government needs to step in and provide professional counseling to such individuals. In addition, it should also consider training for caregivers on how best to cope with the depression of the sick as the first responders to this problem. Counseling for persons who have recently been diagnosed as having contracted HIV or AIDS, or those who are living with the disease, should be provided by the state as a priority. This service is not always forthcoming, and clearly factors such as underdevelopment, poverty and inadequate resources can hamstring the delivery of such services. These factors notwithstanding, Airhihenbuwa laments: "More than twenty years into the epidemic, many governments have yet to assume leadership in promoting policy that protects the human rights of persons living with HIV/AIDS in their countries" (Airhihenbuwa 2007, 159).

Although one does not expect the state to provide the sole support for these efforts, there has to be the constant pressure of citizens to ensure that these urgent public health policies are addressed. In this regard, there is clearly a need for the state to use its influence and its control of the means of communication to promote community awareness of human rights violations that may undermine prevention. In the Dominican Republic there was a widespread practice of HIV testing without informed consent. Human Rights Watch had to raise this issue in the Dominican Republic in 2004. Human Rights Watch argued: "The Directorate for Control of Sexually Transmitted Infections, HIV and AIDS (*Dirección General de Control de las ITS/VIH y SIDA*, DIGECITSS) should launch awareness campaigns to inform the public about women's human rights violations that contribute to the spread of HIV/AIDS, such as domestic and sexual violence, subordinate social status, and sex discrimination in the workplace and in access to work and services" (Human Rights Watch 2004, 3).

Another way that the state could contribute to the way care is provided and shared is by creating the appropriate environment in which people feel comfortable rendering such services. Caribbean governments cannot afford to suppress discussion of the extent of the problem of AIDS and HIV in the region because of the possible backlash on the tourism industry. There is no denying the importance of tourism to the economies of the region, but to de-emphasize the issue of the spread of a devastating disease because it might scare away some tourists, represents a failure to understand how the muting of such discourses undercut the efforts of prevention. Moreover, people are less inclined to be willing to offer care when doing so stigmatizes them as families, as persons, and especially as men. There is a clear case in Jamaica where homophobia and violence represent specific barriers to the delivery of care both institutionally and privately. Human Rights Watch noted that health workers often mistreated people living with HIV/AIDS; even doctors were refusing to conduct certain types of examination, and health workers tended to release confidential information to other patients (Human Rights Watch 2004). These practices cannot be allowed to continue. In such a cultural context, it would be more than foolhardy to think that men would be open to the idea of becoming more involved in sharing responsibility when they could be vilified, or worse, beaten for providing care for a highly stigmatized group of people in society. The EGM observed in this regard: "Fear of stigma and discrimination cause many to provide care in secrecy, leading to further isolation for the carer and the patient. Both family and volunteer caregivers suffer similar stigmatization and discrimination to that experienced by their patients. HIV/AIDS related stigma can also be found where there is limited understanding of the nature, cause and transmission of HIV" (Division for the Advancement of Women, United Nations 2008, 23). In short, the social environment has to be cleansed of such bigotry before the idea of change of this type could be introduced.

We should therefore welcome the initiative of governments in the region to address some of these issues brought on by the spread of HIV/AIDS in the Caribbean. One such initiative is the Pan Caribbean Partnership Against HIV/AIDS (PANCAP). PANCAP was established in February 2001 at the annual Meeting of the Caribbean Community Heads of State, and was endorsed by the Nassau Declaration on Health. According to its charge it was established to advocate for HIV/AIDS issues at the governmental level, to coordinate the regional response, mobilize resources, and increase the level of resources in individual countries to deal with this problem. PANCAP has also been responsible for establishing a Caribbean Regional Strategic Framework for HIV/AIDS. These are important initiatives that should be encouraged, but we should continue to push for efforts that would facilitate greater sharing of responsibilities such as the building of daycare centers at sites that are conducive to easy access of parents who are working, or the provision of work arrangements and schedules that do not have the impact of bifurcating the relationship of work and family responsibility.

Lastly, trade unions should become more involved in the process of promoting greater equality of responsibility between men and women. After all, the rationale behind trade unionism is to improve the conditions under which people work, but more specifically, to address the needs of the whole person. Issues of sharing responsibility between men and women should be central to their charge. Some unions have taken on these issues, others have not been as involved. It is incumbent on trade unions to push for the rights of migrant workers who are, for example, moving from Haiti to the Dominican Republic, or from Guyana to most of the Eastern Caribbean. The undocumented status of many of these workers simply exacerbates their vulnerabilities and opens them to myriad forms of abuse. The Caribbean trade union movement must also be in the vanguard of the struggle against discrimination at work of those persons living with HIV/AIDS. These are issues that broaden the scope of operation of some unions, and for some, there is always the temptation to get bogged down in the so-called bread and butter matters of collective bargaining. As important as terms and conditions of employment are, the other concerns mentioned in this chapter address some of the most fundamental issues of distributive justice, democratization, and the human rights that constitute the foundation of trade unionism. The Caribbean trade union movement would do well to support the recent call by the International Trade Union Confederation (ITUC), to employers and trade unions to work toward realizing the full potential of workplace-based prevention and education (ITUC 2011). In addition to promoting the idea that work-related activities should fully be a part of the overall response to HIV-AIDS, the ITUC also articulated a six point plan of action to achieve this objective:

- reduction of stigma and discrimination on the basis of real or perceived HIV status in recruitment, employment and occupation—as a part of the "getting to zero discrimination" strategy;
- increased access to prevention services through workplace HIV service delivery, including workplace peer education—as a part of the "getting to zero new infections" strategy;
- supporting countries in responding to HIV/AIDS within broader plans and actions related to the Millennium Development Goals (MDGs), poverty reduction strategies and development, including scaling up of national workplace HIV policies as outlined in the ILO HIV and AIDS Recommendation No. 200;
- scaling up social protection strategies and access to treatment, care and support through workplace HIV/AIDS service delivery, including access to mother to child transmission (MTCT) treatment—as part of the "getting to zero new AIDS-related deaths" strategy;
- continuous HIV reviews by the UN and ensuring that HIV and human rights issues retain priority in the broader health context, including the development and ratification of a set of human rights indicators for national monitoring, accountability and budgeting (ITUC 2011).

Caribbean trade unions therefore must come to terms with these broader and more pressing issues occasioned by the deepening process of global capitalism and its social relations.

Conclusion

Pushing for equal sharing of responsibility between men and women and a new ontology of familial care are of course not new issues; the women's movement has been making this case for sometime now. What is perhaps new is the urgency of the matter. We cannot afford for this disparity to continue without serious challenge. The burden of responsibility and care is simply overbearing at this stage for women to assume on their own. Sharing of responsibility frees up time for other productive activities of benefit to families and society. Men and boys must increasingly come to understand how inequities with respect to sharing responsibilities limit options for those who shoulder the bulk of these undertakings. There are clearly economic, political, social, ethical and philosophical imperatives pushing us inevitably in the direction of change. Change however is not expected to be easy. Equal sharing of responsibility is a process that will come up alongside an entrenched system of the gendered division of labour, and an encrusted system of patriarchy which some are deftly determined to defend. Change has to be negotiated on several fronts simultaneously. Men and women must demonstrate a willingness to invest in a new kind of democratic order. Trade unions must use their power of mobilizing workers to think differently about the nature of productive activity and responsibility. The state must become the site of struggle for these material improvements in people's lives, and to the extent that we invest faith in a notion of civil society not as some autonomous space, but as a vehicle for mobilizing the popular will, it too must be called on to promote transformation of these social relations between men and women. The present is the history of the future we wish to create.

Notes

1. Capital is being used here to refer to wealth that is in the process of being created. In this sense therefore, capital represents the expansion of value, which is in turn converted to profit.

14

Between Café and Cigarillos

Notes towards mapping the research trajectory and the intellectual legacy of Fernando Ortiz through a study of his select works

David Gómez Arredondo and *Hari Nair**

Fernando Ortiz is the undisputed figure of reference in the ever widening horizon of contemporary Cuban and Caribbean culture. Ortiz's reputation stems from his monumental ethnographical and historical research on Indo-Cuban and Afro-Cuban cultures. His oeuvre is a veritable treasure trove of information and ideas. Since his death, Cuba has not witnessed another attempt that is as vast or as ambitious as that of Ortiz in studying Cuban culture, especially Afro-Cuban culture. The persistence of religious, linguistic and cultural practices of African origin in Cuba has converted the work of Ortiz into an ineluctable referent despite the fluctuating fortunes of a variety of paradigms and theories within Cultural Anthropology.

Besides the historical and ethnographical scholarship, Ortiz is credited with conceptualizing the idea of "transculturation." In this chapter, we shall critically look at the history of this idea but

* This chapter proceeds from the preliminary notes of an ongoing project engaged in studying and translating the works of Fernando Ortiz. It is based on the current consensus of its authors and that in turn is nourished by caffeine and tobacco—the "two anodynes of fatigue in modern civilization"—according to Heinrich Jacobs, 1934, *Sage und Siegeszug des Kaffees: Die biographie eines Weltwirtschaftlichen Stoffes* as cited in (Ortiz 2002, 453).

that cannot be done without locating it within the particular context of Cuba and the Caribbean. Given the unimpeachable relevance of Ortiz for the study of Cuban culture as well as for the current theoretical debates within Culture Studies, we trust that a critical revision of the work of Ortiz is necessary because it will aid in our appreciation of both contemporary Cuba and the Caribbean.

Fernando Ortiz: A Profile of the Scholar and his Discourse

Fernando Ortiz (1881-1969), a Creole scholar, is best known for his penetrating analysis of the elements that constituted the Cuban identity. Fernando was born in Havana, and spent the greater part of his early adulthood shuttling across the Atlantic between Spain and Cuba. After graduating in law from the University of Barcelona in 1895, Ortiz completed his doctoral research in the same discipline in 1901 from the Universidad Central de Madrid.

The true legacy of Fernando Ortiz has been his pioneering contributions to the study of Afro-Cuban society. These studies ranged from the legal, criminological and penal through oral history and philology to economic history, sociology, ethnology, archaeology and anthropology. One of the most striking aspects of his trajectory was the instance of intellectual moulting, when he shed his criminological perspective in studying Afro-Cuban society and focused on its cultural elements. This metamorphosis also aided the vindication of Afro-Cubans.

The intellectual moulting of Ortiz was a consequence of his many empirical studies. These studies gave rise to the concept of "transculturación." With the aid of this concept, Ortiz explained Cuban history as a complex process, wherein multiple cultures permanently interacted with each other. If Cuba was a microcosm of Latin America, what was true for Cuba could possibly be true for other parts in the region as well. Thus, generations of scholars employed the concept of transculturation towards understanding almost every other society in Latin America.

Scholars have claimed that in the second volume of the work *Hampa Afro-cubana* titled *Los negros esclavos* (1916), Ortiz laid the foundations for an historical and eclectic methodology that eventually led to the concept of *transculturación* (Font, Quiroz and Smorkaloff 2005, xiii-xiv). But, it was with the publication of *Contrapunteo cubano del tabaco y el azúcar: Advertencia de sus contrastes agrarios, económicos, históricos y sociales, su etngrafía y su transculturación* (1940) that the neologism of transculturation entered the academic discourse in the Atlantic world. Its use, however, became more frequent only since the early 1980s.

Within this academic context, transculturation became increasingly appreciated for its rejection of the racist tendencies that were prevalent in the Social Sciences during the late 19th and early 20th centuries. However, before Ortiz enunciated this concept, he had himself entertained a prejudiced view of Afro-Cuban culture, at least, until ca. 1920s. What was the intellectual context before Ortiz underwent his intellectual moulting? That context was the Italian school of Positive Criminology (or Criminal Anthropology), which percolated from Cesare Lombroso and Enrico Ferri through to Ortiz.

Immediately after completing the doctoral dissertation in law, Fernando Ortiz was drawn towards the "mala vida en La Habana" (the criminal or underworld of Cuban society). But one particular event of 1904 seemed to have troubled Ortiz. A white girl named Zoila was murdered in a Cuban sugar plantation by a black sorcerer (Leo 2005, 41). This incident prompted Ortiz to further investigate the Cuban *hampa afrocubana* (the secretive Afro-Cuban underworld). Consequently, Ortiz published two books with the same title *Hampa Afro-cubana*; vol. 1 *Los negros brujos* (1906) and vol. 2 *Los negros esclavos* (1916).

Although the two volumes of *Hampa Afro-cubana* were located within a Euro/ethnocentric discourse, it marked the beginning of Ortiz's life-long research engagement with the African elements in Cuban history and society. Notwithstanding the ethnocentrism present in these studies, the work of Ortiz underwent a paradigmatic shift during the decade of the 1920s. He moved away from a discourse determined by race towards one of culture, as he began studying religious rituals, music, dance, feasts, games, slang and the language of the Afro-Cubans. As a result of this paradigmatic shift, Ortiz became convinced that race was a deceptive category as employed in the Social Sciences. Let us look at some of the circumstances that resulted in this radical reorientation in the ethnography of Fernando Ortiz.

Jorge Castellanos has summed up the ideological transition in the ethnographical orientation of Fernando Ortiz between 1906 and 1937 (Castellanos 2003, 109-52). Castellanos refers to an anecdote dating back to 1901, when Ortiz was asked to comment on "la mala vida" of Havana, in the context of a discussion on the book *La mala vida en Madrid* authored by Constancio Bernaldo de Quirós. Although Ortiz spoke about the ñáñigos on that occasion, he confessed little knowledge about them and so decided to study this subject closely. The result was a long series of studies on Afro-Cubans.

Ortiz recognized that the study of Afro-Cubans was a difficult task, because it invited ridicule and was monetarily unrewarding. After a short period of direct observation, Ortiz drafted a text, which became the book *Hampa Afro-cubana: Los negros brujos* (1906). This work was pioneering because it opened up a new field for study—the Afro-Cuban religion. But, like many pioneering works, it too suffered from many errors of omission and interpretation.

The interpretative framework of *Los negros brujos* was fundamentally prejudiced against the Afro-Cubans. In this work, Ortiz located an entire community of people as part of "la mala vida cubana," and described the Afro-Cuban religion as malefic, amoral, criminal and, by definition, antisocial. Hence, this religion had to be eliminated because it was contagious—argued Ortiz (Castellanos 2003, 112-17). The racism immanent in the first volume of *Hampa Afro-cubana* titled *Los negros brujos* persisted into its second volume, *Los negros esclavos*. The following passage is suggestive enough:

> In Cuba, an entire race entered the underworld. (In Europe, an analogous phenomenon can be observed in the social life of the gypsies, although different in many aspects. [Foot note]) When the Blacks reached Cuba all of them entered the Cuban underworld, not as fallen beings from a superior moral plane rather as inept, for the moment at least, to aspire to that level. [...]
>
> In love, the Blacks were summarily lascivious; their marriages bordered on polygamy; prostitution did not deserve repugnance; their families lacked cohesion; their religion led them to human sacrifices, to the plunder of sepulchres, to anthropophagi, and to the most brutal superstitions. Human life inspired in them little respect.... [...]
>
> But the inferiority of the Negros, which subjected them to the underworld was due to the lack of an integral civilization because so primitive was their morals, intellect, desires etc. It is this character that distinguishes them from

> the individuals in the underworld of those societies formed exclusively by Whites (Ortiz 1916, 13-14).[1]
>
> [...] The African Negro was brought to Cuba in complete physical and psychological nudity [...] The Negro was, as Girard de Rialle said, "a grown-up child subject to momentary impulses and an absolute slave of his passions. The most surprising contradictions in his conduct manifested themselves thus. He is shallow, inconsistent, jolly, lover of frenetic passion, crazy for dance, noise, and gaudy clothes." The ethnologists completed these pieces painting the African people, who were subjected to an abominable treatment, as naturally indolent, excessively sensuous, lacking forethought, being superstitious without limits, with an intelligence that was hardly awakened and as enemies of abstract ideas, as being timid before the unknown although brave before real danger, charitable, lovers of their roots and captives of nostalgia for the native country while in foreign lands, full of devotion for kids and, given to good friendship. [...] Such seem to have been the salient psychological characteristics of the virgin races—according to the ethnographers—over whom slavery flourished in the Indies (Ortiz 1916, 54-55).[2]

This explicit ethnocentrism that characterized the early interpretative framework of Ortiz was due to the influence of a particular current of criminal anthropology within the Italian school of Positivist criminology,[3] which was in vogue during the last quarter of the 19th century. According to Enrico Ferri (1908), the founding scholar of Positive criminal anthropology was Cesare Lombroso (1835-1909).[4] From the results of his studies of criminals themselves, Lombroso argued that the anatomical, psychological and anthropological factors converted one into a criminal. The passage given below exemplifies how Lombroso had conceived of the Positive School of criminal anthropology:

> The Modern, or Positive, School of Penal Jurisprudence, on the contrary, maintains that the anti-social tendencies of criminals are the result of their physical and psychic organization, which differs essentially from that of normal individuals; and it aims at studying the morphology and various functional phenomena of the criminal with the

> object of curing, instead of punishing him. The Modern School is therefore founded on a new science, Criminal Anthropology, which may be defined as the Natural History of the Criminal, because it embraces his organic and psychic constitution and social life, just as anthropology does in the case of normal human beings and the different races (Lombroso 1911, 5).

Lombroso believed that criminal tendencies could be inherited, and these could be detected through studies of physiognomy because an innate criminal would possess the physical characteristics reminiscent of early humans within the evolutionary chain. Lombroso himself described how he arrived at this conclusion. The following paragraphs contain his recollections:

> I began dimly to realize that the *a priori* studies on crime in the abstract, hitherto pursued by jurists, especially in Italy, with singular acumen, should be superseded by the direct analytical study of the criminal, compared with normal individuals and the insane.
>
> [...] On his death [that of the famous brigand Villela] one cold grey November morning, I was deputed to make the *post-mortem*, and on laying open the skull I found on the occipital part, exactly on the spot where a spine is found in the normal skull, a distinct depression which I named *median occipital fossa*, because of its situation precisely in the middle of the occiput as in inferior animals, especially rodents. This depression, as in the case of animals, was correlated with the hypertrophy of the *vermis*, known in birds as the middle cerebellum.
>
> [...] At the sight of that skull, I seemed to see all of a sudden, lighted up as a vast plain under a flaming sky, the problem of the nature of the criminal—an atavistic being who reproduces in his person the ferocious instincts of primitive humanity and the inferior animals. Thus were explained anatomically the enormous jaws, high cheek-bones, prominent superciliary arches, solitary lines in the palms, extreme size of the orbits, handle-shaped or sessile ears found in criminals, savages, and apes, insensibility to pain, extremely acute sight, tattooing, excessive

> idleness, love of orgies, and the irresistible craving for evil for its own sake, the desire not only to extinguish life in the victim, but to mutilate the corpse, tear its flesh, and drink its blood (Lombroso 1911, xiv-xv).

This idea is known as atavism. Although it has since been entirely rejected, Ortiz was at that time clearly influenced by the work of Lombroso, who prefaced both the first and the second editions of *Los negros brujos*. However, the penal orientation of *Los negros brujos* was diminished in *Los negros esclavos*—the second ethnographical work of Ortiz.

Perhaps, the most significant difference in the framework of analysis between *Los negros brujos* and *Los negros esclavos* was that the latter work tended towards a historical analysis of the Afro-Cubans, although it relied not so much on documents from the archives as on existing travel literature, 19th century novels, government reports, Spanish legislation and works of Creole criminal anthropology (Castellanos 2003, 124).

The nucleus of *Los negros esclavos* dealt with the history of Afro-Cuban slavery (chapters IV-VI and chapter X), the treatment of the Blacks (chapters VII-IX), rural slaves (chapters XI-XVI), urban slaves (chapter XVII), those emancipated from slavery (chapter XVIII), the juridical status of Afro-Cuban slaves through history (chapters XIX-XXI) and the history of resistance of Afro-Cuban slaves (chapters XXII-XXIII).

At the end of the book, while taking stock of his study, Ortiz mentioned that sections dealing with music, dance, morality, religion, social organizations and other themes were missing. These subjects would in fact occupy the mind of Ortiz for the rest of his life. Out of those emerged a gigantic scholarly production in the form of *La africanía de la música folklórica de Cuba* (1950), *Los bailes y el teatro de los negros en el folklore de Cuba* (1951), *Los instrumentos de la música afrocubana* (1952-22 in 5 volumes). No less important than these books was the personal intellectual transformation that Fernando Ortiz himself underwent as a consequence of the study of Afro-Cuban culture. That transformation, though gradual, was total in its rejection of racism.

Between 1920 and 1925, Ortiz was immersed in ethnography and published a number of studies on Afro-Cuban religious rituals, socio-political organizations, and the use of slang and language. This period coincided with the Harlem Renaissance and the resurgence of Afro-Cuban art in the form of music, dance and literature. Ortiz was widely read by the artists of the Afro-Cuban movement as well by its political leaders notably Gustavo Urrutia. While Ortiz became an inspirational figure for the Afro-Cubans, he in turn mingled with them, especially the young artists. This conviviality convinced him of the futility of race as a social category and the need to substitute it with that of culture.

These years were also politically tumultuous for Cuba and Ortiz was actively present in the national political forum since the end of World War I until his exile to the United States (1931-3). The struggle against the dictatorship of Gerardo Machado required a united opposition of all Cubans, across classes and "races." Consequently, in his speech as the president of the Sociedad Económica de Amigos del País on 9th January 1929 he contrasted race against culture (Castellanos 2003, 127-28). Here, Ortiz was beginning to hark back to what José Martí had so wisely written nearly forty years earlier. On the subject of races and racism, Martí wrote thus:

> There should be no hatred for races because there are no races. Stunted thinkers sitting at lamp-lit desks cook up races for book-shelves that a true traveler and an empathetic observer search in vain in nature's justice, where only the universal identity of man is highlighted by the all-conquering love and turbulent appetite. The soul emanates, equally and eternally, from bodies varying in form and colour. He who foments and propagates opposition and hatred against races is sinning against humanity (Marti 2004, 73).[5]

In a number of his writings since 1929, Fernando Ortiz repeatedly attacked racism, xenophobia, and race as a category. In many of these attacks, he all too frequently returned to José Martí. Of those writings, especially noteworthy are *Martí y las razas* (1942), "Cuba, Martí, and the race problem" published in *Phylon* (1942), "Por la integración cubana de blancos y negros," his lecture at Club Atenas delivered on 12 December 1942 and published in *Ultra* (1943), "Martí y 'las razas de librería"' published in *Cuadernos Americanos* (1945), and *El engaño de las razas* (1946).

During the decade of the 1950s, Ortiz published monumental works dedicated to the study of Afro-Cuban culture. In these anthropological writings, he established how the dominant classes in Cuba used terms such as "mala vida," "hampa afro-cubana" and, adjectives like retrograde, savage, primitive, atavistic etc. for continuously marginalizing the Afro-Cubans.

Elements of a Research Lexicology

The productive period of Fernando Ortiz extended from 1901 to 1959. In these six decades, Ortiz produced an oeuvre that was both gigantic in quantity and scope. How could one begin a study of his writings? Perhaps, an acquaintance with the research lexicology of Ortiz could be the most viable entry point because this could offer us a panoramic perspective of the conceptual world of Fernando Ortiz.

Therefore, in this section, we shall characterize the semantic implications of his research lexicology. In doing so, we must necessarily be selective. So, we have restricted ourselves to terms that are most representative of his thought. These are "Afrocubano," "Contrapunteo" and "Transculturación." The first term was used as an intellectual category, the second as a rhetorical *topos* with a polemical intent, and the third term was employed as a theoretical concept.

Afro-Cuban

Ortiz borrowed the term Afro-Cuban from Antonio de Veitía, who had used it as early as 1847 (Robaina 2005). [6] The term was employed by Ortiz more as an intellectual category, rather than as one of identity, for explaining the dual nature of a particular socio-cultural community that Ortiz wanted to study. Afro-Cuban referred to the "psychological community" that was formed when the pre-existing divisions between peoples of African origin receded away as they adopted a new home in Cuba and were adapting to the new circumstances. The adoption of Spanish, which was the language of the dominant culture, marks the birth of this new community.

The use of the term was apparently anachronistic for two reasons. First, the majority of the Blacks and Mulattoes did not consider themselves to be Afro-Cubans. Second, Cuban intellectual and political leaders urged their countrymen to eliminate racial differences and to consider themselves as Cubans for the sake of national unity. The debate regarding the appropriateness of the term is still current. Notwithstanding, Tomás Fernández Robaina insists that the term Afro-Cuban "illustrates the result of an ongoing process of influences among African cultures in Cuba and the dominant Eurocentric cultures" (Fernández Robaina 2005, 177-78).

Contrapunteo/Counterpoint

The word "counterpoint" is derived from a binary opposition—point and counterpoint. Counterpoints are normally posited against points in a verbal dispute. In Spanish, then, it should have been "punto y contrapunto." However, Ortiz used the word "contrapunteo" instead of contrapunto because it is a Cuban expression—a typical "cubanismo."

There was yet another reason for the choice of "contrapunteo" besides mere patriotic sentiment. In Cuban folk music, the playful rivalry or dialogue between two or more voices or instruments is common. This is known as *controversia*. It is also present in poetry, dance, drama, liturgy ... and ... in life! No elaboration of the term "contrapunteo" could match the characterization of the term by Ortiz, which is given below:

> This type of dialogued composition which carries the dramatic dialectic of life into the realm of art has always been a favourite of the ingenous folk muses in poetry, music, dance, song, and drama. The outstanding examples of this in Cuba are the antiphonal prayers of the liturgies of both whites and blacks, the erotic controversy in dance measures of the rumba, and in the versified counterpoint of the unlettered *guajiros* and the Afro-Cuban *curros* (Ortiz 2003, 3-4).

> Al fin, siempre fue muy propio de las ingenuas musas del pueblo, en poesía, música, danza, canción y teatro, ese género dialogístico que lleva hasta el arte de la dramática dialéctica de la vida. Recordemos en Cuba sus manifestaciones más floridas en las preces antifonarias de las liturgias, así de blancos como de negros, en la controversia erótica y danzaría de la rumba y en los contrapunteos versificados de la guajirada montuna y de la currería afro-cubana (Ortiz 2002, 136).

As is evident from its title *Contrapunteo del tabaco y el azúcar* (*Cuban counterpoint: Tobacco and sugar*), the book is a contrasting study of tobacco and sugar, two very important agricultural products, which according to Ortiz have shaped the economic history of Cuba. The book is divided into two parts: a literary essay followed by a historical study. The study is divided into a parallel set of chapters; where one set is dedicated to tobacco and the other to sugar.

Both the essay and the study seek to be comprehensive despite the disclaimers of Ortiz. But, the essay is a "pícaro" (truant/playful) defence of tobacco—America's very own plant. The essay and the study contrast the parallels between tobacco and sugar—their history, their agrarian and botanical features, their commerce and industry, their individual and social uses, and in fact, a lot more.

The contrast, or the binary opposition, between sugar and tobacco in the essay ends on a truant note, as a third Cuban character enters the stage. Ortiz says that the friendly bickering between Don Tobacco and Doña Sugar ended in a fairly tale marriage. Out of this wedlock was born alcohol, "conceived by the Unholy Ghost, the devil, who is the father of tobacco in the sweet womb of wanton sugar." Hence, "the Cuban Trinity: Tobacco, Sugar and Alcohol" (Ortiz 2003, 93).

While the historical study aims at satiating a demanding scholar, the essay would delight a reader accustomed to the wit and ways of Hispanic-American baroque literature (Santi 2002, 94-103).[7] Given below are three passages that sample the desire of Ortiz to deliver sensuous pleasure to his readers but these do indeed reflect a unique craft of writing.

> Sugar cane was the gift of the gods, tobacco of the devils; she is the daughter of Apollo, he is the offspring of Persephone (Ortiz 2003, 6).

> For this reason, if long ago the savages censed their idols in caves with tobacco to placate their fury with adulation, today one burns the incense of tobacco in the hollows of one's own skull to calm one's worries and breathe new life into one's illusions (Ortiz 2003, 10).

> Poets who have been smokers have sung of the rapt ecstasy that comes over them as they follow with eyes and imagination the bluish smoke rising upward, as though from the ashes of the cigar, dying in the fire like a victim of the Inquisition, its spirit, purified and free, ascending

> to heaven, leaving in the air hieroglyphic signs like ineffable promises of redemption (Ortiz 2003, 9).
>
> La caña fue obra de los dioses, el tabaco lo fue de los demonios; ella es hija de Apolo, él es engendro de Proserpina... (Ortiz 2002, 139-40).
>
> Por esto, si atańo se ahumaban ritualmente con tabacos los ídolos salvajes en las cavernas para aplacarles sus furias por el incienso de la adulación, hogaño se sahúmo con tabaco el espíritu propio en el antro del cráneo para calmarle sus congojas y avivarle sus ilusiones (Ortiz 2002, 145).
>
> Además, los poetas fumadores han cantado el éxtasis contemplativo que experimentan siguiendo con la vista y la fantasía el humo azuloso que sube, como si el tabaco, al morir por el fuego como un endemoniado, su espíritu, ya purificado y libre, ascendiera al cielo escribiendo con hieráticos signos de nube inefables promesas de redención (Ortiz 2002, 144).

Transculturation

Transculturation was a term that Fernando Ortiz used for explaining the complex transmutations of culture that took place in Cuba (Ortiz 2002, 254-60).[8] Ortiz argued that when two different cultures interacted with each other, it sometimes resulted in the loss or uprooting of the preceding culture (de-culturation), and the birth of a third cultural phenomenon (neo-culturation). De-culturation and neo-culturation are the main components of the concept of transculturation, which Ortiz derived from his studies of Cuban history.

Ortiz highlighted a number of cultural transmutations that occurred in Cuba all through its history. First, was the transculturation of the Palaeolithic Indian communities (Ciboneys and Guanajabibes) and the Neolithic ones (Taino Indians). This was followed by the coming of the Spaniards in the late 15th century. The arrival of this "hurricane of culture from Europe" resulted in the complete elimination of the indigenous population in Cuba. Consequently, an entirely different set of population came to inhabit the islands.

The arrival of the Spaniards also witnessed a steady stream of African Negroes coming from all the coastal regions of Africa. The Negroes were deprived of their original socio-cultural environment and were faced with the problem of maladjustment and readjustment in Cuba. The Negroes were not accompanied by their institutions unlike the Spaniards, who came with their religion and kinsmen.

The uprooting of the Negroes from their original home and the brutal treatment that they received at the hands of slave traders filled them with a longing for freedom. However, they had no option but to adopt the pretence of submission. In the centuries following the discovery of Cuba by the Spaniards, there were waves of immigrants from other parts of Europe and Asia.

For describing this long drawn process of cultural change in Cuba, Ortiz preferred the term transculturation as opposed to acculturation. This was because the former expressed the process of transition from one culture to another better than the latter, which merely implied the acquisition of another culture. The acquired culture was often the dominant one, and hence it was considered as being "superior." Is this interpretation of the terms transculturation and acculturation valid? Towards the end of our chapter, we might recognize that Ortiz was being imprecise in his understanding of acculturation.

The concept of transculturation was neither restricted to an academic understanding of the history of Cuba nor to a sociological analysis of Cuban society. It also had a more pragmatic use. That use was for serving the purpose of Cuban nationalism through an integration of Blacks and Whites. Towards explaining the manner in which he understood Cuban transculturation Ortiz resorted to the allegory of the *ajiaco*.

Ajiaco is a dish with many ingredients, very much like Cuban society. But, *cubanidad* for Ortiz, did not lie in the broth of the *ajiaco*; rather, in the cooking, in the constant integration and disintegration of the ingredients in the cooking pot, in the constant blending of cultures and human lineages (Rojas 2005, 65-71). In other words, the goal of *cubanidad* for Ortiz was clearly not homogenization; its aim was neither in being a mulatto/a, nor in becoming one. Transculturation understood thus is indeed a valuable insight.

Transculturation in 'Play'

Ortiz's concept of transculturation was recovered and employed by later scholars for resolving their own research problems. The concept resonated in the experience of many different societies in Latin America, beyond Cuba. This shows that transculturation as a concept is indeed pertinent. Therefore we shall now turn our attention to see how this theoretical concept played out in practice—all within the works of Ortiz. The instances or themes selected for this purpose are tobacco, Afro-Cuban music and "cabildos."

Tobacco and Transculturation

Most people agree that the use of tobacco is indeed very injurious to health. Yet, more than a billion people ingest it into their bodies every day in a variety of forms. Is tobacco truly "sublime" as Lord Byron once described it (Byron 1823, 41)? Or, was he abusing poetic license in praising a "diabolic" invention? While non-users might dismiss Byron's description as an exaggeration, tobacco continues to be an antidote to our "Age of Anxiety" (Klein 1995, 27). If we set aside both the laudatory defence of tobacco and its loathing, one cannot but recognize that tobacco is indeed part of the universal human culture. Its history is laid out in the *Contrapunteo cubano del tabaco y el azúcar* (Ortiz 2003, 103-254 and 283-209; Ortiz 2002, 261-535, 655-722, and 739-49).

This book does not contain a straightforward history of tobacco, but is instead the history of the transculturation of tobacco. What does Ortiz mean by that? Transculturation of tobacco is an examination of the stimuli and means that resulted in the transfer of tobacco from the New World to the Old. While Europe colonized America and its indigenous inhabitants, chocolate, corn, papaya, potato, tomato and many other original American products conquered the world and became an essential part of human society. Yet, tobacco remains singular because it has been an enduring force to date. This makes the history of tobacco an extraordinary case for understanding the process of transculturation (Ortiz 2003, 183-84).

Tobacco was originally used for religious and medicinal purposes by the natives of America. However, when tobacco reached Europe and other parts of the world, it had entirely lost its religious purpose. It became a symbol of high social status, acquired an aesthetic appeal before becoming all too popular. During the European religious conquest of America, most of the native religions were stereotyped as "false," "idolatrous" and even "diabolic." Nonetheless, it is interesting to know from Ortiz that Christian friars doubled up as tobacco smugglers. In the 17th century, convents were often raided in search of contraband tobacco (Ortiz 2003, 307).

Tobacco smuggling was a profitable enterprise because there were heavy taxes on tobacco. From the early decades of the 16th century, Spanish colonizers cultivated tobacco, which made it taxable by the State. Due to the high demand for tobacco, taxing it helped satiate the monetary needs of the governments.

> [...] the Indian plant was not completely grated on the trunk of the culture of white people, nor naturalized among them, until a wholly new use was found for it, that of serving as a great source of tax revenue to satisfy the monetary needs of government. With this tobacco became a complete social institution among the white nations. What among the Indians had been a social institution of a magic-religious character became among the whites an institution of economic character, a characteristic phenomenon of complete transculturation (Ortiz 2003, 219-20).

> [...] in Euro-Asiatic nations the opposition to tobacco, which went to the lengths of making its cultivation punishable by death, disappeared when tobacco was brought under a system of production and taxation favourable to the established social and political interests (Ortiz 2003, 230).

Even the Papal States exploited tobacco for fiscal reasons, and in some places, the Pope established a monopoly over tobacco trade. Thanks to these measures, it appeared that tobacco had more followers than Christ (Ortiz 2003, 247-48). But, were men of religion really tolerant towards tobacco?

Ortiz referred to how the Muslims in Turkey were outraged by the use of tobacco; how the patriarchs of the Eastern Church spoke of it as the devil's plant; and how the clergy in the Old World were fanatically intolerant of tobacco. He also alluded to the anti-tobacco diatribes of the Protestants. Although the Roman Catholic Church was generally tolerant towards tobacco because it was a source of income, Ortiz mentioned a number of decrees by popes and synods addressed to the clergy on the appropriate modes concerning the use tobacco. Apparently, the Holy Office of the Inquisition hardly ever took any action against the use of tobacco (Ortiz 2003, 231-37).

It is indeed very interesting to read that at one time European doctors were the "stoutest defenders of tobacco." Ortiz noted that perhaps Dr. Nicolás Monardes, a Spanish physician of the late 16th century, was tobacco's greatest advocate. Tobacco was thought to provide immunity against the contagion of plague during the Great Plague in England (1665); to alleviate pain during pregnancy and childbirth; enemas of smoke were administered in Switzerland, Germany and other countries of Europe; and many doctors believed tobacco to be a panacea, and administered it in the form of compound, poultice, infusion, powders, as well as for chewing, fuming and inhaling (Ortiz 2003, 242-47). Today, empirical studies have confirmed that smoking tobacco causes emphysema, and could lead cancer and a painful death. Such is the curious history of the transculturation of tobacco.

Another interesting instance of the transculturation of tobacco was that "the Negroes adopted the use of tobacco from the Indians before the Whites did" (Ortiz 2003, 192). In fact, Ortiz argued that the Indians' characteristic manners of using tobacco are to be found in Africa (Ortiz 2003, 194). Ortiz referred to the use of tobacco by Africans in the following manner:

> And even though the Negroes in Africa did not know tobacco, or the custom of smoking it, they quickly grasped, by easy analogies, its religious sense, its magic significance, its use as a narcotic or stimulant to induce states of supernatural possession or in the magic rite of physiological and spiritual catharsis. And while they did not incorporate tobacco into their rites, which were archaic and did not admit of exogenous innovations, they had not hostility towards it (Ortiz 2003, 195).

Ortiz extensively analysed the religious and medicinal uses of tobacco amongst the natives of the Caribbean islands, Mesoamerica, Peru, South and North America. He relies on voluminous ethnographical accounts of travellers, priests and government officials who lived in those lands. There are long passages on how Indians consumed tobacco, how it was rolled for smoking, how it was smoked, and how the tobacco smoke was exhaled. He then proceeded to compare the different modes of tobacco consumption amongst Europeans during the 17th and 18th centuries. He highlighted practices that have survived and those that have not, as well as practices and products, like the cigarette, that were newly invented.

Neither the Negroes nor the Whites acquired the religious meanings that the Indians in the Caribbean had attached to tobacco before the arrival of the Spaniards. But within a few decades of their arrival, many native communities in the Antilles were completely wiped out, partly due to disease but partly due to the brutal treatment meted out to them. When Columbus first arrived on these islands, some of those Indians offered tobacco leaves to the Spaniards, as a sign of friendship. That practice however has survived amidst the complex history of the transculturation of tobacco. Even today, tobacco in the form of cigars and cigarettes are offered to break ice and make friends while it is at the same time "the soldier's most faithful friend."

An Analysis of Afro-Cuban Cabildos in the Light of Transculturation

Although it was around 1940 that Ortiz defined the concept of transculturation, we could to a certain extent trace the trajectory that allowed him to articulate this concept. In reality, the emergence of the concept of transculturation in his work was a response to the difficulties and discoveries that arose in the context of his ethnographical and historical studies. Thus, his analysis of the Afro-Cuban *cabildos* (councils), although prior to *Contrapunteo cubano del tabaco y el azúcar*, could be a propitious terrain for exemplifying and exploring the theoretical model of transculturation (Ortiz 1973, 121-34).[9] In the analysis of cabildos, Ortiz complies with the phases and the components that he would later make explicit with the neologism of transculturation: acquisition, loss, and synthesis in the terrain of culture.

Ortiz began by explaining what constituted the cabildos. It was an association formed by Negro slaves belonging to the same "tribe" or "nation." During festivals, the cabildos met, and in these reunions its members played instruments like the tambor, sang and danced. The cabildos collected funds and individual members were assigned to posts through elections. These features of the cabildos point to a hierarchically structured organization, where the oldest member of the tribe or nation was generally the "king," or head, of the cabildo.

In his various studies, Ortiz explicitly highlighted the form in which relations of power and domination were exercised within a social system characterized by slavery. This was the background to his ethnographical observations on Afro-Cuban cabildos.

> The king enjoyed considerable power within the short radius of action that lay outside the influence of the social power of the Whites (Ortiz 1973, 122).[10]

The king of the cabildo was in charge of the funds and had the powers of sanctioning his subjects with fines. In the hierarchy of the cabildo, the king was followed by the queen. There were a few other posts of ceremonial character, which were not well defined, amongst which was the flag bearer, a post that was created when the flag was admitted as the symbol of the cabildo.

Let us make an aside for capturing the ethnographical description of Ortiz. As we have seen, the concept of transculturation arose principally within the context of the study of cultural survivals and transformations related to African slavery in Cuba. This presupposed a comparison between the distinctive characteristics of the African communities based on their origin and cultural features that could be recognized amongst the slaves already transplanted in the Caribbean, particularly, in Cuba. Ortiz frequently noted that the African slaves in Cuba, in their attempt at acculturation and adaptation to the new socio-historical ambience, acquired European elements and lost their African features. It is worth emphasizing that this loss was not in any sense total because all through the history of slavery African elements were constantly being transferred to Cuba.

In the case of the cabildos, this understanding of the African cultural components allowed Ortiz to establish a few hypotheses. Against the presupposition sustained by a certain author that the king of the cabildo complied with both the ceremonial and religious functions, Ortiz argued that it was reasonable to sustain the hypothesis that there was a "division of the priestly and royal powers vested in the authorities of the cabildos as was common amongst the original communities from whence came the Afro-Cubans" (Ortiz 1973, 123).[11] In this manner, Ortiz concluded that certain organizational and cultural aspects that were peculiar to the African context had been transplanted to Cuba, although these were transformed to some extent. According to Ortiz, the hypothesis concerning the division of powers within the cabildo conformed to the attire worn by the kings—frock-coats, robes, ties, double-coned hats—all of which originated from within the European social terrain "without exhibiting any remnant of religious character."

With regard to attire, we may note how Ortiz recognized a phenomenon that he would later designate as being characteristic of transculturation. It is the acquisition of cultural elements proceeding from an alien cultural matrix. Those African slaves, who belonged to the cabildos utilized European military attire, particularly the king of the cabildo. This appropriation of European cultural elements was especially notable on the "day of the kings," when the king of the cabildo in his ceremonial attire recalled the indelible imprint of colonial Europe in the Congo:

> On the "day of the kings", the "Congo king" was attired in frock-coat and trousers, double-coned hat, long, ornate baton etc. While these were of European origin, the royal cloak and the sceptre were those of the African king of Congo, received as a souvenir from the king of Portugal in 1888.[12]

This ethnographical observation makes one realize that the phenomenon of transculturation, so precisely described by Ortiz in the context of the multiplicity of co-existing cultures in Cuba, was without doubt simultaneously taking place alongside the processes of European colonialism in Africa. Ortiz became a lucid observer of the cultural implications related to one of the facets of the Modern World System, which was associated with the configuration of a world market that employed slavery and forced labour extracted from various parts of Africa over a period of four centuries. But, his point of view was always located within the context of Cuba. That was his outlook, the context from within which he perceived certain cultural processes that sparked off his interest on the subject of slavery.

Perhaps, it is necessary to highlight here that the theoretical model of transculturation—which Ortiz explicitly developed in his *Contrapunteo cubano del tabaco y el azúcar* but was also clearly anticipated in his preceding work—must be considered as an exercise in historical research. In other words, transculturation does not deal with statically capturing the form in which different cultural elements congregated or interacted, rather it must be located as unfolding within a dynamic framework. The processes of transculturation that developed all through history have their own origins and inflections.

Consequently, Ortiz always delimited his research questions within a time frame and pondered over the chronological order of the phenomena he studied. And, his exploration of the Afro-Cuban cabildos does not represent an exception to this rule:

> Let us see what could have been the origin of such Afro-Cuban cabildos. Surely, these did not spontaneously arise in Cuba. Today, we can be certain that the origin of African cabildos dates back to the 14th century, more than a hundred years before the discovery of America (Ortiz 1973, 126).[13]

During his historical (diachronic) research on the cabildos, Ortiz discovered that this same institution was functioning in Seville ca. 1390, and this organization was notoriously similar to the cabildos extant in Cuba towards the end of the 19th century. The African cabildos that were functioning in Seville in the last decade of the 14th century also celebrated festivals and dances, and these also had the "mayoral"—a figure of authority similar in all respects to the king of the Afro-Cuban cabildos. According to the chronicle of Ortiz de Zúñiga, alluded to by Ortiz, the mayoral of African cabildos in Seville functioned both as the leader and the judge of the members of the organization (Ortiz 1973, 126).[14]

But, the African communities, divided by tribal, national and ethnic affiliations, were not the only ones that were organized into cabildos in Seville ca. 1390. Ortiz demonstrated the existence of cabildos of gypsies, who were also incorporated into such a type of organization by the royal authorities. Here, an interesting aspect of the historical and ethnographical research of Ortiz was brought to light, which he explicitly dealt with a few decades later, in his studies on folklore and Afro-Cuban music (Ortiz 2001, 5-12).[15] Ortiz was evidently sensitive in his description of social hierarchy, in such a manner that while describing an institution such as the cabildo, he did not avoid highlighting the manner in which power and domination criss-crossed ethnic and communal affiliation.

> Gypsies and Negros in Seville had shared experiences, given the analogous social inferiority in which they found themselves in, for their exotic language and customs, their colour, their contagious superstitions, their tribal

> affiliations etc. It is not surprising that the Whites organized them into cofradías and cabildos and that the chiefs of the gypsy tribes, as those of the nucleus of the nation, called them king or captain, and both elected the king and the queen. The social organization of the Afro-Cuban cabildo, and likewise, their kings and captains, was what Spain gave and that was how Spain recognized foreign immigrants on their own soil, particularly those belonging to uncultured and subjected peoples.[16]

With regard to this text of 1921, it is worth noting that Ortiz was progressively moving away from his positivist stance that was notoriously evident in *Los negros brujos* of 1906. Some of his positivist premises led him to classify cultures within an evolutionary framework, which he did not ever abandon completely. This is evident in an important section on transculturation in *Contrapunteo cubano del tabaco y el azúcar* (Ortiz 1978, 92-97).

For example, we have already seen that in "Los cabildos afrocubanos," Ortiz highlighted the subordinate role of Africans and gypsies. The organization of these peoples into *cofradías* (fraternal associations) and cabildos was a clear indication of their subaltern role in Seville at that time. At the end of this passage, Ortiz referred to "naciones incultas" (uncultured nations), which was an unfortunate expression that was incompatible with his general outlook.

One could affirm that Ortiz was articulating with ever greater precision a frontal attack against the Cuban Creole society that enforced an inferior role to Afro-Cubans. He did so through an exhaustive research that clarified the cultural contributions of the Afro-Cubans. This method of rational and scientific elucidation became his principal weapon. Thus, by virtue of his theoretical labours and research endeavours, Ortiz was being identified within the Cuban ideological scene as a powerful critic of secular racism prevalent in Cuba.

Notwithstanding, it is also necessary to highlight the epistemological scope and limitations of his thought, which was in good measure linked to cultural anthropology of his time. The distinction between "advanced" and "primitive" cultures was a distinction based on a value scale that relied on criteria such as a social and technological sophistication. For Ortiz, the scientific work of cultural anthropology rested on this premise. In this sense, the horizon of cultural anthropology was one which Ortiz could not transcend as an anthropologist.

Instead, perhaps, one should inquire whether the evolutionary premises that permeated his studies constituted, in the last instance, an obstacle to that goal which really mattered to Ortiz. The goal was to recognize and value Afro-Cuban identities, which were historically undervalued by the Creole thinking that was dominant in Cuba.

At this juncture, it is equally important to emphasize that the concept of transculturation as proposed by Ortiz in 1940 implied a gigantic step towards recognizing the subordinate cultures in Cuba, especially, the Afro-Cuban culture. The dominant anthropological currents of the time could only capture the form in which a collective group acquired a new culture, or how a group was accultured by receiving elements from another culture.

According to this approach, the accultured group received a new identity by renouncing its previous cultural identity. Ortiz regarded this explanation to be insufficient in recognizing the complexity of the phenomenon of cultural contact. His capacity to capture all or a great majority of the cultural elements that influenced those socio-historical processes that he studied may be discerned in his analysis of the Afro-Cuban cabildos.

We have already noted that Ortiz found the origins of the Afro-Cuban cabildos in those associations formed by the decision of royal authorities in Seville. More than a century before the emergence of America in the horizon of Europe and before the arrival of African slaves to the Caribbean, it was possible to establish the existence of African cabildos and cofradías in Seville. Ortiz noted thus the transculturation of Afro-Cuban cabildos:

> And from Seville, where there was a great nucleus of Africans, came the African cabildos and cofradías to the Indies, wherein the metropolitan organization was reproduced.[17]

In the ethnographical descriptions of the Afro-Cuban cabildos we can see that Ortiz moved across different levels. To begin with, it was necessary to precisely characterize the nature, structure and functions of the cabildos. This was followed by shedding light on its features and historical origins. But, perhaps, the most relevant aspect of his historical and ethnographical descriptions lay in the manner in which the process of transculturation was unravelled.

This allowed the reader to perceive the asymmetries and the power relations that existed in Cuban society of the time.

Although Afro-Cuban cabildos comprised of Negro slaves of the same national and ethnic origin, the institution itself was of European provenance. Some of the practices of the members of the cabildos reflected the presence of European cultural elements, like, in the case of the military attire. This meant that the Afro-Cuban cabildos, when considered as a cultural phenomenon, exemplified with great clarity the process of transculturation. While the Negro slaves that belonged to these cabildos adopted European cultural practices they lost African cultural elements in the process. In the end, the Afro-Cuban cabildo was a synthesis of its own—an institution with both African and European features.

Afro-Cuban Music and Transculturation

One of the principal historical and ethnographical interests of Fernando Ortiz was African music in Cuba. He dedicated voluminous studies to this subject, which resulted in *Los instrumentos de la música afrocubana*—a monumental work in five tomes. The penetrating and minutely detailed descriptions contained therein allowed Ortiz to understand and exhaustively explain the characteristics of *tambores* and other musical instruments of African origin.

Ortiz acquired such precision in his knowledge of the details regarding the manufacture of Afro-Cuban tambores that he could infer the ethnic origin of a tambor from an analysis of the *clavija* (peg/pin/bolt) used for tightening the membrane of the instrument. In his analysis of the characteristics of tambores Arará—one of the African ethnic identities transcultured in Cuba—Ortiz compared two types of clavijas used in the making of the tambor and concluded that the morphological difference between the clavijas corresponded to their distinct ethnic origins (Ortiz 1997, 8).[18]

In his studies of Afro-Cuban music, Ortiz swam against the current of cultural and ideological tendencies that were dominant at that time. He was particularly interested in recognizing the African contributions to Cuban music because these were often obviated or minimized. The larger research project of Ortiz on Afro-Cuban music produced three different studies.

In *La africanía de la música folklórica cubana*, Ortiz dealt with certain aspects of the transculturation of African elements in Cuban music. This prepared the terrain for a detailed examination of some of its elements, which were explored in *Los bailes y el teatro de los negros en el folklore de Cuba*. Once the ground was cleared with these two studies, Ortiz plunged into a careful and minute analysis of each one of the Afro-Cuban instruments about which he had any information at all, and produced his magnum opus *Los instrumentos de la música afrocubana*.[19]

The scope of this research project on Afro-Cuban music was so vast that the above-mentioned studies were located at the thresholds of many fields that shared their borders with what strictly belonged to the field of music. This was so because Ortiz was always interested in the social history of music so much so that he incorporated into his study elements that were extraneous to music. However, these alien elements served to clarify aspects pertaining to music.

For example, while studying melodies, canticles, rhythms and instruments of Afro-Cuban music, Ortiz highlighted their religious meanings and implications. Thus, his analysis of the features of Afro-Cuban instruments and the materials utilized for making these were complimented by a hermeneutic of occasions propitious for playing these instruments. Such questions were otherwise generally referred to within a study of religious practices transplanted from Africa to Cuba.

Besides this preoccupation with the social history of music, which permitted an appreciation of the social totality, Ortiz also proceeded towards studying other Afro-Cuban expressions that were closely linked to music. In *Los bailes y el teatro de los negros en el folklore de Cuba*, Ortiz proffered a detailed ethnographic description of the "pantomimes" and dances associated with the *Orichas, Yoruba* or *Lucumí* deities, which were transplanted to the Caribbean via the slave trade.

Within the framework of the *Lucumí* ceremonies in Cuba, the staging and representation of the *Orichas* were subjected to multiple rules and prescriptions. These were described and analysed minutely by Ortiz. In other words, the ethnographical approach to Afro-Cuban music demanded that the totality of the phenomenon be recognized. In this way, Ortiz extended the horizon of his studies on music to include descriptions of the theatrical performances, the "pantomimes," the dances as well as the clothing and attire.

We have seen that the theoretical model of transculturation, utilized by Ortiz explicitly since 1940, stemmed from his preceding historical and ethnographical research. However, his studies on

Afro-Cuban music were written after he had already characterized the meaning of the concept of transculturation. This enabled Ortiz to demonstrate that Afro-Cuban music was a fertile terrain for exploring it as a phenomenon of transculturation.

Consequently, in the description of the transculturation of African tambores in Cuba, the scope of the concept of transculturation was delimited when compared to what was on offer in *Contrapunteo cubano*....[20] Ortiz inquired why African musical instruments were prohibited from the Creole social milieu of Cuba while African rhythms were accepted.

> Let us observe what happened in Cuba. Since the time of the first contacts, African rhythms were accepted and the country's music was progressively being turned into mulatto because of the irresistible influence of those rhythms in dances and songs. But, Negro musical instruments were not accepted. Why?[21]

For answering this question, Ortiz developed distinct responses. He showed that African tambores had a religious character during the period when slavery was in vogue. This made it difficult for the tambores to be played on any occasion other than that of the meetings of the cabildos, in which only those Negro slaves of the same nationality and ethnicity participated. Towards exemplifying this, Ortiz referred to the tambores *batá* of the *Lucumí*, who made up one particular group of the Afro-Cuban ethnicity. It was not until 1936, when during a public performance organized by Ortiz did the tambores *batá* cross the portals into the world of the profane.

Ortiz also sought to explain this absence of the African musical instruments from the Creole ambience of Cuba by alluding to the nature of the instrument itself. Many slaves were from Congo and Angola. Their tambores were enormous in size and potency (for percussion). These were "neither easily portable nor their drumming in walled enclosures possible" (Ortiz 1993, 182).[22]

But the most important impediment that prevented the diffusion of the African tambores amongst the Creoles and the *peninsulares* in Cuba was explained by virtue of the relations of ethnic domination. In this matter, Ortiz was very clear while underlining that the cultural appropriation could be seen limiting or made impossible due to the social hierarchy and the domination of one ethnic group over another.

> If the Negros did not like to profane their tambores, the Whites, although unable to resist the suggestive rhythms and dances, did not adopt their tambores due to certain difficulties, and because they did not want to 'belittle' themselves into strumming 'Negro instruments', *i.e.,*-with the criteria then prevalent-of vile people, of barbarians and savages [...] They could dance everywhere, the steps and the swagger of the *zarabanda,* and many other similar dances, because these, although of the same Negro lineage, had already been naturalized by the Spanish people [...] Yet, if the African tambores were adopted, not even the so-called 'Whitening', Christianization o nationalization could have disguised the non-Hispanic or native exoticism and the pagan nature of the dance, nor would it have been possible to dance in the court of Philip II with Negro instruments from Congo (Ortiz 1993, 183).[23]

Thus, Ortiz demonstrated that the processes of transculturation could be favoured or impeded depending on the prevalent social values. In this explanation of transculturation, he introduced an important factor that must be noted. While considering the social asymmetries and the relations of power, the panorama of the processes of transculturation was modified. The historical encounter between two or more groups, differentiated between themselves, was insufficient for setting off a process of transculturation, at least in certain specified contexts. Thus, if the African rhythms were indeed transcultured and were "whitened" in a number of dances as was the case with the incorporation of certain percussive elements of Cuban music, this did not occur with the musical instruments owing to the "social conventions" prevalent at the time (Ortiz 1993, 183).

Mapping the Broad Contours of the Reception of Contrapunteo Cubano... in Anthropology and Literature

As Fernando Ortiz was redacting the text that would eventually become the book *Contrapunteo cubano...*, he met with the anthropologist Bronislaw Malinowski in Cuba. The year was 1939. Their ensuing correspondence encouraged Malinowski to sketch an introduction for the Spanish edition (1940). That "introduction" reappeared in the English translation (1947), and in all subsequent editions of *Contrapunteo cubano*.... Despite the apparent congruence between the positions of Ortiz and Malinowski, their relationship is a telltale on the nature of academic collaboration and the production of knowledge.

Ortiz wrote to Malinowski seeking the latter's approval for the use of the neologism "transculturation."[24] And in the book, Ortiz explicitly refers to this act of seeking and having received the approbation of the Polish anthropologist (Ortiz 2003, 103).[25] Fernando Coronil perceived this scholarly engagement between Ortiz and Malinowski within the international network of knowledge production (Coronil 2003, xxx). The endorsement of a metropolitan authority could favour the fate of a work produced in the periphery; as it perhaps did in the case Ortiz. However, the favour did not come without a price.

Malinowski (mis)appropriated *Contrapunteo cubano*... into his own theoretical project of 'functionalism' despite insufficient evidence to label Ortiz as a functionalist. For a functionalist like Malinowski, the relevance of human institutions was located by emphasizing their current significance. This implied a neglect of the history of these institutions. A student of Ortiz, Julio Le Riverend, claimed that Ortiz had insisted that he was not a functionalist (Coronil 2003, xxxv). This was because, unlike Malinowski, Ortiz attached a great importance to the historical study of human institutions and culture.

Thus, the differences between Ortiz and Malinowski were not incidental but of emphasis. In that case, the misinterpretation of Ortiz by Malinowski does not seem innocuous, and especially so in the light of recent studies. Evidence mounts against Malinowski in the context of the correspondence between Ortiz and Melville Herskovits (1895-1963)—the pioneering American anthropologist of African and Afro-American culture.

Herskovits gained a lasting reputation for having aided the entry of African and Afro-American studies into mainstream academics in the United States. As a student under Franz Boas, he received a doctoral degree in 1923 from Columbia University.[26] His research output since the mid 1920s consistently attacked ethnocentrism as well as cultural hierarchy. He argued for a mutual respect of cultures and actively criticized American foreign policy with regard to Africa since World War II (Gershenhorn 2004). Ortiz certainly would have concurred with the inclinations of Herskovits, or so one would imagine. Nonetheless, Herskovits and Ortiz seemed to have been oblivious to each other until the publication of *Contrapunteo cubano....*

As soon as *Contrapunteo cubano...* came out of the press, Ortiz mailed a copy of the book to Herskovits along with a covering letter, which received an impassioned response. In his response, Hershkovits strongly resented against the manner in which Malinowski understood the term "acculturation" as being "inculcation," whereby a "superior" civilization was promoting elements of its culture to "savage" peoples. Herskovits wrote thus to Ortiz (2002, 786-87):[27]

> Certainly, it is necessary for me to enter a very strong demur to the implications of the term "acculturation" advanced on pages xvi-xvii by Malinowski. It is significant, I think, that he does not document this passage; certainly, in our use of the term in this country there is no implication of handing down a superior civilization to a "savage" folk. The term as we use it in our scientific work is indeed entirely colourless and in my book I have stressed the necessity for studies in this field which concern the results of contact between two primitive folk. One of my students who has worked in West Africa has investigated the problem of the results of contact between non-European culture among the Hausa of Nigeria, while I am hoping to send another student to Honduras to study the cultural amalgalm resulting from contact between the Carib Indians and Africans. If anybody has been guilty of discussing cultural contact in terms of "inculcation"—to use Malinowski's own word—it has been his own students writing of "culture contact" rather than those of us in this country who are concerned with the scientific problem of acculturation.

This letter reflects certain details that we cannot pass over lightly. While Ortiz might have been ignorant of the implications of Herskovits' studies on acculturation/- culture contact, Malinowski certainly was not. Yet, Malinowski very clearly omitted any reference to Herskovits in his "introduction" to *Contrapunteo cubano....* Instead, there is a mere solipsistic allusion to his work.

This omission was grave not only because Herskovits had authored or co-authored at least three studies on cultural exchange in the years immediately preceding the publication of *Contrapunteo cubano*... rather because Malinowski misinterpreted the term "acculturation" and in the process led Ortiz down the road of semantic imprecision regarding "acculturation" vis-à-vis "transculturation."[28]

Malinowski's behaviour could be explained variously but the differences underlying British and North American schools concerning Applied Anthropology were central (Santí 2002, 85-91). Although Malinowski veered closer towards the North American school between 1936 and 1939, he was nonetheless reluctant to employ the term "acculturation" as enunciated and understood by the American anthropologists and instead chose the term "culture contact." And when Ortiz introduced the term "transculturation," this neologism generated in the periphery would have sounded sweet to Malinowski amidst the noise generated by quibbles over terminology between metropolitan anthropologists.

Although the correspondence between Ortiz and Herskovits show that they were needlessly talking past each other on the question of acculturation/transculturation, the duo indeed acknowledged each other's works. Herskovits alluded to the studies of Fernando Ortiz in *The Myth of the Negro Past* (1941) and *Man and his works: The science of cultural contact* (1948). Robin Moore has suggested that Ortiz went beyond drawing on Herskovits' study *Acculturation: The study of culture contact*. Some of his later writings referred to the works of Herskovits, as well as those of Harold Courlander amongst others (Moore 1994, 44-45).

Yet, it remains to be confirmed, through a perusal of the studies and archives of Ortiz and Herskovits, whether these two scholars further alluded to or engaged with or influenced each other; and if so, to what extent. This is because in the terrain of ethnography as well as in the theoretical orientations concerning the study of the African elements in the Atlantic world, the true counterpart of Fernando Ortiz was Melville Herskovits; and other Boasian anthropologists, like Sidney Mintz and his works on the Caribbean region and, sugar, in particular (Mintz 1985). The conjunctions and disjunctions in the research trajectories of Ortiz and the American anthropologists need to be mapped further.

If one moves from the United States towards Spanish America, it is odd that the influence of Ortiz over Latin American anthropologists, outside Cuba, has been considerably less than what one would expect. Andrés Medina, a Mexican anthropologist, pondered over this oddity nearly twenty years ago (Medina 1993).

Medina wondered why Fernando Ortiz and—others such as Miguel Othón de Mendizábal and José María Arguedas—have remained inadequately recognized, although their works articulate an original yet specifically Latin American trajectory of thought. In fact, their names do not even appear in introductory courses in Anthropology at most universities. Medina explained this anomaly as arising out of a conglomeration of different factors, but the most important one was the lop-sided relationship between core and the periphery (between hegemonic and developing countries) in the production of knowledge and culture.

To this general explanation must be added a specific fact concerning the fortune of Ortiz's idea of transculturation. Gonzalo Aguirre Beltran, a former student of Herskovits and a leading Mexican anthropologist during the 1950s and 1960s, depreciated Ortiz's concept of transculturation (Beltrán 1957). Other blind spots of professional anthropologists, in the whole American continent, with regard to the work of Ortiz are listed by Jorge Ibarra and Fernando Coronil (Ibarra 1990, 1347-49 and Coronil 2003, xxxvi-xxxvii).

Having said that, Ortiz's iconographical study of the deity *Huracán*, in his *El huracán: Su mitología y sus símbolos* (1947), was widely read by scholars of Mesoamerica. And more recently, Antonio Garcia de Leon Griego in his *El mar de deseos: El Caribe hispano musical. Historia y contrapunto* (2002) employed the Ortizian insight of viewing the terrain of culture as extending beyond national boundaries.

If anthropologists were delayed in their appraisal of the work of Fernando Ortiz, that was not the case with writers. Through writers, the ideas and works of Fernando Ortiz filtered into literary criticism and thus re-entered the academe. Here, we shall restrict ourselves to the incidence of Ortiz upon Alejo Carpentier and Alfonso Reyes although C.L.R. James, the Trinidadian writer and political activist, referred to Ortiz as having ushered the Caribbean into the mind of the 20th century.

The Cuban writer Alejo Carpentier claimed to have devoured the books of Ortiz, especially considering their shared interests in Afro-Cuban music. In his *La música en Cuba* (1946), Carpentier referred to the exaltation of Afro-Cuban folklore generated in part at least by the studies of Ortiz. Alfonso Reyes, whom Jorge Luis Borges, described as amongst the greatest Spanish prose-writers of all time, wrote a prologue to *Los bailes y el teatro de los negros en el folklore de Cuba* (1951). Reyes invited the reader to relish the African elements in American culture through the writings of the erudite Ortiz.

The engagement of Carpentier and Reyes with the works of Ortiz altered the fortune of *Contrapunteo cubano...* within the discipline of literary studies. Evidence to this effect is prompted by the fact that a few decades later, the Uruguayan literary critic Ángel Rama published *Transculturación narrativa en América Latina* (1982). In this work, Rama recovered the idea of transculturation, as conceived originally by Ortiz, and employed it to explain the nature of Latin American narratives. Rama's book eventually became a foundational text of literary criticism.

The last decades of the 20th century were momentous. The *quintocentenario* of the European discovery of America generated debates over the subject of "culture contact." It was also a time when disciplinary boundaries were disintegrating and theoretical currents in literature were being vitalized in the interdisciplinary fields of Latin American, Caribbean, Post-Colonial and Culture Studies. In this complex atmosphere, the ideas and works of Fernando Ortiz began to receive scholarly attention. Many of his works were reprinted, translated anew, critically appreciated, widely read and discussed. This burgeoning scholarly interest forms the background as well as the introduction to our own project of critically reviewing and translating the works of Fernando Ortiz.

As we end this coda, it is worth reminding ourselves that the ethnographical and historical research of Ortiz sprouted and flourished from within Cuban history, and his concept of transculturation arose as a consequence of his attempts to understand the cultural processes that took place in Cuba as well as within the larger context of the multiplicity of complex cultural matrices that congregated in the Caribbean over five hundred years.

Notes

1. En Cuba toda una raza entró en la mala vida. (En Europa un fenómeno análogo puede observarse en la posición social de los gitanos, aunque diversos bajo muchos aspectos. [nota a pie]) Al llegar los negros entraban todos en la mala vida cubana, no

como caídos de un plan superior de moralidad, sino como ineptos por el momento al menos, para trepar hasta él. [...]

En sus amores eran los negros sumamente lascivos, sus matrimonios llegaban hasta la poligamia, la prostitución no merecía su repugnancia, sus familias carecían de cohesión, su religión los llevaba a los sacrificios humanos, a la violación de sepulturas, a la antropofagia, y a las brutales supersticiones; la vida del ser humano les inspiraba escaso respeto [...]

Pero la inferioridad del negro, la que le sujetaba al mal vivir era debida a la falta de civilización integral, pues tan primitiva era su moralidad, como su intelectualidad, como sus voliciones etc. Este carácter es lo que más lo diferencia de los individuos de la mala vida de las sociedades formadas exclusivamente por blancos. (Ortiz 1916, 13-14)

2. [...] el negro africano fue traído a Cuba en la más completa desnudez física y psicológica. [...] El negro era como decía Girard de Rialle "un niño grande entregado a la impresión del momento y absolutamente esclavo a sus pasiones. Así, se manifiestan en él las contradicciones más sorprendentes en su conducta. Es ligero, inconsistente, alegre, reidor, amante del placer con frenesí, loco por el baile, el ruido y los vestidos chillones y llamativos." Los etnólogos completan esos trazos pintándonos los pueblos africanos que dieron su carne a la trata abominable, como naturalmente indolentes, de sensualidad desbordante, faltos de previsión, supersticiosos sin límites, de inteligencia poca despierta y enemigos de las ideas abstractas, tímidos de espíritu ante lo desconocido, aunque valerosos ante el peligro real, caritativos, amantes de su terruño y presa de añoranzas en tierras extrañas por el recuerdo del país nativo, llenos de devoción a los hijos y dados a la buena amistad. [...] Tales parecen ser los rasgos psicológicos salientes que, según los etnógrafos, tenias las razas vírgenes sobre las cuales se cebó la trata esclavista de estas Indias. (Ortiz 1916, 54-55)
3. The positive school of criminology maintains, on the contrary, that it is not the criminal who wills; in order to be a criminal it is rather necessary that the individual should find himself permanently or transitorily in such personal, physical and moral conditions, and live in such an environment, which become for him a chain of cause and effect, externally and internally, that disposes him toward crime. This is our conclusion, which I anticipate, and it constitutes the vastly different and opposite method, which the positive school of criminology employs as compared to the leading principle of the classic school of criminal science. Ferri, Enrico. "The Positive School of Criminology" the first of three lectures delivered at the University of Naples on 22 April 1901. Published in Ferri, Enrico.

The Positive School of Criminology. Translated by Ernest Untermann. Chicago: Charles H. Kerr & Company, 1908. Accessed August 9, 2011. Project Gutenberg http://www.gutenberg.org/files/10580/10580-h/10580-h.htm

4. The anthropological factor: It is precisely here that the genius of Cesare Lombroso established a new science, because in his search after the causes of crime he studied the anthropological condition of the criminal. This condition concerns not only the organic and anatomical constitution, but also the psychological, [which] represents the organic and psychological personality of the criminal. Every one of us inherits at birth, and personifies in life, a certain organic and psychological combination. This constitutes the individual factor of human activity, which either remains normal through life, or becomes criminal or insane. The anthropological factor, then, must not be restricted, as some laymen would restrict it, to the study of the form of the skull or the bones of the criminal. Lombroso had to begin his studies with the anatomical conditions of the criminal, because the skulls may be studied most easily in the museums. But he continued by also studying the brain and the other physiological conditions of the individual, the state of sensibility, and the circulation of matter. And this entire series of studies is but a necessary scientific introduction to the study of the psychology of the criminal, which is precisely the one problem that is of direct and immediate importance. It is this problem which the lawyer and the public prosecutor should solve before discussing the juridical aspect of any crime, for this reveals the causes which induced the criminal to commit a crime. At present there is no methodical standard for a psychological investigation, although such an investigation was introduced into the scope of classic penal law. But for this reason the results of the positive school penetrate into the lecture rooms of the universities of jurisprudence, whenever a law is required for the judicial arraignment of the criminal as a living and feeling human being. And even though the positive school is not mentioned, all profess to be studying the material furnished by it, for instance, its analyses of the sentiments of the criminal, his moral sense, his behaviour before, during and after the criminal act, the presence of remorse which people, judging the criminal after their own feelings, always suppose the criminal to feel, while, in fact, it is seldom present. This is the anthropological factor, which may assume a pathological form, in which case articles 46 and 47 of the penal code remember that there is such a thing as the personality of the criminal. Ferri, Enrico. "Of Criminology" the second of three lectures delivered at the University of Naples on 23 April 1901. Published in Ferri, Enrico.

The Positive School of Criminology. Translated by Ernest Untermann. Chicago: Charles H. Kerr & Company, 1908. Accessed August 9, 2011 via Project Gutenberg http://www.gutenberg.org/files/10580/10580-h/10580-h.htm

5. No hay odio de razas, porque no hay razas. Los pensadores canijos, los pensadores de lámparas, enhebran y recalientan las razas de librería que el viajero justo y el observador cordial buscan en vano en la justicia de la naturaleza, donde resalta en el amor victorioso y el apetito turbulento, la identidad universal del hombre. (Martí 2004, 73)
6. Cf. Fernández Robaina. "The term *Afro-Cuban*: A forgotten contribution." In *Cuban Counterpoints: The legacy of Fernando Ortiz*, edited by Mauricio A. Font and Alfonso W. Quiroz, 171-79. Lanham: Lexington Books, 2005.
7. Enrico Mario Santí offers an erudite appreciation of this essay along with a revision of existing studies by other literary critics. See the section "Cierre: Neobarroco" in "Introducción" to Ortiz *Contrapunteo cubano.*, 2002, pp. 94-103.
8. See Ortiz, "Del fenómeno social de la transculturación y de su importancia en Cuba" in *Contrapunteo cubano...*, 2002, pp. 254-60.
9. "Los cabildos afrocubanos" was first published in *Revista Bimestre Cubana* in 1921, and also in Ortiz, *Etnia y Sociedad*, 1993, 64-75. But here, we have cited the version available in *Órbita de Fernando Ortiz* edited by Le Riverend 1973.
10. El rey disfrutaba de considerable poder dentro del corto radio de acción que le dejaba el poder social de los blancos (Ortiz 1973, 122).
11. [...] la division de los poderes sacerdotal y real en las autoridades de los cabildos como es común en los pueblos de donde procedían los asociados (Ortiz 1973, 123). Here, Ortiz is referring to the author R. Meza, 'El día de Reyes' published in *Diario de la Marina de la Habana*, 8 January 1903.
12. El 'día de Reyes', el 'rey congo' vestía casaca y pantalones, sombrero de dos puntas, alto bastón borlado, etc. Todos esos atributos de origen europeo y, además, un manto real y un cetro, eran propios del rey congo africano, recibidos en obsequio del rey de Portugal en 1888. (Ortiz 1973, 123)
13. Veamos cuál pudo ser el origen de tales cabildos afrocubanos. Con seguridad no surgieron espontáneamente en Cuba. Bien puede hoy asegurarse que los *cabildos* de africanos se remontan al siglo XIV, *más* de cien años antes del descubrimiento de América (Ortiz 1973, 126).
14. Cf. Ortiz de Zúñiga, *Anales eclesiásticos y seculares de Sevilla*, lib. XII, cap. 10 cited in Ortiz, (1973, 126).
15. Although Ortiz wrote this work between 1947 and 1949, it was published only in 1954.

16. Gitanos y negros tuvieron en Sevilla cosas comunes por la análoga inferioridad social que hallaron, por su exótico lenguaje y costumbres, su color, sus supersticiones contagiosas, sus agrupaciones tribales, etc. No se extrañe pues que los blancos los organizaran también en *cofradías* y *cabildos* y que los jefes de las tribus gitanas, como a los de núcleos de nación les llamaran *rey* o *capitán* y que ambos eligiesen *rey* y *reina*. La organización social del cabildo afro cubano, así como sus reyes y capitanes, fue la que España dio y reconoció en su propio suelo a los inmigrados extranjeros, especialmente a los de naciones incultas y sometidas (Ortiz 1973, 127).
17. Y de Sevilla vinieron los *cabildos* y *cofradías* negras a las Indias, reproduciéndose la organización metropolitana donde hubo gran núcleo de africanos (Ortiz 1973, 129).
18. Es probable que esta diferencia morfológica de las clavijas responda a distintas procedencias étnicas (Ortiz 1997, 8).
19. *Los instrumentos de la música afrocubana,* vols. 1-3, 1952; vol. 4, 1954; vol. 5, 1955.
20. For what follows in this section, cf. Ortiz, "La transculturación de los tambores de los negros." In *Etnia y sociedad,* 1993, 181-8. This text was published in Venezuela in 1952.
21. Observemos lo que pasa en Cuba. Se aceptan desde los primeros contactos los ritmos africanos y la música del país se va amulatando, debido a la irresistible influencia de aquellos en los bailes y canciones; pero no se aceptan los instrumentos negros. Por qué? (Ortiz 1993, 181)
22. [...] no se prestaban al transporte fácil ni a su tañido en los recintos cerrados. (Ortiz 1993, 182)
23. Si los negros no gustaban de profanar sus tambores, los blancos, a pesar de no poder resistir la sugestión de sus ritmos y bailes, no adoptaron sus tambores por sus dificultades y porque no querían 'rebajarse' a tañer 'instrumentos de negros', es decir—con el criterio de aquel entonces—de gente vil, de bárbaros y salvajes [...] Se pudieron bailar en todas partes los pasos y los contoneos de la *zarabanda,* y de muchos otros bailes de igual condición, porque éstos, aun cuando de negra estirpe ya habían sido naturalizados por el pueblo español [...] Mas si se hubieran adoptado los tambores africanos, aquel blanqueamiento, cristianización o nacionalización no hubiera podido disimular entonces la oriundez exótica y pagana del baile, ni habría sido permitido que en la corte de Felipe II se bailara con instrumentos de los negros del Congo (Ortiz 1993, 183).
24. Letter of Ortiz to Malinowski dated 25 November 1939, "Appendix I" (Ortiz 2002, 767).
25. When the proposed neologism, *transculturation,* was submitted to the unimpeachable authority of Bronislaw Malinowski, the

great figure in contemporary ethnography and sociology, it met with instant approbation. Under his eminent sponsorship, I have no qualms about putting the term into circulation (Ortiz 2003, 103).

26. Incidentally, Columbia University awarded an honorary degree to Fernando Ortiz in 1954.
27. Letter of Melville Herskovits to Fernando Ortiz dated 29 October 1940, "Appendix XIV-a" (Ortiz 2002, 786-87).
28. Cf. Herskovits, M, R. Redfield and R. Linton. 1936. "A memorandum for the study of acculturation." *American Anthropologist* 38:149-52. Herskovits, M. 1937. "The significance of the study of acculturation for anthropology." *American Anthropologist* 39:259-64; and, Herskovits, M. *Acculturation: The study of culture contact*. New York: J.J. Augustin, 1938.

15

The Haitian Challenge to Regional Security

Predicaments of a Failed State

Aparajita Gangopadhyay

On 12 January 2010 Haiti suffered an unprecedented disaster when a massive earthquake struck the country killing nearly 250,000 people, injuring an equal number and displacing more than 2.3 million people from their homes (MINUSTAH n.d.). Haiti brings forth a picture of destruction, devastation, poverty, hunger, illnesses and a general atmosphere of chaos and catastrophe. It is an image which reinstates that both God and man have forsaken these people, and who have nothing but a future of hopelessness and despair in store for them. Haiti is a rare country in the Caribbean region which perpetuates a tone of despondency among scholars, observers and lay persons alike. This is not incidental or the outcome of an individual researcher's predicaments and biases that gives Haiti this image necessitating a probe into the conjecture that historical circumstances have imparted Haiti it's much unfortunate birthmarks.

By the end of the Second World War and in the subsequent Cold War parlance, Haiti along with its neighbours Dominican Republic and Cuba were valued as "strategic assets" in the Caribbean. Even before the onset of the Cold War and the consequent ideological rivalry that was encouraged and sustained between the two blocs, the region and islands of the Caribbean were already considered as prized "possessions" for the United States. The Caribbean continued to be regarded by the U.S. as part of its "backyard," tracing it to the unilateral declarations by the Americans like the Monroe Doctrine and the Roosevelt Corollary.

Since its independence from French colonial rule, Haiti has long lived in the shadows of the United States. From the very beginning, unlike its neighbours, the trajectory of Haiti's development and growth as a nation was skewed. A close scrutiny of its development as a nation clearly brings forth the challenges that Haiti has faced, created by events unfolding in within the region as well as by those destabilising forces operating in the country. Such factors, both domestic and international, compelled Haiti on a path thereon which was augmented by misfortunes and total instability. Keeping this as its backdrop, this chapter will attempt to understand the predicament that Haiti suffers today and its causes/roots which are embedded in its historical past. The chapter will trace the evolution of Haiti since 1804 followed by a close examination of the challenges and constraints that surfaced during the Cold War years. An attempt is also made to evaluate the response of the world community towards Haiti's trials and tribulations. In this context, an analysis of the challenges of human development faced by the island nation and the corresponding initiatives taken by the United Nations, the Organisation of American States and CARICOM towards re-construction and revival of the Haitian polity, society and economy will be examined. The final section will assess the future of Haiti in the given circumstances.

Haiti: History Gone Awry

Haiti was one of the most valuable possessions that the French had overseas during the 17th century and one the first countries in the region of the Caribbean to get independence from colonial rule. "Born out of the economic recesses of slavery, and the political violence of the French revolution, Haiti emerged in 1804 as an independent nation" (Fauriol 1990, 562). Nearly two centuries after acquiring independence Haiti remains the most impoverished country in the western hemisphere. Pictures of destruction, devastation and poverty are probably the most visible images emerging out of Haiti. The aftermath of the slave uprising that began in 1789 and culminated in Haitian independence in 1804, left the country in total ruin. The removal of the colonial authority also deprived Haiti of any workable political and economic institutions. In addition, the massive importation of slave labour required for Haiti's sugar plantation economy had prompted profound social and racial divisions within the society that persist until today.

Haiti is a country of contrasts. Among other factors, geography has played a significant role in maintaining this isolation within the region. The irregular coastline which extends through the northern and southern peninsulas had literally become an invisible line of division, partitioning the society into different sections and peoples, separated from each other and the mainstream Haitian life. With difficulties in internal communications, and a rural life remarkably resistant to change, largely all progress in the port towns remained localised. Haiti had the poorest overall infrastructure per capita of any country in the Western hemisphere. In addition, a closer scrutiny of the country also revealed that historically and geographically Haiti has been isolated despite and because of the border that it shares with Dominican Republic, and the close proximity to Cuba and the United States (Rotberg 1988, 97). In comparison to the other countries of the region, Haiti resisted efforts at modernization and Westernization. Centuries of economic and political chaos and misadventures have left Haiti essentially a rural country with a failed countryside no longer productive to feed its teeming millions; Haiti is stripped bare of trees, long cut down for firewood and charcoal; its mountain tops denuded and slopes badly eroded. Agricultural productivity has declined drastically since 1960. Ironically, Haiti has one of the highest densities of populations worldwide and one-third of all Haitians are urban (D'Agostino 2003).

The absence of identifiable political and economic strategies, lead by the Haitian state since its independence, makes any study of its experience very frustrating. A cursory glance at the review of literature on Haiti suggests that a very small and generally organised political and economic elite had effortlessly worked towards maintaining in its own fragile status quo as well as sustaining a limited enclave of export orientated commercial activities. Writers have used terms such as "kleptocracy" or "predatory state," and "politics of squalor" to describe Haiti's impasse. Others have used terms such as "colonial," or "self colonised" character of the Haitian society to explain its despondent condition (Fauriol 1990, 564; Nicholls 1979; Rotberg 1988).

Politics in Haiti reflect the constraints and difficulties consequent to many physical and socio-economic hardships that the nation has faced since its independence. Haiti is a nation that has known despotism and terror more than elections and power-sharing. Conceived in harsh slavery, born of revolution and nurtured in decades of hostility, Haiti knew turbulence and corruption before it experienced order. It has never known effective two party or multi-party competitions, with honest elections or benevolent government (Rotberg 1988, 99). According to diplomatic historian Rayford Logan, Haiti started out as a "power and enigma" and turned into an "anomaly," because of a "threat," and ultimately was an "outcast" among the comity of nations (Logan 1971, 210). Lacking viable institutions, Haiti initially evolved a remarkable collection of powerful personalities who shaped the nation's style of governance—authoritarian, personalist and anchored in coercive power. Ideas of nationhood and common good had very few takers. With no means of communicating the needs of the state, and with no funds to extend it beyond the controlling elite which dominated all processes, almost all presidents carried their presidency with the rights to pillage and plunder thus easing the path for the elites to follow, i.e., a license to plunder. The governments became increasingly unstable. Although Haiti projected an image of homogeneity, class consciousness, sectionalism and political and social differences were carried to the extremes. Nation-building and creation of a sustainable state was thus never realised. Consequently the post-independence economic decline pushed Haiti deeply into debt. By the dawn of the 20th century, Haiti was in debt to the French, the German, and the U.S. financial interests. As most of their imports came from the United States, the American influence had grown immensely and even expanded into the banking sectors as well.

The escalating political strife, lack of governance and the economic downfall prompted the U.S. intervention in Haiti. The U.S. intervened in July 1915 and ruled there until 1934. The other factors that prompted the intervention also included the United States' fear of German presence fuelled by the outbreak of World War I. The United States pacified, administered, and introduced new methods of solving old problems, providing an array of technological improvements, building decent roads and introducing proper telephone and telegraphic services. It refurbished hospitals and schools, tried to upgrade the living standards, and like colonial powers in Africa, tried to impose its own cultural ideas on Haitian society (Rotberg 1988, 103). Although the U.S. president Woodrow Wilson declared that the intervention in Haiti constituted a humanitarian response to the total collapse of indigenous abilities to maintain law and order, the manner of intervention, and the way in which the Americans subsequently dealt with the Haitians, suggests an overriding concern for the protection of U.S. national interests in a disturbed world. The Americans were inexperienced colonisers, and the Marine Corps, which provided the local leadership and were the grand commissar during most of the occupation, proved more amateur than most, as has been stated by one scholar:

> Their horizons were narrow, and the maintenance of law and order—at a time when US funds were short—seemed more important than preparing Haiti for economic and political growth. The American occupation was thus without plan, and disappointing to those who had hoped that it would transform a society too long isolated from the current world progress. It also perpetuated the atmosphere of arbitrary authoritarianism to which Haitians were long accustomed (Rotberg 1988, 104).

Haitians resented the occupation, not least because of the failure of the Americans to prepare either Haitians or Haiti for its end, but for the total lack of sensitivity towards the local populations. No attempt was made to involve the locals in the country's political process or to plan with Haitians for their eventual resumption of sovereignty. During the occupation, elections were held locally, but they were rigged; after 1917, the ballot was denied on the national level. Presidents ruled by fiat on behalf of the occupiers, constitutional amendments were farcically ratified, and the press was censored (Rotberg 1988).

Political chaos and instability was the way of life in Haiti prior to the American intervention. Of the twenty-two presidents who served between 1843 and 1915, one finished his term in office, three died of natural causes while in office, one was blown up in the presidential palace, another one was probably poisoned, one hacked to pieces, and one resigned. The fourteen others were overthrown. The sorry state of Haitian finances was also perceived by Washington as a Trojan horse for European intervention in the Caribbean (Fauriol 1990, 565). The overt object of the U.S. action had not been to expose Haiti to U.S. exploitation, but to promote Haitian political stability, financial rehabilitation, and economic developments. Yet, Haiti was one of the United States' least successful interventions. Subsequently, a financial order was established, debt was reduced, and administrative infrastructure was improved, but the U.S. presence did not lead to democratic virtues or greater management capabilities among the Haitian elite.

Violent and anti-U.S. feelings triggered a review of U.S. policy in 1930. Both Presidents Hoover and FDR became determined that U.S. would exit from Haiti's tropical imbroglio as quickly as possible (Fauriol 1990, 562). The U.S. decision to withdraw in 1934 was specifically spurred by anti-American protests in Haiti, and F.D. Roosevelt's *Good Neighbor Policy* towards Latin America and the Caribbean in general.

The United States had failed to change Haiti. Nineteen years might have proven sufficiently long to have demonstrated the superiority of Anglo-Saxon political approaches. American tutelage might have brought about lasting alterations in Haitian practices. However, according to Rotberg (1988, 104), "the Americans had ruled arbitrarily, perhaps more openly and without the venality, but still in the manner of earlier Haitian dictators. The US had given Haitians no obvious and easily imitated model of political responsibility." The level of local participation in politics remained low and unrepresentated. As far as most Haitians were concerned, one clique had replaced another: power was power (Rotberg 1988).

As tutors, the Americans had reinforced retrogressive stereotypes. The Americans had not broadened the base of political participation; the same type of factions operated in Haitian politics as they had always operated. The Haitian political elite's greed for power was visible in many occasions. For instance, President Sténio Vincent, a wealthy mulatto who had assumed office under the Americans, transformed himself into a dictator in 1933.[1] It was only the U.S. pressures and threats of an intervention that kept Vincent out. Subsequently, the Haitian ambassador to the U.S. was elected as President and he was followed by Dumarsais Estimé, a reformer, in 1949. He encouraged trade unions and rural cooperatives and even nationalised large U.S. companies. However, he was removed from power by the army when it was realised that he was an "opportunist and not a true popularist" and was replaced by the General Paul Magloire, a U.S. marine trained General of the Haitian army (Rotberg 1988, 105).

The intervention also brought forth the glaring fact that the U.S. marines took nearly one month to establish order. During the period of the American occupation, the U.S. maintained veto power over any government decisions within Haiti. The twenty year occupation also saw the concentration of commercial power within Port-au-Prince which resulted in facilitating the eventual establishment of an autocratic government by François Duvalier in the years to come. The U.S., however, failed to foster the development of democratic institutions which paved the way for the election of Duvalier in 1957.

The Caribbean is the only region where the U.S. economic, political and military presence which includes interventions has been constant throughout history (Muñiz and Beruff 1994, 113). Historically, the geopolitical importance of the Caribbean has gone beyond mere proximity. The U.S. policy towards the Caribbean was based on its national security, defined in terms of strategic and economic concerns (Muñiz and Beruff 1994, 115). The heart of the policy was constant: deterring any hostile extra- or intra-hemispheric power from establishing a military or geopolitical presence perceived to threaten the continental United States. The Caribbean hosted key sea lines of communications for trade to and from the United States and through the Panama Canal as well as for power projection in the Atlantic toward Europe and Central and South America. Also deemed of great value were the American investments in the region, and energy and mineral resources, particularly petroleum and bauxite. Thus, geographic contiguity, sea lines of communications, economic linkages, and natural resources conjoined to make the Caribbean strategically important for the United States (Muñiz and Beruff 1994; Loesch 2001, 8). As George Danns (1989, 22) puts it:

> [The] United States has redefined its geopolitical space as the Caribbean Basin. The concept links the Caribbean to Central America and imports into the region...Caribbean policy-makers must cope, therefore, with the perception that vital United States interests are under threat in their area, whether or not they themselves believe this to be the case.

Overall, Haiti's diplomacy was an isolationist policy. It had been characterised by a strong disinclination to be visibly associated with the mainstream of Third World politics, including the Non-Aligned Movement and the North-South disputes. These factors alone greatly differentiated Haitian policy from the policies of the country's Caribbean and Latin American neighbours. Haiti's main concern remained the management of its ties with the preponderant centre of power, the United States (Fauriol 1990, 571).

Duvalier Regime and the Haitian Crisis

During the period of the Cold War, Haiti was essentially part of the larger efforts to keep communism at bay. Containment of communism and the Duvalier policies at home, i.e., crushing any communist uprising, kept the Americans basically contented with the status of Haiti. The U.S. preoccupation with Cuba and its close proximity with Haiti increased the latter's strategic value for the Americans. Economically, Haiti was of no great importance to the United States, and thus ignored generally. The Duvalier era began in 1957 when "Papa Doc" or François Duvalier became the president for life.[2] He took over presidency in a period of political confusion that included the collapse of the previous government of Paul Magloire, violence and fraudulent elections. Duvalier was a champion and product of a movement towards the return of a black culture, a movement that emerged during the U.S. occupation of Haiti.

Duvalier was determined to bring forth the nation's primordial black heritage which subsequently isolated Haiti in the international arena and from all sources of foreign assistance. But in Duvalier was created a tyrant, and "Duvalierism" was made up of a curious combination of negritude, quasi-radical nationalism and fascist tendencies. The search for such a "new equilibrium" signalled a shift in political and economic power—from the prominent mulatto elite to a new black middle-class acting in the interest of the peasant masses. However, most of the gestures were in name only and Duvalier's regime was synonymous with corruption, income inequalities, illiteracy and environmental degradation compounded by brain drain. This period also witnessed the repression of all opposition with declining power of the former mulatto elite as well as the political power of the Roman Catholic Church. Duvalier introduced a powerful paramilitary organisation called the Volontaires de la Securité Nationale (VSN) or popularly known as Tonton Macoutes which was established to protect the regime and enforce its directives (Fauriol 1990, 570).

Papa Doc was succeeded by his son Jean-Claude Duvalier, also called "Baby Doc," who was surrounded by his father's advisers, family members and security personnel who played a major role in influencing him during this period. He embarked on a "new" economic model that was aimed to turn the fortunes of Haiti through an "economic revolution." However, the ambiguity of the design alongside attempts to modernise the economic structure corroborated with the political reforms which lead to further disintegration of the Haitian society. Baby Doc's policy called for a greater aid from the major economic donors especially the United States.

Haiti's emergence as the focus of American foreign policy in the Caribbean emerged in the period immediately after Castro's declaration of his allegiance to Moscow. Although President Duvalier had certain serious issues with the Kennedy administration which had been critical of his oppressive and dictatorial government, the Americans subsequently overlooked the regime's excesses once the Duvalier administration used the same methods (oppressive, cruel and dictatorial) to contain communism in Haiti. The American government continued their support post-Kennedy, and this rose to new heights by 1971 when the U.S. naval vessels patrolled off the coast of Haiti to ensure smooth transition of the presidency from François Duvalier to his son Jean-Claude. The U.S. also increased their aid to the island nation as a response to decreased violence in the initial years of Jean-Claude's presidency (Fauriol 1990, 571).

The Ronald Reagan administration was inclined to reassess its ties with the Duvalier regime, and the latter was disposed to cooperate, shaken as it was by the refugee crisis, economic downturn and troubles with foreign aid. The U.S. administration showed a willingness to accept slow progress toward political reform if gains could be achieved in three other areas: the immigration issue, Haitian economic and social development, and the U.S. foreign aid. In tandem, Duvalier announced a framework for gradual "democratisation." The details were vague, but the timing was important, for it preceded Haiti's incorporation into the Caribbean Basin Initiative, a major framework of U.S. foreign policy in the region (Fauriol 1990). Duvalier had to soon deal with the Catholic Church militancy and the visit of Pope John Paul II to Haiti when he sermonised from the airport of the injustices meted out to the Haitians. It seemed to indicate that the Church was keen to champion an active political role in Haiti. The Church encouraged the Haitians to protest in the streets and cooperated actively with the international and U.S. human rights groups to focus on the regime's corruption and human rights abuses.

Soon within the United States, a majority of U.S. congressional members became sceptical of the U.S. government's vague optimism about Haiti's political progress. The racial element of U.S.-Haitian relations also played a crucial role in changing U.S. perceptions of Duvalier, for U.S. Blacks took a special interest in change in Haiti (Fauriol 1990, 572). Racial, religious, and humanitarian concerns had, in fact, captured the attention of the U.S. Black community as a whole early on. Ultimately, the Duvalier regime's overall ineptitude isolated it from much of its traditional key sources of economic support (the United States, West Germany, France, and Canada). When merged with racial and humanitarian considerations this isolation left the Duvalier regime undefended.

The actual collapse of the Baby Doc regime began in November 1985 with a series of spontaneous riots in Gonaives that turned into a major anti-government protest. Duvalier fled from Haiti and interestingly it was the American military aircraft C-141 that took Duvalier to France when he decided to go into exile on 6 February 1986. However, when it came to developing a transition regime the list of possible leaders was frighteningly small. Even though the U.S. embassy mid-wifed a changeover of government whose leadership (headed by General Henri Namphy) appeared agreeable to Duvalier, the broader picture turned out to be much more uncertain. In the post-Jean-Claude period the Reagan government supported the National Council of Government with an increased military aid of U.S. $ 2.8 million. This government was short lived and Haiti fell to chaos and uncertainty once again (Loesch 2001, 11). The U.S. Secretary of State George Shultz's call for democracy in Haiti a week before Duvalier's collapse had covered up the fact that this objective could not be accomplished in the near future. Policy designs were catapulted into the future without defining the full-term progress and Haiti paid the price of this lack of definition when elections in late 1987 did not live up to expectations. The short-lived 1988 government under the civilian president Leslie Manigat subsequently gave way to General Namphy.[3] Following this, in March 1990 General Avril resigned and was replaced by Ertha Pascal-Trouillot, the only woman judge who sat on Haiti's Supreme Court. The provisional president stated that her only goal was to lead the country to early elections. The U.S. ambassador called it "a great day for this country, a great day for democracy" (New York Times 1990).

Meanwhile, the economic well-being of Haiti did not show any significant change when compared to the previous decades. Although Haiti did manage some foreign direct investment, it was however limited to assembly plants mostly in the garments, sporting goods, electronic toys and other peripheral industries. FDI entered Haiti simply because the labour was cheap, besides certain import privileges and a favourable tax regime. The Haitian market was however in a constant state of decline mainly due to lack of any significant industrialization combined with the high degrees of corruption, lack of basic infrastructure, and increased competition from other nations. In addition, the embargo imposed on Haiti during the period of 1991-94 in real terms killed the economy (Loesch 2001, 8).

With President Bill Clinton in office, the U.S. offered Haiti some incentives which brought about the election of President Jean-Bertrand Aristide. Apart from holding elections, the specific objectives of the other projects included efforts at re-conceptualizing Haiti's diplomatic ties to the United States, attempting to promote intellectual cooperation between Haiti and the U.S., efforts at modernizing Haiti's religious mores, and finally encouraging efforts at stimulating changes through the creation of a community-based development model (Loesch 2001, 8). The then Senator John McCain of Arizona, complained: "Without that global strategy, we keep getting our-selves involved in peripheral matters such as Northern Ireland and Haiti" (Loesch 2001, 10). What McCain had failed to realize was that Northern Ireland and Haiti had slipped to the periphery of Clinton administration's foreign policy for a while even though events there attracted a great deal of media attention (Brinkley 1997, 124). According to Humberto García Muñiz and Jorge Rodríguez Beruff (1994, 119), what the Clinton administration's critics failed to see was that the events in both Somalia and Haiti were holdovers from President Bush's multinational "new world order."

In the last decade and half of the 20th century the U.S. had stealthily moved away from the affairs of Haiti. The successive American administrations continue to make a number of promises and voice oft-repeated reassurances. The end of the Cold War no longer meant that Haiti would be able to enjoy its previous isolation; American interests in Haiti are now focused on a new set of security challenges, namely, illegal immigration, drugs and infectious diseases (Loesch 2001, 8). However, an in-depth examination of the U.S. policy postures would reveal that Haiti has been receiving relatively empty promises over the years. No doubt the aid that Haiti receives will continue to be substantial for various humanitarian programme and initiatives but it will be unimaginable if not impossible to forecast any direct intervention by the U.S. in Haiti to ensure peace and stability.

Haiti and the United States: An Ambivalent Disengagement?

The process of stabilization and securitization embarked on in Haiti was expected to be strengthened by the swearing-in of the new President Michel Martley on 14 May 2011. There have been certain anomalies and a pattern of deviant behaviour on the part of the U.S. vis-à-vis Haiti in the last decade or so of the 20th century. The United States has always been keen to prevent the emergence of any hostile powers as well as the presence of any failed nations in its neighbourhood. In a recent hearing of the Subcommittee on the *Western Hemisphere, Peace Corps, and Global Narcotics Affairs* of the Senate Committee on Foreign Relations, the U.S. Assistant Secretary of the Bureau of Western Hemisphere Affairs, Arturo Valenzuela, testified on 17 February 2011, that the U.S. commitment to:

> Haiti will be sustained...the role of the United States in the unprecedented bilateral and multilateral cooperation in support of Haiti. Since the earthquake, the U.S. government has spent $1.1 billion in humanitarian relief assistance and...$406 million in recovery assistance toward job creation, rubble removal, shelter solutions, health and other priorities....the U.S. government has pledged $1.15 billion in new money toward reconstruction...disbursed more than $332 million to provide debt relief and contribute to the Haiti Reconstruction Fund (Valenzuela 2011).

Despite these commendatory words citing the American commitment to Haiti's future, it is clear that the U.S. has no real commercial or national security interests anymore in the country. The security interests in Haiti can no longer be analysed from a traditional Cold War perspective. Currently, the two primary concerns of the U.S. on Haiti are of non-traditional/non-military nature, i.e., enormous immigration out of Haiti which continues unabated and to a small degree, nonetheless equally important, of drugs like cocaine that finds their way into the United States through Haiti.

The United States has seen over the past decades a huge immigration out of Haiti via small boats. The enormity of the situation was visible in the 1970s when the numbers rose to 20,000 or more. Haiti's periods of instability, violence and unrest coupled with abject poverty, illiteracy and unemployment had forced thousands of people to seek a better life in the United States. They landed in Florida, with no skills to speak of and thus not welcomed into the American society. The reasons for the resentment stemmed from a number of other factors as well. Above and beyond that, the Haitians were a great health hazard with communicable diseases, in particular HIV/AIDS that made them extremely vulnerable in this new society. For instance, after the 1991 coup in Haiti, due to the political persecutions against Jean-Bertrand Aristide's supporters alongside the worsening economic conditions created by the economic embargo, there was a dramatic increase in the illegal migration into the United States. Initially the American government treated the Haitians as political refugees seeking asylum and this "benevolent" U.S. policy encouraged more Haitians to follow suit. However, Guantanamo Bay which was the home-stop for such refugees could not accommodate any more and subsequently, President George Bush in 1992 through an executive order asked all interdicted Haitians to return home, putting a stop to this exodus. President Bush faced severe criticism at home from human rights groups, Haitian-Americans, even democrats such as the democratic candidate Bill Clinton. It is estimated that about 600,000 Haitians live in the U.S. not including the illegal immigrants (Miller 2004).

Although, the illegal immigration had declined considerably, in the recent past the U.S. has relaxed its immigration rules following the Haitian earthquake of 2010. The U.S. interests in Haiti in the recent years have been because of the island nation's increasing role in the drug trade. Haiti is not essentially a producer of drugs but rather is used as a trans-shipment locale for of these drugs. Successive corrupt governments, weak in enforcing law, the inaccessible and hostile terrain with an unsecured coastline makes Haiti the new "emergent" trans-shipment hub in the Caribbean. Haiti is thus used to ship drugs out of Colombia, Venezuela and other countries in the region. It is estimated that about 8 per cent of all cocaine entering the U.S. is through the Haiti/Dominican Republic route (Perito and Maly 2007). The largest part of the cocaine consignment enters through the Mexican/Central American route. The Haitian government's inability to deal with the drug trafficking problem was visible when on 16 March 2007 President Préval joined leaders from the neighbouring countries and representatives from Europe and the United States in a regional summit on Drugs, Security and Cooperation in the Caribbean, and stated, "If we are left alone, the drug trafficking giants are going to devour us in one bite" (Perito and Maly 2007). Following this, in a Haitian Flag Day speech, on 18 May 2007, he declared a "war without end" against corruption, smuggling and drug-trafficking (Perito and Maly 2007). In fact, on the one hand the post-earthquake scenario has meant increased trafficking than before, while on the other it has also meant less active role by the Haitian government to control it.

While the United States had been withdrawing from Haiti, it was steadily encouraging those of the United Nations and other regional organisations to deal with the Haitian imbroglio. Interestingly, the U.S. which had intervened in Haiti many times earlier had willingly accepted to permit regional bodies like the Caribbean Community or CARICOM, and the Organization of American States (OAS) to play a central role in the process of reconstruction and development in Haiti. In its defense, the United States cited that the crisis in Haiti was a regional security and stability issue, and thus making it mandatory for regional organizations like the OAS and the CARICOM which were best suited to deal with the Haitian question.

The United Nations and other regional organizations have played a joint role in Haiti. The first UN intervention was in February 1993 when the United Nations along with the OAS deployed a joint International Civilian Mission in Haiti. In September 1993, the Security Council established the first peacekeeping operation, the UN Mission in Haiti (UNMIH). Furthermore, in July 1994, the Security Council authorised by resolution 940, the deployment of a 20,000 strong multi-national force to facilitate the prompt return of legitimate Haitian authorities, maintain security and stability and encourage the rule of law on the island. This multinational force was followed by a series of UN missions from 1994 to 2001, including in March 2005, the UN Support Mission in Haiti (UNSMIH), the UN Transition Mission in Haiti (UNTMIH) and the UN Mission of the Civilian Police in Haiti (MIPONUH). All such efforts were to reinstate a stable government in the civil-war torn country including helping all such efforts at reinstating President Aristide.

This initially resulted in certain positive developments. Among many, the transfer of power between two democratically elected presidents, the apparent development of a multi-faceted civil society and the increased participation in building a political culture based on democratic values. However, the successes were short-term and failed and the expected "peace" did not happen. On 29 February 2004, the Permanent Representative of Haiti to the United Nations submitted a request for assistance from the interim president. At the behest of the Security Council international troops entered Haiti with the adoption of Resolution 1529 that permitted the deployment of a multilateral interim force. Since then, the United Nations Stabilization Mission in Haiti or MINUSTAH remains deeply entrenched providing assistance and support on all fronts in Haiti. The MINUSTAH responsibilities have multiplied manifold in the post-earthquake period.

The other organizations involved in the reconstruction of Haiti were the OAS and CARICOM, both regional organizations geared to play a positive and constructive role there. In his opening remarks, on 15 October 1994, the OAS Secretary General noted that he had accompanied President Aristide on his return to Haiti from exile. For the OAS, this represented the culmination of a task that it had pursued since the 1991 coup. The Secretary General emphasized that throughout the period of 1991-95, the OAS had strengthened its ties to Haiti. The establishment of MICIVIH in 1992 demonstrated the ability of the two international organizations to work together closely in the field of human rights. The June 1994 *ad hoc* meeting of OAS Foreign Ministers was held in Haiti, as was the 1995 OAS General Assembly. In December 1994, the OAS presented Haiti with recommendations intended to consolidate democracy in the country, with the result that the OAS would provide technical cooperation and support for Haitian government's priorities and immediate needs in the areas of strengthening of the state, human rights promotion and civic education.[4] The OAS undertook an electoral observation mission at the request of the Haitian government, with a final report being issued discussing the results. The OAS had also followed closely the electoral process in Haiti and Aristide's handover of power to another freely-elected successor.

In a similar vein, the OAS and CARICOM had also contributed in all possible manners to make Haiti safe and secure. The OAS was also a member of the group of multilateral institutions and governments supporting and financing development in Haiti. In his closing remarks at Washington D.C., Ambassador César Gaviria, the Secretary General of the OAS in the mid-1990s, reinforced the organization's commitment to democracy in Haiti and noted that "the underlying problem was in finding an institutional expression for popularly-held democratic values and translating them into the structures of the state" (Democratic Forum 1995). The OAS observed elections in Haiti as follows during the decade of the 1990s: 1991 (Presidential), 1995 (Presidential, Legislative and Municipal), 1996 (Parliamentary, Municipal), 1997 (Legislative and Municipal) and 2000 (Parliamentary, Municipal and Local).[5]

The OAS General Assembly, at the 4th Plenary Session in San Jose, Costa Rica adopted an important resolution calling for a solution to the electoral crisis in Haiti.[6] This was entitled *Support for Democracy in Haiti*. This resolution summarized developments in Haiti and the international agencies as well as the Haitian government activities surrounding the crisis up to that date. Especially noteworthy in this General Assembly Resolution were the references to consultations with CARICOM, the creation of a *Group of Friends*, and the establishment of a *Special Mission*. All of these recommendations soon fructified in the form of the international community and hemispheric nations support of the OAS and Haiti. In a particularly important move on 26 February 2004, just before Aristide's departure from Haiti, the OAS Permanent Council urged the UN Security Council to take the necessary and appropriate urgent measures to address the crisis in Haiti. This resolution was adopted by consensus. It was an acknowledgement that the situation in Haiti had gone beyond what the OAS could achieve there through its own offices alone.

Over the last few years, regional partners have played a greater role in Haiti. In fact, it is the regional giants like Brazil who have stepped in to play a significant role in there. Brazil led the UN force in 2005 and also contributed close to 1200 troops for the multi-national force. This replaced the small contingent troops from the U.S., France and Canada. Alongside were troops from Argentina, Chile and Uruguay. These troops tried to curtail the violence, keep order, disarm the populations and facilitate the authorities to prepare for the forthcoming general elections.

Haiti: A Failed State

Haiti's tragic history does not permit any hope for the island nation.

Like all its successors, the past and present regimes have been totally incapable of dealing with Haiti's political, economic and ecological challenges. Haiti's track record of dealing with the emergent and ongoing crises is poor, leaving the people with limited choices. Humanitarian concerns continue to dominate. It is clear to observers and scholars on Haiti that it is an uphill and seemingly impossible task for any government to successfully address. Successive governments and even international agencies in Haiti find it impossible to deal with such enormous upheavals unfolding simultaneously throughout Haiti. The question arises as to which should be of primary concern: political stability and security or humanitarian concerns? Haiti is in a perfect catch-22 situation and it is overwhelmingly clear that new and implausible issues are emerging everyday and only multiplying to the already untenable situation there. Future governments may want to change Haiti in a fundamental political sense. But the human and the historical aspects are so fragile that no re-molding of Haiti for the better can be predicted with confidence. Given its legacy of overpopulation, deforestation, infrastructural neglect and devastation and a general weariness, Haiti hardly presents a likely case of economic take-off (Rotberg 1988, 103). Haiti continues to need a great deal of support from international donors to reconstruct the country and the economy. Despite huge capital being committed by the U.S., the European Union, and the World Bank, the committed funds remain unspent. The international financial organisations blame it to the lack of projects and poor accountability, while the local authorities complain that they need much more time to produce viable results.

The United States seems to be quite satisfied to hand out humanitarian aid towards the reconstruction of Haiti post the earthquake of 2010. The U.S.' *volte-face* has been due to a number of factors and changes in the international scenario. The end of the Cold War did not merely end the ideological divide among the nations but forced them to re-evaluate the strategic importance of their position in the fast-changing international arena. Countries like those located in the Caribbean and Central America actually began to disappear from the American radar. Haiti's absence of strategic value in the "new world order" along with its unattractiveness as a potential economic and commercial partner made the United States disengage from their affairs in "real" terms. Communism was gone, Haiti's strategic location was long lost, and thus any thought of shouldering the Haitian burden was no longer appealing. In addition, the transition in international politics also witnessed the volatility of the Middle-East and the consequent American pre-occupation with that region's problems and issues. At the same time the U.S. was also particularly caught-up with China and the others around the globe. Latin America and the Caribbean were generally abandoned and Haiti disappeared totally out of the American national concerns which were now dominated by the fall-outs of the economic crises. However, the United States could not totally abandon Haiti. Nevertheless, sustained commitment will be necessary in order to introduce good governance and even possibly a democracy.

Haiti becomes the test case for any scholar to predict its future. It is quite clear that the priority for any new government now is to find a way out of the chaos in the aftermath of the earthquake. The government will also need to generate employment, slowly eradicate illiteracy, find means to deal with poverty and the list is endless. Undoubtedly, Haiti's survival and its security will continue to challenge international relations in the next few decades.

Notes

1. The Americans had introduced the Haitian Constitution that only permitted two terms for a president but Vincent wanted a third term for himself. This brought forth the American influence to dissuade him from seeking a third term.
2. Papa Doc became President for life in 1964. He died in 1971 and had remained as president for life till then.
3. General Namphy was himself thrown out of office by another military commander, General Prosper Avril, in September 1988 leading to further chaos and instability in Haiti.
4. As a result of the OAS reorganization undertaken in 2004, this entity was renamed the Office for the Promotion of Democracy (OPD), under the Department for Democratic and Political Affairs (DDPA).
5. OAS web site, http://www.oas.org/key_issues/eng/GAelections.htm
    a. 16 December 1990-20 January 1991 presidential elections were held with Jean-Bertrand Aristide coming to power as president.
    b. In 1995, local and legislative elections were held in many rounds. 25 June, 13 August and 17 September 1995 respectively. The presidential elections were held on 17 December 1995 and president Rene Préval was sworn in on 7 February 1996.

c. The parliamentary elections were held on 6 April 1997.
d. The legislative elections were held in two rounds, 21 May and 9 July 2000. The presidential elections were held on 26 November 2000. Jean-Bertrand Aristide had won the lections with a landslide victory.

6. The OAS's 31st Regular Session was held in 3-5 June 2001 at Costa Rica and the agreement was called AG/RES.1831 (XXX-O/01).

16

Crime and Justice in the Caribbean

The Case of Trinidad and Tobago*

Ramesh Deosaran

This chapter on crime and justice in a Commonwealth Caribbean country provides a brief background to its location and system of government, then examples of crime and prison trends, and finally, a discussion on police governance.

Trinidad and Tobago is an English-speaking twin-island state. It is the southernmost country in the Caribbean archipelago of islands, northeast of the South American country of Venezuela and south of Grenada in the Lesser Antilles. With a population of approximately 1.3 million people and unlike most other English-speaking Caribbean countries, Trinidad and Tobago is primarily industrialized. Its economy is based strongly on petroleum and petrochemicals, natural gas, and methanol, with tourism and manufacturing also important sectors.

Both islands were originally settled by Amerindians of South America. Trinidad was claimed by Christopher Columbus in 1498 for Spain. There were many European wars for the island that included the French, Dutch and British. The island of Tobago also had a similar past. Trinidad was ceded to Britain in 1802. In 1889, the islands of Trinidad and Tobago were made into a single colony. Partial self-government was instituted in 1925 and from 1958 to 1962 the nation was part of the West Indies Federation. Trinidad

* The research assistance of Ian Ramdhanie (B.Sc., M.Sc.) is gratefully acknowledged by the author.

and Tobago gained its independence in 1962 from England and its republican status in 1976.

Driven largely by the need for cheap labour (slave and indentured) during the 18th and 19th centuries, the country now has a diverse ethnic population—38 per cent of African descent and 40 per cent of East Indian descent, 20 per cent mixed, and small proportions of Caucasian, Chinese, Syrian/Lebanese, Portuguese, etc. The people also have a wide variety of religious backgrounds. These include Roman Catholic, Hindu, Anglican, Muslim, Baptist, Pentecostal, Presbyterian, Seventh Day Adventist, and Jehovah Witness. The country is well-known for its pre-Lenten Carnival and it is the birth place of steelpan, calypso, soca and limbo. It celebrates several cultural festivals like Eid, Hosay and Divali.

Government

Trinidad and Tobago is a parliamentary democracy whose Republican Constitution dates from August 1, 1976. The country's legal system is based on English common law. All citizens are eligible to vote at age 18. The country's head of state is a president, elected by an electoral college comprising members of the House of Representatives and the Senate. The head of government is a prime minister, usually the majority party leader in the House after elections are held. The doctrine of separation of powers, inherited from the British Westminster system, provides for the executive, a bi-cameral legislature and the judiciary.

Criminal Justice System

The criminal justice system consists of the police (law enforcement), courts (prosecutors, defense attorneys, judiciary), and corrections (prisons, probation, etc.). Generally, the criminal justice system operates free from interference by the executive although the executive has direct control over the police and corrections; that is, they both fall under the Ministry of National Security. The judiciary does not fall under any government ministry and has recently gotten some control over its own budget (www.ttlawcourts.org).

Recently, there have been complaints from some members of the criminal justice system, as well as from opposition parties, against the government's attempts to interfere in the criminal justice system especially with regard to the police and the courts. One example was the attempt by the prime minister in 2006 to impeach the chief justice for alleged misbehaviour in public office. The matter was eventually won by the chief justice. This was the first time in the history of the Commonwealth countries that efforts were made to impeach a sitting chief justice. There is another example whereby the chief magistrate refused to give testimony in the court after he made allegations that the chief justice tried to influence his ruling.

Over the last five to seven years, the criminal justice system has also witnessed police investigations, charges, arrests, court trials, and imprisonment of several members of Parliament, both on the government and opposition sides. Added to this is the frequent revelation of police officers, defense force personnel, and prison officers being involved in a wide range of criminal activities, for example, murder, drug trafficking, kidnapping, robberies, rapes, etc. As a result, the criminal justice system has been subjected to intense public controversy.

Policing

The country is served by the Trinidad and Tobago Police Service (TTPS) with approximately 7,000 police officers, a police-citizen ratio of 1:185.

An independent body appointed by the president, called the Police Service Commission, looks over the efficiency and effectiveness of the roles, functions, and performance of the commissioner of police and the deputy commissioners of police and, by extension, the entire police service. Another independent body, the Police Complaints Authority, hears complaints about the conduct of police officers. It also monitors the investigation of complaints and determines disciplinary measures where appropriate.

There was also another policing unit called the Special Anti-Crime Unit of Trinidad and Tobago (SAUTT) established in 2003 to support the TTPS. This was recently disbanded. The military is called the Trinidad and Tobago Defense Force. Its various units include the Trinidad and Tobago Regiment and the Trinidad and Tobago Coast Guard, which includes the Air Wing Operations. The military falls under the Ministry of National Security. Its strength is approximately 2,000 members. There are several joint police and military operations with regard to anti-narcotic operations, street patrols, raids and searches, etc. In fact, there is an established Inter-Agency Task Force for these purposes.

Crime

Classification of Crimes

In Trinidad and Tobago, crimes can be either indictable or non-indictable. Crimes are further categorized into three administrative groupings: serious crimes, minor crimes, and minor offenses. Serious crimes are all crimes that carry a penalty of five or more years, for which prosecutions have been instituted in the High Court. Examples include murder, rape, incest, felonious wounding, kidnapping, treason, robbery, burglaries and break-ins, larceny of over TT $2,000.00 (approx. USD $328), and trafficking of dangerous drugs over a certain quantity. Minor crimes are all crimes carrying a penalty of less than five years for which prosecutions have been instituted in a Magistrate Court or in the High Court. Examples include indecent assault, unlawful wounding and inflicting, possession of firearm and ammunition, larceny of under TT $2,000 (approx. USD $300), and trafficking of dangerous drugs within a certain quantity. Minor offenses are all offenses for which prosecutions have been summarily instituted in the Magistrate's Court. Examples include loitering, assault by beating, armed with a weapon, breaches of the peace, malicious damage of TT $1,000 (approx. USD $150) and under, cruelty to animals, and gambling and betting.

Crime Statistics

The latest crime statistics available by the Trinidad and Tobago Police Service are for the year 2010 (www.nationalsecurity.gov.tt). The provisional statistics show the number of crimes that were "reported," and the number of crimes that were "detected." "Detected" does not mean convicted or solved. It means that for a crime, a person has been arrested after police investigations.

In 2010, there were 472 murders reported and 104 detected, which is a 22 per cent detection rate. For rape, incest, and sexual offenses, 696 incidents were recorded and 346 were detected, for a 50 per cent detection rate. For burglaries and break-ins, 5,207 incidents were reported and 521 were detected, which is a 10 per cent detection rate. For narcotics crimes, 499 incidents were reported and a similar number (499) were detected for a 100 per cent detection rate.

As can be seen in Table 16.1, from 2000 to 2010 total serious crimes in Trinidad and Tobago increased by 15 per cent, total minor

Table 16.1: Crime Rates Per 100,000 Residents, 2000-2010

	2000	2010
Total Serious Crimes	1,318	1,511
Total Minor Crimes	1,203	836
Total Minor Offences	1,606	1,165 (2009)
Murder	9	36
Rape, Incest and Sexual Offences	42 (2001)	53
Wounding and Shooting	38 (2001)	47
Narcotic Offences	37 (2001)	38
Robbery	315 (2001)	385
Larceny	228 (2001)	460
Kidnapping	12 (2001)	9

Source: Trinidad and Tobago Police Service, 2000-2010.

crimes decreased by 31 per cent and total minor offenses decreased by 27 per cent. Murder increased by 300 per cent; in fact, 2008 had the highest number of murders ever (544) for Trinidad and Tobago. For a relatively small country, with a population of approximately 1.3 million persons, having an average of more than one murder per day is high. Closer examinations of the situations of murders in Trinidad and Tobago suggest that there is a notable connection between murders, gang warfare, and drug trafficking.

Rape, incest, and sexual offenses increased by 26 per cent from the 2001 to 2010 and wounding and shooting increased by 24 per cent, which coincides with an increasing use of illegal firearms. Narcotic offenses increased by 3 per cent. The geographic location of Trinidad and Tobago at the southern end of the Caribbean archipelago of islands, close to the South American continent, makes it a strategic transshipment point from the main suppliers of cocaine from South America (Columbia to Venezuela to Caribbean) to the consumers in North America and Europe.

Also shown in Table 16.1, robberies increased by 22 per cent and larceny by 102 per cent while kidnapping decreased by 25 per cent. The year 2005 had the highest number of kidnappings in the country's history with 240 (19 per 100,000 residents). Trends suggest that small- and medium-size business owners and their families are the main targets of kidnapping for ransom.

While crime occurs throughout Trinidad and Tobago, trend data suggest that murders, wounding and shooting, and gang violence, for example, take place more often in certain urban communities. The most typical crimes in urban areas are robbery, wounding and shooting, murders, narcotics, and illegal possession of firearms and ammunition. The most typical crimes in rural areas are larceny, burglary and break-ins, rapes, incest, and other sexual offenses. Further, robberies tend to increase in certain months than others. For example, during the Carnival season (January to March annually) the police find an increase in robberies. This is especially the case in certain urban areas where some *mas* (masquerade) players need to acquire money to purchase carnival costumes and to attend music concerts and other festivities. Also, during the Christmas season, when there are a lot of commercial activities in the urban centers, robberies also increase.

Drug Offenses

In Trinidad and Tobago, the two major illegal drugs are marijuana and cocaine. Persons can be charged with trafficking, possession, as well as using these drugs. There have also been a small number of incidents with trafficking of heroin. Along with the illegal drugs, illegal firearms and ammunitions are also trafficked.

Trinidad and Tobago does not produce cocaine. It serves as a trans-shipment point alongside other Caribbean islands from South America through the Caribbean to North America and Europe. In comparison to cocaine, however, marijuana is grown and produced in Trinidad and Tobago for trafficking as well as for local consumption.

In Trinidad and Tobago, there are also users of cocaine and marijuana. Any quantity of these drugs is illegal to traffic, possess, and use and they carry prison sentences upon being found guilty in the courts. The courts in Trinidad and Tobago are very strict when it comes to sentencing for drug offenses.

Finding of Guilt

All criminal cases start with the filing of a complaint in the summary court. Minor offenses are tried before the magistrate. For more serious offenses, the magistrate holds a preliminary inquiry. If there is sufficient evidence, the accused goes to trial before a judge and jury of the High Court.

In the Constitution, there is the explicit right to a fair trial. An independent judiciary vigorously enforces this right. All criminal defendants have the right to an attorney. The judiciary is independent of the other branches and free from outside interference. Criminal defendants are generally presumed innocent until proven guilty and are afforded the right to representation by counsel (www.legalaffairs.gov.tt). There are a few exceptions, for example, with possession of illegal drugs, the accused must prove innocence.

Rights of Accused

In Trinidad and Tobago some crimes, such as the use of obscene language, can only be tried in a Magistrate Court. Other crimes—for example, murder, rape, kidnapping—can only be tried in a High Court with a judge and jury. For some other crimes—for example, dangerous drugs—the accused has the right to elect whether he or she wants the matter to be tried by a magistrate or a High Court with a judge and jury.

For some crimes, the accused has an option to plea guilty to a lesser offense in a criminal matter before the courts. However, it is up to the prosecutor and the presiding officer (magistrate or judge) to accept the plea. For example, after a preliminary inquiry in the magistrate court for murder, and after the deposition is completed with a statement of the evidence, the accused may plea to the lesser count of manslaughter to which the prosecutor and the presiding officer may agree.

In Trinidad and Tobago, the accused has no right to a speedy trial. The accused must follow the case management system for his or her matter before the court.

Defense

The accused has the right to an attorney and if he or she cannot afford one, one will be appointed to him or her. The accused does not have the right to choose an attorney that is allocated by the state. The Legal Aid and Advisory Authority appoints an attorney for the accused upon application. This authority provides legal advice and court representation from a panel of attorneys before coroners, magistrates, and judges and juries, in matters of probation, family law, civil and criminal law where costs are defrayed wholly or partly out of monies provided by an act of Parliament. This act aims to make legal aid and advice readily available to persons of small and moderate means. The Legal Aid and Advisory Authority is a unit of the Ministry of Legal Affairs. Any member of the public can visit any of the nine branches across Trinidad and Tobago. There is a TT $10.00 (approx. USD $1.64) application fee.

In matters before a magistrate court or in proceedings before a High Court or Court of Appeal, a magistrate or judge must decide if an accused is eligible for legal aid or representation. In High Court civil matters, eligibility is based on the applicant's means and the merits of the matter.

Investigation and Prosecution of Cases

The police service conducts the investigation of criminal cases in Trinidad and Tobago. For some crimes, the police may prosecute in the Magistrate Courts only. The police officer must be of a certain rank. Further, police officers are also allowed to conduct preliminary inquiries in the Magistrate Courts.

For all High Court matters, attorneys from the Office of the Director of Public Prosecutions (DPP) prosecute while the police do the investigation of the cases. There is also the provision whereby the DPP's office can retain the services of private attorneys to represent the state on court matters.

Criminal Law Department

The Criminal Law Department is headed by an independent public officer, the Director of Public Prosecutions (DPP), who has the power to initiate and undertake criminal proceedings against any person before any court with respect to any offense against the laws of Trinidad and Tobago, to take over and continue any such criminal proceedings that may have been instituted by any other person of authority, and to discontinue at any stage before judgment is delivered any such criminal proceedings instituted or undertaken by himself or any other person or authority.[1] The DPP may allow an attorney-at-law in private practice to prosecute on application.

The mission of the department is to serve the state by representing it in criminal matters before the courts in Trinidad and Tobago, and where necessary, abroad. Further, it provides advisory services on matters of a criminal nature to government departments and agencies. The objectives of this department are to appear in all criminal matters at all levels, to advise all departments (police, customs, immigration, town and country, and price control) in criminal matters, to represent police officers on cross charges, and to assist the police in prosecution where difficult points of law are involved in the Magistrates' Court.

Alternatives to Trial

In Trinidad and Tobago, there are alternatives to going to trial, such as plea bargaining. This is where the accused and the prosecutor can bargain an agreement for a plea of guilty to a lesser offense, or they can make an agreement whereby the accused testifies against other accused persons for a reduced sentence, or immunity, etc.

Another alternative to going to trial is community-based mediation. For certain crimes, magistrates may offer the accused and the victim the opportunity to refer their matter to mediation. A trained mediator will try to resolve the main contention between both parties. If both parties do not agree to go to mediation, then the matter is tried by the court. Both parties must agree to abide by the decisions of the mediation process. There is a time limit set by the magistrate to have the matter settled by mediation and if the matter is not resolved within the time frame, the mediator can ask the magistrate for an extension if he or she believes that some additional time is required. If after the time allocated has expired, and the matter is not resolved, the matter is returned to the court for trial.

When the accused is deemed to be medically unfit to stand trial, he or she is sent via the courts to medical institutions for diagnosis and treatment. It is also possible when the accused are deemed to be medically unfit to have their cases discharged.

Incarceration Before or Awaiting Trial

In Trinidad and Tobago, there are primarily two criminal acts in which the accused does not have the right to seek bail. These are murder and treason. For some other offences like kidnapping for ransom or an accused having a certain number of previous matters listed before the court, or has a lengthy criminal record, bail can be denied. For other crimes, the accused can apply for bail. After the accused has been arrested and charged by the police, he or she can apply for bail. If he or she cannot afford bail or until he or she obtains bail, the accused is incarcerated. An accused has a right to appeal to a High Court judge if he or she is not granted bail by a magistrate.

If an accused is held in prison before conviction, that is, while awaiting trial, he or she is placed in a separate section in the prisons called remand. Upon conviction, the prisoner is transferred to another section in the prisons for convicted persons.

System for Juveniles

There is no statutorily-defined juvenile court. However, appropriate arrangements are made in the Magistrate Court to facilitate the trial of matters directly affecting juveniles. In comparison to adults, the names of accused juveniles are not allowed to be featured in the media.

Punishment

Types of Punishment

In Trinidad and Tobago, several forms of punishment are listed on the books. These include fines, prison sentences, probation, treatment, corporal punishment/flogging, house arrest, reparations, compensations, community service, etc. They are used to varying degrees. The most frequently used punishments are prison sentences and fines.

Typical Punishments

The punishment for murder in Trinidad and Tobago is execution by hanging. However, there have been a number of judgments by the Privy Council in London, England, which have placed some restrictions on its implementation. As a result, there are many persons who have been convicted of murder serving life-time sentences in prison. There have been no executions in the last five years.

The typical punishment for rape is a relatively long prison sentence between 15 to 25 years for each conviction of rape. It should be noted that there have been some questionable inconsistent sentences where convicted rapists have been given relatively short sentences that produced much public outcry. There have also been sentences where judges have prescribed long prison terms accompanied by corporal punishment.

The typical punishment for serious theft, burglary, and robbery is a relatively long prison sentence from five years to 15 years. For the most serious drug offenses, the typical punishment will be lifetime imprisonment.

Probation

There is also a probation system in Trinidad and Tobago. Probation is a suspended jail sentence where instead of serving time in prison, the criminal will be returned to the community for a period in which they will have to abide to certain conditions set forth by the court under the supervision of a probation officer. General conditions may include maintaining employment, abiding by a curfew, living where directed, abstaining from unlawful behaviour, following the probation officer's orders, not absconding, and refraining from contact with other individuals, who may include victims of the original crime, potential victims of similar crimes, potential witnesses, or those who have partnered with the offender in the earlier crime. Usually the offender is supervised by a probation officer to monitor his or her performance during the probation period. The probation officer helps the offender to adapt to living in the community and to behave in a lawful and responsible way. Trinidad and Tobago does not yet have a parole system. This is being considered by the relevant authorities.

Prison

In Trinidad and Tobago, the prison population in 1988 was 2,855. It rose steadily and peaked at 4,474 in 1998, which was a 57 per cent increase. After 1998 there was a gradual decline to 3,411 in 2010, representing a decrease of 24 per cent. The prison population per 100,000 residents was 259 in 2010 (Deosaran 2007).

There are seven prisons in Trinidad and Tobago. Six prisons are for convicted persons and one is for remand; that is, those awaiting trial. These prisons are the Carerra Convict Prison, Port of Spain Prison, Maximum Security Prison, Golden Grove Prison for male convicts, Golden Grove Women's Prison, and Tobago Prison and Golden Grove Prison for remand.

There are three juvenile institutions for convicted juveniles. The first institution is the St. Michael's School for Boys, which caters to males between the ages of 10 to 16 years old. The second institution, St. Jude's School for Girls, serves 10-16 year old girls. Males 16 to 18-years-old are sent to the Youth Training Center. Girls aged 16 to 18 years are sent to the women's adult prison.

The biggest prison in Trinidad and Tobago is the Maximum Security Prison. It is located in Arouca in the main island of Trinidad. Arouca is within the Tunapuna/Piarco Regional Corporation. It can accommodate approximately 2,000 prisoners. It has state-of-the-art security systems. The facilities and physical infrastructure at this prison are better than the other prisons. There is no problem of overcrowding in this prison in stark comparison to the other prisons. The prison has classrooms, recreational facilities, a library, sports facilities, a computer laboratory, religious facilities, a kitchen, dining hall, sick bay, etc.

Characteristics of Prisoners

A study in 2003 reported the following characteristics of adult prisoners in Trinidad and Tobago (Deosaran, Ramdhanie, and Lall 2003). The majority of the prisoners were males and almost thirty per cent of the prisoners were between 17 and 26 years old (see Figure 16.1). The majority of prisoners were Afro-Trinidadians followed by prisoners who were Indo-Trinidadians and mixed ethnicities.

Most prisoners were single (84 per cent). Fifteen per cent were married and some 60 per cent had children. The vast majority of prisoners had a low socio-economic background. The highest proportion of prisoners resided in the northern region of Trinidad (46 per cent). This was followed by those who lived in the southern region of Trinidad (31 per cent) and the central region of Trinidad (17 per cent). Five per cent lived in the island of Tobago and one per cent was foreign nationals.

The same study also found that a majority of the prisoners (56 per cent) were recidivists. These prisoners would continuously

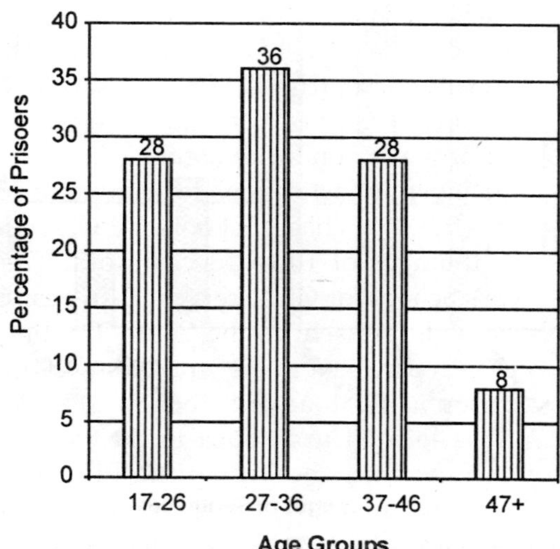

Figure 16.1: Age Distribution of Prisoners

Source: Deosaran, R., 2007.

return to prison to serve sentences for committing other crimes upon release. Thirty-nine per cent were in prison for the first time while five per cent had "other" statuses, such as awaiting appeal, prohibited immigrants, adjourned cases, etc. The highest proportion of prisoners was imprisoned for narcotics-related crimes, followed by larceny-related crimes, and then personal crimes.

Twenty-five per cent of prisoners were serving sentences of less than one year and 23 per cent were serving one to three years (see Figure 16.2). Overall, 94 per cent had sentences of hard labour,

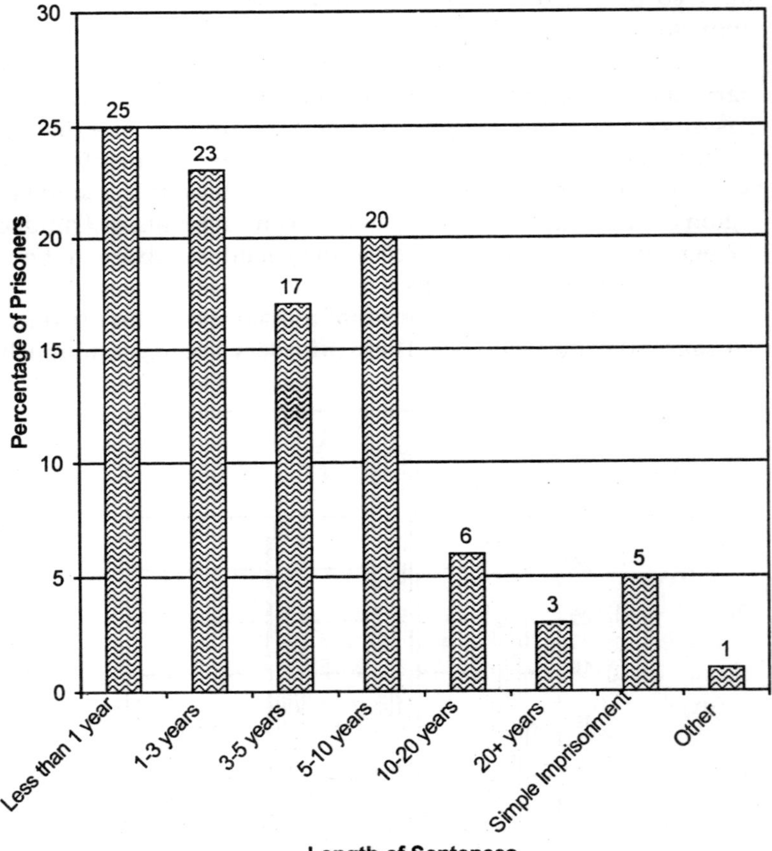

Figure 16.2: Length of Sentence of Inmates (All Prisons)

Note: Simple imprisonment means thirty days or less.

Source: Deosaran, R., 2007.

while six per cent had other types. Of this 94 per cent with hard labour, 73 per cent had only hard labour, 12 per cent had hard labour or a fine, six per cent had hard labour and a fine and three per cent had hard labour and strokes (whipping).

Labour and Vocational Activities in Prisons

Although most prisoners' sentences may stipulate hard labour as part of the sentence, this typically involves cleaning up the surroundings, ensuring a regular supply of water on the compound, kitchen duty, agriculture, rearing animals and so on. It is not compulsory that prisoners work on the prison compound. Depending on the attitude and disposition of the prisoners, as well as the availability of prison staff to supervise them, prisoners may be called upon to do work. Some prisoners are selected to perform certain duties in the prison. Those selected wear different colour apparel to distinguish them from the others. In fact, some of them are called orderlies and work in the prison officers' offices, living quarters, etc. These prisoners have to be trusted over time before they are given these work assignments.

Some prisoners are allowed to work outside or away from the prison compound itself. For example, they do cleaning jobs at various coast guard and army sites. Prisoners who work are paid a small stipend by the prison service. They receive such monies when they are ready to be discharged. Due to the shortage of prison officers to supervise prisoners when they are out of their prison cells doing work, this aspect of working is quite limited to a relatively small number of prisoners. This number varies from prison to prison.

Prisoners are allowed to attend classes that are offered on their prison compound. These classes are taught by prison officers, volunteers, ex-prisoners, and even other prisoners. Some of these classes include academic, skills and training, religious/spiritual, counseling, literacy, pottery, tailoring, electrical, computers and other types of studies. In fact, there are several instances whereby prisoners were able to undertake national and international examinations while in prison and were quite successful. Further, many prisoners have been able to gain entry into local and foreign universities from passing examinations from the prison.

Visiting Policies and Privileges

The visitation policies of the various prisons are slightly different from one another. However, the general policy is that if an inmate is serving a longer sentence, he or she has a longer length of time for the visit. Generally, each inmate will be allowed one visit every four to six weeks with a maximum of three persons for any visit. The shortest time allowed for a visit is 15 minutes and the longest time is 45 minutes.

The actual area set aside for visits varies from prison to prison. In some prisons, prisoners are allowed to interact with the visitors, while in others they communicate via telephone lines and a glass window barrier between prisoner and visitor. Conjugal visits are not allowed in Trinidad and Tobago's prison system. The prison authorities also have a system for special visits. These will include special days like birthdays, Mother's Day, Father's Day, Christmas, etc.

Some of the other privileges that prisoners can access include mail and the ability to attend funerals of very close relatives under the escort of a prison officer. Prisoners are also allowed to receive toiletries and food items from family and friends when they visit them. For female prisoners who give birth to babies while in prison or who have recently given birth to babies just before entering prison, they are also given special visitation privileges to take care of the newly born.

Prisoner Transfer

Prisoners serving sentences in prisons in Trinidad and Tobago who are nationals of other countries can have a request made by the relevant authorities in their diplomatic missions to have them serve their sentences in their home country.

Police Governance

Apart from the crime and prison statistics, the country has recently experienced extensive debate over the new mode of police governance. The Constitution previously provided, as an oversight body, for an independent Police Service Commission appointed by the country's President. This body had powers to appoint, promote, transfer and discipline police officers, except in the case of the Police Commissioner where the Prime Minister had a veto.

Five years ago, both Government and Opposition co-operated on new legislation which changed the Constitution (Act No. 6 of 2006, Act No. 12 of 2007) so that:

1. The Parliament now has to approve or reject the President's nominees to the Police Service Commission. The President, however, has the exclusive power to appoint the Commission's chairman from the appointed members.
2. The Parliament also now has the power to approve or reject the nominees for Commissioner of Police and the three Deputy Commissioners.

The new Police Commissioner now has "complete powers" to manage the Police Service and exert promotion and disciplinary actions over officers up to the rank of Assistant Commissioner. The Police Service Commission now has powers to appraise, monitor, evaluate and discipline the Police Commissioner and the three Deputy Commissioners. The Police Service Commission is also empowered to require a special report from the Commissioner on any matter of concern to which the Commissioner must respond in writing within a stipulated period. The Police Service Commission can terminate the contract of the Commissioner or any of the three Deputies if their performance is assessed to be unsatisfactory. The Minister of National Security, however, is responsible for setting policies for the Police Service (Section 85, Constitution).

These new developments are important since previously the Police Commissioner persistently complained that he had responsibilities but no powers to manage the Service. That is, he is accountable but without powers. Secondly, the oversight of the Police Service was found to be deficient, such that incidents of corruption, inefficiency and public dissatisfaction kept mounting without any visible relief. It is hoped that with these new Constitutional amendments things will improve.

There are two over-arching issues which have some bearing on police governance and performance but which are outside the scope of this chapter. That is (i) the politics of crime and (ii) the basis for developing public policy on crime. In the first issue, a matter of structure, it is important to note the extent to which the adversarial nature of the country's political system contributes to the imperfections in public policy. The second issue, a matter of process, deals with the tendency of producing crime-related policies without sufficient or reliably-derived evidence for such policies. These issues require a separate discussion but together with other structural factors in the country would help provide a bigger picture for the country and the Caribbean as a whole.

17

Crime, Violence, and the Global Proliferation of Terrorism

A Descriptive Overview of the Caribbean

M. Raymond Izarali

The Caribbean eludes many of us who live outside the region. Promoted by the tourism industry as a vacation haven for fun and play, honeymoons, alluring white sand and blue waters and its rich botanic features, the Caribbean is generally perceived by Westerners and others as a superb diversion from the productivity-driven demands of their society. Such depictions are emphasized because of vested interests, both for the tourism industry and for the national revenue of many Caribbean countries. But they also carve an image of the region to those outside as a place that has sublime qualities, using its natural endowments of pristine waters and lush vegetation to create an impression that veils other characteristics such as the true nature of local life, socio-economic conditions, challenges to liberty, crime and violence, education, and access to justice. As Andy Knight remarks in chapter two: "Outsiders from the Caribbean region usually think of this area primarily as a haven for tourists, as a tropical paradise." Certainly, some parts and features of the Caribbean make for an illusion of paradise. Even Christopher Columbus was so enwrapped by its majestic atmosphere that he requested his remains be buried in Santo Domingo.

It is interesting to recall Columbus as we conclude this volume, considering that subsequent to his initial, mistaken voyage to the region and other voyages, that despite the region's picturesque features it became a place of much horror and mistreatment for so many people from Africa, India and elsewhere, and to natives who had already inhabited the place before Europeans began staking claims of "discovery." Its vast expanse of arable and fertile lands resonated with Europe's appetite for sugar and other goods, led to external economies both in human cargo and agricultural yields, and became the basis of a sub-human system of justice and oppression. Most notable was the establishment of sugar plantations. This undertaking germinated into generations of cruelty in establishing the slave trade there and an economy of the enslaved to work these plantations, and subsequently a system of indentureship. While sugar production in the current times has been on the decline, it is significant to recall that, as Knight notes, "the Caribbean became the world's largest source of sugar."

Africa was plundered for its human richness, its young and most fit of them, to toil in these plantations, producing a sweetness to satiate European taste and an economy that demarcated the dehumanization of Africans in law and practice. An estimated 12 million black Africans were uprooted from their families in places like Ghana, Senegal, Nigeria and Angola to ply the tide of the Triangular Trade, of which about two million did not survive the journey (Thompson 1997, 6-7). About 90 per cent of them are said to have been routed to the Caribbean and South America. With the abolition of slavery, crude indentureship programmes were tried with others (e.g., Chinese and Javanese) but India became the focal point, leading to hundreds of thousands of Indians being voyaged to places like Trinidad, Guyana, Guadaloupe, Suriname, Martinique, St. Lucia, and Grenada, as Satnarine Balkaransingh has pointed out in chapter three. Thus the majestic beauty of the Caribbean that makes it illusory in tourism promotions has been imprinted with a history of violence, human enslavement and mistreatment that were sanctified in law for the benefit of the white colonialists. As Dr. Eric Williams (1942) observed, so strange that an article so sweet turned out to be the basis of so much crime and bloodshed.

The preceding chapters suggest that the region as it stands is a complex place. It could be understood as purely the Caribbean, the Caribbean Basin, or the circum-Caribbean—identified in geographical, cultural, or political/regional terms. Indeed contributors to this volume have conceptualized it in various ways. The Caribbean in contemporary times is home to a vast array of peoples and cultures, different languages, ethnicities, and religions

(Tulchin and Espach 2000, 10-11). It might be regarded as a place that perhaps best identifies with an earlier wave of globalization which ushered people from Africa via the slave trade (Dunn 1972; Williams 1942; Thompson 1997); from India, Indonesia, and China through indentureship programmes (Roopnarine 2007; Thompson 1997); and from Europe (Spain, France, Netherlands, England) through a colonizing and proselytizing political psychology. Not surprisingly, segments of the Caribbean may be delineated as Spanish, French, Dutch, and English, reflecting the transitions and remnants of the different/rival European powers over time (UNDP 2012; Thompson 1997, 7). Interestingly, the Caribbean is also now discussed in terms of its diaspora in debates about transnational relations to address the idea of "transnational families" and political economy, as elaborated earlier by Timothy Shaw in chapter one. These attributes thus identify a very heterogeneous place and so the idea of commonality at large may make for a vexing question.

Although the Caribbean has evolved from the colonial expansionism of Europe it is not clear whether these power structures have altogether disappeared. While official control was ceded in many instances decades ago, some scholars insist that the yoke of Western powers remained through what has been dubbed neo-colonization—the economic structures of control maintained by the West during the post-colonial period (Thompson 1997, 9). Others are of the view that the impact of colonization carried on in the social psychology of many Caribbean people in what may be regarded as the colonization of consciousness (see Itwaru 1989; Fanon 1967), characterized by the way people conceive of themselves and their capacities relationally to whites, especially since they were imbued for generations with the idea that white is emblematic of race and epistemic superiority. Ironically, many see whites in this way but try to imitate some of the white man's behaviour toward their own people.

Certainly, some such discourses attempt to identify the manner in which, following the departure of colonial rule, governance and strata of relations among many Caribbean governments and people mimicked the postures of oppression and the behaviourism of the colonialists in ways that abused political sovereignty and subverted self-determination at the individual level, and have given rise to many contemporary woes. Political oppression, corruption, racism, blatant violations of human rights, and perversion to institutions of justice coupled with the flight of colonialist capital and economic exploitation have all mired the social landscapes of the contemporary Caribbean in an abyss of challenges. While it is instructive to be mindful of the role of the West in fuelling divisions among Caribbean peoples for their own aggrandizement and greed in what is understood generally as the "divide and conquer" or "divide and rule" philosophy, it is critical that such invocations not overlook the social injustices carried out by Caribbean people/ leaders on their own people or whittle down their moral accountability. Countries like Guyana and Haiti in the case of Forbes Burnham and the Duvaliers and elsewhere come to mind. If this were to happen, we would be misguided in identifying the fault-lines that have given rise to many contemporary issues, which have served as a catalyst to the migration of so many people to seek a better life for themselves and their children in places like England, Canada, and the U.S.; such migration interfaced them with circumstances of crude cultural alienation, marginalization, and emasculation in their adopted country while the new political oppressors in the Caribbean feasted inconsiderately on power at the expense of the security and wellbeing of the public.

The spawning of the flight of human and intellectual capital is glaringly evident in the large diaspora populations in the Metropoles and in the hundreds of thousands of Caribbean people who dream of or await visas to migrate. As Andy Knight has already pointed out in chapter two, Caribbean people account for 10 per cent of all foreign nationals in the U.S. According to Statistics Canada, Canadians of Caribbean heritage comprised by 2001 about two per cent (or half a million) of the national population (Statistics Canada 2007). Of these, 42 per cent have origins in Jamaica, 16 per cent in Haiti, 10 per cent in Guyana, 10 per cent in Trinidad and Tobago, and five per cent in Barbados. Overall, 55 per cent of the people of Caribbean heritage in Canada were born outside Canada. In the context of Jamaica, Natasha Parkins has already given a lucid account in chapter eight of some of the push and pull factors of professionals in respect to migration. Timothy Shaw has likewise remarked that there are about as many Guyanese in Canada and the U.S. combined than there are in Guyana: plus or minus 700,000.

The point here should not be lost: while repercussions of colonialism may still prevail, it is not a sufficient basis to excuse the roles and responsibilities that the political establishments in the contemporary Caribbean have in shaping a present and a future that are asymmetric to the injustices of the past. To wholly impute the wraths of contemporary times to the white man or the colonialists is to have a cock-eyed view of the violence and hardship inflicted on Caribbean people by their own, whether it has been through institutionalized racism, corruption, greed, or inebriation from power.

Many of the variables that characterize the complex nature of the contemporary Caribbean have been addressed by a diverse range of contributors to this volume. Some focus on the presence, significance, and networks of major players like India, China, and the West in the Caribbean. Some address factors that inspire emigration and the possible role of Caribbean embassies in growth stimulation. Rhoda Reddock addresses the issue of gender construction in the Caribbean in the age of globalization. Linden Lewis urges us to revisit the culture of care in the face of HIV/AIDS, arguing for a new social contract that is fair to women and girls and that obliges men to absorb their fair share of responsibilities. As psychologists, Jaipaul Roopnarine and Ambika Krishnakumar outline key elements to Caribbean family life, highlighting the dynamics of parent-child relationships, harsh discipline, mental health, violence, the factors that negatively and positively impact education development, and the measures required for sustained human development; their study underscores the pervasiveness of violence in domestic and social settings and its deleterious effects on the goal of cultivating a just, socially hospitable, and progressive society. Kalowatie Deonandan furnishes an account of the Emerging Economies pursuing megaprojects in Guyana, the concomitant social harms leveraged on indigenous communities through preferential and non-transparent arrangements by the government to major foreign corporations, and the loss of anticipated economic returns to the nation—what one might call "crimes of globalization" (see Friedrichs 2002; Ezeonu 2008).

Others have focused on crime and violence in particular settings, in different ways. David Arredondo and Hari Nair, for example, highlight the relevance of the works of Fernando Ortiz on culture and criminology to understanding contemporary Cuba. Aparajita Gangopadhyay discusses the urgent problems of crime, violence, and political instability in Haiti and the challenge posed to regional security. Ramesh Deosaran crystallizes the framework of crime and justice in Trinidad and Tobago. Roger Hosein, Jeetendra Khadan, and Nicholas Paul apply an economic approach to argue that resource investments in sporting activities such as athletics and olympics training can yield greater social cohesion and significantly dilute the plague of violence and deviance in the CARICOM community.

Drugs, Crime, and Violence

It is significant that in almost all of these discussions on the Caribbean, the idea of crime and violence surfaces in one way or another to conceptualize and contextualize social and political life in the region. Indeed this is not accidental but rather reflective of the tribulations faced by Caribbean peoples and governments and the extent to which these experiences have been etched in the subconscious. Alvin Thompson (15) once wrote that: "Any serious study of the history of the Caribbean will soon reveal the depth and breadth of the violence which has engulfed the region." While he had in mind the violence that played out during the almost 500 years of colonization of the region, it is lamentable that the same remark applies to the current times. Studies carried out by the United Nations and the World Bank emphasize crime as the foremost problem of the contemporary Caribbean, with illicit drugs trans-shipment originating from South America to the United States and Europe being the drive-wheel. The extent to which crime pervades the Caribbean is such that it undermines development, deters investment, inspires outbound migration, engenders a felt-sense of insecurity, and reduces national revenue, among other things. As many Caribbean states are heavily dependent on tourism for national revenue, a high prevalence of crime has the effect of being burdensome on the state to implement security measures for both local citizens and tourists, and of deterring prospective tourists when their confidence in security erodes. The situation is characterized by Ivelaw Griffith (2002, 138) in his claim that:

> There is near-universal agreement among Caribbean officials that the top security concern in the region relates to drugs. The drug phenomenon involves drug production, consumption and abuse, trafficking, and money laundering. However, it is the trafficking that best highlights the region's strategic value.

Ronald Sanders (2003, 370), a former diplomat of Antigua and Barbuda, in his clarion call for attention to the problem underscores the impact when he writes:

> If the Caribbean is not provided urgent assistance to confront the overwhelming problem of crime, this idyllic region...may well become an area shunned by tourists and investors, with all the disastrous consequences both domestically and internationally that such an unfortunate development would cause, including the possible creation of a base for international terrorism and financial crime.

While serving as prime minister of Jamaica, P.J. Patterson acknowledged in his 2006 New Year's address that: "Without a doubt, the high level of violent crime remains our most troubling and pressing problem" (UNODC 2007, i). At the heart of it drugs and drug gangs appear to be key players in criminality. Trinidad and Tobago imposed a national curfew in the latter part of 2011 to deal with the overwhelming magnitude of crime. Guyana for its part has been struggling to stay at pace with drug dealers and other criminal elements; more recently, a major drug baron, Shaheed "Roger" Khan, a Guyanese citizen, was arrested by police in Suriname while in hiding, transported to Trinidad and Tobago which has an extradition arrangement with the US, and subsequently extradited to the US to face trial. He is now serving three 15-year prison sentences concurrently. As Timothy Shaw has already pointed out, the drug baron Christopher "Dudos" Coke (officially Michael Christopher Coke) of Jamaica was also extradited from Jamaica to the US to stand trial, after much civil unrest in Tivoli Gardens, Kingston. Ironically, both men were portrayed by some as Robin Hood-like characters in the way they engaged in social life but both were at the helm of major drug enterprises.

The strain on Caribbean states is made heavier when we consider that corruption is rampant, prisons are overcrowded, and courts are severely backlogged (Bagley, 2004, 33; UNODC 2007; UNDP 2012; Griffith 2011; UNODC 2011; Morris 2008; Maguire *et al.* 2010; Pino and Johnson 2011; Harriott 2002). As Verna St. Rose-Greaves, Opposition Senator in 2010 in Trinidad and Tobago, noted of the Port-of-Spain jail that was built in 1812: "This place is not fit for animals, let alone human beings. Men sleeping head-to-toe in a cell, packed in like sardines, some without mattresses and without proper bedding layered from ceilings in hammocks straight down to the floor on cardboard. The stench of human and cat urine soaked into a hundred-year old concrete floor" (Douglas 2010). In the context of Jamaica, Amnesty International (2000) notes:

> Conditions in Jamaica's detention centres fall well below international standards. Prisons are so overcrowded and insanitary that incarceration amounts to cruel, inhuman or degrading treatment. The two main prisons on the island, St. Catherine's District Prison and Kingston General Penitentiary, remain severely overcrowded, having been built for 650 and 850 inmates respectively but currently housing approximately 1225 and 1378.

In 1993, Ivelaw Lloyd Griffith (1993, 244), a leading scholar on security in the region, wrote: "The use and misuse of drugs like alcohol and tobacco have long been problematic for countries in the Caribbean. Yet the drugs with security implications are primarily cocaine, marijuana, heroin, and their derivatives, such as crack." This perspective was echoed again at the Thirteenth Annual Eric Williams Memorial Lecture at Florida International University in his lecture "Drugs and Crime as Problems Without Passports in the Caribbean: How Secure is Security, and How Sovereign is Sovereignty?" (Griffith 2011). By 1993, the places with the most prominent marijuana cultivation were Belize, Guyana, Jamaica, and Trinidad and Tobago (Griffith 1993, 244). In one instance in May 1992, about 799,700 pounds of marijuana valued at G$1 billion were seized along the Berbice River; two months prior to that, 60,000 pounds were seized up the Mahaica River and police uncovered ten fields and 160,000 marijuana plants alongside the Maduni Creek (Griffith 1993, 244). In respect to cocaine, Griffith (1993, 247) reports that seizures in Guyana were a mere 400 grams in 1987 but catapulted to 3,575 grams the following year. Moreover, to highlight the implications of drug use, he indicated that: "the registration of addicts seeking rehabilitation in Barbados rose from seven in 1986 to 115 in 1988; hospital admission of cocaine and marijuana addicts in Trinidad and Tobago rose from 376 in 1983 to 1,041 in 1989; and the number of 'crack bases' in Jamaica has been increasing dramatically" (Griffith 1993, 247). Jamaica, for its part, was said to have become "a cocaine and crack market for both residents and tourists" (Carl Stone, cited in Griffith 1993, 247). The underlying point here is that the drug problem is not a sudden phenomenon but one that seems to have emerged more heavily in the 1990s, as is the concomitant perversion of law enforcement and justice institutions and political corruption—notably, in the Bahamas, Antigua and Barbuda, Trinidad and Tobago, Jamaica, St. Lucia, and the Turks and Caicos. Because of the large amount of money involved, it should not be surprising to learn of the scope in which the problem pervaded Caribbean countries. Marijuana, for example, generated about US$ 2 billion in Jamaica and about US$350 million in Belize by 1993 (Griffith 1993, 293).

The prevalence of high crime and insecurity stemming from illicit drugs is attributed to the Caribbean's proximity to the Andean region of South America which hosts the world's largest source of cocaine (UNODC 2007; Manwaring 2011; Griffith 1993; Haughton 2007). Colombia in particular has for some time produced most of the global supply of cocaine but new data indicate that its production level has diminished significantly over the years. According to the *World Drug Report 2010 (UNODC 2010, 16)*, the area used for coca cultivation in Colombia between 2000 and 2009 shrunk by 58 per cent as a result of eradication measures by the government but at the same time Peru showed a cultivation increase of 38 per cent and the Plurinational State of Bolivia 112 per cent.

The Figure 17.1 highlights cocaine production from 1990 to 2008. As at 2009, Colombia accounted for 43 per cent of global cocaine cultivation, followed by Peru at 38 per cent and Bolivia at 19 per cent (UNODC 2010, 16). Thus while Colombia has been showing a declining trend it still stands strong in global coca cultivation; furthermore, despite its diminished supply on the world market, the complementary production in Peru and Bolivia still makes the Andean region a global organ of cocaine production. The irony, however, is that the production is not so much intended for local consumption but rather for foreign markets.

The largest cocaine market in the world is North America, which by the year 2008 hosted 6.2 million users, followed by Europe which showed between four and five million users for the same year (UNODC 2010, 16). The Figure 17.2 gives a 10-year overview of cocaine demand in North America in metric tons (mt).

North America alone required 196 mt of pure cocaine in 2008 to meet its demands. North America and Europe pose a heavy demand on cocaine production. Given that cocaine carries a high street value coupled with the fact that traffickers are paid in kind and not necessarily in cash, the burdens imposed on Caribbean societies can be enormous—on the healthcare system, law enforcement, deviance and crime, heightened insecurity—because traffickers will sell to locals in order to generate an income from their share of the pie, thus leading to consumption and addiction

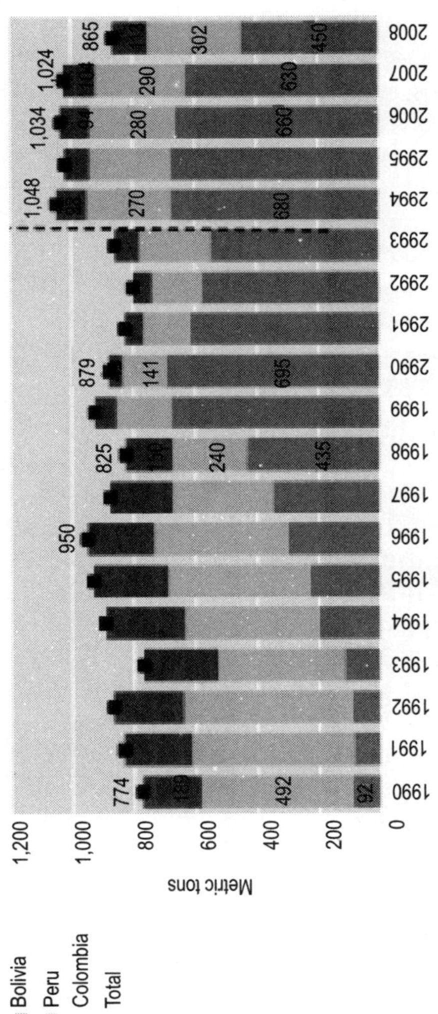

Figure 17.1: Global Potential Cocaine Production (mt) 1990-2008

Source: Word Drug Report 2010 (UNODC 2010, 66).

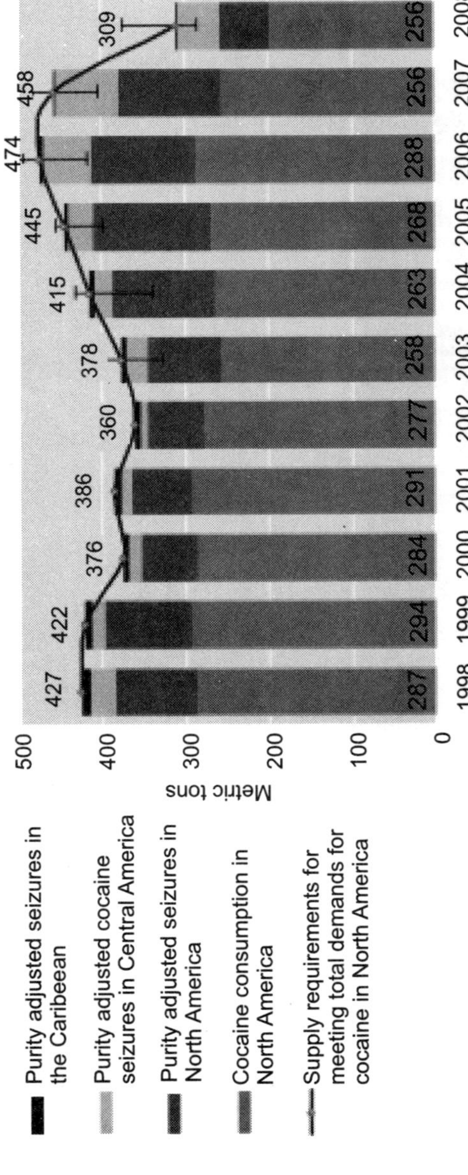

Figure 17.2: Cocaine Demand (Consumption and Seizures): North America, 1998-2008

Source: World Drug Report 2010 (UNODC 2010, 76)

problems locally and stress on families and social systems. As the *World Drug Report 2010* (UNODC 2010, 16) states of North America and Europe: "These two regions, with 70 per cent of the demand and 85 per cent of the total value, play the main role in shaping the evolution of the global cocaine market. Another 2.7 million users are found in South America, Central America and the Caribbean." The social baggage of crime and violence that are attached to this scenario may be appreciated when this data is understood in financial terms. For the year 2008 the North American market was valued at $US 37 billion while the European market was valued at US$34 billion, compared to a global cocaine market at the time of approximately US$ 88 billion (UNODC 2010, 16). Huge as the financial value of the market is, it is worth bearing in mind that about 70 per cent of the profit generated from cocaine is in transactions between mid-level dealers and consumers in the US while 1.5 per cent is made by Andean farmers, and 13 per cent by international traffickers including Caribbean countries.

As can be seen in the pie figure 17.3 above, the lion share of profits as well as the greater proportion of consumption is anchored in the US (UNODC 2010, 18). Thus it would be a myth to conceive of the Andean farmers as being recipients of huge profits from such a high-priced industry.

Notwithstanding the financial value of the market, shipping the drug from its source of production to its principal consumer markets is a matter of some innovation, and in this regard Caribbean countries suffer bitterly as a result of being used as a major transit point for the drug (Manwaring 2011; Griffith 1993 and 2011; Haughton 2007; Agozino *et al.* 2009; Pino and Johnson 2011; Block and Griffin 1999). Drugs are channelled by air and sea to places like Jamaica and the Dominican Republic through Guyana, Trinidad and Tobago, the Bahamas and other Caribbean countries to be further transported to the US directly, or to Puerto Rico in the hope that they will enter the mainland US easier because of ease of customs clearance of cargo from Puerto to the mainland US; Puerto is an overseas territory of the US with commonwealth status. Countries like the Bahamas and Guyana are lucrative trans-shipment points because of their geography and their limited resources to patrol the perimeters of their boundaries. As Griffith (1993, 249) notes: "The geography of the Bahamian archipelago makes it an excellent candidate for drug transhipment, given its 700 islands and cays, and its strategic location in the airline flight path between Colombia and South Florida."

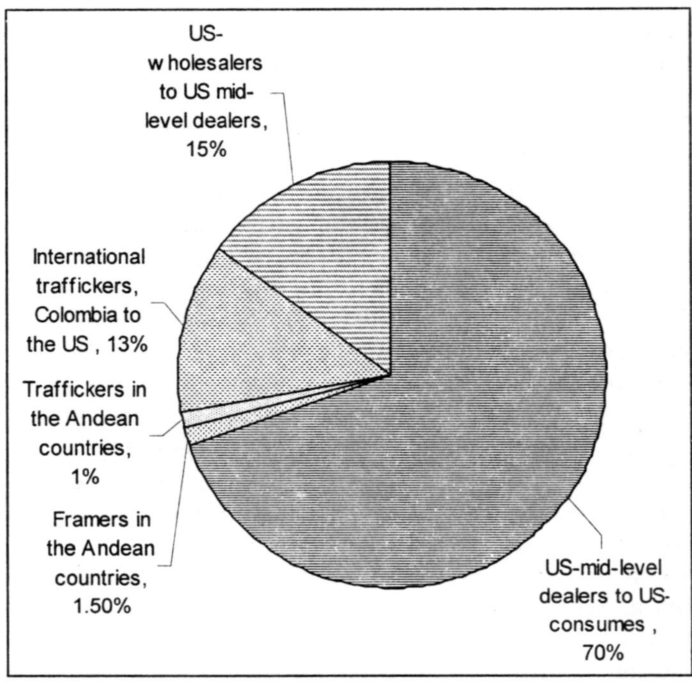

Figure 17.3: Distribution of Gross Profits (in %) of the US$ 35 Billion US Cocaine Market, 2008

Source: *World Drug Report 2010* (UNODC 2010, 18).

The *International Narcotics Control Strategy Report 2011* (INCSR 2011, Vol. 1, 284) noted that: "Guyana is a transhipment point for cocaine from Colombia and Venezuela destined for North America, Europe, and the Caribbean. Generally, small aircraft transporting cocaine land at remote airstrips in Guyana's unpopulated interior highlands or coastal savanna regions to refuel and continue on to offshore destinations. Due to weak land and maritime border controls and the vast unpatrolled interior, drug traffickers are able to conduct operations without significant interference from law enforcement agencies." Similarly, the report states that: "Trinidad and Tobago's location off the coast of Venezuela, porous air and sea borders and direct air or sea routes to Europe, West Africa, the U.S., Canada, and the Caribbean make it ideally suited for drug transhipment" (536). Accordingly, trafficking of cocaine and marijuana from South America and smaller amounts of heroin is notable. The report likewise claims the Dominican Republic is a major transit country for drugs from

South America destined to Europe and North America: "Illicit drugs continue to arrive in the Dominican Republic via aircraft and increasingly by sea aboard maritime conveyances such as go-fast boats, privately owned fishing and recreational vessels, and cargo containers" (INCSR 2011, Volume 1, 215). Certainly, the report findings are not limited to these countries. The point is simply to illustrate the problem of trans-shipment in the face of the open expanse of the geography of Caribbean countries and the problems this engender for Caribbean governments and people.

The financial value makes the trans-shipment both innovative and aggressive. For example, in October 2011 a vessel, MV Vega Azurit, that departed Guyana to Jamaica was found with 50 pounds of pure cocaine worth US$560,000 by Jamaican authorities (Kaiteur News, 14 October 2011). The drug was found in boxes that had been labelled as "coke," "pepsi," and "Canada Dry" in a 40-foot refrigerated container that was declared as empty. The same vessel was found with 122 kilograms of cocaine in a timber consignment from Guyana in March of the same year and, on another occasion in March, with 112.5 kilograms of cocaine, all by Jamaican authorities. In April 2011, a sting operation by the Drug Squad in a St. James residence in Barbados found 94 pounds of powder-form cocaine in wooden pallets (Stabroek News, 3 April 2011). In another instance in September of 2010, a container was found in Bridgetown, Barbados with 2700 pounds of Marijuana worth over $11 million, for which a man from St. Thomas was charged for trafficking (Stabroek News, 3 April 2011). In 2004, some 700 kilograms of "high-purity" cocaine worth over 35 million British pounds were found in steel drums of molasses in a container in the Netherlands that came from Guyana. The container was said to have left Guyana with organic sugar but by the time it reached the Netherlands the sugar was replaced with cocaine. A 59 year old UK-based man named Simon Price was sentenced to 28 years imprisonment in the UK for this incident (Caribbean 360, 18 July 2005). In February 2012, about 20 kilograms of cocaine shipped from Guyana in boxes of star apples and attentioned to a falsified business in the Toronto area were found by the Royal Canadian Mounted Police (RCMP 2012). Of course, it is worth remembering that on March 15, 1993, US authorities found 117 pounds of cocaine in the panelling of a Guyana Airways Corporation plane (flight GY714) that arrived in New York from Guyana (Griffith 1993b, p. 79). The bottom line is clear: Caribbean countries for some time have been seen as having a lucrative geography to migrate drugs from South America to North America and Europe, and given the high financial value, drugs create both a strong appeal to traffickers and a huge problem for Caribbean countries. While Mexico has become a major geography of funnelling drugs to the U.S., Caribbean countries are not exempt from the pains of drug trafficking nor is there any clear sign that the problem will be eradicated immediately. As a joint 2007 report by the World Bank and the United Nations Office on Drugs and Crime puts it: "Despite their diversity, one thing all Caribbean countries have in common is that they have long been caught in the crossfire of international drug trafficking. The Caribbean suffers greatly from the supply from the south and the demand in the north" (UNODC 2007, 15).

Indeed, it must be noted that the problem is not just on its impact on the proliferation of crime and the harm to social life but also economic in terms of punitive financial measures imposed on economic entities that are victimized in trans-shipment, something which is perhaps often invisible to the public. In one case where nearly 100 pounds of marijuana was found in a Guyana Airways plane that arrived in New York in January 1992, US Customs imposed a fine of US$1.2 million dollars on Guyana Airways Corporation (Griffith, 1993, 263). Griffith (1993, 263-4) provides an account of punitive fines imposed on Jamaica in the past that are worth quoting at length because they also capture the strain such fines have on the local economy in terms of jobs, industry and transport facilities:

- "In 1986 two Air Jamaica planes were impounded in Miami and New York and a U.S. $657,000 fine was levied.
- In 1986, the now defunct Eastern Airlines was fined U.S. $900,000 after marijuana was found on a cargo flight. Three weeks later it was fined U.S. $1.6 million for the same infraction. Cargo flights from Jamaica were then suspended.
- In 1988, Sea-Land Services paid the United States Customs U.S. $85 million in fines.
- In 1989 the United States Customs imposed a U.S. $96 million charge against Sea-Land Services following the discovery of 12,000 pounds of marijuana shipped from Jamaica. Sea-Land subsequently withdrew its services from Jamaica.
- In April 1989 an Air Jamaica plane was impounded in Miami and a U.S. $28.8 million fine imposed."

While these examples are of an earlier vintage, they do underscore the history of the problem, the economic strain posed to air transport, and the demands placed on states to combat the aggressive pursuit of drug traffickers to migrate the drugs from the source of supply to the source of demand. It should not be surprising therefore that many Caribbean countries have spent a significant proportion of their national revenue combating problems relating to drugs. Neither should it be a surprise that, given the financial value of drugs, corruption is fostered on many levels (particularly in light of low-paying high status jobs in the civil service), violence proliferates, and criminal gang activities are spawned. This situation is especially troubling in light of the fact that CARICOM countries have 64 per cent of their population below age 30 (UNDP 2012, 45); such a social context suggests that the youth are exposed to both a social plague and a luring path to quick money. This problem is compounded by the fact that hardly any proper, substantive official data is available to determine the number of gangs, their membership size, and their influence on society and the youth as well as on how gangs are inspired and proliferated in the region. As Katz, Maguire, and Choate (2011, 2) have observed in their attempt to carry out a systematic comparison of gangs between two communities in the US and two in the Port of Spain area of Trinidad, "Scholars have lamented the paucity of research on the contributions of gangs to violence in the Caribbean region." Yet the problem of gangs pervades the region. Moreover, in trying to study gangs, or crime and violence in the Caribbean for that matter, applying Western theories which are heavily invested in understanding such problems in Western cultures to Caribbean societies may not have as much yield value. The dynamics among gangs and the context of social life in the Caribbean are somewhat asymmetric to those in the US (Deosaran 2008; Katz *et al.* 2011), and so there is need for a Caribbean criminology (Deosaran, 2004; Pryce 2007) that can help us to better comprehend the nature and context of crime and violence in the Caribbean. As Katz *et al.* (2011, 3) put it: "The dearth of research on gangs in developing nations has resulted in poor theoretical development about gangs and gang-related problems in these areas...The lack of research on gangs in the Caribbean in particular is somewhat surprising, given that the region has the second highest homicide rate in the world...and gangs are believed to be the primary factor driving the violence." Trinidad and Tobago according to the Trinidad and Tobago Police Services (TTPS) is said to have a minimum of 95 gangs, which are behind 60 per cent of the country's homicides and are the principal players in the local firearm markets (Katz *et al.*, 2011, 4). Some of the differences in gang culture and violence between the US and the Caribbean may be delineated from a finding by Katz *et al.* (2011, 12) in the comparison between the two US jurisdictions and the two Trinidad jurisdictions:

> Gang members in Trinidad were significantly more likely to have been the victim of a violent crime in the past 12 months than U.S. gang members. In particular, Trinidadian gang members were more likely to have been shot (28.6% T&T, 9.5% U.S.), threatened with a gun (66.7% T&T, 37.8 U.S), injured with a weapon other than a gun (52.4% T&T, 27.0% U.S.), and robbed (42.9% T&T, 18.9% U.S.) than U.S. gang members. A similar pattern was observed for the frequency of victimization. When compared to U.S. gang members, Trinidad gang members were threatened with a gun two times more often, shot 10 per cent more often, injured with a weapon 2.3 times more often, and robbed 5.96 times more often.

Thus, these differences may suggest, at a minimum, that gangs in the Caribbean as are perhaps gangs in developing countries are both driven and affected by factors that are not fully consistent with those in the US counterpart. At the very least we notice in the above findings that violence is encountered more by gangs in the Port of Spain area of Trinidad than they are in the US. Indeed, Katz *et al.* have clearly acknowledged that no generalizations across the Caribbean region or between the US and Trinidad could be made from their study. Of course, one must acknowledge both the difficulty and paucity of literature on international comparison of gangs (Klein 2011; Hagedorn 2005).

Notwithstanding these considerations, it is significant that a study carried out by Katz, Choate, and Fox in 2010 (in UNDP 2012, 71) found that in Trinidad 42 per cent of the youth who joined gangs did so because of friendship, 29.4 per cent did so for the sake of protection and safety, 8 per cent did so to make money, 3.8 per cent had a sibling in a gang, and 2.1 per cent had a parent (s) in a gang. This situation confirms some sense that the presence of gangs may be regarded by a proportion of the youth as a common feature of daily life on account of a friendship with someone who is already a member of a gang. In such a situation, the youth could be more subtly derailed to a path of deviance and crime. Given the negligible size and population of many Caribbean countries, it is rather disconcerting that there are estimated to be as many as

95 gangs in Trinidad and Tobago with a membership of 1,269; 268 gangs in Jamaica with a membership of 3,900; 150 gangs in Barbados with a membership of 4000; and 15 gangs in Antigua & Barbuda with a membership of between 264 to 570 (UNDP 2012, 70). Not to mention the unspecified amounts in places like Guyana, St. Lucia, the Bahamas, and the Dominican Republic. The problems posed to youth by drugs trans-shipment in terms of fostering gang proliferation and being derailed from a moral path of life are perhaps, in the absence sufficient scientific analysis, embodied in the perceptions of citizens of the Caribbean, as shown in the Figure 17.4 (UNDP 2012, 68).

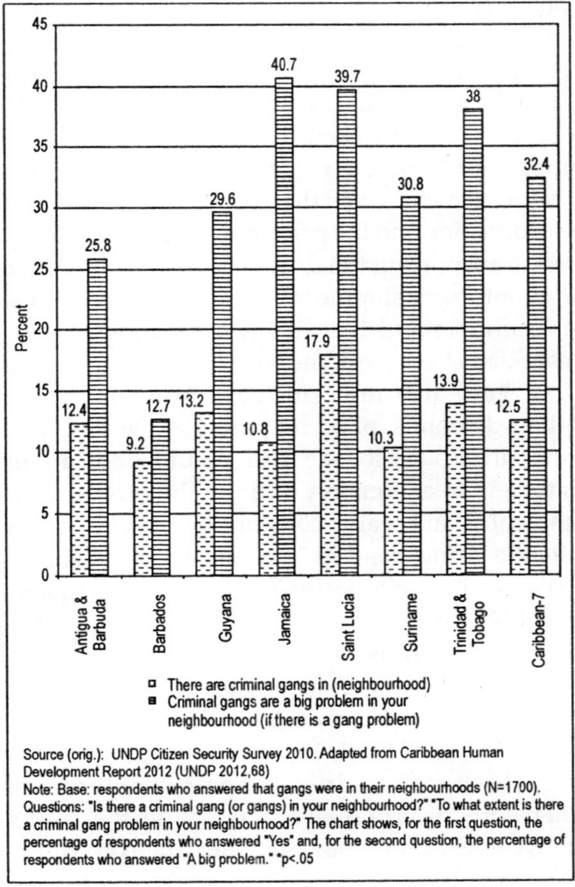

Figure 17.4: Perceptions of the Street Gang Problem, 2010.

Source: Extracted from *Caribbean Human Development Report 2012* (UNDP 2012, 68)

Whatever one's view of the actual number of gangs, it must be said that while in some instances gangs may lead one to believe that they are more reliable for community protection and safety as is at times said of Shaheed "Roger" Khan in Guyana and Christopher "Dudos" Coke in Jamaica, gangs tend to hold society under a degree of siege. Gangs emerge for specific objectives and rarely are those objectives benevolent. Gangs and their rivalry may significantly narrow the scope of social liberty, proliferate violence and drug trafficking, and define limits on the free movement of the civilian population in everyday life (Hagedorn 2005; Manwaring 2011). Thus, a sense of the perception factor of gang problems by members of the community is an important measure of people's sense of security.

Altogether, we may say that in light of the profit breakdown previously highlighted, illicit drugs demanded by North America and Europe that are trafficked through the Caribbean underpin several important issues. First, the cocaine market has a huge financial value. Second, given that the Andean region is the centre of cocaine production and the principal markets are North America and Europe, transporting the drug poses enormous problems for Caribbean countries, as shipment is done both by air and sea. Third, if we are to understand that drugs are a plague to Caribbean societies especially because of the region's proximity to the Andean region, it suggests that the principal consumer markets are, in virtue of their demands, part and parcel of the problem of crime and violence in the Caribbean and should dedicate effort and resources to help to adequately address the problem. While data patterns indicate that cocaine consumption in the US has been on the decline, the rising trend in Europe continue to keep demand steady and as such inspire more innovative ways to keep supply at pace. All things considered, "It is not surprising, then, that of the 20 countries identified as major drug transit or major drug producing countries by the United States government in 2006, four are in the Caribbean: the Bahamas, the Dominican Republic, Haiti, and Jamaica" (UNODC 2007, 19).

Since the discussion on drugs is a precursor to understanding some dimensions of crime and violence in the contemporary Caribbean, we now turn to some statistical data on crime provided by the UN/World Bank to sketch an overview of the issue in the region, some of which have already been provided in earlier chapters, notably by Timothy Shaw and by Roger Hosein *et al.* A descriptive as opposed to a theoretical account of crime in the

Caribbean is furnished here because, as has been noted earlier, there is need for a Caribbean criminology as opposed to the application of popular Western theories of crime to properly understand the nature and context of crime in the region. Crime as noted by Griffith and Sanders and a slate of others paints a stark picture of the Caribbean. At the same time, crime data for the region are not a simple task to gather and interpret because of the different frames of reference to the Caribbean (i.e., which countries are included in one's notion of the Caribbean), definitional differences in respect to certain crimes (some are lumped together while some may be individuated and differently defined), the lack of sufficient and reliable data archiving, population concentration amongst the different countries, under-reportage of crime, different techniques in gathering and reporting data, and reliability of the institutions providing the data in determining a more accurate reflection.

This complexity is illustrated in a case highlighted by the UN's Office on Drugs and Crime (UNODC 2007, 8): "According to WHO data Jamaica has one of the lowest rates of intentional violence in the world. According to the police statistics, however, the homicide rate was 56 per 100,000 residents in 2005—one of the highest rates in the world..." Furthermore, relying on police data especially in places that have high crime rates may not give a clear picture, since police data will be based on reported cases whereas a significant amount of cases may go unreported on account of factors like distrust or low confidence in the police, fear of retaliation or repercussions, or a sense that nothing may become of the matter if reported; in some instances, members of the public may suspect the police and other law enforcement officials to be in collusion with the criminals whom they wish to report (Maguire *et al.* 2010; Pino and Johnson 2011; UNDP 2012). In August 2009, for example, three Coast Guards of the Guyana Defence Force (GDF) were charged for the murder of 23 year old Dweive Kant Ramdass of Bartica, after they allegedly robbed him of the G$17 million in the Essequibo River with which he was travelling to Bartica to conduct business on his employer's behalf (Haniff and Harris, 2009). Ramdass was aboard a passenger boat that had just departed the Parika Stelling; the boat was intercepted by the GDF Coast Guard boat and Ramdass was singled out. The event made for quite a tragedy to the family and an embarrassment for the Guyana Defence Force. In March 2012, two constables of the Guyana Police Force were placed under close arrest at Eve Leary Police Station for allegedly demanding G$56,000 from a Brazilian national after requesting to see his passport (Kaieteur News, 8 March 2012). Despite having a valid passport, it is alleged that they demanded $10,000 then snagged the remainder of his money which the victim claimed to be in the amount of $46,000. Upon arriving at the police station in Georgetown to make a report, the victim recognized the vehicle in the parking lot that had been used by the individuals who apprehended him and also encountered the two individuals inside the station.

In addition to these factors, some countries comprise a much larger population while the population of others may be quite small, and thus regional generalizations of statistical data may give an especially skewed depiction of crime occurrences and the types of crimes, something that is clearly outlined in the joint World Bank/UN 2007 report on crime in the region. Cuba, for example, has 11 million people whereas Montserrat has 4,000 (UNODC 2007, 3). As the report notes, "While there are 20 to 30 countries and territories in the Caribbean (depending on how they are counted) some 88 per cent of the population is found in just five countries..." (UNODC 2007, 2). Moreover, while jurisdictionally the English-speaking segment of the region comprise the majority of countries and territories, the majority of the population of the Caribbean is actually Spanish (UNODC 2007, 3). Aside from these elements that problematize regional comparisons on a global level, standardized data furnished by the UN's Office on Drugs and Crime suggest that the Caribbean endures more murder on a per capita basis than elsewhere in the world, at 30 per 100,000 population. Southern and West Africa, for example, has a rate of 29, South America at 26, North America at 7, and so on (See Figure 17.5).

Standardized time series data for the Dominican Republic, Trinidad and Tobago, and St. Lucia in respect to homicide rate from 1999 to 2005 show a sharp upward pattern (UNODC 2007, 11). In 1999, the homicide rate for the Dominican Republic was 14 per 100,000 persons; by 2003 it escalated to 19 and by 2005 to 27 per 100,000. Likewise in Trinidad and Tobago, it was 7 per 100,000 in 1999 but by 2003 it escalated to 18, and by 2005 it rose to 30 per 100,000. St. Lucia stood at 9 in 1999 and moved to 21 per 100,000 in 2003.

The time-series Figure 17.6 highlights the dynamics of some Caribbean countries in respect to homicide rates.

Jamaica for its part carried a high murder rate for some time and had come to be viewed by some as the murder capital of the

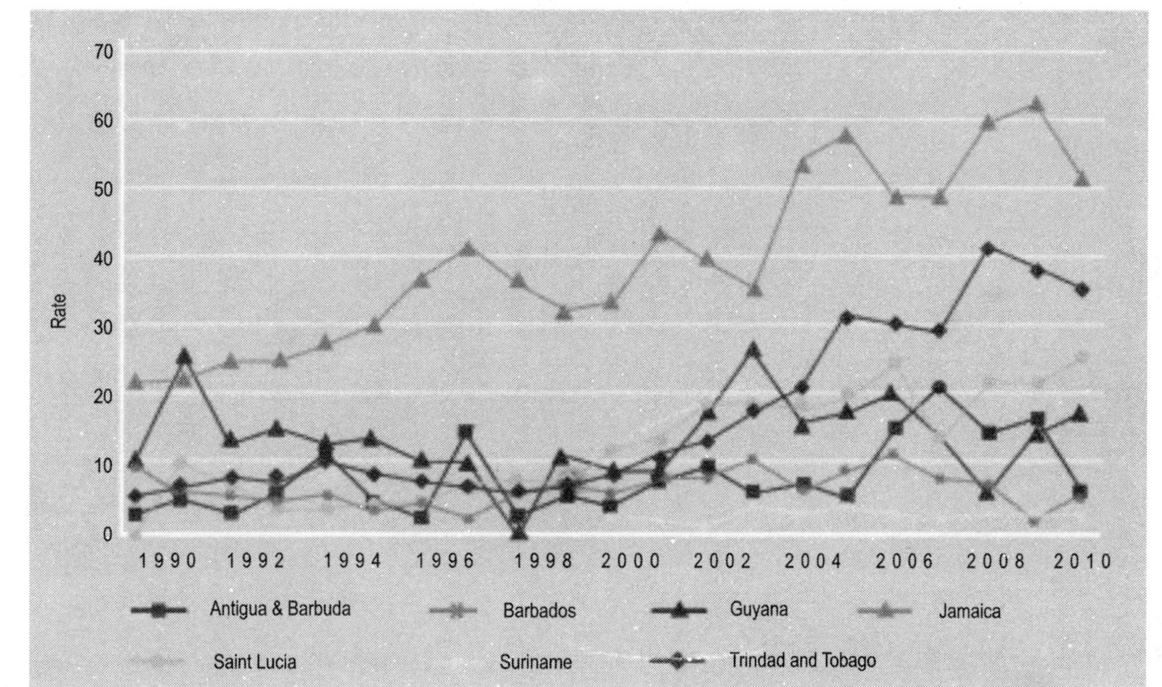

Figure 17.5: Homicides Rates in the Dominican Republic, ST. Lucia and Trinidad and Tobago: 1999-2005

Source: *Crime, Violence, and Development: Trends, Costs and Policy Options in the Caribbean* (UNODC, 2007, 11)

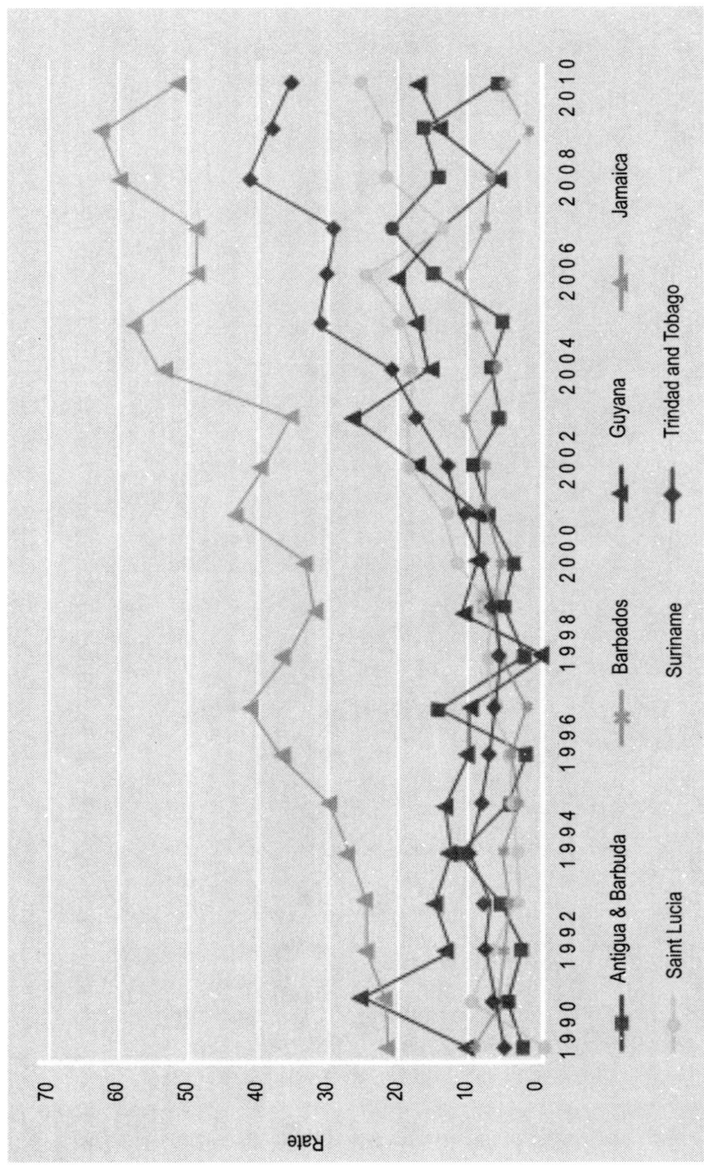

Figure 17.6: Homicide Rates Per 100,000 Population, 1990-2010

Source: Caribbean Human Development Report 2012 (UNDP 2012, 21)

world (BBC Caribbean, 3 January 2006; *The Economist*, 20 March 2008). However, data furnished by the Jamaica Constabulary Force as part of its Periodic Major Crime Statistics Review indicate a rather interesting dynamic for the period of January to May over the last three years. From January to May of 2009, there were 594 murders whereas for the same period in 2010 there were 684 and in 2011 there were 399. A peculiar statistics is also shown in respect to shooting in Jamaica. Gun was the implement used in 71.2 per cent of those murders in 2011, compared with a knife used for 14.3 per cent. However peculiar the numbers for Jamaica, it must be observed that crime management is far from a simple task, as evident in the large amount of murders and other major crimes for which police are faced. As the Commissioner of Police of Jamaica noted in a release of 9 March 2012, "Between 2007 and 2012, 5,820 Jamaicans were murdered by criminals using illegal firearms. During the same period, 8,574 Jamaicans were shot by criminals with illegal firearms but survived those injuries. In the same period, there were 25,448 major crimes committed with the use of illegal guns. Between 2007 and 2012 the security forces seized 3,102 illegal firearms of various types and 48,868 rounds of ammunition from criminals. Over the same period, 62 police personnel were killed on duty by criminals while another 127 were shot and injured" (Commissioner of Police, 9 March 2012). While Jamaica has shown a diminishing rate of murders in recent times it nevertheless bears a high rate at some 60 murders per 100,000 persons, giving Jamaica the highest rate of homicide in the Caribbean and the third highest in the world (UN News Service, 8 February 2012).

Of course, it must be kept in mind that while homicide rates have kept the alarm sounding when it comes to crime in the Caribbean, there are other crimes that keep the public uneasy such as robberies and burglaries and break-ins. In some countries such as Jamaica, Guyana and Barbados, occurrences of these crimes are said to be somewhat stable (though this does not necessarily mean low) but in others such as Trinidad and Tobago and Antigua and Barbuda, the rates have increased. As the *Caribbean Human Development Report 2012* (UNDP 2012, 23) states: "Within the Caribbean region, citizens are most likely to be victimized by burglaries and robberies, crimes that involve high social, economic and personal costs among victims." The time-series Figures 17.7 and 17.8 below illustrate the trend of burglary and break-ins in select countries.

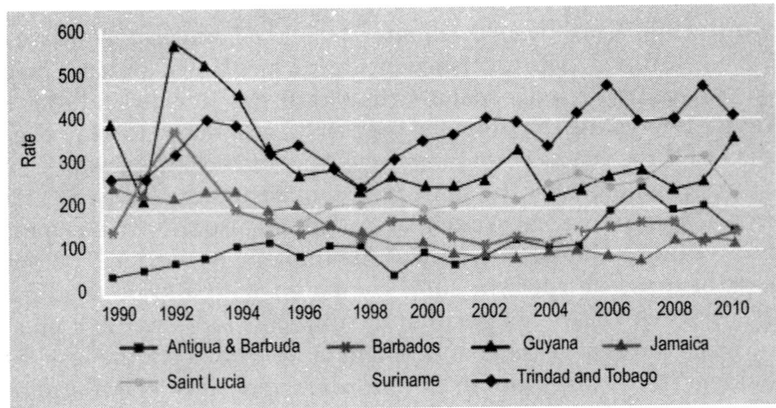

Figure 17.7: Burglary and Break-in Rates per 100,000 Population: Selected Caribbean Countries, 1990-2010

Source: *Caribbean Human Development Report 2012* (UNDP 2012, 24).

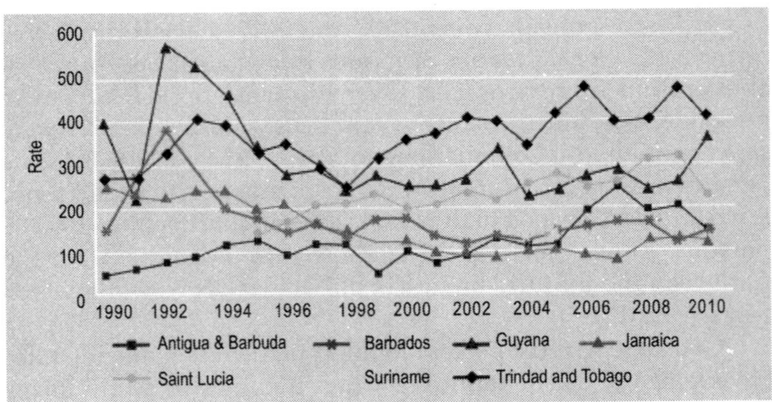

Figure 17.8: Robbery Rates Per 100,000 Population, 1990-2010

Source: Extracted from *Caribbean Human Development Report 2012* (UNDP 2012, 23)

Robberies, burglary and break-ins, and property crime in general are understandably a major cause of concern for the public. Indeed, murders do take place within the context of such crimes. But at a deeper level, the occurrence of such crimes and the fear engendered as a result of these crimes threaten the population at large at both a macro and micro level. On the one hand, such crimes are injurious to investment and business operations because they imply serious risks as well as costs to protect one's business such as private security, expensive grillwork, surveillance systems, etc. They also undermine Gross Domestic Product. On the other hand, they can elevate the level of fear in a country such that people are left feeling that they are somewhat under a state of siege—fearful of what will happen to their person and chattels when they leave home; whether their homes will be burglarized in their absence; fearful to sleep too comfortably at night because of the prospect of violent break-ins; worried in such a climate when they go to bed whether they will be part of the death statistics the next day because of their general inability due to lack of resources to protect themselves from the dangers of break-ins; frightful to have any sign of material progress noticeable because one could become a target to predators, and so on. In these ways, it may be said that in a fundamental respect Caribbean societies live a different culture of ease in the day than in the night. While the daylight hours are not without threat, since such crimes also take place in broad daylight, the quiescence and darkness coupled with individual and national inability to adequately curb crime makes for very haunting nights and especially so as many Caribbean countries endure unstable if not periodic supply of electricity at night. Such experiences are at least a legion in Guyana. The continuous trauma such experiences precipitate and the scar they etch in the psyche of children who must endure this fate as daily life ought not to be overlooked. It should therefore not surprise us that citizens report high degrees of fear when it comes these crimes. The Figure 17.9 maps out a survey of citizens in select countries in respect to fear of burglary and robbery.

Given the extent to which gangs have saturated in the different countries of the Caribbean and the problems of violence they pose, it should not surprise us either that citizens in Caribbean countries have a high degree of fear of gangs. The Figure 17.10 from a UNDP Citizens Security Survey of 2010 gives a helpful depiction of perceptions of street gang problem to help visualize the fear people have in particular countries, with Jamaica containing the highest level at 40.7.

The scaling down of one's degree of autonomy, of imposing limits on liberty, of stagnating growth and undermining internal sovereignty on account of widespread crime bring to mind an observation made by philosopher Thomas Hobbes (1991, Chapter

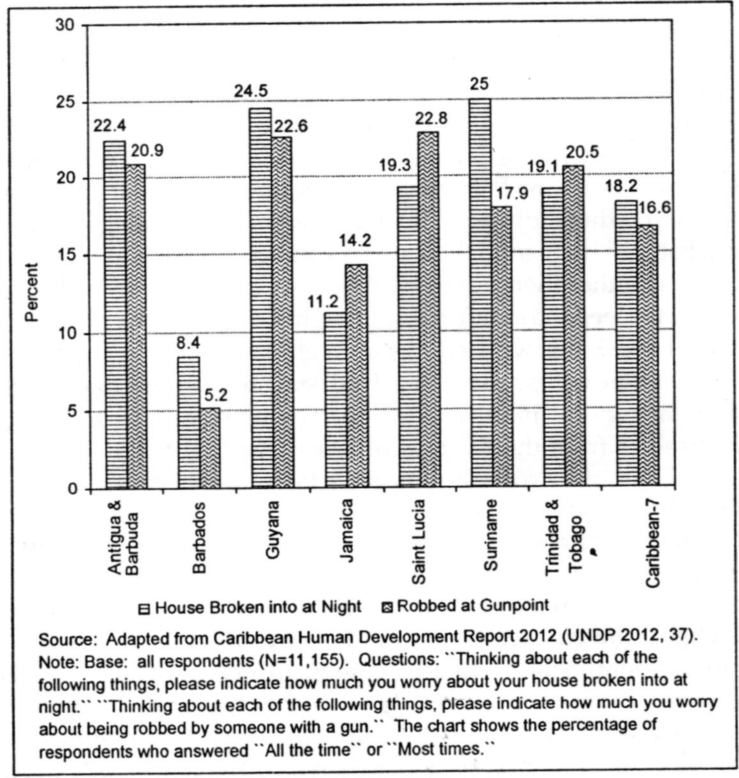

Source: Adapted from Caribbean Human Development Report 2012 (UNDP 2012, 37).
Note: Base: all respondents (N=11,155). Questions: "Thinking about each of the following things, please indicate how much you worry about your house broken into at night." "Thinking about each of the following things, please indicate how much you worry about being robbed by someone with a gun." The chart shows the percentage of respondents who answered "All the time" or "Most times."

Figure 17.9: Fear of Burglary and Robbery, 2010

Source: Extracted from the *Caribbean Human Development Report 2012* (UNDP 2012, 37).

XIII, 89) quite sometime back, that resonates with the contemporary Caribbean:

> Whatsoever therefore is consequent to a time of Warre, where every man is Enemy to every man; the same is consequent to the time, wherein men live without other security, than what their own strength, and their own invention shall furnish them withal. In such condition, there is no place for Industry; because the fruit thereof is uncertain; and consequently no Culture of the Earth; no Navigation, nor use of the commodities that may be imported by Sea; no commodious Building; no

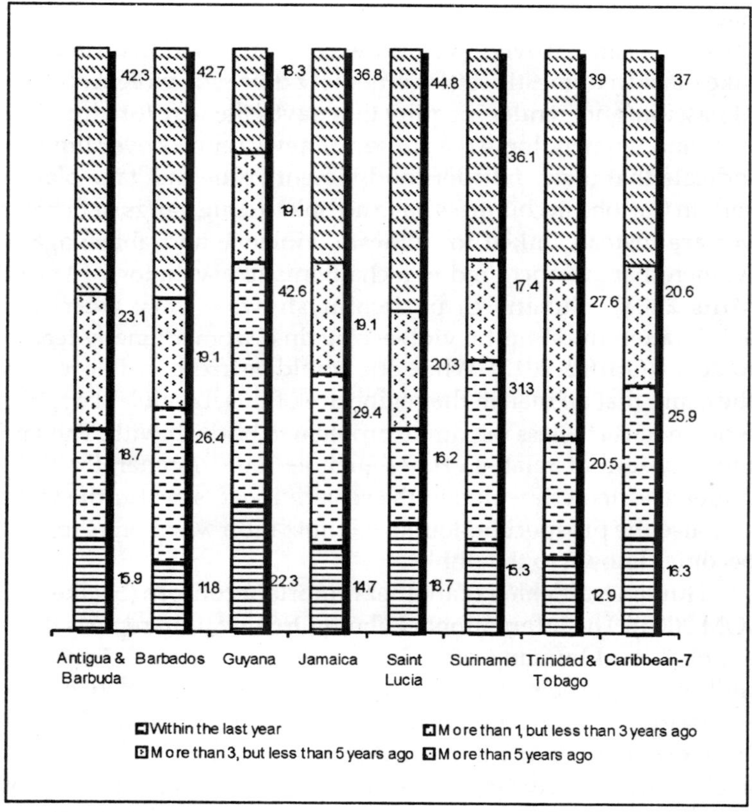

Figure 17.10: The First Appearance of the Gang Problem in Neighbourhoods, Caribbean-7, 2010

Source: Caribbean Human Development Report 2012 (UNDP 2012, 69.

> Instruments of moving and removing such things as require much force; no Knowledge of the face of the Earth; no account of Time; no Arts; no Letters; no Society; and which is worst of all, Continuall feare, and danger of violent death; And the life of man, solitary, poore, nasty, brutish, and short.

In sum, we might say that crime in the Caribbean is a huge problem that demands urgent and collective attention. But while problems of gangs, drugs, and property crimes are notable and have captured both attention and fear, no discussion on crime in the Caribbean can overlook murders and other serious crimes that take place in domestic settings, notably domestic violence, crimes of passion, and gender inequity that paves the way for atrocity on girls and women. Indeed a survey of news reports over time will indicate that many murders and violent crime that take place in certain Caribbean countries have no link to drug gangs or burglary but are instead linked to domestic violence and abuse against women that are anchored in a chauvinistic psychology (Arscott-Mills 2001). Guyana in particular shows a very worrisome acceleration in domestic violence against women, many leading to death (Griffith 2012). While one would be irresponsible to make the claim that all men in the region are of this ilk, violence against women nevertheless remains a problem to be dealt with. The same must be said of related crimes such as rape, a generally highly underreported crime due to the sensitivity at issue for the victim and also the prospect of double victimization when one's identity becomes known to the public.

Human trafficking is another important concern (Seelke 2009; IOM 2005). The International Labour Organization reports that at a global level human trafficking is the cause of an estimated 2.5 million people being victims of forced labour which also includes sexual exploitation (cited in UN.GIFT). Of this amount, 250,000 or 10 per cent take place in Latin America and the Caribbean (cited in UN.GIFT). Moreover, it is estimated that an annual global profit of US$31.6 billion from the exploitation of forced labour, of which US$1.3 billion or 4 per cent is generated in Latin America and the Caribbean. Given the relatively small size of the Caribbean population, the proportion estimated of human trafficking jointly for Latin America and the Caribbean cannot be ignored, especially since the majority of the victims who are trafficked globally are said to be between the age of 18 and 24. The Organisation of America States (OAS) anticipates an increase in human trafficking among Caribbean countries because of the relatively free movement of people within the CARICOM community (Caribbean News Now, 16 October 2012). In light of the fact that the population in the Caribbean Community (CARICOM) is such that 64 per cent of it is comprised of persons who are under the age of 30 and that 30 per cent of the population is between 18 and 30 years old, it is paramount to chart a course for an improved quality of life so as to inculcate values in the young that can promote a better vision of their future.

In the present state of affairs, it is lamentable that the problem of crime and institutions of justice and political offices have deteriorated to such a dire level that the people have lost a tremendous degree of confidence in official systems (Hylton and Young 2007; Pino and Johnson 2011; Griffith 2002 and 1993). Whereas the impact of the crime problem itself is a major issue to live with, the extent of corruption decays the hope citizens have in the system and people that/who are to protect them and implement measures for justice to take its course. This situation is especially made evident in a UNDP Citizen Security Survey of 2010, in which 11,155 people were randomly surveyed about their perception of corruption in the country. The results are evident in the Figure 17.11 below:

Country	*Judges are corrupt*	*Justice system is corrupt*	*Powerful criminals go free*	*Politically connected criminals go free*
Antigua & Barbuda	32.3	44.3	37.8	44.8
Barbados	24.5	33.8	40.1	41.9
Guyana	39.0	47.7	46.9	51.8
Jamaica	36.3	57.3	52.7	57.8
Saint Lucia	33.7	48.1	47.7	51.3
Suriname	35.6	45.8	38.9	47.0
Trinidad & Tobago	58.7	69.8	61.6	702
Caribbean-7	37.2	49.6	47.0	52.5

Figure 17.11: Perceptions of Corruption (Percent), 2010

Source: Extracted from *Caribbean Human Development Report 2012* (UNDP 2012, 78).

Source: UNDP Citizen Security Survey 2010.

Note: Base: all respondents (N = 11,155), Questions: "Using a scale from 1 to 5 (1 = Strongly disagree, 2 = Disagree, 3 = Don't know, 4 = Agree, 5 = Strongly agree), indicate your assessment of the performance of the criminal justice system on the following (fairness, integrity, effectiveness): 'The judges are not corrupt', 'The justice system is free of corruption'. 'The justice system is unable to convict powerful criminals', 'Powerful criminals are likely to go free', and 'Politically connected criminals are likely to go free'." The chart shows the percentage of respondents who answered "Strongly disagree" or "Disagree".

The response in respect to perception of crime are perhaps not startling to people living in the region but they nevertheless point to a low level of confidence in the notion of fairness and impartiality and, as such, suggest a low level of expectation that justice will be delivered through official systems.

Terrorism in/from the Caribbean

It need hardly be said that the Caribbean has had some episodes of undesired visibility by the Western world and indeed by its own citizens in recent times when allegations surfaced of terrorism plots by persons of Caribbean background to bomb the fuel tanks and pipelines at the JFK Airport in New York. The terror plot resulted in a life sentence being handed down on December 15, 2010 to 58 year-old Abdul Kadir (a/k/a Aubrey Michael Seaforth), a Guyanese citizen of Linden and former parliamentarian, and to 67 year-old Russell Defreitas (a/k/a Mohammed), also of Guyana, on February 19, 2011 (FBI Press Releases, 15 December 2010, and 17 February 2011).

Both men were charged with conspiring to attack a public transportation system, conspiracy to destroy a building by fire or explosive, conspiracy to attack aircraft and aircraft materials, conspiracy to destroy international airport facilities, and conspiracy to attack a mass transportation facility. FBI investigations indicate that both conspired to wreak havoc that would rival 9/11 but that Defrietas was the master-mind behind the plot. Another accomplice, 60 year-old Abdel Nur (a/k/a Compton Eversley), who is a Guyanese citizen was sentenced to 15 years imprisonment because he pleaded guilty the day prior to trial for supporting the plot (FBI Press Release, 17 February 2011). Nur's attorney Daniel Nobel had requested a sentence below the maximum in view of Nur's ailment with lung cancer but no such concession was granted. At the time of the sentencing, a fourth accomplice, 65 year-old Kareem Ibrahim, who is a citizen of Trinidad and Tobago was awaiting a separate trial in connection with the same plot, as the matter was delayed due to health issues incurred by the accused (FBI Press Release, 17 February 2011). He was later sentenced to life imprisonment (FBI Press Release, 13 January 2012).

The FBI's press releases state that Defrietas previously worked at the airport as a cargo handler for Evergreen Airlines. Between 2006 and 2007 Defreitas is said to have made numerous trips to

Guyana and Trinidad and during this time recruited Kadir and others. Kadir, who testified in his own defense, was faced with myriad circumstantial evidence including letters he had written to Iranian officials that linked him to Iran (Sulzberger, 2 August 2010). The FBI press release further indicates that evidence was produced during trial in support of the claim that Defreitas attempted to garner the support of Abu Bakr of the Jamaat Al Muslimeen group of Trinidad and Tobago, of Adnan El Shukrijumah who is deemed an al Qaeda leader by the U.S. (who was born in Saudi Arabia but whose father is from Guyana), and of others from Iranian authorities (FBI Press Release, 17 February 2011; Washington, 2008).

An FBI press release issued 15 December 2010 states that Defreitas undertook video surveillance of the JFK International Airport in New York and transported them to Guyana for perusal by Kadir, himself a trained engineer, and others. Kadir, the press release states, admitted on cross-examination to passing on information to authorities in Iran on sensitive matters such as the Guyanese military. Kadir and Nur made several trips to Guyana and Trinidad. Kadir was headed to Iran to an Islamic conference via Venezuela (where he was to pick-up his Iranian visa); he was arrested in Trinidad on 2 June 2007 aboard a Venezuela-bound aircraft. The plane was ordered to turn back and he was subsequently arrested and had charges read to him in the Port of Spain Magistrates Court (Stabroek News, 26 October 2008). He was then extradited to the United States. Defreitas was arrested in New York on 1 June 2007.

The plot was foiled and processed in court with evidence furnished by a secret FBI informant, Steven Francis, who had recorded the men while on airport surveillance and international trips that were intended to acquire the finance and logistical support to carry out the plan (Sulzberger 2010). A CBS News report indicates that the informant was convicted twice on drug trafficking charges but had been working since 2004 with the government (Klatell 2009).

There have been other cases of material interest, namely, the deportation of Sheik el-Faizal from Britain to Jamaica on the basis of preaching extremism, and of Willie Brigitte of Guadaloupe who was deported from Australia to France for allegedly having been involved in plotting terrorism activity in Australia. El-Faizal was found guilty in a British court of three charges of soliciting the murder of Jews, Americans and Hindus, and two charges of using threatening words to incite racial hatred (BBC News, 25 May 2007). The tapes apparently were the principal basis for the prosecution.

In an interview on *Religious Hard Talk*, a television programme in Jamaica, el-Faizal claimed he did not believe in killing innocent people and condemned the 9/11 attacks on the basis that they killed innocent people and thus had strayed from the path of Islam. He further noted that Western forces have committed atrocities on Muslims around the world, as in the war on Iraq which the UN deemed illegal, but when attention is drawn to them by people like himself, they are vilified as terrorists and as preaching hatred while those who commit the atrocities are viewed as legitimate (Religious Hard Talk, YouTube Video).

Willie Brigitte of Guadaloupe was given a nine-year jail sentence by a Paris court for plotting to blow-up Australia's only nuclear research power station, located in Lucas Heights. He was also accused of plotting to destroy a US-Australian intelligence surveillance station at Pine Gap as well as military establishments across Australia (BBC News, 15 March 2007; Liz Jackson, 2004). According to the BBC News, "France's top anti-terrorist judge, Jean-Louis Bruguiere, accused Brigitte of setting up a terror cell in Australia in alliance with the Pakistani Islamic militant group, Lashkar-e-Toiba" (BBC News, 15 March 2007). Brigitte was deported from Australia to France to stand trial after being arrested in 2003.

Such high profile cases encourage suspicious eyes on the Islamic community and people of Middle Eastern heritage at large in the Caribbean region. In the Bahamas, for example, members of the Muslim community complain they have found themselves under the radar of the U.S. Embassy in Nassau for suspicion of terrorist activities, so much so that their U.S. visas are being revoked without explanation; even their desire to establish a mosque gets scrutinized for its funding sources (McCartney 2011; Huste 2007).

Terrorism in the Caribbean has been largely ignored by scholars; many focused on terrorism in Latin America in relation to drugs and political ideology, notably of Leftist groups. In the context of transnational terrorism, the focus has been on whether there are either sympathizers in the region to extremist, Islamist groups or whether networks have been established in the region by such groups. In so doing, attention tends to be drawn either methodologically or explicitly to the size of the Muslim population in determining whether the region poses a threat. But terrorism, it must be said, comes in many guises and is not restricted to religious zeal or retaliation of oppression and injustice that may be perceived as experienced by members of a faith elsewhere in the world; this is evident in terrorism carried out by the Revolutionary Armed Forces of Colombia (FARC), Shining Light (Sendero Luminoso) of Peru, the Tupamaros of Uruguay, the Liberation Tigers of Tamil Elam (LTTE) in Sri Lanka, the Basque ETA of Spain, and so on. It must also be remembered that insofar as religion is infused with terrorism, such forms of terrorism are not restricted to any one faith. The historic feud between the Catholics and Protestants in Ireland over nationalism, self determination and religious identity and the various acts of terrorism championed by leaders such as Michael Collins are very telling, though often ignored in social commentaries. The case of Ireland involved denominations belonging to the same faith.

In the current times, globalization and cyber space may prove to be instrumental in the global proliferation of terrorism and in this regard the Caribbean is not exempt (Nassar 2005). Flynn and Bryan (2001) capture the point well when they write that "national borders are porous to terrorism—no one need claim responsibility for attacks—and globalization and technology have opened up new possibilities for terrorists."

Bagley (2004, 34) echoes the point when he writes: "In most of Latin America and the Caribbean, the dynamics of globalisation over the last two decades have resulted in almost ideal conditions for the rapid penetration and spread of transnational and organised crime." Some research suggests there are links between global criminal networks and "Islamic terrorists" in the Tri-border Area—Argentina, Brazil and Paraguay—(Bagley 2004; Huste 2007). Given the proximity of the Tri-Border Area, infiltration of international terrorism to the region cannot be ignored. The Caribbean is very volatile to stringent measures taken in the West, measures that can drastically rupture its much relied-on travel industry and trade and, as such, the livelihood and security of Caribbean people (Girvan 2001; Albuquerque and McElroy 1999; Pratt 2003). Thus, aside from security concerns, it has repercussions on national revenue.

Aside from the issue of international terrorism emanating from the Caribbean against the US and Europe, it needs to also be acknowledged that people from the circum-Caribbean were also victims of 9/11. Early data (Griffith 2004, v) provided by various consular officials and embassies indicate at least the following fatalities: Antigua and Barbuda, 3; Barbados, 5; Belize, 1;

Bermuda, 2; Colombia, 20; Dominica, 1; Guyana, 26; Haiti, 14; Jamaica, 22; St. Lucia, 2; St. Vincent, 1; and Trinidad and Tobago, 12. From this point of view, Caribbean families also grieved direct losses from the 9/11 attacks, a fact not much known amongst Caribbean people themselves. A social work study conducted in New York in the period following the attacks indicates that many Caribbean families in New York experienced a hard time coping with the trauma associated with the 9/11 attacks (Matthews 2004).

It must also be acknowledged that 9/11 was not the first event of terrorism that bereaved and aggrieved Caribbean people. Caribbean people have already endured a direct terrorist attack over Caribbean waters when Cubana Airways flight CU455 was planted with two bombs which exploded over the coast of Barbados on 6 October 1976, killing all aboard (Phillips 1991, 209; Bagoo 2011; Guyana Graphic, 6 October 2006). Aboard the aircraft were the Cuban Olympic fencing team and several students from Guyana, among others (Landau and Smith 2001). The same group carried out the bombing of the Guyana Consulate in Port-of-Spain (1 September 1976) and the BWIA office in Barbados (14 July 1976). Four people were implicated in the disaster: Orlando Bosch, Freddy Lugo, Hernan Ricardo, and Luis Posada Carriles. All were allegedly Cuban exiles based in Venezuela who were taking actions against Caribbean governments that they deemed as being sympathetic to Fidel Castro (Griffith 2002; Phillips 1991). The bombs placed on Cubana Airways CU455 detonated 11 minutes after take-off, causing the plane to crash into the sea (Phillips 1911, 211). All the passengers—57 Cuban athletes, 11 Guyanese many of whom were students studying in Cuba, 5 North Koreans, and 5 crew members—died (Phillips 1999, 211; Griffith 2002; Guyana Graphic, 6 October 2010). There were also a number of Cuban government officials aboard the plane. The participants of the Cubana Airways bombing were part of an amalgamated commando.

Forward Looking

As we look at current and past issues we must also look ahead to determine ways of moving forward. The Caribbean has been experiencing difficult times for a while now due to high crime rates, huge debt, political corruption, and poverty. As we have noted earlier, the trans-shipment of drugs from the Andean region to North America and Europe through the Caribbean has been a major part of the problem of crime and insecurity. Both adults and the youth are victims of these problems. As we look to the future for a better, even prosperous Caribbean, we have to be mindful that there are internal differences in the Caribbean. Different countries may have different views on how to enhance themselves and so this may not embody a vision that captures the larger Caribbean. Certainly there are also cultural tensions among Caribbean countries and however covert these tensions may be, they suggest that the prospect of political and economic collaboration may be marred by such tensions (see, for example, Harewood 2010). At the same time, it must be emphasized that there are some problems which no single country in the Caribbean can tackle on its own, notably the problem of drugs and the climate of crime that drugs precipitate. For this reason, a collaborative approach on some issues are obligatory. Furthermore, since the drug problem is directly linked to North America and Europe it would be foolish to think that the problem could be solved independent of the cooperation and resource support of the West. One might choose to argue that if the production and supply of such drugs were to stop the demand will likewise fade, but the same could be said the other way around, notably that if the demand were to stop the production and supply would fade. Clinging to such chants in polarised positions on the issue will likely not get us far in addressing the problem. There at least needs to be greater public education on both sides and collaborative undertakings to prosecute perpetrators, treat addicts, properly rehabilitate offenders to avoid recidivism, and incapacitate the structural apparatus of criminal networks. At the same time, consideration has to be given to the need for certain narcotics that are needed for medicinal purposes, for example narcotics used for the alleviation of chronic pain. While there is a desire to see the scourge of illicit drugs vanish from the Caribbean, there appears to be a deficit in treatment centres to properly treat and rehabilitate those who have been consumed by such drugs. Similarly, there needs to be a reformed attitude of care when addressing such persons, and therefore appropriate training for those who are placed on the frontline to provide treatment and public education. In respect to the threat of terrorism in/from the Caribbean, it is likewise plausible to say to that no one country can tackle this problem on its own. International terrorism is a reality and one need hardly say that it ought to be of concern to Caribbean governments and peoples and the West and that there is need for a collaborative approach to it, one that is mindful not to marginalize/persecute people and groups simply on the basis of their ethnicity/religion/race.

Bibliography

INTRODUCTION

Alleyne, Dillon, Kelvin Sergeant *et al. Economic Survey Of The Caribbean 2010-2011: Improving Economic Prospects Amid Global Recovery*. Economic Commission for Latin America and the Caribbean (ECLAC) Subregional Headquarters for the Caribbean, 2011.

Bishop, Matthew Lewis, Norman Girvan *et al. Caribbean Regional Integration: A Report*. Port of Spain: UWI Institute of International Relations (IIR), April 2011. Accessed March 20, 2012. http://www.iadb.org/intal/intalcdi/PE/2011/08559.pdf.

ECLAC. *India and Latin America and the Caribbean: Opportunities and Challenges in Trade and Investment Relations*. Santiago: UN, 2011.

——. *Migration in the Caribbean, What Do We Know?* (Expert Group Meeting on International Migration and Development in Latin America and the Caribbean) UN/POP/EGM-MIG/2005/09, 13 January 2006.

Griffith, Ivelaw Lloyd, Norman Girvan, Richard L. Bernal, G. Philip Hughes, and Paget deFreitas. "Is the Caribbean Community in Danger of Collapsing?" *Inter-American Dialogue, Latin America Advisor*, March 19, 2012. Accessed March 20, 2012. http://www.the dialogue.orgpage.cfm?pageID=32&pubID=2906.

Heine, Jorge. "Playing the India Card." In *Which Way Latin America? Hemispheric Politics Meets Globalization*, edited by Andrew Cooper and Jorge Heine. pp. 122-139. New York: United Nations University Press, 2009.

Jadeja, Daulatsinhji P. (ed). *India and Latin America: Partners in Progress*. New Delhi: TransAsia Publications, 1988.

Kirpalani, Murli J. (ed). *Indian Centenary Review. One Hundred Years of Progress: 1845-1945, Trinidad, B.W.I.*Port of Spain: Indian Centenary Review Committee, 1945.

Lederman, Daniel, Marcelo Olarreaga and Guillermo E. Perry (eds.) *China's and India's Challenge to Latin America: Opportunity or Threat?* Washington DC: World Bank, 2009.

Nettleford, Rex. *Engagement of Diversity and Dilemma of Difference: Educating the Next Generation*, Speech Delivered to the Education for Peace-building Session, Commonwealth People's Forum, Trinidad and Tobago, November 24, 2009.

Payne, A., and Sutton, P. *Repositioning the Caribbean within Globalisation*, Waterloo, Ontario, Canada: Centre for International Governance Innovation (CIGI) Caribbean Paper No. 1. Accessed March 12, 2012. http://www.cigionline.org.

Phillips, Nicola. "Coping with China." In *Which Way Latin America? Hemispheric Politics Meets Globalization*, edited by Andrew Cooper and Jorge Heine. pp. 100-121. New York: United Nations University Press, 2009.

Premdas, Ralph R. *Ethnicity and Identity in the Caribbean: Decentering a Myth.* Working Paper #234, The Helen Kellog Institute of International Studies, December 1996. Accessed March 12, 2012. http:/ kellogg.nd.edu/publications/ workingpapers/WPS 234.pdf.

Stoneman, Richard, Duke Pollard and Hugo Inniss. *Turning Around CARICOM: Proposals to Restructure the Secretariat. FINAL REPORT.* CARICOM Secretariat, January 2012.

CHAPTER 1

HOW MANY CARIBBEANS IN 2020: VULNERABLE? RESILIENT? INFORMAL? AND/OR ILLEGAL?

Aalto, Pami (ed). *The EU-Russian Energy Dialogue: Europe's Future Energy Security.* Aldershot: Ashgate, 2008.

Bagley, Bruce B and William O Walker (eds). *Drug Trafficking in the Americas.* Miami: University of Miami N-S Center, 1994.

Bernstein, Steven and Benjamin Cashore. "The Two-Level Logic of Non-State Market Driven Global Governance." In *Authority in the Global Political Economy,* edited by Volker Rittberger and Martin Nettesheim, 276-313. London: Palgrave Macmillan, 2008.

Bishop, Matthew Louis. *The Political Economy of Eastern Caribbean Development.* London: Palgrave Macmillan, forthcoming, 2011.

—— and Anthony Payne. "Caribbean Regional Governance and the Sovereignty/ Statehood Problem." Waterloo: CIGI. Caribbean Paper #8, 2010.

Brereton, Bridget. *From Imperial College to UWI: A History of the St Augustine Campus, Trinidad and Tobago.* Kingston: Ian Randle for UWI, 2010.

Bronfman, Alejandra. *On the Move: The Caribbean Since 1989.* Halifax: Fernwood, 2007.

Brown, Stuart S. *et al.* "Non-State Transnational Transfers: Types and Characteristics." *International Studies Review,* 11(2) June (2009): 402-450.

Cooper, Andrew F. *Internet Gambling Offshore: Caribbean Struggles Over Casino Capitalism.* London: Palgrave Macmillan, 2011.

—— and Timothy M Shaw. "The Summitry of Small States: Towards the 'Caribbean Summit."'Waterloo: CIGI, Policy Brief # 15, April 2009.

—— (eds). *The Diplomacies of Small States: Between Vulnerability and Resilience.* London: Palgrave Macmillan, 2009.

De Lombaerde, Philippe and Michael Schulz (eds). *The EU and World Regionalism: The Makability of Regions in the 21st Century.* Farnham: Ashgate, 2009.

Dingwerth, Klaus. "Private Transnational Governance and the Developing World: A Comparative Perspective." *International Studies Quarterly,* 52(3) September (2008): 607-634.

ECLAC. *Economic Survey of the Caribbean 2008-2009.* Port of Spain: ECLAC, October 2009.

Economist. "Nobody's Backyard: The Rise of Latin America." *Economist,* 396(8699) 11 September (2010): 13 and Special Report (1-18).

Farer, Tom (ed). *Transnational Crime in the Americas.* New York: Routledge for Inter-American Dialogue, 1999.

Fiorentini, Gianluca and Sam Peltzman (eds). *The Economics of Organized Crime.* New York: CUP for CEPR, 1997.

Friman, H Richard (ed). *Crime and the Global Political Economy.* Boulder: LRP, 2009.

— — and Peter Andreas (eds). *The Illicit Global Economy and State Power.* Lanham: Rowman and Littlefield, 1999.

Gaens, Bart (ed). *Europe-Asia Interregional Relations: A Decade of ASEM.* Aldershot: Ashgate, 2008.

Gale, Fred and Marcus Haward (eds). *Global Commodity Governance: State Responses to Sustainable Forest and Fisheries Certification.* London: Palgrave Macmillan, 2011.

Gibbon, Peter, Stefano Ponte and Evelyne Lazaro (eds). *Global Agro-Food Trade and Standards: challenges for Africa.* London: Palgrave Macmillan, 2010.

GIIDS. *Small Arms Survey 2009: Shadows of War.* Cambridge: CUP for GIIDS, 2009.

Girvan, Norman. "Reinterpreting the Caribbean." In *The Caribbean Economy: A Reader* edited by Dennis Pantin, 304-318. Kingston: Ian Randle, 2005.

— — "Caribbean Dependency Thought Revisited." *Canadian Journal of Development Studies* 27(3) (2006): 329-352.

Glenny, Misha. *McMafia: A Journey through the Global Criminal Underworld.* Toronto: Anansi, 2009.

Griffith, Ivelaw (ed). *Caribbean Security in the Age of Terror: Challenge and Change.* Kingston: Ian Randle, 2004.

Hall, Kenneth O and Myrtle Chuck-A-Sang (eds). *CARICOM: Policy Options for International Engagement.* Kingston: Ian Randle for UWI-CARICOM Project, 2010.

Harriott, Anthony (ed). *Understanding Crime in Jamaica.* Mona: UWI Press, 2003.

Herz, Monica. *Organization of American States.* Abingdon: Routledge, 2010.

Hettne, Bjorn and Andras Inotai. *The New Regionalism: Implications for Global Development and International Security.* Helsinki: UNU-WIDER, February 1994.

Hettne, Bjorn, Andras Inotai and Osvaldo Sunkel (eds). *Globalism and the New Regionalism.* London: Macmillan, 1999.

Hillman, Richard S. "Introduction." In *Understanding the Contemporary Caribbean* edited by Richard Hillman and Thomas J D'Agostino, 1-18. Boulder: Lynne Rienner. Second edition, 2009.

IBRD. *Global Economic Prospects: Economic Implications of Remittances and Migration.* DC: IBRD, 2006.

IDB. *Remittances in Times of Financial Instability: Impact of the Financial Crisis on Remittances to Latin America and the Caribbean.* IDB, 2009.

Iheduru, Okechukwu C. "The 'New' ECOWAS: Implications for the Study of Regional Integration." In *Ashgate Research Companion to Regionalisms,* edited by Shaw, Andrew Grant and Scarlett Cornelissen. Farnham: Ashgate, 2011.

Keohane, Robert O. and Joseph S. Nye (eds). *Transnational Relations and World Politics.* Cambridge, MA: Harvard University Press, 1971.

Khagram, Sanjeev and Peggy Levitt (eds). *The Transnational Studies Reader.* New York: Routledge, 2007.

Laursen, Finn (ed). *Comparative Regional Integration: Europe and Beyond.* Farnham: Ashgate, 2010.

Macdonald, Laura and Arne Ruckert (eds). *Post-Neoliberalism in the Americas.* London: Palgrave Macmillan, 2009.

Mace, Gordon, Andrew F Cooper and Timothy M Shaw (eds). *Inter-American Cooperation at a Crossroads.* London: Palgrave Macmillan, 2010.

Madsen, Frank. *Transnational Organized Crime.* Abingdon: Routledge, 2009.

Meeks, Brian and Norman Girvan (eds). *The Thought of New World: The Quest for Decolonization.* Kingston: Ian Randle, 2010.

Mohammed, Patricia. *Imaging the Caribbean: Culture and Visual Translation*. Oxford: Macmillan Education, 2009.

Naim, Moises. *Illicit: How Smugglers, Traffickers and Copycats are Hijacking the Global Economy*. New York: Anchor, 2006.

Naylor, R T. *Wages of Crime: Black Markets, Illegal Finance and the Underworld Economy*. Ithaca: Cornell UP, 2005.

OECD. *Latin American Economic Outlook 2011: Middle Classes and Development*. Paris: OECD, 2011.

Pantin, Dennis (ed). *The Caribbean Economy: A Reader*. Kingston: Ian Randle, 2005.

Payne, Anthony and Paul Sutton. "Repositioning the Caribbean within Globalization." Waterloo; CIGI. Caribbean Paper #1, 2007.

Reis, Michele. "Theorizing Diaspora: Perspectives on "Classical" and "Contemporary" Diasporas." *International Migration*, 42(2) (2004): 41-60.

Scher, Philip W. (ed). *Perspectives on the Caribbean: A Reader in Culture, Migration and Representation*. Malden: Wiley-Blackwell, 2009.

Shaw, Timothy M. "Commonwealth and Global Development: Contributions to Private Transnational Governance?' *Commonwealth and Comparative Politics*, 48(1) (2010a): 91-111.

—— "New Regionalisms Post-EPAs: What Prospects for Sustainable Development in Africa and the Caribbean?" In *Comparative Regional Integration: Europe and Beyond*, edited by Finn Laursen, 193-211. Farnham: Ashgate, 2010b.

—— (2010c) ""New Regionalisms" Informed by Caribbean Perspectives." Port of Spain: ACS, 2010c.

—— J. Andrew Grant and Scarlett Cornelissen (eds). *Ashgate Research Companion to Regionalisms*. Farnham: Ashgate, forthcoming, 2011.

Thomas-Hope, Elizabeth (ed). *Freedom and Constraint in Caribbean Migration and Diaspora*. Kingston: Ian Randle, 2009.

Townsend, Dorn. "No Other Life: Gangs, Guns and Governance in Trinidad and Tobago." Geneva: SAS. Working Paper #8, 2009.

UNDP. *Human Development Report 2009 Overcoming Barriers: Human Mobility and Development*. New York: Palgrave Macmillan, 2009a.

—— "Opening Spaces for Citizen Security and Human Development; HDR for Central America, HDRCA 2009-2010," Bogota, October, 2009b.

UNODC *Annual Report 2010: Promoting Health, Security and Justice*. Vienna: UNODC, 2010a.

—— *World Drug Report 2010*. Vienna: UNODC, 2010b.

Vlcek, William. *Offshore Finance and Small States: Sovereignty, Size and Money* London: Palgrave Macmillan, 2008.

Wiltshire, Rosina. "Implications of Transnational Migration for Nationalism: The Caribbean Example." *Annals of the NY Academy of Sciences, Towards a Transnational Perspective on Migration*, 645 (2006): 175-187.

World Bank. *Migration and Remittances Factbook 2008*. Washington DC: World Bank, 2008.

Zank, Wolfgang (ed). *Clash or Cooperation of Civilizations? Overlapping Integration and Identities*. Farnham: Ashgate, 2009.

www.acs-aec.org
www.caic.org.tt
www.canari.org
www.caricom.org
www.caricomimpacs.org
www.cfatf-gafic.org

www.cries.org
www.cris.unu.edu
www.eclac.org
www.fatf-gafi.org
www.garnet-eu.org
www.globalwitness.org
www.interpol.int
www.netris-acp.org
www.normangirvan.info
www.organized-crime.org
www.smallarmssurvey.org
www.thecropperfoundation.org
www.uncaccoalition.org
www.undp.org
www.unodc.org
www.uwi.edu

CHAPTER 2
THE WEST IN THE CARIBBEAN

"Regional Sugar Industry Faces Serious Challenges," Caribbean News Now, 21 December 2010. Accessed December 12, 2011. http://www. caribbean newsnow.com/topstory-Regional-sugar-industry-faces-serious-challenges-4091.html

Alderson, Andrew. "Best Selling Tony Blair Goes House Hunting in Barbados". *The Telegraph,* 13 December 2011. Accessed December 14, 2011. http://www.telegraph.co.uk/news/politics/tony-blair/7969464/Bestselling-Tony-Blair-goes-house-hunting-in-Barbados.html

Bakker, Caroline, Martina Elings-Pels and Michele Reis, *The Impact of Migration on Children in the Caribbean,* UNICEF Office for Barbados and Eastern Caribbean, paper No. 4. August 2009.

Cardoso, Fernando Henrique and Enzo Faletto. *Dependência e Desenvolvimento na América Latina.* Rio de Janeiro: Zahar, 1970.

ECLAC. *Migration in the Caribbean—What Do We Know?* Expert Group Meeting on International Migration and Development in Latin America and the Caribbean, Population Division, Department of Economic and Social Affairs, United Nations Secretariat, Mexico City (30 November-2 December 2005), UN/POP/EGM-MIG/2005/09, 13 January 2006.

— — *Emigration of Nurses from the Caribbean: Causes and Consequences for the Socio-Economic Welfare of the Country: Trinidad and Tobago—a Case Study,* LC/CAR/G.748. ECLAC, August 2003.

— — *Migration in the Caribbean: Brain-Drain—Remittances—Diaspora.* ECLAC, 2006. Accessed January 5, 2012. http://www.eclac.org/publicaciones/xml/3/28873/L.107.pdf.

European External Action Service, "EU Cooperation with Trinidad and Tobago". Accessed December 12, 2011. http://eeas.europa. eu/delegations/trinidad/eu_trinidad/tech_financial_ cooperation/index_en.htm.

Evans, J.M. "Immigration Act 1971," *The Modern Law Review,* 35 (5), 1972: 508.

Fekete, Liz. "The Emergence of Xenoracism," *IRR News.* 28 September 2001. Accessed December 12, 2011. http://www.irr. org.uk/2001/september/ak000001.html.

Ferguson, James. *Caribbean*. Mass: Interlink Books, 2008.

Gmelch, George. *Behind the Smile: the Working Lives of Caribbean Tourism*. Bloomington, IN: Indiana University Press, 2003.

Grant, Edward. *The Foundations of Modern Science in the Middle Ages: Their Religious, Institutional, and Intellectual Contexts*. Cambridge: Cambridge University Press, 1996.

Hale, Edward Everett. *The Life of Christopher Columbus: From His own Letters and Journals and other Documents of his Time*. Fairfield, Indiana: Ist World Library—Literary Society, 2006.

Kindred, Kathy. "Factors Influencing Tourism in the Caribbean," *eHow*, 13 December 2011.

Lentin, Alana and Gavan Titley. *The Crises of Multiculturalism: Racism in a Neoliberal Age*. London: Zed Books, 2011.

Lentin, Alana."Racism in a Post-racial Europe," *Eurozine*. 7 December 2011. Accessed December 12, 2011. http://www. eurozine.com/articles/2011-11-24-lentin-en.html.

Mintz, Sidney W. "Slave Life on Caribbean Sugar Plantations". In *Slave Cultures and Cultures of Slavery*, edited by Stephan Palmie, 12-22. University of Tennessee Press, 1995.

Mishra, Prachi. *Emigration and Brain Drain: Evidence from the Caribbean*. IMF, 2006. WP/06/25.

Mitchell, Donald. Sugar in the Caribbean: Adjusting to Eroding Preferences, Development Prospects Group, World Bank Policy Research Working Paper 3802, The World Bank, December 2005.

Mittelman, James (ed). *Globalization: Critical Reflections*. Colorado: Lynne Rienner Publishers, 1997.

Padilla, Mark. *Caribbean Pleasure Industry: Tourism, Sexuality and AIDS in the Dominican Republic*, Chicago: University of Chicago Press, 2007.

Papal Decree. Accessed December 11, 2011. http://www.uintah basintah.org/usdocuments/doc4.pdf

Pattullo, Polly. *Last Resorts: The Cost of Tourism in the Caribbean*. London: Cassell, 1996.

Prebisch, Raúl. "Commercial Policy in the Underdeveloped Countries," *American Economic Review* 49, May 1959: 251–273.

Schmid, Karoline. *Migration in the Caribbean: Brain Drain, Remittances, Diaspora*. ECLAC Subregional Headquarters for the Caribbean, 1997.

Sharpe, Peter. *Sugar Cane: Past and Present*. Illinois: Southern Illinois University, 1998. Accessed December 11, 2011. http://www.siu.edu/~ebl/leaflets/sugar.htm,

Sydelle, John. "Factors influencing Caribbean tourism growth," *eHow*, 2 April 2011. Accessed December 12, 2011. http://www.ehow.com/info_8155365_factors-influencing-caribbean-tourism-growth.html.

Taliman, Valerie. "Revoke the Inter Cetera Bull," *Turtle Quarterly*. Fall-Winter (1994): 7-8.

Thomas-Hope, Elizabeth. Regional Special Topics Monograph on International Migration, Analysis of the 2000 Round Census Data of Eighteen Caribbean Countries CARICOM Secretariat, 2009.

Travis, Alan. "David Cameron Launches Immigration Crackdown," *The Guardian*. 10 October 2011. Accessed December 12, 2011. http://www.guardian.co.uk/uk/2011/oct/10/david-cameron-immigration-crackdown.

UNESCO. *General History of the Caribbean: New Societies: The Caribbean in the Long*

Sixteenth Century, vol. II. The University of Michigan—UNESCO Publishing, 1999.
Vaughan, Erin. "Constraints Affecting Tourism in the Caribbean," *eHow*, 7 February 2011. Accessed December 12, 2011. http://www.ehow. com/ info_7903496_constraints-affecting-tourism-caribbean.html,
Williams, Earl. *From Columbus to Castro: The History of the Caribbean*. New York: Vintage, 1984.

CHAPTER 3
INDIA-CARIBBEAN RELATIONS WITH EMPHASIS ON TRADE AND COMMERCE BETWEEN INDIA AND TRINIDAD AND TOBAGO

Arasaratnam, S. *Maritime Commerce and English Power (South East India 1750-1800)*. Asian Studies Association of Australia South Asian Publication Series No11. New Delhi: Sterling Publishers Pvt. Ltd., 1996.
Anthony, Michael. *Port of Spain in a World at War 1939-1945: The History of Port of Spain Vol.2*. Port of Spain: Paria Classics, 1978.
Balkaransingh, Satnarine. "Trinidad Space Speaking Through Indo-Trinidadian Rituals and Festivals: 1990-2009." Unpublished PhD Dissertation. University of Trinidad and Tobago, 2010.
—— Address to potential Indian investors entitled, "Exploring Trinidad and Tobago and India's Cultural Relations With A View To Enhancing Further Co-Operation." Grand Hotel Delhi, March 23, 2007.
—— "The contribution of Indian Culture with Special Reference to the Role of the Arts in Influencing the Development of the Trinidad and Tobago and the Caribbean Aesthetic". Paper presented at International Conference entitled, *Origins-Creating Tracks of the Indian Diaspora*, hosted by Indira Gandhi National Centre for the Arts (IGNCA) January 2007.
Braithwaite, Lloyd. *Social Stratification in Trinidad: A Preliminary Analysis*. Kingston: ISER UWI, 1975.
Central Bank of Trinidad and Tobago. Summary Economic Indicators, September 2011.
Chittick, Neville. "East Africa and the Orient: ports and trade before the arrival of the Portuguese." *Historical Relations across the Indian Ocean*: Reports and papers of the meeting of experts organized by UNESCO at Port Louis, Mauritius, from 15 to 19 July 1974. Belgium: UNESCO, 1980.
Dabydeen, David and Samaroo, Brinsley (eds). *India in the Caribbean*. London: Hansib Publishing Ltd., 1987.
Danvers, F.C. *A Century of Famines*. India Office, 1877.
Demas, William *et al., Imperatives of Adjustment: Draft Development Plan 1983-1986*. Report of the Task force appointed by Cabinet to formulate a multi-sectoral development plan for the Republic of Trinidad and Tobago Volumes I and II. Trinidad: Republic of Trinidad and Tobago, 1983.
Dutt, Ramesh Chunder. *The Economic History of India. Volume I*. New Delhi: Publications Division, Ministry of Information and Broadcasting, 2006.
—— *The Economic History of India. Volume II*. New Delhi: Publication Division, Ministry of Information and Broadcasting, Government of India, 2006.
FICCI. "Monthly Review of Indian Economy April 2011." *India at a Glance*. Economic Affairs and Research Division, Accessed November 20, 2011. http://www.indiainbusiness.nic.in/know-india/india-at-a-glance.htm#1.

Forrest, W.A. George. *History of The Indian Mutiny Volumes I, II and III*. New Delhi: Asian Educational Services, 2006.

Gadgil, D.R. *The Industrial Evolution of India in Recent Times, 1860-1939*. Bombay: Oxford University Press, 1971.

Galaal, Musa H.I. "Historical Relations between the Horn of Africa and the Persian Gulf and the Indian Ocean Islands through Islam." *Historical Relations Across the Indian Ocean*: Reports and papers of the meeting of experts organized by UNESCO at Port Louis, Mauritius, from 15 to 19 July 1974. Belgium: UNESCO, 1980.

Gooptar, Primnath. "75 Years of Indian Cinema in Trinidad and Tobago." PhD Diss. University of Trinidad and Tobago (UTT), 2011.

Gosine, Mahin. *The Coolie Connection*. New York: Windsor Press, 1992.

Hart, Daniel, "Historical and Statistical View of the Island of Trinidad," *Port of Spain Chronicle*, 1866.

Jacob, Debbie. "Vulgarity is killing the Music". Interview with Ras Shorty. *Indian Express*. Monday February 26, 1996.

Jha. J.C. "India and Us". *Art and Culture: Quarterly Journal of National Cultural Council*. Trinidad: National Cultural Council, 1971.

Kemp, Peter. Ed., *The Oxford Companion to Ships and the Sea*. Hong Kong: OUP, 1976.

Keswani, D.G. "Indian cultural and commercial influences in the Indian Ocean from Africa and Madagascar to South-East Asia." In *Historical Relations Across the Indian Ocean*: Reports and papers of the meeting of experts organized by UNESCO at Port Louis, Mauritius, from 15 to 19 July 1974. Belgium: UNESCO, 1980.

Kirpalani, Murli J. (ed). *Indian Centenary Review. One Hundred Years of Progress: 1845-1945*, Trinidad, B.W.I. Port of Spain: Indian Centenary Review Committee, 1945.

La Guerre, John, (ed). *Calcutta to Caroni*. (St Augustine: UWI, 1985 [1974]).

Lal, Brij V. *The Encyclopaedia of the Indian Diaspora*. India: Oxford University Press, 2007.

Look Lai, Walton. *Indentured Labour, Caribbean Sugar: Chinese and Indian Migrants to the British West Indies 1838-1918*. Baltimore: John Hopkins Univ. Press, 1993.

Majumdar, Ranjana. "Kamla: Indian company set to invest $1b in T&T." Trinidad Express Newspaper January 14, 2012.

Mansingh, Ajay and Lakshmi. *Home Away from Home*. Jamaica: Ian Randle Publishers, 1999.

Mollat, Michael. "Historical Contacts of Africa and Madagascar with South and South-East Asia: The Role of the Indian Ocean." In *Historical Relations Across the Indian Ocean*: Reports and papers of the meeting of experts organized by UNESCO at Port Louis, Mauritius, from 15 to 19 July 1974. Belgium: UNESCO, 1980.

Nehru, Jawaharlal. *The Discovery of India*. New Delhi, 1973.

Ramdeen Sunil *et al.*, (eds). "Doing Business-India/Trinidad Chamber of Commerce." *Inaugural Magazine*. Trinidad: India-Trinidad and Tobago Chamber of Industry and Commerce, 2009.

— — *et al.* (eds). "India and Trinidad and Tobago Economic and Trade Relations." *Inaugural Magazine*. Trinidad: India-Trinidad and Tobago Chamber of Industry and Commerce, 2009.

— — (eds)., "Interview with H.E. Malay Mishra." *Inaugural Magazine*. Trinidad: India-Trinidad and Tobago Chamber of Industry and Commerce, 2009.

Riviere, William Emanuel. "Labour Shortage in the British West Indies after Emancipation," *Journal of Caribbean History*. No. 4, 1972.

Samaroo, Brinsley. "Chinese and Indian Coolie Voyages in the Caribbean". *Journal of Caribbean Studies* Vol. 14, Nos. 1 and 2, 1999.

— — "Eric Williams East Indian Academic Concerns, Conference on Independence and After: Eric Williams and the Making of Trinidad and Tobago". Paper presented at the Institute for the Study of the Americas, Senate House, London University 2011.

— — "Two Abolitions: African Slavery and East Indian Indentureship." *India in the Caribbean*, edited by David Dabydeen and Brinsley Samaroo. London: Hansib Publishing Ltd, 1987.

Sookdeo, Neil. *Freedom, Festivals and Caste in Trinidad After Slavery—A Society in Transition*. USA: Xlibris Corp., 2000.

Singh, Sherry-Ann. "The Ramayan Tradition and Socio Religious Change in Trinidad, 1917-1990." PhD Diss. St Augustine, University of the West Indies, 2005.

Tagore, Rabindranath. *The Meaning of Art*. London: Oxford University Press, 1926.

Tinker, Hugh. *A New System of Slavery: The Export of Indian Labour Overseas 1830-1920*. London: Hansib Publishing Ltd., 1993.

Vertovec, Steven. *Hindu Trinidad: Religion, Ethnicity and Socio-Economic Change*. London: Macmillan Education Ltd., 1992.

— — "Hinduism and Social Change in Trinidad." PhD Diss. London, 1987.

World Economic Forum. Global Competiveness Report 2011-2012. "T&T More Competitive," *Daily Express*, September 8, 2011.

CHAPTER 4
AN OVERVIEW OF SINO-CARIBBEAN RELATIONS

Goldstein, Avery. *Rising to the Challenge: China's Grand Strategy and International Security*. Stanford: Stanford University Press, 2005.

Mei, Xin Yu. "Problems China Should Pay Attention to in Foreign Direct Investment." *China Finance*, 18(2005).

Weiss, John. People's Republic of China and its Neighbors: Partners or Competitors for Trade and Investment. *ADB Institute Discussion Paper*, No. 13 (2004).

Ma, Xiuhong. "The New Chapter of Cooperation in Trade and Economy between China and Caribbean." *Economy Daily*. September 6, 2007, sec. 3.

— — "Deepening Cooperation in Trade and Economy and Filling Mutual Development", *Light Daily*. September 9, 2007, sec. 5.

Bárcena, Alicia and Osvaldo Rosales. "The People's Republic of China and Latin America and the Caribbean: Towards a Strategic Relationship." Santiago, Chile: Economic Commission for Latin America and the Caribbean (CEPAL) May 2010. Accessed January 18, 2011 http://www.eclac.org/publicaciones/xml/1/39521/China_Latin_America_Caribbean_strategic_relationship_906.pdf.

People's Daily Online, "Growth Rate of China's Trade with Latin America and Caribbean Decreased in 2008." *People's Daily Online*. Accessed January 18, 2010. http://english.peopledaily.com.cn/90001/90778/90857/90861/6605991.html.

Ministry of Foreign Affairs, People's Republic of China. "Countries to Establish Diplomatic Relations with the People's Republic Date Summary." June 12,

2010. Accessed January 25, 2011. http://www.fmprc.gov.cn/chn/pds/ziliao/2193/.

China-Caribbean Economic and Trade Cooperation Forum. "Sino-Caribbean Economic and Trade Relationship." October 29, 2004. Accessed January 06, 2011. http://cncforum.mofcom.gov.cn/aarticle/duzdc/jingjidongtai/200410/20041000298250.html.

Tong, Li. "Rapid Development in Sino-Caribbean Economic and Trade Relationship: Investment from China to Latin America Amounted to US$24.774 Billion," *People: Multinational Channel*, August 28, 2009. Accessed January 07, 2011. http://mnc.people.com.cn/GB/9946592.html.

Trade Development Bureau of Ministry of Commerce, People's Republic of China. "China's Status in the World Economy and its Relationship with Latin America," October 22, 2008. Accessed January 10, 2011. http://www.tdb.org.cn/news/245022.

National Bureau of Statistics of China. *China Statistic Year Book 2009*. http://www.stats.gov.cn/tjsj/ndsj/2009/html/R1708e.htm. Accessed January 18, 2011

China FTA Network. The Rapidly Development of Sino-Latin America Economic and Trade Relationship" January 2, 2009. Accessed July 31, 2011. http://fta.mofcom. gov.cn/article/ftazixun/200909/989_1.html,

Ministry of Commerce of the People's Republic of China. "Introduction of the Bilateral Economic and Trade Relationship between China and Caribbean Area," *Invest in China*. March 27, 2006. Accessed January 18, 2011. http://www.fdi.gov.cn/pub/FDI/tzfu/rdwt/dwtz/t20060423_27325.htm.

—— "Sino-Caribbean Trade Volume Breaks US$ 5 Billion for the First Time", Department of American and Oceanian Affairs, March 3 2008. Accessed January 21, 2011. http://mds.mofcom.gov.cn/aarticle/zcfb/200803/20080305407201. html.

Xinhua Net. "Dai Bingguo Attended the 50th Anniversary Celebration of the Establishment of Diplomatic Relations between the People's Republic of China and the Latin American and Caribbean Countries", *Xinhua Net*, October 12, 2010. Accessed January 14, 2011. http://news.xinhuanet. com/world/2010-10/12/c_12652266.htm.

CHAPTER 5

THE EMERGING ECONOMIES AND CARIBBEAN DEVELOPMENT: THE CASE OF GUYANA'S MEGAPROJECTS

Avendaño, Rolando and Gøril Bjerkhol Havro. "Latin America's Asian Opportunity." *Policy Insights* (OECD) No. 53. October 2007. Accessed March 7, 2011. http://www.oecd.org/dataoecd/62/28/39564143.pdf.

Boyd, Gavin. "Grounding Globalization: The Perils of Linking Economic Processes of Globalization to Economic Outcomes." *Economic Geography*. July 78(3) (2002): 361-38.

Brack, Duncan, Chantal Marijnissen and Saskia Ozinga. "Controlling Imports of Illegal Timber: Options for Europe." Brussels: The Royal Institute of International Affairs (Chatham House), 2002. Accessed July 27, 2011. http://www.chathamhouse.org/sites/default/files/public/Research/Energy%2C%20Environment%20and%20 Development/options_for_europe2. pdf

Bulkan, Janet. "Exporting Guyana's Timber to Create Wealth in India." [Letter to the Editor]. *Kaieteur News*. April 12, 2011. Accessed April 17, 2011. http://

www.kaieteurnewsonline.com/2011/04/12/exporting-guyana%E2%80%99s-timber-to-create-wealth-in-india/

Castaneda, Sebastian. "China's Policy Paper on Latin America and the Caribbean." Council of Hemispheric Affairs (COHA). July 29, 2009. Accessed January 20, 2011. http://www.coha.org/china%E2%80%99s-policy-paper-on-latin-america-and-the-caribbean/.

Central Intelligence Agency. *The World Factbook: Guyana.* 2011. Accessed June 8, 2011. https://www.cia.gov/library/publications/the-world-factbook/geos/gy.html.

Colchester, Marcus. *Guyana—Fragile Frontier, Loggers, Miners and Forest People.* New York: Latin American Bureau, 1997a.

—— "Guyana: Fragile Frontier." *Race and Class* 38(4) (1997b.): 33-56.

Colchester, Marcus, Jean La Rose and Kid James. "Mining and Amerindians in Guyana." Final Report of the APA/NSI project on 'Exploring Indigenous Perspective on Consultation and Engagement within the Mining Sector in Latin America and the Caribbean. Ottawa: North South Institute, 2002. Accessed July 14, 2008. http://www.nsi-ins.ca/english/pdf/guyana/guyana_final_report.pdf.

Colchester, Marcus amd Jean La Rose. "Our Land Our Future: Promoting Indigenous Participation and Rights in Mining, Climate Change and other Natural Resource Decision-making in Guyana." Final report of the APA/FPP/NSI project 'Indigenous Perspectives on Consultation and Decision-Making about Mining and Other Natural Resources: Toward Community Strengthening, Dialogue and Policy Change,' 2010. Accessed February 20, 2011. http://www.forestpeoples.org/sites/fpp/files/publication/2010/08/guyanaourlandourfuture jun10eng.pdf.

Conway, Dennis. "Small Islands: Can Past Experience Help Subvert the Neo-Liberal Agenda ?" Paper presented at the *Latin American Studies Association XX International Congress*, Guadalajara, Mexico, April 17-19, 1997.

CIA World Fact Book. "Guyana 2011." Accessed July 27, 2011. https://www.cia.gov/library/publications/the-world-factbook/geos/gy.html

The Daily Herald. "Forestry Deal with India's Coffee Maker Raises Questions." April 10, 2011. Accessed April 21, 2011. http://www.thedailyherald.com/regional/2-news/15744-forestry-deal-with-indias-coffee-maker-raises-questions.html.

Deonandan, Kalowatie. "Guyana's PPP: From Socialism to National Democracy." In *Revolutionary Movements to Political Parties: Case Studies from Latin America and Africa*, edited by Kalowatie Deonandan, David Close and Gary Prevost. New York: Palgrave, 2007.

Department of Foreign Affairs and International Trade (DFAIT), Canada. "Mining in Developing Countries—Corporate Social Responsibility: The Government's Response to the Report of the Standing Committee on Foreign Affairs and International Trade." October, 2005. Accessed February 13, 2008. http://www.pdac.ca/pdac/advocacy/csr/roundtables-background. pdf.

"Expert: Donors Must View Amaila Falls as Part of a Larger Scheme." *Development Today*. November 16, 2010. Accessed April 25, 2011. http://www.bicusa.org/en/Article.12256.aspx.

The Economic Commission for Latin America and The Caribbean (ECLAC). *Economic Survey of Latin America and the Caribbean 2009-2010.* ECLAC, 2010. Accessed June 8, 2011. http://www.eclac.cl/publicaciones/xml/4/40254/2010-637-EEI_Book_WEB-1.pdf.

"Trinidad Seeks India's Investment in Energy Search." *Economic Times*, February

9, 2011. Accessed March 20, 2011. http://articles.economictimes.indiatimes.com/2011-02-09/news/28433887_1_trinidad-and-tobago-energy-sector-energy-development.

The Environmental Investigation Agency (EIA) and Telepak. "Timber Trafficking: Illegal Logging in Indonesia, South East Asia and International Consumption of Illegally Sourced Timber." 2001. Accessed June 11, 2011. http://www.eia-international.org/files/reports26-1.pdf.

Forest Peoples Programme (FPP). "Illegal Logging Discovered in Guyana." April 1998. Accessed March 13, 2011. http://ces.iisc.ernet.in/hpg/envis/doc98html/biodguy427.html.

Frederick, Colin. "Peril in Paradise: The Caribbean, the Fragile Third Border of the Drug Trade." Council on Hemispheric Affairs (COHA), July 20, 2010. Accessed March 8, 2011. http://www.coha.org/peril-in-paradise-the-caribbean-the-fragile-third-border-of-the-drug-trade/

Gafar, John. "Guyana: From Cooperative Socialism to Economic Liberalization and Growth: 1976-1994." *The Journal of Developing Areas*, 31 (1) (1996): 41-74. Autumn.

Global Timber. "Guyana." 2011. Accessed March 23, 2011. http://www.globaltimber.org.uk/guyana.htm.

— — Accessed April 2,2011. 2007a. http://guyan aforestryblog.blogspot.com/2007/02/global-timber-website-modified.html.

— —"China-Illegal Imports and Exports." 2007b. Accessed April 19, 2011. http://www.globaltimber.org.uk/ChinaIllegal ImpExp.htm.

Goodland, Robert. "Guyana, Amaila Falls Hydro: Social and Environmental Aspects." October 19, 2010. Accessed March 10, 2011. http://www.google.com.gt/search?q=Guyana%3A+Amaila+Falls+ Hydro%3A+Social +and+Environmental+ Aspects.+Robert+ Goodland&ie=utf-8&oe=utf-8&aq=t&rls=org.mozilla:en-US:official&client=firefox-a.

Government of Guyana. *Forests Act*. 1998. Accessed June 8, 2011. http://www.gina.gov.gy/gina_pub/laws/Laws/cap6701.pdf.

Graham, Melissa. "China Looks South: Problematic Investments in Latin America." Council of Hemispheric Affairs (COHA). November 8, 2010. Accessed January 15, 2011. http://www.coha.org/index.php?s =1&s=China+Looks+South%3A+Problematic+ Investments+in+Latin+America&submit=Search.

Greenpeace. "An Overview of Asian Companies in Guyana." 1997. Accessed January 27, 2007. http://archive.greenpeace.org/comms/97/forest/asian_companies_ guyana.html.

Guyana Chronicle. "Norway Retracts Comment on Barama Operations." August 27, 2010. Accessed April 21, 2011. http://www.guy anachronicleonline.com/site/index.php?option =com_content& view=article&id=17836:norway-retracts-comment-on-barama-operations&catid=4:top-story&Itemid=8.

Inforpress Centroamericana. "Hydroelectricity: A Potential Tool for Local Development." *Central America Report*. July 15, 2005.

International Human Rights Clinic. "All that Glitters: Gold Mining in Guyana, the Failure of Government Oversight and the Human Rights of Amerindian Communities." March Cambridge, Mass: Human Rights Program, Harvard Law School, 2007. Accessed January 30, 2011. http://www.law.harvard.edu/programs/hrp/documents/AllThatGlitters.pdf.

International Monetary Fund (IMF). Regional Economic Outlook: Western Hemisphere Washington, D.C.: IMF, 2010. Accessed March 11, 2011. http://www.imf.org/external/pubs/ft/reo/2010/WHD/eng/pdf/wreo1010.pdf.

— — "IMF Executive Board Concludes 2010 Article IV Consultation with Guyana." Public Information Notice (PIN) No. 11/29. March 4, 2011. Accessed June 13, 2011. http://www.imf.org/external/np/sec/pn/2011/pn1129.htm.

— — *World Economic Outlook Database.* April 2011. Accessed July 27, 2011. http://www.imf.org/external/pubs/ft/weo/2011/01/weodata/index.aspx

Jagan, Cheddi. "Interview with Cheddi Jagan." Interview by Fred Rosen and Mario Maurillo. *NACLA* 31 (1) (1997). Accessed February 9. 2001. http://jagan.org/articles4c.htm.

Kaieteur News. "Govt. Insists Nothing Secret about Concessions." April 13, 2011. Accessed April 23, 2011. http://www.kaieteurnewsonline. com/?s=clico.

Kuecker, Glen David. "Fighting for the Forests: Grassroots Resistance to Mining in Northern Ecuador." *Latin American Perspectives,* Issue 153, 34(2) (2007): 94-107.

McLean, Norman. "Omai Gold Mines Limited: 'Departing With Dignity.' Presentation to the Mining Conference sponsored by the Guyana Geology andMines Commission. Georgetown, Guyana, August 22, 2005. (Document in Author's Possession).

National Development Strategy (Guyana). *National Development Strategy 2001-2010: Eradicating Poverty, Unifying Guyana.* Chapter 16. NDS, 2000. Accessed March 15, 2011. http://www.ndsguyana.org/document.asp.

Nauth, Priya. "Guyana Hosting International Workshop on Amazon Protection." *Guyana Chronicle Online.* April 20, 2010. Accessed April 1, 2011. http://www.guyanachronicleonline.com/site/index.php?option =com_content &view=article&id=12297:guyana-hosting-international-workshop-on-amazon-protection&catid=2: news&Itemid=3.

Omai Gold Mines Limited (OGML). "Direct Payments to Government: 5% Royalty Paid in Gold." Georgetown: Public Communications Department OGML, 2005. (Document in Author's Possession).

Organization for Economic Cooperation and Development (OECD). "China, India and the Challenge of Specialisation." *Latin American Economic Outlook (LEO) 2008.* OECD, 2008. Accessed February 12, 2011. http://www.oecd.org/document/8/0,3746,en_2649_33973_ 38789800_1_1_1_1,00.html.

Palmer, John and Janette Bulkan. "Guyana—Amaila Falls Hydropower Dam and Access Road: Notes for Advisory Expert Panel of Inter American Development Bank." February 28, 2011. Accessed March 10, 2011. http://www.redd-monitor.org/wordpress/wp-content/uploads/2011/03/AmailaFalls_notes_for_REDD-Monitor_28Feb2011.pdf.

Public Statement by participants in a Training of Trainer Workshop on Indigenous Peoples Rights, Extractive Industries and National Development Policies in Guyana. Georgetown, Guyana, March 2-8, 2010. Accessed March 10, 2011. http://www.forestpeoples.org/sites/fpp/files/publication/2010/08/guyanaapawshopstatement-mar10.pdf.

Rabe, Stephen. *U.S. Intervention in British Guiana: A Cold War Story (New Cold War History).*Chapel Hill, NC: University of North Carolina Press, 2005.

Ram, Christopher. "The Amaila Falls Road Project-Whose Synergy." *Stabroek News.* May 9, 2009. Accessed March 18, 2011. http://www.stabroeknews.com/2010/features/05/09/the-amaila-falls-road-project-%E2%80%93-whose-synergy/.

— — "Strangling the Gold(en) Goose." *Stabroek News.* September 12, 2010. Accessed March 21, 2011. http://www. stabroeknews.com/2010/features/09/12/strangling-the-golden-goose-2/

Ramdas, Krishna. Author Interview. Linden, Guyana, July 29, 2010.

Ramessar, Candace Rowena. "Water is More Important than Gold: Local Impacts and Perceptions of the 1995 Omai Cyanide Spill, Essequibo River, Guyana." M.A. Thesis. Blacksburg, Virginia: Virginia Polytechnic Institute and State University, 2003.

Robinson, William I. "Latin America and Global Capitalism." *Race and Class*, 40 (2-3) (1999): 111-131.

Sánchez, Alex. "The Oil Race is On: China Signs Multi-Billion Dollar Oil Contract with Venezuela, But India Also Wants Latin American Oil." Council of Hemispheric Affairs (COHA) September, 2007. Accessed March 7, 2011. http://www.coha.org/the-oil-race-is-on-china-signs-multi-billion-dollar-oil-contract-with-venezuela-but-india-also-wants-latin-american-oil/.

Sanders, Sir Ronald. Settling the China Question: A Caribbean Challenge. *BBC Caribbean.Com*. May 5, 2008. Accessed January 14, 2011. http://www.bbc.co.uk/caribbean/news/story/2008/05/printable/080502_sanders0505.shtml.

Scott-Joseph, Ankie, Juliette Melville, Patrick Kendall and Elmer Harris. "Debt Sustainability in Caribbean Countries: An Exploration of Alternative Methodologies." Social and Economic Research Unit, Caribbean Development Bank, August 2006. Accessed June 8, 2011. http://www.caribank.org/titanweb/cdb/webcms.nsf/AllDoc/BADCC4CFA13C8A360425741E00525397/$File/DebtSustainability% 5B1%5D.pdf.

Sherwood Forrest Inc. *Draft ESIA Report*. 2010. Accessed March 12, 2011. http://www.epaguyana.org/index2.php?option=com_docman& task=doc_view&gid=116&Itemid=29.

Scholte, Jan Aart. 2005. "The Sources of Neoliberal Globalization," UN Research Institute for Social Development (UNRISD) Programme Paper No. 8, 2005. Accessed August 15, 2008. http://www.unrisd.org/unrisd/website/document.nsf/0/9E1C54 CEEB19A314C12570B4004D0881?Open Document.>

Stabroek News. "US Company Granted State Forest Permit." January 8, 2008a. Accessed March 17, 2011. http://www.stabroeknews.com/2008/news/stories/01/08/us-company-granted-state-forest-permit/.

—— "Guyana's Indigenous peoples: Still languishing on the Periphery." May 28, 2008b. Accessed July 20, 2010. <http://www. stabroeknews.com/2008/guyana-review/05/28/guyana%E2%80%99s-indigenous-peoples/.

—— "Proposed Sherwood Logging Project will Entail Loss of Wildlife ESIA." August 9, 2010a. Accessed March 15, 2011. http://www.stabroeknews.com/2010/news/stories/08/09/proposed-sherwood-logging-project-will-entail-loss-of-wildlife-esia/.

—— "GGMC, GGDMA clash over enforcement of mining regulations." April 30, 2010b. Accessed February 25, 2011. http://www.stabroeknews.com/2010/business/04/30/ggmc-ggdma-clash-over-enforcement-of-mining-regulations/print/.

—— "Synergy got Amaila Road Contract on Evidence it would Hire Experts." August 17, 2010c. Accessed March 18, 2011. http://www.stabroeknews.com/2010/news/stories/08/17/asynergy-got-amaila-road-contract-on-evidence-it-would-hire-experts-source/print.

—— "PM Lauds Ties Between China and Guyana." September 29, 2010d. Accessed January 4, 2011. http://www.stabroeknews.com/2010/news/stories/09/29/pm-lauds-ties-between-china-and-guyana.

—— "External Debt to Exceed US$1B by Year End." February 13, 2011. Accessed June 8, 2011. http://www.stabroeknews. com/2010/news/stories/02/13/external-debt-to-exceed-us1b-by-yearend/.

Thornton, Allan. "Chinese Involvement in African Illegal Logging and Timber Trade." Testimony before the US House of Representatives, Committee on International Relations, Subcommittee on Africa. Global Human Rights and International Operations. July 28, 2005. Accessed April 14, 2011.http://www.eia-global.org/PDF/testimony—ChinaAfricahearing—forests—jul05.pdf

Toni, Ana. Overview of Asian Companies, in particular Malaysian Companies. Report Commissioned by Greenpeace to be presented to the External Commission on Foreign Companies in the Amazon Comissiao Externa de Investigacao de Madeireiras na Amazonia). May 1997. Accessed March 23, 2011. http://archive.greenpeace.org/comms/97/forest/asian_companies_contents.html.

Transparency International. "Corruption Perceptions Index." 2010. Accessed April 11, 2011. http://www.transparency.org/policy_ research/surveys_indices/cpi/2010/results.

World Travel Online. "Trinidad and Tobago Become a Hotspot for Chinese Overseas Investment —Trinidad and Tobago Business Forum successfully held in Shanghai." September 28, 2010. Accessed February 15, 2011. http://news.travel168. net/travel_fair_review/20100928/25320.html.

World Bank. A Time to Choose Caribbean Development in the 21st Century. Report No. 31725-LAC. 2005. Accessed March 3, 2011. http://siteresources.worldbank.org/LACEXT/Resources/317250LAC.pdf.

—— "International Development Association Country Assistance Strategy for Guyana for the Period FY 2009-2012." April 15, 2009. Accessed March 18, 2011. http://www-wds.worldbank.org/external/default/WDSContent Server/WDSP/IB/2009/05/22/000350881_ 20090522101401/Rendered/PDF/479830CAS0P106101Official0Use0 Only1.pdf.

Yagenova, Simona V. and García, Rocío. "Guatemala: El pueblo de Sipakapa Versus la empresa Minera Goldcorp." OSAL 10, 25 April 25, 2009. Accessed August 15, 2009. http://bibliotecavirtual.clacso. org.ar/ar/libros/osal/osal25/05yage.pdf.

CHAPTER 6

PRIMACY OF POLITICS IN DEVELOPMENT AND POVERTY REDUCTION IN THE CARIBBEAN

Bangura, Yusuf. "First Global Poverty Summit Examines Strategies in Poverty Reduction," United Nations Research Institute for Social Development (UNRISD), 31 January 2011. <http://www.unrisd.org/80256B3C005BE6B5/search/132D0887051DDA70C125782900 3BEE0E?OpenDocument> Accessed August 20, 2011.

Bourne, Compton. "Poverty and Its Alleviation in the Caribbean," Lecture at the Alfred O. Heath Distinguished Speakers' Forum, University of the Virgin Islands, Monday, March 14, 2005.

Britto, Tatiana Feitosa de. "The Challenges of El Salvador's Conditional Cash Transfer Programme, *Red Solidaria*", Country Study Number 9. Brasilia: International Poverty Centre, United Nations Development Programme, 2007.

Caribbean Development Bank. *Government of the Commonwealth of Dominica, Country Poverty Assessment, Final Report,* June 2003. London: Halcrow Group Limited, 2004.

— — *Government of Anguilla Country Poverty Assessment, Final Report,* June 2002. London: Halcrow Group Limited, 2002.

Craig, D. and D. Porter. *Development Beyond Neoliberalism? Governance, Poverty Reduction and Political Economy*. New York: Routledge, 2006.

Díaz-Cayeros, Alberto and Beatriz Magaloni. "Aiding Latin America's Poor," *Journal of Democracy,* 20(4) (2009): 36-49.

Dookeran, Winston. "Politics and Development: A Strategic Conversation on the Missing Politics in Development." In *Leadership and Governance in Small States: Getting Development Right,* edited by Winston Dookeran and Akhil Malaki. Saarbrucken: VDM Verlag Dr. Muller Aktiengesellschaft & Co. KG, 2008: 24-28.

Dookeran, Winston and Manfred D. Jantzen, *Power, Politics and Performance: A Partnership Approach for the Development of Small States*. Kingston: Ian Randle Publishers, 2012.

Hickey, Sam. "The Return of Politics in Development Studies I: Getting Lost within the Poverty Agenda?" *Progress in Development Studies,* 8 (2008): 349-58.

IMF, *Dominica: Poverty Reduction Strategy Paper,* IMF Country Report No. 06/289, August 2006. Accessed September 2, 2011. http://www. imf.org/external/pubs/ft/scr/2006/cr06289.pdf

Leftwich, Adrian, *Developmental States, Effective States and Poverty Reduction: The Primacy of Politics,* United Nations Research Institute for Social Development (UNRISD) Project on Poverty Reduction and Policy Regimes, Geneva, Switzerland: UNRISD, 2008.

Marshall, Richard and Bernard Walters, *Evaluating Ten Years of "Strategizing" for Poverty Reduction: A Cross-sectional Appraisal of the Poverty Reduction Strategy Paper (PRSP) Initiative,* The Brooks World Poverty Institute (BWPI) Working Paper 143, March 2011.

Moore, Mick and Graham Teskey, "The CAR Framework: Capability, Accountability, Responsiveness. What Do These Terms Mean, Individually and Collectively?" DFID Governance and Conflict Advisers, October 2006. Accessed September 2, 2011. http://www2.ids.ac.uk/gdr/cfs/pdfs/CARframeworkDRCweb.pdf

Pathak, R.D., P. Subba Rao *et al.* "State and Poverty Alleviation in South Asia and South Pacific: A Comparative Perception Survey of Civil Servants", *The Role of Public Administration in Building a Harmonious Society,* Network of Asia-Pacific Schools and Institutes of Public Administration and Governance (NAPSIPAG), Annual Conference 2005, Beijing, PRC, 5-7 December 2005.

Sachs, Jeffrey, *Ending World Poverty,* New York: Penguin, 2005.

Sen, Amartya K. *Development as Freedom*. New York: Alfred A. Knopf, 1999.

Soares, F.V., and Tatiana Britto. "Confronting Capacity Constraints on Conditional Cash Transfers in Latin America: The Cases of El Salvador and Paraguay." Working Paper 44, Brasília: International Poverty Centre, 2007.

Singh, Priti. "Elusive Justice: Denial Frame for Tribal Poor in India." In *Strengthening Governance through Access to Justice,* edited by Amita Singh and Nasir Aslam Zahid. New Delhi: PHI Learning Private Learning, 2009.

CHAPTER 7

CARIBBEAN EMBASSIES: BRIDGING THE GAP BETWEEN THE CARIBBEAN DIASPORA AND THE HOME COUNTRY AS PART OF AN INITIATIVE TO STIMULATE GROWTH AND DEVELOPMENT IN THE REGION

Ancien, Delphine, Mark Boyle and Rob Kitchin. "Exploring Diaspora Strategies: Lessons for Ireland." Paper presented at workshop entitled Exploring Diaspora Strategies, National University of Ireland, Maynooth, January 26-28, 2009.

Briney, Amanda. "Embassies and Consulate—An Overview, Embassies and Consulates are the Diplomatic Offices of a Country." Accessed October 20, 2010. http://geography.about.com/od/political geography/a/embassy.htm.

Belai, Bathseba, H. "Enabling Diaspora Engagement in Africa: Resources, Mechanisms and Gaps, Case Study: Ethiopia." Ottawa: The Association of Higher Learning and Development, 2007. Accessed September 15, 2010. http://www.aheadonline.org/enablingdiaspora engagementmay 2007.pdf.

Bourne, Compton. "Poverty and its Alleviation in the Caribbean." Paper presented at Alfred O. Heath Distinguished Speakers Forum, University of Virgin Islands, March 14, 2005.

Brand, Laurie, A. *Emigration and the State in the Middle East and North Africa.* Cambridge: Cambridge University Press, 2006. Accessed December 17, 2010. www.cambridge.org.

CARICOM. *CARICOM Statistics 2009*. Accessed April 04, 2011. http://www.caricomstats.org/.

Caribbean Development Bank. (CDB). *Social and Economic Indicators, Borrowing Member States, Volume XVI.* Economics Department, Barbados: Caribbean Development Bank, 2006.

Cohen, Robin. *Global Diasporas: An Introduction.* Oxford and New York: Routledge, 2008.

Docquier, Federic and Abseslam Marfouk. "Measuring the International Mobility of Skilled Workers-release 1.0." Policy Research Working Paper No. 3381. World Bank, August 2004.

Downes, Andrew. "Human Resources Development in the Caribbean: Overcoming the Unemployment Problem." *Journal of Education and Development in the Caribbean* 4 (1) (2000): 19-39.

—— "Caribbean Labour Market Challenges and Policies." CEPAL Series—Macroeconomia del desarrollo. Santiago, Chile: UN Economic Development Division, March 2006.

Fagen, Weiss, Patricia, Carlos Dade, Kathleen Felix, David Nicolas and Noriac Dathis. "Haitian Diaspora Associations and their investments in Basic Social Services in Haiti." Paper prepared for the Inter-American Development Bank, January 2009. Accessed September 15, 2010. http://isim.georgetown.edu/Publications/PatPubs/Haitian% 20Diapora%20Associations.pdf.

Grey, Atim. "Creating a Conducive Environment for Diaspora Contributions: The Experience of Ghana." Paper prepared by the National Population Council, Ghana for UNFPA/UNITAR/IOM Workshop on the Contribution of Diasporas, New York, May 11, 2006.

Heijmans, Maaike, and Jan Melissen. "Foreign Ministries and the Rising Challenge of Consular Affairs: Cinderella in the Limelight." Clingendael Diplomacy

Papers. The Hague: Netherlands Institute of International Relations, Clingendael, 2006.

Ionescu, Dina. "Engaging Diasporas as Development Partners for Home and Destination Countries: Challenges for Policymakers." Geneva: International Organization for Migration, 2006.

International Monetary Fund (IMF). "International Transactions in Remittances: Guide for Compilers and Users." Washington DC: Statistical Department, International Monetary Fund, 2009.

International Labour Organization. *2009 Labour Overview Latin America and the Caribbean.* Lima: International Labour Office, Regional Office for Latin America and the Caribbean, Peru, 2009.

Kethar, Suhas, L. and Dilip Ratha. "Development Finance via Diaspora Bonds Track Record and Potential." Paper presented at the Migration and Development Conference at the World Bank, Washington DC, May 23, 2007.

Latapi, Escobar and Eric Janssen. "Migration, the diaspora and development: The case of Mexico." Discussion Paper DP/167/2006. Geneva: Decent Work Research Programme, International Institute of Labour Studies, 2006.

Levitt, Peggy. "Social Remittances: Migration Driven Local-Level Forms of Cultural Diffusion." *The International Migration Review,* 32(4) (1998): 926-948.

Maphosa, France. The Impact of Remittances from Zimbabweans Working in South Africa on Rural Livelihoods in the Southern Districts of Zimbabwe. Forced Migration Working Paper Series No. 14. Witwatersrand, South Africa: University of Witwatersrand, 2005.

Nurse, Keith. "Migration, Diaspora and Development," Universidad Autonoma de Zacatecas & Canadian Foundation for the Americas, Zacatecas, Mexico, October 2004.

Sheffer, Gabriel. *Modern Diasporas in International Politics.* London: Croom Helm, 1986.

Somerville, Will, Jamie Durana and Aaron Matteo Terrazas. "Home Town Association: An Untapped Resource for Immigrant Integration." Migration Policy Institute Insight, July 2008.

United Nations. "Expert Group Meeting on International Migration and Development in Latin America and the Caribbean." Mexico City: UN Department of Economic and Social Affairs, November 2005.

—— "Migration in the Caribbean—What Do We Know?" Population Division of the United Nations Secretariat. International Migration. Wallchart, 2002. ST/ESA/SER.A/219, Sales No. EO3. XIII.3.

United Nations Development Programme (UNDP). *Human Development Report* 2007/2008. New York: Palgrave Macmillan, 2007.

United States Agency for International Development. "Framework for Leveraging Migrant Resources for Effective Development and Diplomacy." Diaspora Networks Alliance, 2008. Accessed September 24, 2010. http://pdf.usaid.gov/pdf_docs/PDACM860.pdf

United States Department of State Cultural Heritage Center. 2010. Accessed September 23, 2010. http://exchanges.state.gov/heritage/index.html.

Williams, Eric. *Capitalism and Slavery.* North Carolina: The University of North Carolina Press, 1944.

World Bank. World Development Indicators. Washington DC: World Bank, 2009. Accessed April 02, 2011. http://databank.world bank.org/ddp/home.do.

CHAPTER 8
THE PUSH AND PULL FACTORS OF MIGRATION: WHY JAMAICAN PROFESSIONALS ARE LEAVING JAMAICA

Alkire, Sabina. *A Conceptual Framework for Human Security*. Oxford: Centre for Research on Inequality, Human Security and Ethnicity, 2003.

Anderson, Patricia. *Youth Unemployment in Jamaica*. Geneva: International Labour Organisation, 1997.

Ayoob, Mohammed. "Defining Security: A Subaltern Realist Perspective." In *Critical Security Studies*, edited by Keith Krause and Michael C. Williams, 121-146. Minneapolis, MN: University of Minnesota Press, 1997.

Bajpai, Kanti. *Human Security: Concept and Measurement*. Occasional Paper 19. Notre Dame, IN: Kroc Institute for International Peace Studies, 2000.

Beine, Michel, Frédéric Docquier and Maurice Schiff. *Brain Drain and its Determinants: A Major Issue for Small States*. Bonn: Institute for the Study of Labour (IZA), 2008. Accessed December 23, 2010. http://ftp.iza.org/dp3398.pdf

Castles, Stephen, and Mark Miller. *The Age of Migration*. New York: The Guilford Press, 1998.

Commission on Human Security. *Human Security Now*. New York, 2003. Accessed December 23, 2010. http://www.humansecurity-chs.org/finalreport/English/FinalReport.pdf

Degazon-Johnson, Roli. "The Trade in the Highly Skilled: The Case of the Commonwealth Caribbean." *Paper presented at the Institute of Commonwealth Studies Seminar, London, United Kingdom* July 12, 2007. Accessed January 3, 2011. http://www.thecommon wealth.org/files/182462/FileName/ICPS-SmallStates Presentation-July2007.pdf

Docquier, Frédéric., and Abdeslam Marfouk."International Migration by Educational Attainment (1990-2000)." In *International Migration, Remittances and Development*, edited by C. Ozden and M. Schiff, 1-44. New York: Palgrave MacMillan, 2005.

Fawcett, James T. and Fred Arnold. "Explaining Diversity: Asian and Pacific Immigration Systems." In *Pacific Bridges: The New Immigration from Asian and the Pacific Islands*, edited by James T. Fawcett and Benjamin Carino, 453-478. New York: 1987

Foong Khong, Yeun. "Human Security: A Shotgun Appraoch to Alleviating Human Misery." *Global Governance*, 7 (2001): 231-236.

Geertz, Clifford. *The Interpretation of Cultures*. New York: Basic Book Incorporated, 1973.

Griffith, Ivelaw. "Security, Sovereignty and Public Order in the Caribbean." *Security and Defense Studies Review*, 2 (2002): 1-18.

Harriott, Anthony. "Citizen Security and Human Development in the Caribbean: Some Thoughts". Accessed December 21, 2010. http://www.jm.undp.org/files/Anthony_Harriot-Citizen_Security_ Report.pdf

Hunger, Uwe. *The "Brain Gain" Hypothesis: Third-World Elites in Industrialized Countries and Socioeconomic Development in their Home Country*. Germany: University of Muenster, 2002.

International Organization for Migration. *World Migration 2008: Managing Labour Mobility in the Evolving Global Economy*. Geneva, Switzerland, 2008.

Jamaica Constabulary Force. National Intelligence Bureau, 2009.

Jolly, Richard and Deepayan Basu Ray. "The Human Security Framework and National Human Development Reports: A Review of Experiences and

Current Debates". *NHDR Occasional Paper 5*. Human Development ReportOffice of the UNDP, 2006.

Kapur, Devesh, and John McHale. *Give us your Best and Brightest: The Global Hunt for Talent and its Impact on the Developing World*. Washington: Center for Global Development,2005.

Kritz, Mary M., Lin Leam Lim and Hania Zlotnik. *International Migration Systems: A Global Approach*. New York: Oxford University Press, 1992.

Lee, Everett, S. "A Theory of Migration". *Demography*. 3(1) (1966): 47-57.

Lowell, B. Lindsay. *Some Developmental Effects of the International Migration of Highly Skilled Persons*. Geneva: International Labour Office, 2001.

—— and Allan Findlay. *Migration of Highly Skilled Persons from Developing Countries: Impact and Policy Responses*. International Migration Branch. Geneva: International Labour Office, 2001.

Marshall, Dawn. "A History of West Indian Migrations: Overseas Opportunities and "Safety-Valve" Polices." In *The Caribbean Exodus*, edited by B.B. Levine, 15-31. New York· Praeger Publishers, 1987.

Martin, Philip, and Gottfried Zürcher. "Managing Migration: The Global Challenge." *Population Bulletin*, 63 (1) (2008): 1-19.

Massey, Douglas, Joaquin Arango, Graeme Hugo, Ali Kouaouci, Adela Pallegrino and J. Edward Taylor."Theories of International Migration: A Review and Appraisal". *Population and Development Review*, 19 (3) (1993): 431-466.

McFarlane, S. Neil and Yuen Foong Khong. *Human Security and the UN: A Critical History*. Indiana: Indiana University Press, 2006.

Nurse, Keith. "Diaspora, Migration and Development in the Americas." Canadian Foundation for the Americas, 2004. Accessed November 20, 2010. http://www.focal.ca/pdf/migration_Nurse_diaspora% 20migration% 20development%20Caribbean_September%202004_FPP-04-6.pdf

Paris, Roland. "Human Security: Paradigm Shift or Hot Air?" *International Security*, 26(2) (2001): 87–102.

Parkins, Natasha C. "The Push and Pull Factors of Migration: Why Jamaican Professionals are Leaving Jamaica." M.Sc. Thesis. University of the West Indies, 2009.

Piore, M.J. *Birds of Passage: Migrant Labour in Industrial Societies*. Cambridge: Cambridge University Press, 1979.

Planning Institute of Jamaica. "An Assessment of the Emigration of Highly Skilled Workers from Jamaica". *The Labour Market Information Newsletter of Jamaica*. No. 54. (2007)

—— *Economic and Social Survey*. Kingston: Jamaica Printing Services Limited, 2008.

Potter, Robert, Tony Binns, Jennifer Elliott and David W. Smith. *Geographies of Development*. Harlow: Pearson Education Limited, 2004.

Ritchie Dawson, Laura. "Brain Drain, Brain Circulation, Remittances and Development: Prospects for the Caribbean". Caribbean Paper No. 2. INTAL, 2007. Accessed November 20, 2010. http://www.cigionline. com/sites/default/files/2.%20Brain%20Drain,%20Brain% 20Circulation,%20Remittances %20and%20Development %20 Prospects%20for%20the%20Caribbean.pdf

Quinn, Michael, A. and Stephen Rubb. "The Importance of Education-Occupation Matching in Migration Decisions." *Demography*, 42(1)(2005): 153-167.

Schmid, Karoline. *Migration in the Caribbean: Brain Drain-Remittances-Diaspora*. ECLAC, 2006. Accessed November 21, 2010. http://www.eclac.cl/publicaciones/xml/3/28873/L.107.pdf

Skeldon, Ron. *Globalization, Skilled Migration and Poverty Alleviation: Brain Drains in Context*. Brighton: Development Research Center on Migration, Globalisation and Poverty, University of Sussex, 2005. Accessed November 21, 2010. http://www.migrationdrc.org/publications/working_papers/WP-T15.pdf

Planning Institute of Jamaica. *The Labour Market Information Newsletter of Jamaica*. Jamaica: Pear Tree Press, 2005.

The World Bank. *The Road to Sustained Growth in Jamaica*. Washington DC: The World Bank, 2004.

Thomas-Hope, Elizabeth. "Trends and Patterns of Migration to and from Caribbean Countries". Paper prepared for the Simposio Sobre Migracíon Internacional En Las Americas, Sponsored by the United Nations, CEPAL, and ECLAC, San José, Costa Rica, September 2002.

—— *Skilled Labour Migration from Developing Countries: Study on the Caribbean Region*. Geneva: International Labour Organisation, 2002. Accessed November 23, 2010. http://www.ilo.org/public/english/protection/migrant/download/imp/imp50e.pdf

United Nations Development Programme (UNDP). *Human Development Report 1994—New Dimensions of Human Security*. New York: Oxford University Press, 1994.

—— *Human Development Report 2009 Overcoming Barriers: Human Mobility and Development*. New York: Palgrave MacMillan, 2009.

United Nations Office on Drugs and Crime. *Crime, Violence and Development: Trends, Costs and Policy Options in the Caribbean*. A Joint Report by the United Nations Office on Drugs and Crime and the Latin America and the Caribbean Region of the World Bank. UNODC, 2007. Accessed November 24, 2010. http://www.unodc. org/pdf/research/Cr_and_Vio_Car_E.pdf

Wallerstein, Immanuel. *The Modern World System: Capitalist Agriculture and the Origins of the European World Economy in the Sixteenth Century*. New York: Academic Press, 1974.

CHAPTER 9

INDIAN MIGRATION TO THE CARIBBEAN: REFLECTIONS ON THE FORMATION OF ETHNIC IDENTITY

Abramson, Harold J. *Ethnic Diversity in Catholic America*. New York: Wiley, 1973.

Beachey, R.W. *The British West Indian Sugar Industry in the late Nineteenth Century*. Oxford: Oxford University Press, 1957.

Bronkhurst, H.V.P. *Among the Hindus and Creoles of British Guiana*. London: T. Woolmer, 1888.

Chickrie, Raymond S. "Muslims in Suriname: Facing Triumphs and Challenges in a a Plural Society," *Journal of Muslim Minority Affairs*, 31 (2011): 79-99.

Erikson, E.L. "The Introduction of East Indian Coolies into the British West Indies," *Journal of Modern History*, 6 (1934): 48-59.

Freeman, L.A. "Land Tenure in British Guiana," in *Caribbean Land Tenure Symposium*, published by the Caribbean Research Council, Port of Spain, Trinidad (1946): 357-66.

Gafar, John. 1998. "Growth, Inequality and Poverty in Selected Caribbean and Latin American Countries, with Emphasis on Guyana," *Journal of Latin American Studies*, 30 (1998): 591-617.

Gibson, Kean. *The Cycle of Racial Oppression in Guyana*. Lanham, MD: University Press of America, 2003.

Greeley, Andrew. *Ethnicity in the United States*. New York: Wiley, 1974.

Hoefte, R. *In Place of Slavery: A Social History of British Indian and Javanese Labourers in Suriname*. Gainsville: University Press of Florida, 1998.

Hoerder, Dirk. *Cultures in Contact: World Migrations in the Second Millennium*. Durham, NC: Duke University Press, 2002.

Jagan, Cheddi. *Forbidden Freedom: The Story of British Guyana*. Georgetown: Hansib Publishing, 1994.

Kolff, Dirk H.A. "From Hindustani Diaspora to Indian Expansion: The Context of the First Phase of the Transition" Working Paper presented at the workshop on South Asian Labour at *the International History of Social History*, Amsterdam, 1995.

Luckhoo, J.A. "The East Indian in British Guiana," *Timheri* (The Journal of Royal Agricultural and Commercial Society of British Guiana), 7 (1921): 20-28.

Markovits, Claude. "Indian Merchant Networks outside India in the Nineteenth and Twentieth Century: A Preliminary Survey," *Modern Asian Studies*, 33 (1999): 883-911.

— — *The Global World of Indian Merchants, 1750-1947*. Cambridge, UK: Cambridge University Press, 1966.

McKeown, Adam. "Global Migration, 1846-1940." *Journal of World History* 15 (2004): 155-189.

Merton, Robert. *The Sociology of Science: Theoretical and Empirical Investigations*. Chicago: University of Chicago Press, 1973.

Meyer, David S. *et al.* (eds). *Social Movements: Identity, Culture, and the State*. New York: Oxford University Press, 2002.

Nath, Dwarka. A History of Indians in British Guiana. London: Thomas Nelson & Sons, 1950.

Nugent, Walter. *Crossings: The Great Transatlantic Migration, 1870-1914*. Bloomington: Indiana University Press, 1919.

Portes, Alejandro and Ruben Rumbaut. *Immigrant America: A Portrait*. Berkeley: University of California Press, 1996.

— — *Legacies: The Store of the Immigrant Second Generation*. Berkeley: University of California Press, 2002.

Ryan, Selwyn. *Race and Nationalism in Trinidad and Tobago: A Study of Decolonization in a Multiracial Society*. Toronto: University of Toronto Press, 1972.

Scoble, John. *British Guiana: Facts! Facts! Facts!* London, 1840.

Sen, Amartya. *Rationality and Freedom*. Cambridge, MA: Belknap Press, 2004.

Singh, Kelvin. "East Indians and the Larger Society," In *Calcutta to Caroni*, edited by John La Guerre, 39-68. Trinidad: Longman Caribbean, 1974.

Skocpol, Theda. *States and Social Revolutions*. Cambridge, Cambridge University Press, 1979.

Smith, Raymond T. "Review of Social and Cultural Pluralism in the Caribbean." *American Anthropologist*, 63 (1961): 155-157.

Speckmann, John D. "The Caste System and the Hindustani Group in Suriname," pp. 201-12 In *Caste in Overseas Indian Communities*, edited by B.M. Schwartz. San Francisco: Chandler, 1967.

— —"Dutch Colonial Policy and the East Indians in Suriname," *Colloques Internationaux du CNRS: Asie du Sud Traditions ET Changements* 582 (1972): 605-09.

Stipriaan, Alex van. *Suriname Contrast: Exhaustion and Survival in a Caribbean Plantation Economy 1750-1863*. Leiden, Netherlands: KITLV Uitgeverij, 1993.

Swan, Michael. *British Guiana: The Land of Six Peoples*. London: HMSO, 1957.
Taylor, Michael (ed.), *Collected Works of Herbert Spencer*. London: Thoemmes, 1996.
Thomas, W.I. and F. Znaniecki, *The Polish Peasant in Europe and America*. Urbana: University of Illinois Press, 1996.
Traa, A van. *Suriname 1900-1940*. Deventer, Netherlands: W. van Hoeve, 1974.
United Nations Development Programme. *Human Development Report, 2002*. New York: Oxford University Press, 2002.
Wengen, G.D. van. *The Cultural Inheritance of the Javanese in Suriname*. Leiden, Netherlands: E.J. Brill, 1975.

CHAPTER 10

BLING, BRANDS AND HYPERSEXUALITY: GLOBALIZATION AND CULTURAL CONSTRUCTIONS OF CARIBBEAN MASCULINITIES AND FEMININITIES

Allen, Caroline, F. "Caribbean Bodies: Representation and Practice." In *Caribbean Portraits: Essays on Gender Ideologies and Identities* edited by Christine Barrow. Kingston: Ian Randle Publishers and The Centre for Gender and Development Studies, UWI, 1998.
Antrobus, Peggy. "Women and Global Restructuring: Impacts on Human Security" Presentation to Women's Studies 100, Trent University, 26, March, 2003.
Bairner, A. *Sport, Nationalism, and Globalization: European and North American Perspectives*. Albany: State University of New York Press, 2001.
Ballerino B., Cohen, C., Wilk, R. and Stoeltje (eds). *Beauty Queens on the Global Stage: Gender, Contests, and Power*. London: Routledge, 1996.
Benn, Denis and Kenneth Hall (eds). *Globalisation: A Calculus of Inequality: Perspectives from the South*. Kingston: Ian Randle Publishers, 2000.
Brown, Aggrey. "Caribbean Cultures and Mass Communication Technology: Re-Examining the Cultural Dependency Thesis." In *Globalization, Communications and Caribbean Identity* edited by Hopeton Dunn. Jamaica: Ian Randle Publishers, 1995.
Brown, Hilary. "American Media Impact on Jamaican Youth: The Cultural Dependency Thesis." In *Globalization, Communications and Caribbean Identity* edited by Hopeton Dunn. Kingston, Jamaica: Ian Randle Publishers, 1995.
Buvuniæ, Mayra and Andrew R. Morrison. "Living in a More Violent World", *Foreign Policy*, 118 (2000): 58-72.
Cock, Jacklyn. "Gun Violence and Masculinity in South Africa", Robert Morrell (ed.) *Changing Men in Southern Africa*. London: Zed Books, 2001.
Demers, David P. *Global Media: Menace or Messiah?* New Jersey: Hampton press, Cresskill, 1999.
Downes, Aviston. "Boys of the Empire: Elite Education and the Socio-Cultural Construction of Hegemonic Masculinity in Barbados, 1875-1920" in R. Reddock (ed). *Interrogating Caribbean Masculinities*. The UWI Press, Kingston, 2003.
Dunn, Hopeton (ed). *Globalization, Communications and Caribbean Identity*, Jamaica: Ian Randle Publishers, 1995.
Ferguson, Harry, Jeff Hearn, Øystein Gullvåg Holter, Lars Jalmert, Michael Kimmel, James Lang, Robert Morrell. *Ending Gender-based Violence: A Call to Action to involve men: A Summary of Research*. Stockholm, SIDA, 2004.

Girvan, Norman. "Globalisation and Counter-Globalisation: The Caribbean in the Context of the South." In *Globalisation: A Calculus of Inequality: Perspectives from the South* edited by Dennis Benn and Kenneth Hall, 65-87. Kingston: Ian Randle Publishers, 2000.

Green, Charles. *Manufacturing Powerlessness in the Black Diaspora: Inner-city Youth and the New Global Frontier.* Walnut Creek: Altamira Press, 2001.

Gunst, Laurie. *Born Fi' Dead: A Journey through the Jamaican Posse Underworld.* New York: Henry Holt, 1986.

Harcourt, W. "Editorial: The Global Network Society: New Freedoms or Old Limitations?" *Development*, Special Issue—*Mediating Citizenship in the Global Network Society*, 46 (1) (2003): 9-16.

Hobsbawm, Eric and Terence Tanger (eds). (1983). *The Invention of Tradition,* Cambridge University Press, Cambridge.

Holmberg Carl B.. *Sexualities and Popular Culture, Sage Publications, California,* 1998.

Hosein, Gabrielle. *Gender, Generation and Negotiation: Adolescence and Young Indo-Trinidadian Women's Identities in the late 20th Century* (Unpublished), 2003.

—— Personal Communication, 2006.

Girls Women and the Media Web-site "What the Problem? Facts about Women, Girls and the Media." Accessed June 2, 2011. http://www.mediaand women.org/problem.html

International Herald Tribune."Editorial: Inching Toward Trade Fairness", August 16-17, 2003, p. 6.

International Monetary Fund. "Globalization: A Framework for IMF Involvement", IMF Issues paper, 02/01. Accessed June 2011. http:// www.imf.org/np/exr/ib/2002/031502.htm

Jain, Devaki. 'Nuancing Globalisation or Mainstreaming the Downstream or Reforming Reform', Working Paper No. 3 May, CGDS, Cave Hill, UWI, 2000.

Khan, Shireen. "The Ugliness of Beauty Contests: The Miss Indias these days do not look or act very "Indian"" in *Little India,* April 16, 2003. Accessed June 2, 2011. http://www.littleindia.com/india/July2k/uglybeauty.htm.

Klak, Thomas. "Thirteen Theses on Globalization and Neo-Liberalism." In *Globalization and NeoLiberalism: The Caribbean Context* edited by Thomas Klak. Lanham: Rowman and Littlefield, 1998.

Kempadoo, Kamala. *Sexing the Caribbean: Gender, Race and Sexual Labour.* New York and London: Routledge, 2004.

Matthei, Linda and David A. Smith. "Globalization, Migration and the Shaping of Masculinity in Belize." In *Interrogating Caribbean Masculinities: Theoretical and Empirical Analyses* edited by Rhoda Reddock. Kingston: The UWI Press,2004.

Miller, Daniel. "The Young and the Restless in Trinidad: A Case of the Local and the Global in Mass Consumption." In *Consuming Technologies: Media and Information in Domestic Spaces* edited by R. Silverstone and E. Hirsch. London: Routledge, 1992.

Maxwell, Marina Omawale. "Our Revolutions Must be Different." In *Washerwoman Hangs her Poems in the Su: Poems by Women in Trinidad and Tobago edited by* Margaret Watts. self-published, Maraval, 1990.

Mishra, Pankaj. "New Left seeks a Chinese Way on Welfare", *International Herald Tribune,* October 14-15, (2006), p. 2.

Moghadam, Valentine. "Gender and Globalization: Female Labour and Women's Mobilization." *Journal of World Systems Research,* 5(2) (2002): 301-314.

Mohammed-Cherif, Ferjani. "World Plurality and 'War of Cultures,' *CODESRIA Bulletin*, (3 and 4)(2001):6.

Nederveen Pieterse, Jan. "Globalization as Hybridization" Working Paper Series No. 152, Institute of Social Studies, The Hague, The Netherlands, June 1993.

Petras, James and Henry Veltmeyer. *Globalization Unmasked: Imperialism in the 21st Century*. London: Fernwood Publishing, Nova Scotia and Zed Books,2001.

Peiss, Kathy. *Hope in a Jar: The Making of America's Beauty Culture*. New York: Metropolitan Books, *1998*.

Reddock, Rhoda. "Caribbean Masculinities and Femininities: The Impact of Globalisation on Cultural Representations." In *Gender in the 21st Century: Caribbean Perspectives, Visions and Possibilities* edited by Barbara Bailey and Elsa Leo-Rhynie. Kingston: Ian Randle Publishers, 2004.

Robertson, R. *Globalization: Social Theory and Global Culture*. London: Sage Publications, 1992.

Saunders, Patricia, J. "Is not Everything Good to Eat, Good to Talk: Sexual Economy and Dancehall Music in the Global Marketplace." *Small Axe*, No. 13, March 2003.

Shade, L.R. "Who's Global Knowledge? Women Navigating the Net." *Development*, Special Issue—*Mediating Citizenship in the Global Network Society*, 46, (1) (2003): 49-53.

UNDP China and China Institute for Reform and Development. *China Human Development Report: Development with Equity*. UNDP, 2005.

UNESCO Press. "UNESCO in a Globalising World", Executive Board paper, 159 EX/40, Paris, April 28, 2000.

Watkins, Kevin. "Stumbling toward Disaster: The Trade Charade." *International Herald Tribune*, August 16-17, 2003.

Weber, Thomas, J. and Ewart C. Skinner. "Theorizing Reggae and Small Media: Social Movements in Globalisation." In *Culture and Mass Communication in the Caribbean: Domination, Dialogue and Dispersion* edited by Humphrey Regis. University Press of Florida, 2001.

WINAD (Women's Institute for Alternative Development). A Human Security Concern: The Traffick, Use and Misuse of Small Arms and Light Weapons in the Caribbean, 2006. (mimeo).

Wilk, R. (1996). "Connections and Contradictions: From the Crooked Tree Cashew Queen to Miss World Belize." In *Beauty Queens on the Global Stage: Gender, Contests, and Power* edited by B. Ballerino, C. Cohen, R. Wilk, and Stoeltje. London: Routledge, 1996.

CHAPTER 11
OLYMPICS, ATHLETICS AND BUILDING SOCIAL COHESION IN THE CARICOM

Annan, K. Speech by Kofi Annan, Former Secretary General of United Nations in 2002, "Sports Changes Lives." Bali Sports Foundation, 2010. Accessed June 24, 2011. http://www.stiffchilli.com/index.php/foundation.

Balassa, B. "Trade Liberalization and Revealed Comparative Advantage." *The Manchester School of Economic and Social Studies*, 33 (1965): 99-123.

Bernard, A. and M. Busse. "Who Wins the Olympic Games: Economic Resources and Medal Totals?" *Review of Economics and Statistics* 86 (2004): 413-417.

Bian, X. "Predicting Olympic Medal Counts: the Effects of Economic Development on Olympic Performance." *The Park Place Economist* 13 (2005): 37-44.

Bredemeier, B., and Shields, D. "Sports and Character Development." *Research Digest, President's Council on Physical Fitness and Sports,* 7(1) (2006): 1-8.

Cameron, M. and C. MacDougall."Crime Prevention through Sport and Physical Activity." In *Trends and Issues in Crime and Criminal Justice,* 165: 1-6. Canberra: Australian Institute of Criminology, 2000.

Carmichael, D. *Youth Sport vs. Youth Crime.* Brockville: Active Healthy Links Inc.,2008.

Cheeseman, I. *BBC Interview with Dwight Yorke.* BBC Radio Manchester, 18th December 2009. Accessed June 27, 2011. http://www. socawarriors.net/foreign-based/6774-bbc-interview-with-dwight-yorke.html.

China Daily News, September 6, 2008. Accessed June 23, 2011. http://www.chinadaily.com.cn/olympics/2008-09/06/content_7005208.html.

Delaney, L. and E. Keaney. *Sport and Social Capital in the United Kingdom: Statistical Evidence from National and International Survey Data.* Dublin: Economic and Social Research Institute, Institute for Public Policy Research, 2005.

Diana, A. "Youth at Play: Preventing Youth Problem Behaviour through Sport and Recreation." *Microform Publications.* Eugene: University of Oregon, 2000.

Foster, A. "Upgrades Are On Way at GC Foster." *Jamaica Gleaner,* October 5, 2008. Accessed June23, 2011. http://jamaica-gleaner.com/gleaner/20081005/sports/sports6.html.

Franklyn, D. "Sport in Jamaica: A Local and International Perspective." The Grace Kennedy Foundation Public Lecture Series. Kingston Jamaica, West Indies: Grace Kennedy Foundation, 2010.

Gatz, M., M.A Messner., and S.J. Ball-Rokeach. *Paradoxes of Youth and Sport.* SUNY series on Sport, Culture and RocialRelations. New York: State University of New York Press, 2002.

Girvan, N."Four Questions for Regional Integration." Paper presented at theConference on Economic Growth and Transformation, Mona, September 28-30, 2007.

Greenaway, D. and C. Milner. *Trade and Industrial Policy in Developing Countries—A Manual of Policy Analysis.*London: Macmillan, 1993.

Hartmann, D. "High School Sports Participation and Educational Attainment: Recognizing, Assessing, and Utilizing the Relationship." Report to LA84 Foundation. University of Minnesota, Department of Sociology, 2008.

Hawkins, B."Evening Basketball Leagues: The Use of Sport to Reduce African American Youth Criminal Activity." *International Sports Journal,* 2 (1998)(2): 68-77.

Hinloopen, J. and van Marrewijk.C. "On the Empirical Distribution of the Balassa Index." *Review of World Economics,* 137 (2001): 1-35.

Howell, J.C. *Guide for Implementing the Comprehensive Strategy for Serious, Violent and Chronic Juvenile Offenders.* Washington, D.C: Department of Justice, Office of Juvenile Justice and Delinquency Prevention, 1995.

Irving, R. and Charlton.V. "Searching for the Secrets of Jamaica's Track and Field Success." *News from the University of the West Indies, Mona Campus* (2009): 26-28.

Jamieson, L.M. and S.A. Wolter. *Sport in the City.* Conference proceedings. Leisure Industries Research Centre. Sheffield Hallam University, U.K. July 2-4, (1998): 280-294.

Jamieson, L.M. and C.M. Ross."Research Update: Using Recreation to Curb Extremism." *Parks and Recreation Magazine,* 26 (2007): 28-29.

Joseph, K. "Focus on Sport as Community Development Initiative." *Olympism.* June 5, 2009. Accessed June24, 2011.http://svgnoc.org/blogs/olympism.

King, T.C., L. Valerius, and J.R. Collins. "Ground Zero: A Collaborative Substance Abuse Prevention and Intervention Programme for At-risk Adolescent." *Journal of Parks and Recreation,* 16 (3) (1998): 81-94.

Kvalsund, P. "Sport and Peace Building." Paper presented at the 3rd Magglingen Conference on Sport and Development, Geneva, Switzerland, December 2006.

Larkin, A. *Sport and Recreation and Community Building: Literature Review.* Sydney: NSWASR, 2008. Accessed June 27, 2011. http://www.dsr. nsw.gov.au/assets/pubs/industry/study_community building.pdf –

Levermore, R. and A. Beacom. *Sport and International Development.* Palgrave MacMillan, 2009.

Lowrie, T. "How UTech Revolutionized Jamaican Athletics." *Jamaica Observer,* August 24, 2008. Accessed June 27, 2011. https://www.jamaicaobserver.com/news/139402_How-UTech-revolutionised-J-can-athletics.

Ministry of Culture, Youth and Recreation, Saskatchewan. *The Impact of Culture/Arts, Sport and Recreation on Anti-Social Behaviour in Youth: Evidence and Analysis.* Research paper. Strategic Policy and Youth Branch, Ministry of Culture, Youth and Recreation. Province of Saskatchewan, 2003.

Ogi, A. "International Year of Sport and Education." Interview by Jean Michel Jakobowicz, UN Special No. 635, April 2005. Accessed June 27, 2011.http://www.unspecial.org/UNS639/t21en.html

Papoutsy, M. "The Spirit of the Olympics." Hellenic Communication Service, June 26, 2004. Accessed June 27, 2011. http://www. helleniccomserve.com/olympicspirit.html.

Percival, D. "The Power of Jamaica's Track Success." *The Courier,* 2009. Accessed August 11, 2011. http://www.acp-eucourier.info/The-power-of-Jamaica.698.0.html

Ricardo, D. *On the Principles of Political Economy and Taxation.* Variorum edition. In *Works and Correspondence of DavidRicardo, Vol. I.* edited by P. Sraffa. Cambridge: CambridgeUniversity Press, 1951 [orig. London: John Murray, 1817].

Robinson, P.L. *Jamaican Athletics: A Model for 2012 Olympics and the World.* London: Arcadia Books, 2007.

Sheehan, K., J.A. DiCara, S. LeBailly, and K.K. Christoffel. "Adapting the Gang Model: Peer Mentoring for Violence Prevention." *Pediatrics* 104 (2000):50-54.

Soubbotina, T.P. and K.A. Sheram. *Beyond Economic Growth: Meeting the Challenges of Global Development.* Washington: World Bank Development Education Program, 2000.

Sport England."The Value of Sport." *Published by Sport England.* June 1999. Accessed June 24, 2011. http://book.coe.int/ftp/2388.pdf.

Sport for Development and Peace International Working Group. *Harnessing the Power of Sport for Development and Peace: Recommendations to Governments.*2008. Accessed June 22, 2011. http://www.un.org/wcm/webdav/site/sport/shared/sport/pdfs/Final%20 SDP%20IWG%20Report.pdf.

St. Vincent and Grenadines National Olympic Committee (SVGNOC). "CARICOM Sports Commission—An Urgent Necessity." March 13, 2008. Accessed June 27, 2011. http://www.svgnoc.org.

Tcha, M. and V. Pershin. "Reconsidering Performance at the Summer Olympics and Revealed Comparative Advantage." *Journal of Sports Economics,* 4 (3) (2003): 216-239.

Townsend, D."Trouble in Paradise." *Foreign Policy*. March 11, 2010. Accessed June 22, 2011. http://www.foreignpolicy.com/articles/2010/03/11/trouble_in_paradise.

UNAIDS and World Health Organization. *AIDS Epidemic Update.*2009. Accessed June 23, 2011. http://data.unaids.org/pub/Report/2009/JC1700_Epi_Update_2009_en. pdf.

United Nations. *Overcoming Barriers: Human Mobility and Development. Human Development Report, 2009*. Accessed June 24, 2011. http://hdr.undp.org/en/media/HDR_2009_EN_Complete.pdf.

United Nations Children Fund. *Sport for Development in Latin America and the Caribbean.* UNICEF Regional Office for Latin America and the Caribbean, Panama, 2007. Accessed June 27, 2011. http://www.unicef.org/lac/deporte_para_el_desarrollo_ing(1).pdf.

United Nations Inter-Agency Task Force on Sport for Development and Peace. *Sport for Development and Peace Towards Achieving the Millennium Development Goals.* New York: United Nations, 2003. Accessed June 27, 2011. https://www.un.org/wcm/webdav/site/sport/shared/sport/pdfs/task%20force%20report%20english.pdf.

United Nations Office on Drugs and Crime. Press conference on Global Sport Fund of United Nations Office on Drugs and Crime. New York: United Nations. Department of Public Information. News and Media Division. December 12, 2007. Accessed June 27, 2011. http://www.un.org/News/briefings/docs/2007/071212_UNODC.doc.htm.

— — World Drug Report, 2009. New York: United Nations, 2009. Accessed June 18, 2011. http://www. unodc.org/documents/wdr/WDR_2009/WDR2009_eng_web.pdf.

— — World Drug Report, 2010. New York: United Nations Office on Drugs and Crime, 2010. Accessed June 22, 2011. http://www.unodc.org/documents/wdr/WDR_2010/World_Drug_ Report_2010_lo-res.pdf.

Winther, N. and P. Currie. "Northern Fly-In Sports Camps: A joint sport development/crime prevention project." Paper presented at the North American Society for the Sociology of Sport Conference. Edmonton, Alberta. November 5, 1987.

World Development Indicators (various years). Accessed June 24, 2011. http://databank.worldbank.org.

CHAPTER 12

SOCIAL-PSYCHOLOGICAL DIMENSIONS OF CARIBBEAN FAMILY LIFE: SUSTAINABLE HUMAN DEVELOPMENT

Achenbach, T.M. "Cross-cultural Perspectives on Developmental Psychopathology". In *Childhood and Adolescence: Cross-cultural Perspectives and Applications* edited by U.P. Gielen and J. Roopnarine, 411-429. Westport, CT: Praeger, 2004.

Anderson, P. *The Changing Roles of Fathers in the Context of Jamaican Family Life.*

Arnold, E. "Issues in Re-unification of Migrant West Indian Children in the United Kingdom." In *Caribbean Families: Diversity among Ethnic Groups* edited by J.L. Roopnarine and J. Brown, 243-258. Norwood, NJ: Ablex, 1997.

Aunola, K., and Nurmi, J.E. "The Role of Parenting Styles in Children's Problem Behaviour." *Child Development*, 76 (2005): 1144-1159.

Barrow, C. *Family in the Caribbean: Themes and Perspectives.* Kingston: Ian Randle, 1996.

Baumrind, D. "Child Care Practices Anteceding Three Patterns of Preschool Behaviour." *Genetic Psychology Monographs,* 75 (1967): 43-88.

Beckles, H. *Natural Rebels: A Social History of Enslaved Black Women in Barbados.* London: Zed Books, 1989.

—— *Black Masculinity in Caribbean Slavery.* Paper presented at the Construction of Caribbean Masculinity: Towards a Research Agenda Symposium. Trinidad and Tobago, January11-13, 1996.

Belfer, M.L., and Rhode, L.A. "Mental Health in Latin America and the Caribbean: Problems, Progress, and Policy Research." *Pan American Journal of Public Health,* 18 (2005): 359-365.

Blum, R.W., Halcon, L., Beuhring, T., Pate, E., Campell-Forrester, S., and Venema, A. "Adolescent Health in the Caribbean: Risk and Protective Factors." *American Journal of Public Health,* 93(2003): 456-460.

Bosmans, G., Braet, C., Beyers, W., Van Leeuwen *et al.*, "Power Assertive Discipline and Internalizing Problems in Adolescents: The Role of Attachment." *Parenting Science and Practice,* 11 (2011): 34-55.

Bonomi A.E., Anderson M.L., Rivara F.P., *et al.* "Health Outcomes in Women with Physical and Sexual Intimate Partner Violence Exposure." *Journal of Women's Health* 16 (2007): 987–997.

Brenning, K., Soenens, B., Braet, C., Bosmans, G. "The Role Of Depressogenic Personality and Attachment in the Intergenerational Similarity of Depressive Symptoms: A Study with Early Adolescents and their Mothers." *Personality and Social Psychology Bulletin.* 37 (2) (2011): 284-297.

Brerton, B. "The Experience of Indentureship: 1845-1917. In *Calcutta to Caroni: The East Indians of Trinidad* edited by J. La Guerre, 25-38. London: Longman Caribbean, 1974.

Brown, J., Anderson, P., and Chevannes, B. *The Contribution of Caribbean Men to the Family.* Report for the International Development Centre, Canada. Caribbean Child Development Centre, Mona: University of the West Indies, 1993.

Brown, J., Newland, A., Anderson, P., and Chevannes, B. In *Caribbean Families: Diversity among Ethnic Groups* edited by J.L. Roopnarine and J. Brown, 85-113. Norwood, NJ: Ablex, 1997.

Brunod, R., and Cook-Darzens, S. "Men's Role and Fatherhood in French Caribbean Families: A Multi-Systemic Resource Approach." *Clinical Child Psychology and Psychiatry,* 7(2002): 559-569.

Chao, R. "Extending Research on the Consequences of Parenting Style for Chinese Americans and European Americans." *Child Development,* 72(2001): 1832-1843.

Chen, Z., Liu, M., and Li, D. "Parental Warmth, Control, and Indulgence and their Relations to Adjustment in Chinese Children: A Longitudinal Study." *Journal of Family Psychology,* 14(2000): 401-419.

Child Protection Section UNICEF Regional Office for Latin America and the Caribbean (2006). *Violence against Children in the Caribbean: Regional Assessment.* Accessed May 10, 2011. http://www.uwi.edu/ccdc/downloads/Violence_against_children.pdf,

Craton, M. "Changing Patterns of Slave Families in the British West Indies." *Journal of Interdisciplinary History,* X (1979): 1-35.

Crawford-Brown, C. "The Impact of Parent-Child Socialization on the Development of Conduct Disorder in Jamaican Male Adolescents." In

Caribbean Families: Diversity among Ethnic Groups edited by J.L. Roopnarine and J. Brown, 205-222. Norwood, NJ: Ablex, 1997.

Culp, R.E., Little V., Letts, D., and Lawrence, H. "Maltreated Children's Self-Concept: Effects of a Comprehensive Treatment Program." *American Journal of Orthopsychiatry, 61*(1991): 114-121.

Davies, P. T, Harold, G.T., Goeke-Morey, M.C., Cummings, E.M. "Child Emotional Security and Interparental Conflict." *Monographs of the Society for Research in Child Development*, 67(3) (2002):1–104.

Deen, S. Research into Indian Family History in Trinidad. Paper presented at ISER-NCIC Conference on Challenge and Change. University of the West Indies, St. Augustine, Trinidad, 1995.

Desai, S., Dubey, A., Joshi, B., Sen, M., Sharrif, A., and Vannenman, R. *Human Development in India Challenges for a Society in Transition.* New York, NY: Oxford University Press, 2010.

Dominelli, L. *Revitalizing Communities in a Globalizing World.* Aldershot, UK: Ashgate, 2007.

Dutton, D.G. "The Complexities of Domestic Violence." *American Psychologist, 62* (2007): 708-709.

Durbrow, E.H. "Cultural Processes in Child Competence: How Rural Caribbean Parents Evaluate their Children." In *Cultural Processes in Child Development: The Minnesota Symposia on Child Psychology,* edited by A.S. Masten, pp. 97-121. Mahwah, NJ: Erlbaum, 1999.

Eckenrode, J., Laird, M., and Doris, J. "School Performance and Disciplinary Problems among Abused and Neglected Children." *Developmental Psychology, 29 (1993)*: 53-62.

Edwards, V.J., Holden, G.W., Felitti, V.J., *et al.* "Relationship between Multiple Forms of Childhood Maltreatment and Adult Mental Health in Community Respondents: Results from the Adverse Childhood Experiences Study." *American Journal of Psychiatry,* 160(2003): 1453-1460.

Ellsberg M, Jansen HA, Heise L, Watts CH, Garcia-Moreno C; WHO Multi-country Study on Women's Health and Domestic Violence against Women Study Team. Intimate Partner Violence and Women's Physical and Mental Health in the WHO Multi-country Study on Women's Health and Domestic Violence: An Observational Study. *Lancet,* 361 (2008): 1165-1172.

Engle, P., Black, M.M., Behrman, J.R., Cabral de Mello, M., Gertler, P.J., Kapirri, L. *et al.* Strategies to Avoid Loss of Developmental Potential in More Than 200 Million Children in the Developing World." *Lancet,* 369(2007): 229-242.

Frazier, E.F. *The Negro family in the United States.* New York: Dryden Press, 1951.

Garcia-Moreno, C., Jansen, H.A. F.M., Ellsbery, M., Heise, L., and Watts, C.H. "Prevalence of Intimate-partner Violence: Evidence from the WHO Multi-Country Study on Women's Health and Domestic Violence. *Lancet,* 368(2006): 1260-1269.

Garno, J.L., Goldberg, J.F., Rameriz, P.M., and Ritzler, B.A. "Impact of Childhood Abuse on the Clinical Course of Bipolar Disorder." *British Journal of Psychiatry,* 186(2005): 121-125.

Gershoff, E.T. "Corporal Punishment by Parents and Associated Child Behaviours and Experiences: A Meta-Analytic and Theoretical Review." *Psychological Bulletin,* 128(2002): 539-579.

Greenfield, P.M. "Three Approaches to the Psychology of Culture: Where Do they Come From? Where Can they go?" *Asian Journal of Social Psychology,* 3(2000): 223-240.

Handwerker, W.P. "Power and Gender: Violence and Affection Experienced by Children in Barbados, West Indies." *Medical Anthropology,* 17(1996): 101-128.

Haniff, N.Z. Male Violence Against Men and Women in the Caribbean: The Case of Jamaica". *Journal of Comparative Family Studies,* 29(1998): 361-369.

Heyman, R.E. and Slep, A.M.S. "Do Child Abuse and Interparental Violence Lead to Adulthood Family Violence?" *Journal of Marriage and Family,* 64 (2002): 864-870.

Higman, B. "Household Structure and Fertility on Jamaican Slave Plantation: A Nineteenth Century Example". *Population Studies,* 27(1973): 527-550.

Jayawardena, C. *Conflict and Solidarity in a Guyanese Plantation.* London: University of London, Athlone, 1963.

Kalmuss, D. "The Intergenerational Transmission of Marital Aggression". *Journal of Marriage and the Family,* 46(1984): 11–19.

Kim-Cohen, J., Caspi, A., Moffitt, T.E., *et al.* "Prior Juvenile Diagnoses in Adults with Mental Disorder." *Archives of General Psychiatry,* 60(2003): 709-717

Kingston, Jamaica: Planning Institute of Jamaica and the University of the West Indies, 2007.

Lamb, M.E. (ed). *The Role of the Father in Child Development (5th edition).* Hoboken, NJ: Wiley, 2010.

Lansford, J.E., Chang, L., Dodge, K.A., Malone, P S., Oburu, P., Palmerus, K., Bacchini, D., Pastorelli, C., Bombi, A.S., Zelli, A., Tapanya, S., Chaudhary, N., Deater-Deckard, K., Manke, B., and Quinn, N. "Physical Discipline and Children's Adjustment: Cultural Normativeness as a Moderator". *Child Development,* 76(2005): 134-1236.

Leo-Rhynie, E. "Class, Race, and Gender Issues in Child Rearing in the Caribbean. In *Caribbean Families: Diversity Among Ethnic Groups* edited by J.L. Roopnarine, 25-55. Norwood, NJ: Ablex, 1997.

McLoyd, V.C., Kaplan, R., Hardaway, C., and Wood, D. "Does Endorsement of Physical Discipline Matter? Assessing Moderating Influences on the Maternal and Child Psychological Correlates of Physical Discipline in African American Families". *Journal of Family Psychology,* 21(2) (2007): 165-175.

Melancon, C. and Gagne, M.H. "Fathers' and Mothers' Psychological Violence and Adolescent Behavioural Adjustment." *Journal of Interpersonal Violence,* 26(2011): 991-1011.

Milbourn, P., Sharpe, J. Samms-Vaughn, M. "Child and Adolescent Psychiatry." In *Images of Psychiatry in the Caribbean* edited by F. Hickling and E. Sorel. World Psychiatric Association, 2005.

Mohammed, P. "The Idea of Childhood and Age of Sexual Maturity among Indians in Trinidad: A Sociohistorical Scrutiny." In *Caribbean Families: Diversity among ethnic groups* (pp. 115-146) edited by J.L. Roopnarine and J. Brown. Norwood, NJ: Ablex.

Mouton CP. "Intimate Partner Violence and Health Status Among Older Women." *Violence Women,* 9(2003): 1465–1477.

Narine, L. Trinidad and Tobago Child and Family Health Study. Report to the Family Development and Children's Research Centre and the University of the West Indies, St. Augustine, Trinidad and Tobago, 2011.

Nettles, K. "Homework: An Examination of the Sexual Division of Labour in Urban Households of the East Indian and African Guyanese". *Journal of Comparative Family Studies,* 26(1995): 427-441.

Nsamenang, B.A. "Fathers, Families, and Children's Well-becoming in Africa."

In *The Role of the Father in Child Development*. edited by M.E. Lamb. Hoboken, 388-412. NJ: Wiley, 2010.

Nevadomsky, J. "Changes Over Time and Space in the East Indian Family in Rural Trinidad". *Journal of Comparative Family Studies,* 11(1980): 433-456.

Ogbu, J. "Origins of Human Competence: A Cultural Ecological Perspective". *Child Development,* 52(1981): 413-429.

Pant, P., Roopnarine, J.L., Krishnakumar, A. *Parenting Styles among Indo-Guyanese Fathers: Links to Early Cognitive and Social Development*. Paper presented at the Society for Cross-Cultural Research, New Orleans, 2008.

Patterson, O. *The Sociology of Slavery: An Analysis of the Origins, Development and Structure of Negro Slave Society in Jamaica*. London: McGibbon and Kee, 2008.

Pottinger, A.M. "Children's Experience of Loss by Parental Migration in Inner-city. Jamaica". *American Journal of Orthopsychiatry,* 75(2005): 485-496.

Ramdin, R. *Arising from Bondage: A History of the Indo-Caribbean People*. New York: New York University Press, 2000.

Randle, A.A. and Graham, C.A. "A Review of the Evidence on the Effects of Intimate Partner Violence on Men", *Psychology of Men and Masculinity,* 12(2011): 97-111.

Rauf, M.A.. *Indian Village in Guyana: A Study of Cultural Change and Ethnic Identity*. Leiden, Netherlands: E.J. Brill, 1974.

Reddock, R. *Women, Labour, and Politics in Trinidad and Tobago: A History*. London: Zed Books, 1994.

Reynolds, T. "Caribbean Young People, Family Relationships and Social Capital", Special Issue: Social Capital, Migration and Transnational Families. *Journal of Ethnic and Racial Studies,* 29(2006): 1087-1103.

Reynolds, A.J., Temple, J.A., Robertson, D.L., and Mann, E.A. "Age 21 Cost-benefit Analysis of the Title 1 Chicago Child-parent Centers". *Education Evaluation and Policy Analysis,* 24(2002): 267-303.

Rohner, R.P., Kean, K, J., and Cournoyer, D.E. "Effects of Corporal Punishment, Perceived Caretaker Warmth, and Cultural Beliefs on the Psychological Adjustment of Children in St. Kitts, West Indies." *Journal of Marriage and the Family,* 53(1991): 681-693.

Roopnarine, J.L. "Fathers in Caribbean Cultural Communities". In *Fathers in Cultural Context* edited by D. Shwalb, B. Shwalb, and M.E. Lamb. New York: Routledge, in press.

Roopnarine, J.L., and Hossain Z. "African American and African Caribbean Fathers". In *Handbook of Father Involvement* edited by C. Tamis-LeMonda and N. Cabrera, New York: Psychology Press 2012.

Roopnarine, J.L. and Evans, M., and Pant, P. "Parent-child Relationships in African and Indo-Caribbean Families: A Social Psychological Assessment." In *Social Psychological Dynamics,* edited by D. Chadee and A. Kostic. Mona, Jamaica: University of the West Indies Press, 2011.

Roopnarine, J.L., and Krishnakumar, A. "Childrearing Beliefs and Practices in Trinidad and Tobago and Childhood Outcomes". Report to the Family Development and Children's Research Centre and the University of the West Indies, St. Augustine, Trinidad and Tobago, 2011.

—— "Parenting Styles and Childhood Outcomes in Trinidadian and Guyanese Families". Unpublished manuscript, Syracuse University, 2010.

Roopnarine, J., Snell-White, P., Riegraf, N., Wolfsenberger, J., Hossain, Z., and Mathur, S. "Family Socialization in an East Indian Village in Guyana: A Focus on Fathers". In *Caribbean Families: Diversity among Ethnic Groups* edited by J.L. Roopnarine and J. Brown. Norwood, 57-83. NJ: Ablex, 1997.

Samms-Vaughn, M. *The Jamaican Pre-school Child: The Status of Early Childhood*

Development in Jamaica. Kingston, Jamaica: Planning Institute of Jamaica, 2005.

Samuel, P.S., and Wilson, L.C. "Structural Arrangements of Indo-Guyanese Family: An Assessment of the Assimilation Hypothesis". *Journal of Comparative Family Studies,* 40(2009): 439-454.

Sargent, C. and Harris, M. "Gender Ideology, Childrearing, and Child Health in Jamaica." *American Ethnologist,* 19(1992): 523-537.

Sharma, K.N. "Changing Forms of East Indian Marriage and Family Form in the Caribbean". *The Journal of Sociological Studies,* 5(1986): 20-58.

Sharpe, J. and Mohamed, N. "Mental Health in Early Childhood". In *Issues and Perspectives in Early Childhood Education in the Caribbean* edited by C. Logie and J.L. Roopnarine, La Romaine: Caribbean Publishers (in press).

Sinha, D. "Indigenizing psychology". In *Handbook of Cross-Cultural Psychology: Theory and Method* (Volume 1) edited by J. Berry, Y.H. Poortinga, and J. Pandey, Boston: Allyn and Bacon, 1997.

Smith, R.T. *The Matrifocal Family: Power, Pluralism, and Politics*. London: Routledge, 1996.

Sorkhabi, N. "Applicability of Baumrind's Parent Typology to Collective Cultures: Analysis of Cultural Explanations of Parent Socialization Effects". *International Journal of Behavioural Development,* 29(2005): 552-563.

Soyibo, K., Lee, M.G. "Domestic and School Violence Among High School Students in Jamaica". *West Indian Medical Journal,* 49(2000): 232-236.

Spooner, M. "Does Eligibility for Protection Orders Prevent Repeat Abuse of Domestic Abuse Victims in Caribbean States?" *Journal of Family Violence,* 24(2009): 377-387.

Stith, S.M., Rosen, K.H., Middleton, K.A., Busch, A.L., Lundeberg, K., and Carlton, R.P. "The Intergenerational Transmission of Spouse Abuse: A Meta-analysis". *Journal of Marriage and Family,* 62(2000): 640-654.

Straus, M.A. "Sexual Inequality, Cultural Norms, and Wife Beating", *Victimology,* 1(1976): 45-70.

Super, C. and Harkness, S. "The Cultural Structuring of Child Development". In *Handbook of Cross-Cultural Psychology. Vol. 2: Basic Processes and Human Development* (pp. 1-39) edited by J. Berry, P. Dasen, T. Saraswathi, Needham, MA: Allyn and Bacon, 1997.

Thornberry, T.P. "Explaining Multiple Patterns of Offending Across the Life Course and Across Generations". *The Annals of the American Academy of Political and Social Science,* 602(2005): 156-195.

Treyvaud, K., Anderson, V.A., Lee, K.J., Woodward, L.J., Newnham, C., Inder, T.E., Doyle, L.W., and Anderson, P.J. "Parental Mental Health and Early Socio-Emotional Development of Children Born Very Preterm". *Journal of Pediatric Psychology,* 35(2010): 768-777.

Wasik, B.H., Villagomez, A., Berry, S., and Mulholkar, P. "Home Visiting's Role in Early Childhood Education". In *Approaches to early childhood education* (6th edition) edited by J.L. Roopnarine and J.E. Johnson, Columbus, OH: Pearson Education, in press.

WHO-AIMS Report on Mental Health Systems in the Caribbean Region. Pan American Health Organization, Regional Office of the World Health Organization. Canadian International Development Agency, 2011.

Williams, S., Brown, J., and Roopnarine, J.L. Childrearing in the Caribbean. Technical Report, Caribbean Child Support Initiative. Barbados, 2006.

Wilson, L.C., Wilson, C.M., and Johnson, B.M. "Race and Health in Guyana: An Empirical Assessment from Survey Data". *Caribbean Studies*, 38(2010): 37-58.

World Health Organization. *Intimate Partner Violence*, 2002. Accessed May 10, 2011. http://www.who.int/violence_injury_ prevention/violence/world_report/factsheet/en/index.html

CHAPTER 13

FORGING A NEW ONTOLOGY OF FAMILIAL CARE IN THE CARIBBEAN

Airhihenbuwa, Collins O. *Healing Our Differences: The Crisis of Global Health and the Politics of Identity*. Lanham, Boulder and New York: Rowman and Littlefield Publishers, Inc., 2007.

Amnesty International. *Aftershocks: Women Speak Out Against Violence in Haiti's Camps*. London: Amnesty International, 2011.

Caribbean Development Bank. Annual Report, 2010. Barbados: Wildey, 2011.

CARICOM. "The Caribbean Regional Strategic Framework for HIV/AIDS." Accessed on September 28, 2011. http://www.caricom.org/jsp/projects/hiv-aidsstrategicframework.pdf

Division for the Advancement of Women, United Nations, *The Equal Sharing of Responsibilities Between Women and Men, Including Care Giving in the Context of HIV/AIDS*. Report of the Expert Group Meeting. EMG/ESOR/2008/Report

Folbre, Nancy. *The Invisible Heart: Economics and Family Values*. New York: The New Press, 2001.

Gullí, Bruno. *Earthly Plenitudes: A Study on Sovereignty and Labour*. Philadelphia: Temple University Press, 2010.

Human Rights Watch, "A Test of Inequality: Discrimination of Women Living with HIV in the Dominican Republic," Report. 16(4) (2004).

ITUC. "US$ 8 Billion More Needed to Fight HIV-AIDS, Unions Call for More Workplace Action." Online Press Release 129, June 24, 2011.

Makhijani, Arjun. *Manifesto For Global Democracy: Two Essays on Imperialism and the Struggle for Freedom*. New York: The Apex Press, 2004.

UNAIDS. Factsheet: Caribbean, November 23, 2010. Online edition, Accessed September 28, 2011. http://www.unaids.org/documents/20101123_FS_carib_em_en.pdf.

—— *The Status of HIV in the Caribbean*. Trinidad, 2010a.

—— *Report on the Global AIDS Epidemic*. UNAIDS, 2010b. Accessed September 28, 2011. http://www.unaids.org/globalreport/global_report.htm.

UNODC and World Bank, *Crime, Violence, and Development: Trends, Costs, and Policy Options in the Caribbean*. A Joint Report by the United Nations Office on Drugs and Crime and the Latin America and Caribbean Region of the World Bank, Report No. 37820, 2007.

World Bank. *World Development Indicators* 2011. Online edition. Accessed September 28, 2011. http://data.worldbank.org/data-catalog/world-development-indicators.

CHAPTER 14
BETWEEN CAFÉ AND CIGARILLOS: NOTES TOWARDS MAPPING THE RESEARCH TRAJECTORY AND THE INTELLECTUAL LEGACY OF FERNANDO ORTIZ THROUGH A STUDY OF HIS SELECT WORKS

Beltrán, Gonzalo Aguirre, *El proceso de aculturación*. Mexico: Universidad Nacional Autónoma de México, 1957.

Byron, Lord George. *The Island or Christian and his comrades*. 3rd edition. London: John Hunt, 1823.

Castellanos, Jorge. *Pioneros de la etnografía afrocubana*. Miami: Universal, 2003. Accessed May 18, 2011. http://www.hispanocubano.org/cas/pion3.pdf

Coronil, Fernando. "Transculturation and the politics of theory: Countering the Center, Cuban Counterpoint". Introduction to *Cuban Counterpoint: Tobacco and Sugar*, ix-lvi. Durham and London: Duke University Press, 2003.

Ferri, Enrico. "The Positive School of Criminology." The first of three lectures delivered at the University of Naples on 22 April 1901. Published in Ferri, Enrico. *The Positive School of Criminology*. Translated by Ernest Untermann. Chicago: Charles H. Kerr & Company, 1908. Accessed August 9, 2011. Project Gutenberg http://www.gutenberg.org/files/10580/10580-h/10580-h.htm

— — 'Of Criminology', the second of three lectures delivered at the University of Naples on 23 April 1901. Published in Ferri, Enrico. *The Positive School of Criminology*. Translated by Ernest Untermann. Chicago: Charles H. Kerr & Company, 1908. Accessed August 9, 2011. Project Gutenberg http://www.gutenberg.org/files/10580/10580-h/10580-h.htm

Fernández Robaina, Tomás. "The Term *Afro-Cuban*: A Forgotten Contribution." In *Cuban Counterpoints: The Legacy of Fernando Ortiz*, edited by Mauricio A. Font and Alfonso W. Quiroz, 171-79. Lanham: Lexington Books, 2004.

Font, Mauricio A., Alfonso W. Quiroz and Pamela Maria Smorkaloff. "Introduction: The intellectual legacy of Fernando Ortiz." In *Cuban Counterpoints: The legacy of Fernando Ortiz*, edited by Mauricio A. Font and Alfonso W. Quiroz, xi-xix. Lanham: Lexington Books, 2005.

Gershenhorn, Jerry. *Melville J Herskovits and the Racial Politics of Knowledge*. Lincoln: University of Nebraska Press, 2004.

Ibarra, Jorge. "La herencia científica de Fernando Ortiz." *Revista Iberoamericana* (1990) 152-2:1339-51.

Klein, Richard. *Cigarettes are Sublime*. Britain: Picador, 1995.

Leo, Octavio di. "It All Started in Madrid." In *Cuban Counterpoints: The legacy of Fernando Ortiz*, edited by Mauricio A. Font and Alfonso W. Quiroz, 39-54. Lanham: Lexington Books, 2005.

Le Riverend, Julio. (ed). With a Selection of Texts and Prologue to *Órbita de Fernando Ortiz*. La Habana: Unión de Escritores y Artistas de Cuba, 1973.

Lombroso, Cesare. *Criminal Man According to the Classification of Cesare Lombroso Briefly Summarized by his Daughter Gina Lombroso Ferrero*. With an introduction by Cesare Lombroso. New York and London: G.P. Putnam's Sons The Knickerbocker Press, 1911.

Martí, José. *Nuestra América* originally published in *El Partido Liberal*, México, 30 January 1891. Reprinted in Simón Bolívar/José Martí, *Nuestra América*. Presentación de Ana Cecilia Lazcano Ramírez. Mexico: Universidad Nacional Autónoma de México, 2004.

Medina, Andrés. "La etnografía como reflexión en torno a la nación: tres experiencias." *Alteridades* 6(1993):67-72. Accessed July 25, 2011. http://www.uam-antropologia.info/alteridades/alt6-8-medina.pdf

Mintz, Sidney. *Sweetness and Power: The Place of Sugar in Modern History*. New York: Penguin, 1985.

Moore, Robin. "Representations of Afrocuban Expressive Culture in the Writings of Fernando Ortiz." *Latin American Music Review/Revista de Música Latinoamericana* 15: 32-54. Accessed July 22, 2011. http://www.jstor.org/stable/3085947

Ortiz, Fernando. *Hampa Afro-cubana: Los negros esclavos. Estudio sociológico y de derecho público*. Havana: Universal, 1916. Accessed May 20, 2001. http://www.archive.org/details/hampaafrocubana l00ortiuoft.pdf

—— *La africanía de la música folklórica de Cuba*. Havana: Ministerio de Educación, Dirección de Cultura/Ediciones Cárdenas y Cía, 1950.

—— *Los bailes y el teatro de los negros en el folklore de Cuba*. Havana: Ministerio de Educación, Dirección de Cultura/Ediciones Cárdenas y Cía, 1951.

—— *Los instrumentos de la música afrocubana*, 5 vols. Havana: Ministerio de Educación, 1952-5.

—— "Los cabildos afrocubanos" in *Órbita de Fernando Ortiz*, edited by Julio Le Riverend, 121-34. La Habana: Unión de Escritores y Artistas de Cuba, 1973.

—— *Contrapunteo cubano del tabaco y el azúcar*. Caracas: Ayacucho, 1978.

—— *Etnia y sociedad*. La Habana: Editorial de Ciencias Sociales, 1993.

—— "La transculturación de los tambores de los negros." In *Etnia y sociedad*, 181-8. La Habana: Editorial de Ciencias Sociales, 1993.

—— *Los tambores ararás/La conga*. Havana: Editorial Letras Cubanas, 1997.

—— *La africanía de la música folklórica cubana*. Habana: Editorial Letras Cubanas, 2001.

—— *Contrapunteo cubano del tabaco y el azúcar (Advertencia de sus contastes agrarios, económicos, históricos y socials, su etografía y su transculturación)*. Edited by Enrico Mario Santí. Madrid: Cátedra, 2002.

—— *Cuban Counterpoint: Tobacco and Sugar*. Translated by Harriet de Onís with a new introduction by Fernando Coronil. Durham and London: Duke University Press, 2003.

Rojas, Rafael. "Transculturation and Nationalism." In *Cuban Counterpoints: The Legacy of Fernando Ortiz*, edited by Mauricio A. Font and Alfonso W. Quiroz, 65-71. Lanham: Lexington Books, 2004.

Santí, Enrico María. Introduction to *Contrapunteo cubano del tabaco y el azúcar* 23-103. Madrid: Cátedra, 2002.

CHAPTER 15
THE HAITIAN CHALLENGE TO REGIONAL SECURITY: PREDICAMENTS OF A FAILED STATE

Brinkley, Douglas. "Democratic Enlargement: The Clinton Doctrine." *Foreign Policy*, 106 (1997): 110-127.

D'Agostino, Thomas J. "Caribbean Politics." In *Understanding Contemporary Caribbean* edited by Richard S. Hillman and Thomas J. D'Agostino, 85-147. Boulder, Co: Lyne Rienner, 2003.

Danns, George K. 1989. "Militarisation, Conflict and Co-operation", *The Security of the Caribbean: A Case Study*. London: The Centre for Security and Conflict Studies, 220: 21-32.

Democratic Forum, Unit for the Promotion of Democracy, Organization of American States, *One Year After the Return to Constitutional Government: The Challenges to Democratic Consolidation in Haiti.* Washington, D.C.: OAS, 1995.

Dobbins, James. "Charting Future U.S. Haiti Relations", 2004. Accessed April 18, 2011. http://www.rand.org/pubs/testimonies/2005/RAND_CT219.pdf

Fauriol, Georges A. "Haiti: The Failures of Governance." In *Latin American Politics and Development* edited by Howard J. Wiarda and Harvey F. Kline, 562-574. Boulder, Co: Westview, 1990.

Howland, Todd. 'Peacekeeping and Conformity with Human Rights Law: How MINUSTAH Falls Short in Haiti', *International Peacekeeping,* 13 (4) (2006): 462-476. Accessed April 7, 2011. http://www.minustah.org

Klak, Thomas. "Globalization, Neoliberalism and Economic Change in Central America and the Caribbean". In *Latin America Transformed: Globalization and Modernity* edited by Robert N. Gwynne and Cristóbal Kay, 67-92. London: Arnold, 2004.

Knight, Andy W. and Randolph B. Persuad. "Subsidiarity, Regional Governance and Caribbean Security", *Latin American Politics and Society,* 43 (1) (2001): 29-56.

Kreps, Sarah E. "The 1994 Haiti Intervention: A Unilateral Operation in Multilateral Clothes", *The Journal of Strategic Studies,* 30 (3) (2007): 449-474.

Langlais, Daniel P. *The OAS and the 2004 Haiti Crisis.* Washington, D.C.: Inter-American Defense College, Department of Studies, 2005.

Loesch, Jonathan E. *Averting Continuation of Failed U.S. Policy with Haiti.* U.S. Army War College, Strategy Research Project. Pennsylvania: Carlisle Barracks, 2001.

Logan, Rayford W. *The Diplomatic Relations of the United States with Haiti, 1776-1891.* Chapel Hill: University of North Carolina, 1971.

Miller, Jake C. *The Flight of the Haitian Refugees.* New York: Praeger, 1984.

Miller, Sara B. "Haiti's Chaos Reverberates for Expatriates in American Cities", *Christian Science Monitor,* 3 March 2004. Accessed April 7, 2011. http://www.csmonitor.com/2004/0303/p03s02-ussc.html

MINUSTAH, United Nations Stabilization Mission in Haiti, "Restoring a Secure and Stable Environment." Accessed April 7, 2011. http://www.un.org/en/peacekeeping/missions/minustah/

Muñiz, Humberto García and Jorge Rodríguez Beruff. "U.S. Military Policy toward the Caribbean in the 1990s." *Annals of the American Academy of Political and Social Science.* 533 (1994): 112-124.

Nicholls, David. *From Dessalines to Duvalier: Race, Colour, and National Independence in Haiti.* Cambridge: Cambridge University Press, 1979.

Perito, Robert and Greg Maly. *Haiti's Drug Problem.* Center for Post-Conflict Peace and Stability Operations, United States Institute of Peace, June 2007. Accessed April 7, 2011. http://www.usip.org/publications/haitis-drug-problem

Rotberg, Robert I. "Haiti's Past Mortgages Its Future." *Foreign Affairs,* 67 (1) (1988): 93-109.

Treaster, Joseph B. "Civilian Sworn in as Haiti's President." *New York Times* (New York), 14 March 1990.

Valenzuela, Arturo. *U.S. Policy Toward Latin America.* Testimony before the Subcommittee on the Western Hemisphere, Peace Corps, and Global Narcotics Affairs of the Senate Committee on Foreign Relations, Washington, D.C., Bureau of Western Hemisphere Affairs, Assistant Secretary. 17 February 2011. Accessed April 18, 2011. http://www.state.gov/p/wha/rls/rm/2011/156757.htm.

Wrobel, Paulo. "Failed Missions. Failed State". *The World Today*, 61 (2) (2005): 26-27.

CHAPTER 16
CRIME AND JUSTICE IN THE CARIBBEAN: THE CASE OF TRINIDAD AND TOBAGO

Deosaran, Ramesh. (ed). *Crime, Delinquency and Justice: A Caribbean Reader.* Kingston, Jamaica: Ian Randle Publishers, 2007.

Deosaran, Ramesh, Ramdhanie, I.K. and Lall, V. "Crime Statistics, Analysis and Policy Action in Trinidad and Tobago. (Special Research and Policy Reports on Crime Statistics, Community Policing and Police Performance in Trinidad and Tobago)." *Caribbean Journal of Criminology and Social Psychology*, 8(1 and 2) (2003): 1-60.

The Judiciary of the Republic of Trinidad and Tobago
http://www.ttlawcourts.org (July 22, 2011)

The Ministry of National Security—Trinidad and Tobago
http://www.nationalsecurity.gov.tt (July 22, 2011)

Trinidad and Tobago Ministry of Legal Affairs
http://www.legalaffairs.gov.tt (July 22, 2011)

CHAPTER 17
CRIME, VIOLENCE, AND THE GLOBAL PROLIFERATION OF TERRORISM: A DESCRIPTIVE OVERVIEW OF THE CARIBBEAN

Agozino, Biko, Ben Bowling, Elizabeth Ward and Godfrey St. Bernard. "Guns, Crime and Social Order in the West Indies." *Criminology and Criminal Justice*, 9(3)(2009): 287-305.

Albuquerque, Klaus de and Jerome McElroy. "Tourism and Crime in the Caribbean." *Annals of Tourism Research*, 26(4)(1999): 968-984.

Amnesty International International. "Jamaica: Deaths in Prison." 27 April 2000. Accessed January 3, 2000. http://www.amnesty.org/en/library/info/AMR38/003/2000/en

Arscott-Mills, Sharon. "Intimate Partner Violence in Jamaica." *Violence Against Women*, 7(11)(November 2001): 1284-1302.

Bagley, Bruce. "Globalisation and Latin American and Caribbean Organised Crime." *Global Crime*, 6(1)(February 2006): 32-53.

Bagoo, Andre. "CIA Terrorist on Trial." Trinidad and Tobago's Newsday, 6 February 2011. Accessed August 19, 2011. http://www.newsday.co.tt/sunday_special_report/0,135310.html

BBC Caribbean. "Jamaica 'Murder Capital of the World'." *BBC Caribbean.com*, 3 January 2006. Accessed March 1, 2012. http://www.bbc.co.uk/caribbean/news/story/2006/01/060103_murderlist.shtml

BBC News. "Australia Terror Plotter Jailed." 15 March 2007. Accessed June 28, 2011. http://news.bbc.co.uk/2/hi/europe/6454373.stm

BBC News. "Bomber 'influenced' by Preacher." 11 May 2006. Accessed August 10, 2011. http://news.bbc.co.uk/2/hi/uk_news/4762123.stm

—— "Profile: Sheikh Abdullah al-Faisal." 25 May 2007. Accessed May 10, 2011. http://news.bbc.co.uk/2/hi/uk_news/6692243.stm

—— "Race Hate Cleric Faisal Deported." 25 May 2007. Accessed August 10, 2011. http://news.bbc.co.uk/2/hi/uk_news/6691701.stm

—— "Who is Richard Reid?" 28 December 2001. Accessed August 11, 2011. http://news.bbc.co.uk/2/hi/uk_news/1731568.stm

Block, Alan A. and Sean Patrick Griffin. "Build It, and They'll Come: Narcotics and Money Laundering in the Leeward Islands." *Journal of Contemporary Justice,* 15(4) (November 1999): 397-420.

Caribbean 360. "Coke in Guyana Molasses Baron Gets 28 Years for Drug Plot." 18 July 2005. Accessed March 1, 2012. http://www.caribbean360.com/index.php/news/9455.html—5 February 2012.

Caribbean News Now. "OAS Forecasts Increased Human Trafficking in Caribbean." 16 October 2010. Accessed March 2, 2012. http://www.caribbeannewsnow.com/headline-OAS-forecasts-increased-human-trafficking-in-Caribbean-2721.html

Commissioner of Police (Jamaica). "From the Pen of the Commissioner of Police." 9 March 2012. Accessed March 20, 2012. http://www.jcf.gov.jm/news/03/2012/pen-commissioner-police.

Deosaran, Ramesh. "A Portrait of Crime in the Caribbean." In *Caribbean Security in the Age of Terror,* edited by Ivelaw Lloyd Griffith, 104-128. Kingston, Ian Randle: 2004.

—— "Editorial: The Enigma of a Caribbean Criminology." *Caribbean Journal of Criminology and Public Safety,* 13(1)(2) (January-July 2008): i-xvi. Accessed January 5, 2012. http://cjcsp.com/documents/Jan_July_2008_vol13_1_2.pdf

Douglas, Sean. "Verna Shakes Up the Senate." *Trinidad and Tobago News Day,* 17 March 2010. Accessed March 1, 2012. http://www.newsday.co.tt/news/0,117443.html

Dunn, Richard S. *Sugar and Slaves.* New York: W.W. Norton and Company, 1972.

Ezeonu, Ifeanyi. "Crimes of Globalization." *International Journal of Social Inquiry,* 1(2) (2008): 113-138.

Fanon, Frantz. *Black Skin White Masks.* New York: Grove Press, 1967.

Federal Bureau of Investigation (FBI). "Abdul Kadir Sentenced to Life in Prison for Conspiring to Commit Terrorist Attack at JFK Airport, Kadir and Coconspirators Plotted to Explode Fuel Tanks at Airport." U.S. Attorney's Office, 15 December 2010. Accessed August 9, 2011. http://www.fbi.gov/newyork/press-releases/2010/nyfo121510a.htm

—— "Russel Defreitas Sentenced to Life in Prison for Conspiring to Commit Terrorist Attack at JFK Airport, Defreitas and Coconspirators Plotted to Explode Fuel Tanks at Airport." U.S. Attorney's Office, 17 February 2011. Accessed August 9, 2011. http://www.fbi.gov/newyork/press-releases/2011/russell-defreitas-sentenced-to-life-in-prison-for-conspiring-to-commit-terrorist-attack-at-jfk-airport

—— "Kareem Ibrahim Sentenced to Life in Prison for Conspiring to Commit Terrorist Attack at JFK Airport." U.S. Attorney's Office, 13 January 2012. Accessed March 12, 2012. http://www.justice.gov/usao/nye/pr/2012/2012jan13.html

Flynn, Stephen E. and Anthony Bryan. "Terrorism, Porous Boundaries, and Homeland Security." Council on Foreign Relations, 20 June 2011. Accessed

October 22, 2001. http://www.cfr.org/border-and-ports/terrorism-porous-borders-homeland-security-case-us-caribbean-cooperation/p4844

Friedrichs, David O. and Jessica Friedrichs. "The World Bank and Crimes of Globalization: A Case Study." *Social Justice* 29(1-2)(2002): 13-36.

Guyana Graphic. "Today is the 34 Anniversary of the Murder of 11 Guyanese in an Act of Terrorism." *Guyana Graphic*, 6 October 2010. Accessed June 29, 2011. http://www.guyanagraphic.com/News/100620101248.htm

—— "Terrorism in the Sky October 06, 1976." *Guyana Graphic*, 6 October 2006. Accessed June 28, 2011. http://www.guyanagraphic.com/News/10051976-ca.htm

Girvan, Norman. "Terrorism, Tourism and Trade." *The Greater Caribbean This Week.* Accessed June 26, 2011. http://www.acs-aec.org/column/index2.htm

—— "Agenda Setting and Regionalism in the Greater Caribbean: Responses to 9/11." In *Caribbean Security in the Age of Terror*, edited by Ivelaw Griffith. Ian Randle, 2004.

Griffith, Ivelaw. *Quest for Caribbean Security*. New York: M.E. Sharpe, 1993.

—— *Drugs and Security in the Caribbean: Sovereignty Under Seige*. Pennsylvania: Pennsylvania State University Press, 1997.

—— "Security, Poverty, and Public Order." *Security and Defense Studies Review*, 2(2) (Summer 2002): 1-18.

—— "Dedication." In *Caribbean Security in the Age of Terror*, edited by Lvelaw Griffith. Ian Randle, 2004.

—— Drugs and Crime as Problems Without Passports in the Caribbean: How Secure is Security and How Sovereign is Sovereignty? Thirteenth Annual Eric E. Williams Memorial Lecture, Florida International University. School of Public and International Affairs. 28 October 2011. Accessed March 1, 2012. http://www. normangirvan.info/wp-content/uploads/2011/10/griffith-2011-eric-williams-lecture.pdf

Hagedorn, John M. "The Global Impact of Gangs." *Journal of Contemporary Criminal Justice*, 21(2)(May 2005): 153-169.

Haniff, Fareeza and Andrunie Harris. "$17M River Heist...Coast Guard Trio Charged With Murder." *Kaieteur News*, 25 August 2009. Accessed September 1, 2011. http://www.kaieteurnewsonline.com/2009/08/25/17m-river-heist...-coast-guard-trio-charged-with-murder/

Harewood, Susan. "Tings Brown." *Cultural Studies*, 24(2)(March 2010): 214-233.

Harriott, Anthony. "Mission Effectiveness, Environmental Change and the Reconfiguration of the Jamaican Security Forces." *Security and Defense Studies Review*, (2) (Summer 2002): 19-45.

Haughton, Suzette A. "The Jamaica-Britain Border and Drug Trafficking." *The Round Table*, 96(390) (June 2007): 279-303.

Hobbes, Thomas. *Leviathan*. Ed. Richard Tuck. New York: Cambridge University Press, 1991 (Orig. 1651).

Huste, Jean-Paul. "Latin America, The Caribbean, Islamism and Terrorism." European Strategic Intelligence and Security Centre (ESISC), 3 March 2007.

Hylton, Michael and Gladys Young. "Anti-corruption Efforts in the Caribbean: Are We Doing Enough?" *Journal of Financial Crime*, 14(3) 2007: 250-263.

International Organization for Migration (IOM). *Exploratory Assessment of Trafficking in Persons in the Caribbean Region: The Bahamas, Barbados, Guyana, Jamaica, The Netherlands, St. Lucia, and Suriname*. Washington, 2005.

International Narcotics Control Strategy Report (INCSR), Volume 1. United States Department of State: Bureau for International Narcotics and Law

Enforcement Affairs, March 2011. Accessed March 1, 2012 http://www.state.gov/documents/organization/156575.pdf

Itwaru, Arnold. *Critiques of Power*. Toronto: Terebi Press, 1989.

Jackson, Liz. "Willie Brigitte." Four Corners, Australian Broadcasting Corporation, 9 February 2004. Accessed June 28, 2011. http://www.abc.net.au/4corners/content/2004/s1040952.htm

Kaieteur News. "Cocaine Ship Busted for a Third Time in Jamaica." 14 October 2011. Accessed March 1, 2012. http://www.kaieteur newsonline.com/2011/10/14/cocaine-ship-busted-for-a-third-time-in-jamaica/

— — "Cops in Station Identified as Robbers." *Kaieteur News*, 8 March 2012. Accessed March 8, 2012. http://www.kaieteur newsonline.com/2012/03/08/cops-in-station-identified-as-'robbers'/

Katz, Charles, Edward R. Maguire and David Choate. "A Cross-National Comparison of Gangs in the United States and Trinidad and Tobago." *International Criminal Justice Review*, 21(3) (September 2011): 243-262.

Klatell, James M. "4 Charged in New York Airport Plot." CBS News, 10 September 2010. Accessed August 21, 2011. http://www.cbsnews. com/stories/2007/06/02/national/main2877931.shtml

Klein, Malcolm W. "Who Can You Believe? Complexities of International Street Gang Research." *International Criminal Justice Review*, 21(3) (2011): 197-207.

Landau, Anya K. and Wayne S. Smith. "Keeping Things in Perspective: Cuba and the Question of International Terrorism." Centre for International Policy, 20 November 2001.

Maguire, Edward R., William R. King, Devon Johnson, and Charles M. Katz. "Why Homicide Clearance Rates Decrease: Evidence from the Caribbean." *Policing and Society*, 20(4) (December 2010): 373-400.

Manwaring, Max. "Security, Stability and Sovereignty Challenges of Politicized Gangs and Insurgents in the Americas." *Small Wars and Insurgencies*, 22(5) (December 2011): 860-889.

Matthews, Lear. "Working with Caribbean Immigrants After the World Trade Center Tragedy." *Journal of Immigrant and Refugee Services*, 2(3 and 4) (2004): 69-82.

McCartney, Juan. "US Suspected Bahamas Terror Ties." *Caribbean News Now*, 7 June 2011. Accessed June 26, 2011. http://www.caribbean newsnow.com/headline-US-suspected-Bahamas-terror-ties-6555.html

Morris, Patrice.K. "Imprisoned in Jamaica." *International Criminal Justice Review*, 18(4) (December 2008): 435-454.

Nassar, Jamal. *Globalization and Terrorism: The Migration of Dreams and Nightmares*. New York: Rowman and Littlefield, 2005.

Phillips, Dion E. "Terrorism and Security in the Caribbean: The 1976 Cubana Disaster Off Barbados." *Terrorism*, 14(4) (1991): 209-219.

Pino, Nathan W., and Lee Michael Johnson. "Police Deviance and Community Relations in Trinidad and Tobago." *Policing: An International Journal of Police Strategies and Management*, 34(3) (2011): 454-478.

Pratt, Godfrey. "Terrorism and Tourism: Bahamas and Jamaica Fight Back." *International Journal of Contemporary Hospitality Management*, 15(3) (2003): 192-194.

Pryce, Kenneth. "Towards a Caribbean Criminology." In *Crime, Delinquency and Justice*. edited by Ramesh Deosaran. Kingston: Ian Randle, 2007: 3-18.

RCMP. "Cocaine Seizure from Shipment of Apples, Pineapples and Mangoes Leads to Arrests." Toronto: Royal Canadian Mounted Police (RCMP), 6

February 2012. Accessed March 5, 2012. http://www.rcmp-grc.gc.ca/on/news-nouvelles/2012/12-02-06-gta-rgt-drug-drogues-eng.htm

Religious Hardtalk. YouTube. Accessed August 24, 2011. http://www.youtube.com/watch?v=yEL9Tk_KSXc&feature=relmfu

Roopnarine, Lomarsh. *Indo-Caribbean Indenture: Resistance and Accommodation, 1838-1920*. Kingston: University of the West Indies Press, 2007.

Sanders, Ronald. "Crime in the Caribbean." *The Round Table*, 370 (July 2003): 377-390.

Seelke, Clare Ribando. "Trafficking in Persons in Latin America and the Caribbean." Congressional Research Service (CRS Report for Congress), 23 January 2012. Accessed March 21, 2012. http://www.fas.org/sgp/crs/row/RL33200.pdf

Stabroek News. "Guyanese Charged in Huge Bds$13M Barbados Drug Bust." *Stabroek News*, 3 April 2011. Accessed March 1, 2012. http://www.stabroeknews.com/2011/archives/04/03/13m-drug-bust/

— — "JFK Airport Terror Plot." *Stabroek News*, 26 October 2008. Accessed August 21, 2011. http://www.stabroeknews.com/2008/archives/10/26/jfk-airport-terror-plot/#0_undefined,0_

Statistics Canada. "The Caribbean Community in Canada-2007 Number 7." Accessed September 1 , 2011. http://www.statcan.gc.ca/pub/89-621-x/89-621-x2007007-eng.htm

Sulzberger, A.G. "2 Men Convicted in Kennedy Airport Plot." *New York Times*, 2 August 2010.

The Economist. "Caribbean Crime Wave." Accessed March 2, 2012. http://www.economist.com/node/10903343

Thompson, Alvin O. *The Haunting Past: Politics, Economics and Race in Caribbean Life*. Kingston: Ian Randle Publishers, 1997.

Tulchin, Joseph S. and Ralph H. Espach. "Introduction: U.S.-Caribbean Security Relations in the Post-Cold War Era." *Security in the Caribbean Basin*. Lynne Rienner Publishers, 2000.

United Nations Office on Drugs and Crime (UNODC). *Crime, Violence, and Development: Trends, Costs and Policy Options in the Caribbean*. A Joint Report by the United Nations Office on Drugs and Crime and the Latin America and Caribbean Region of the World Bank. March 2007. Accessed July 10, 2010. http://scm.oas.org/pdfs/2008/CP20887E01.pdf

— — *World Drug Report 2010*. New York: United Nations, 2010. Accessed September 1, 2011. http://www.unodc.org/documents/wdr/WDR_2010/World_Drug_Report_ 2010_lo-res.pdf

— — "Prison Reform in Latin America and the Caribbean." 3 August 2011. Accessed March 7, 2012. http://www.unodc.org/unodc/en/frontpage/2011/August/prison-reform-in-latin-america-and-the-caribbean.html

United Nations Development Programme (UNDP). *Caribbean Human Development Report 2012 (UNDP 2012)*. United Nations Development Program. Accessed March 1, 2012 http://www.undp.org/content/dam/undp/library/corporate/HDR/Latin%20America%20and% 20Caribbean% 20HDR/C_bean_HDR_Jan25_2012_3MB.pdf

UN.GIFT (UN Global Initiative to Fight Human Trafficking). "Human Trafficking: The Facts." Accessed March 15, 2012. http://www.unglobalcompact.org/docs/issues_doc/labour/Forced_labour/HUMAN_TRAFFICKING_-_THE_FACTS_-_final.pdf

UN News Service. "Criminal Violence Taking Rising Toll in Caribbean Countries, UN Report Finds." 8 February 2012. Accessed March 25, 2012. http://

www.un.org/apps/news/story.asp?NewsID=41175& Cr=caribbean&Cr1=.

Washington, CMC. "US-Court-Alleged terrorist with Guyanese passport charged in plot to attack US, UK." *Antigua Observer*, 8 July 2010. Accessed June 28, 2011. http://www.antigua observer.com/?p=36711

Weidlich, Thom. "JFK Airport Bomb-Plot Suspect Abdel Nur Pleads Guilty." *Business Week*, 29 June 2010.

Wells, William, Charles M. Katz and Jeonglim Kim. "Firearm Possession Among Arrestees in Trinidad and Tobago." *Injury Prevention* 16 (July 2010): 337-342. DOI: 10.1136/ip.2009.025122.

Williams, Eric. *Capitalism and Slavery*. New York: Perigee Books, 1980 [Orig. 1943].

Contributors

Ambika Krishnakumar holds a Ph.D. from the University of Tennessee and is Associate Professor at Syracuse University, New York. Her research interests include marital conflict, child and adolescent adjustment, school readiness, parent-child relationships, research methodology, development in ethnic, social, and cross-cultural contexts, adolescent parenting, adolescent sexuality, and urban economic hardship. She serves on the reviewer panel of the Journal of Pediatric Psychology and on the editorial board of the Journal of World Health and Population.

Aparajita Gangopadhyay is Associate Professor and Director, Centre for Latin American Studies at Goa University, India. She teaches post-graduate courses in Latin American Studies and International Relations. Dr. Gangopadhyay received her M.A. in International Studies (Politics) and M.Phil. and Ph.D. in Latin American Studies from the School of International Studies, Jawaharlal Nehru University, New Delhi. Her areas of interest are: Argentina-Brazil relations, U.S. foreign policy in Latin America and the Caribbean, foreign policy aspects of Indian diaspora, and security and regionalism in Latin America. She has published in professional journals and has contributed chapters to anthologies and edited volumes. She is the recipient of two prestigious essay awards (one from the Embassy of Argentina and the other from Candido Mendes University, Brazil) and the Publishers and Booksellers Guild of India, Kolkata.

David Gómez Arredondo teaches at the Facultad de Estudios Superiores, campus Iztacala, of the Universidad Nacional Autónoma de México (UNAM). His previous study on Ortiz was published as "Transmigración, transculturación y relato nacional en la obra de Fernando Ortiz" in *Pensares y quehaceres. Revista de políticas de la filosofía* No. 7-8, September 2008 - March 2009, SECNA. A substantial part of Dr. Arredondo's research is comprised of critiques of European philosophy from a Latin American perspective.

Hari Nair is Assistant Professor in the Department of Humanistic Studies, Birla Institute of Technology and Science (BITS), Pilani, India. He holds a Ph.D. from Universidad Nacional Autónoma de México. In December 2011, his doctoral dissertation entitled *Contra imperio: El discurso de derecho natural y la autonomía de los indios americanos* won the special mention "*mención* *honorífica*" of the jury in the competition for the Edmundo O'Gorman Prize, which is awarded annually by the *Instituto Nacional de Antropología e Historia* (National Institute for Anthropology and History, Mexico).

Jaipaul Roopnarine holds a Ph.D. from the University of Wisconsin, and is Jack Reilly Professor of Child and Family Studies and Director of the Jack Reilly Institute of Early Childhood and Provider Education at Syracuse University in New York. His research interests include father-child relationships across cultures; Caribbean immigrant families and schooling; early childhood education in international perspectives; globalization and convergences in childrearing and early socialization, and children's play across cultures. He has served on the editorial boards of Early Childhood Research Quarterly, Journal of Applied Developmental Psychology, and is currently on the editorial board of Fathering. Professor Roopnarine was a Visiting Scholar at The University of the West Indies, Jamaica, Indo-US Subcommission Senior Professor of Psychology at the University of Delhi, Fulbright Scholar to The University of the West Indies in Trinidad, and a consultant to the Roving Caregiver Program in the Caribbean funded by the Bernard van Leer Foundation, The Netherlands. He has also taught at Utah State University, The Pennsylvania State University, Cornell University, The City University of New York, The University of the West Indies, Trinidad, and The University of Wisconsin. He is currently working on an NICHD funded project with Dr. Michael E. Lamb of Cambridge University on parent-infant interactions in African American, European American, and English-speaking Caribbean immigrant families in the United States, and on two other projects that focus on mental health among Caribbean immigrant families in the United States and the Caribbean as well as on parenting styles and academic and social outcomes in Guyanese and Trinidadian families.

Jeetendra Khadan is a graduate of The University of the West Indies, St. Augustine campus (Trinidad and Tobago) and holds a B.Sc. (Hons.) degree in Economics. He is currently completing an M.Phil./Ph.D. in Economics at the same institution. His research focuses heavily on international trade and regional integration issues in the Caribbean. He is also a part-time lecturer on international trade and regional integration and has presented several research papers at major conferences on trade and regional integration issues in the Caribbean.

Kalowatie Deonandan is Associate Professor of Political Studies at the University of Saskatchewan, Canada. Her academic training includes a B.A. and an M.A. from York University in Toronto, and a Ph.D. from Queen's University in Kingston, all in Canada. Her area of regional specialization is Latin America and the Caribbean. She has published several journal articles and book chapters as well as two co-edited volumes: *Undoing Democracy: The Politics of Electoral Caudillismo in Nicaragua* (Englewood, Co.: Lexington Books, 2004) with David Close, and *Revolutionary Movements to Political Parties: Case Studies from Latin America and Africa* (New York: Palgrave, 2007) with David Close and Gary Prevost. Her current research is focused on natural resource extraction and its implications for development and democracy. Dr. Deonandan has served as Head of the International Studies

Program at the University of Saskatchewan and is a former president of the Canadian Association of Latin American and Caribbean Studies (CALACS), the premier academic association on the region in Canada. Currently, she is a member of the editorial board of the CALACS' Journal, The Canadian Journal of Latin American and Caribbean Studies (CJLACS) and an Associate Research Fellow at the Centre for Latin American and Caribbean Studies (CERLAC) at York University, Toronto.

Linden Lewis is Professor of Sociology at Bucknell University in Pennsylvania, U.S.A. He is also a Past President of the Caribbean Studies Association (2010). His research has focused on issues of gender and masculinity, race, globalization, labor and the state in the Caribbean. He has published widely in these areas in such journals as Feminist Review, Caribbean Quarterly, Race and Class, BIM: Arts for the 21st Century, and Caribbean Review of Gender Studies. Professor Lewis has also contributed book chapters in a number of anthologies. Additionally, he has worked as a consultant to UNICEF (Barbados), UNIFEM and the UN Division for the Advancement of Women as a member of its Expert Group in Brazil and Switzerland.

M. Raymond Izarali is a philosopher and Assistant Professor in the Department of Criminology at Wilfrid Laurier University in Ontario, Canada. Dr. Izarali is also the director of the Tshepo Institute for the Study of Contemporary Africa at the same institution. He specializes in the areas of international crime and justice, globalization, and human rights theory. He is currently pursuing research on the the prospect and implications of terrorism in/from the Caribbean. Dr. Izarali teaches courses at both the undergraduate and graduate level pertaining to globalization and social justice, corporate deviance and crime, legal philosophy, and terrorism. He is a member of the editorial board of the International Journal of Technology and Inclusive Education (Infonomics Society, UK) and has also served as an associate editor of the Global Studies Journal.

Martin Franklin is Lecturer in Mathematical Methods and Statistics and Head of the Department of Economics at The University of the West Indies, St. Augustine Campus in Trinidad and Tobago. He has published articles on flexible and distance education, ICT in development, HIV/AIDS, funding of tertiary education, and issues of economic development for small island states in the CARSEA Journal, The Social and Economic Studies Journal, The Journal of Eastern Caribbean Studies, The Caribbean Journal of Education, Global Development Studies, and the Research and Working Paper Series of the Faculty of Social Sciences, University of the West Indies, St. Augustine. In addition, he has also written chapters in six books. He is currently pursuing research on the informal sector, remittances in the Caribbean and the economics of culture. He is a graduate of the University of the West Indies (Mona Campus, Jamaica) and McGill University (Montreal, Canada) where he obtained a Bachelor of Science degree in Mathematics (First Class Honours) and a Master of Science degree in Operations Research. His work experience spans both the public and private sectors and includes both aviation management and operations management.

NAN Yang currently works in the China Merchant Bank as a risk manager in the city of Wenzhou, Zhejiang province in the east of China after he received his Master's degree in the College of Economics at Zhejiang Gongshang University, China in 2011. His research mainly focuses on international trade and finance in developing countries. Among his academic publications, his paper "On the Most Favored Nation Principle in TBT Agreement" has been included by Index to Scientific and Technical Proceedings (ISTP), PA, USA, and another paper "The Conductive Mechanism from Income Tax Rate of Overseas-funded Enterprise to Production — Based on Money Market and Exchange Market" has been published in the Journal of Finance & Trade Economics, one of China's national core journals.

Natasha C. Parkins graduated with a Master's degree in Sociology specializing in Development Studies. Ms. Parkins also holds a Bachelor of Science degree (Upper Second Class Honors) from The University of the West Indies (Mona Campus, Jamaica), majoring in sociology with minors in criminology and psychology. She is a researcher with the Violence Prevention Alliance and is currently working on a joint project with the Alliance and Action on Armed Violence (UK), researching Jamaica's capacity to address the issue of armed violence. Ms. Parkins has lectured in Sociology at the University College of the Caribbean and has tutored a course in Criminal Justice Systems at The University of the West Indies, Mona Campus. She served as a research assistant to the country author on the first Regional Citizens Security Report for the Caribbean, sponsored by the UNDP. In this capacity she researched issues surrounding organized crime and youth violence. Ms. Parkins' research interests are in Jamaican/Caribbean migration and various criminological issues. She has presented her paper on the migration of highly skilled Jamaicans at the annual Derek Gordon Seminar in April 2010 in Kingston, Jamaica and the annual American Society of Criminology Conference in November 2010 in San Francisco, California.

Nicholas Paul is a graduate of The University of the West Indies (St. Augustine Campus, Trinidad and Tobago). He holds a first degree in physics and minors in mathematics and electronics. He is currently completing a Master's degree in statistics in the Department of Mathematics and Statistics at the same institution. His current research involves a number of projects that include developing a mathematics textbook for secondary schools in the Caribbean. He is also a lecturer in mathematics at the University of Trinidad and Tobago, and in biostatistics at the Faculty of Medical Sciences at The University of the West Indies, St. Augustine Campus.

Priti Singh is Assistant Professor in the School of International Studies, Jawaharlal Nehru University, New Delhi. She holds a Ph.D. from the same university. She teaches courses on foreign policies and political economy of Latin America and the Caribbean countries. Recipient of the Australia India Council's Senior Fellowship and the Shastri Indo-Canadian Institute's Faculty Research Fellowship, she has been engaged in research on indigenous communities and government policy. Her primary research interests include comparative studies on policy issues on indigenous peoples, multiculturalism, as well as social movements and international relations.

She is member of editorial advisory boards of reputed journals in India and abroad and has published two books and a number of articles.

Ramesh Deosaran is a Ph.D. graduate of the University of Toronto, Canada. He is currently Chairman of the Police Service Commission and Member of the Teaching Service Commission, two independent bodies, appointed by His Excellency the President of the Republic of Trinidad and Tobago.

Well known internationally for his scholarly work in criminology and the social sciences, he is Professor Emeritus at The University of the West Indies (UWI, St. Augustine Campus) where he served for thirty years, and where he developed among other things the B.Sc. Major in Psychology, and the Graduate Programme (M.Sc., M.Phil. and Ph.D.) in Criminology and Criminal Justice. These two programmes now have among the highest enrollments at the UWI to date. He is founder of both the Ansa McAl Psychological Research Centre and Centre for Criminology and Criminal Justice at the UWI, St. Augustine Campus, where he served as Director for ten-year periods respectively. He also served recently as Programme Professor in Criminology and Public Safety at The University of Trinidad and Tobago (UTT) where he founded the Institute for Criminology and Public Safety and developed the Certificate, Diploma and B.A.Sc. in Criminology and Public Safety.

He is an active researcher and policy analyst in the areas of crime prevention and management, school violence and juvenile delinquency, poverty, penal and police reform, and governance and civil society. He has authored 15 books, and over 300 journal and related reports to date in these and related areas.

Well known for his valuable contributions to the civic life of Trinidad and Tobago, he served as Independent Senator in Parliament for 15 years, and as Chairman of the Joint Select Committee appointed to enquire into Municipal Corporations and Service Commissions. He successfully passed several motions in Parliament including one to review the Death Penalty, another to allow Live Broadcasting of Parliamentary debates and proceedings, and on Election Financing approved by Parliament in 2009.

He was also Executive Director and founding member of the Caribbean Institute of Human Rights (CARIBCARE) (1989-1994).

Professor Deosaran is advisor to several regional and international organizations including the National Crime Commission of St. Lucia, the Association of Caribbean Commissioners of Police (ACCP), the United Nations Office for Drug Control and Crime Prevention (UNODC) on matters of crime prevention and management, and the Organisation of American States (OAS) on campaign finance reform.

Rhoda Reddock is Professor of Gender, Social Change and Development and currently Deputy Principal of The University of the West Indies (St. Augustine Campus, Trinidad and Tobago). She is a former head of the Centre for Gender and Development Studies and lecturer in sociology at the UWI, St. Augustine Campus, and associate lecturer in the Women and Development programme at the Institute of Social Studies, The Hague. She is an activist in the Caribbean Women's Movement and founding member of the Caribbean Association of Feminist Research and Action. A former chair of Research Committee-32 of the International Sociological Association (1994-1998), she has numerous publications including *Women, Labour and Politics in Trinidad and Tobago: A History* (Zed Books, 1994) which was named a CHOICE Outstanding Academic Book for 1995; *Plantation Women: International Experiences* (Berg, 1998, co- edited with Shobhita Jain); *Caribbean Sociology: Introductory Readings* (Ian Randle Publishers, 2000 co-edited with Christine Barrow); and *Interrogating Caribbean Masculinities* (The UWI Press, 2004). In October 2001 she received the UWI Vice Chancellor's Award for All-Round Excellence in Teaching and Administration, Research and Public Service and in July 2002 was recipient of the Seventh CARIÇOM Triennial Award for Women at the Heads of Government Meeting of the Caribbean Community in Guyana. Most recently in 2004, Professor Reddock was a recipient of a distinguished Fulbright New Century Scholars Award and was Visiting Professor at the African Gender Institute of the University of Cape Town in 2005-2006. On 8 March 2008 she received an International Woman of Courage Award from the US Department of State.

Roger Hosein graduated from The University of the West Indies (UWI) and went on to obtain his Ph.D. in economics at Cambridge University in 2000. He joined the Department of Economics at the St. Augustine Campus of UWI later that year and currently holds the position of Senior Lecturer. His research interests focus heavily on International Trade with emphasis on education and economic development in the Caribbean region. He is the founding Coordinator of the Trade and Economic Development Unit within the Department of Economics. He has published some 30 articles in scholarly journals such as the West Indian Journal of Engineering, The Journal of Business, Finance and Economics in Emerging Economies, The Social and Economic Studies Journal, The Journal of Eastern Caribbean Studies, The Construction Management and Economics Journal, The Caribbean Journal of Education, Global Development Studies, and the Research and Working Paper Series of the Faculty of Social Sciences, U.W.I, St. Augustine. In addition, he has written five books and chapters in thirteen other books.

Samantha C. Joseph is a Ph.D. Candidate (Economics) at The University of the West Indies (St. Augustine Campus, Trinidad and Tobago). She holds a Bachelor's degree in Economics and Management (Honours) and a Master's degree in Economics, specializing in International Trade. She has done extensive research and published papers in the areas of migration, remittances, Caribbean diaspora, and on economic development. She has presented her work at a number of conferences including the Caribbean Centre for Money and Finance Annual Conference in Guyana (2009) and Trinidad (2011), the World Association of Sustainable Development Conference in St. Lucia (2010), and the SALISES Annual Conference in Trinidad (2009) and Jamaica (2011). She is also a lecturer in undergraduate economics.

Satnarine Balkaransingh is a former senior public servant in the Government of Trinidad and Tobago; he represented the Government at several international conferences and in negotiations with international lending agencies. He is an economist with significant experience in policy planning, strategic planning and public sector investment programming and management. A trained musician/dancer he has also choreographed, produced and directed over 50 stage and TV productions including ballets, and has performed internationally including for Royalty, Heads of States and Off-Broadway. He is currently a consultant and part- time Lecturer at UWI, St. Augustine. Dr. Balkaransingh has studied in Trinidad, India and the United Kingdom. He holds a BA (Hons.) Economics, Delhi University; Sp Post-Grad Dance, Kathak Kendra, Delhi; M.Sc. Project Planning and National Development (Project Planning Centre, University of Bradford, UK); and a Ph.D. from The University of Trinidad and Tobago (UTT).

Satya Pattnayak is Professor of Sociology and Political Science and Director of the interdisciplinary Latin American Studies Program at Villanova University in Pennsylvania, U.S.A. He holds a Ph.D. from Vanderbilt University. Professor Pattnayak's research interests encompass multiple areas, such as international development, political sociology, democratization, military and society, international terrorism, inequality studies, comparative research methodology, ethnic conflict, Latin America, and South Asia. He is widely published.

Timothy Shaw holds a Ph.D. from Princeton and is presently Adjunct Professor at the University of Ottawa. Having lived an illustrious scholarly career, Professor Timothy Shaw now serves at the University of Ottawa to stay active during retirement. Prior to this post, he served as Director and Professor at the Institute of International Relations at The University of the West Indies (Trinidad and Tobago). He has also served at Dalhousie University (Nova Scotia) from 1971 to 2001. During that time he was Director of the Centre for African Studies at the same institution from 1983 to 1990, Director of the Pearson Institute for International Development (1985-1988), and Director of the Centre for Foreign Policy Studies (1993-2000). He also served as Director and Professor of the Institute of Commonwealth Studies from 2001 to 2006 at the University of London where he is now Professor Emeritus. At the moment he is, concurrently, a Senior Fellow of the Centre for International Governance Innovation at the University of Waterloo, Bank of Uganda Visiting Professor of Development Studies at Mbarara University of Science and Technology in Uganda (2000-), and Extraordinary Professor of Political Science at Stellenbosch University in South Africa (1998-). Professor Shaw has also been a Visiting Faculty at Aolborg University, Denmark (2000-1); Carleton University (1978-9 and 2008); University of Manchester (1991); Nihon University, Japan (1996); Obafemi Awolow University, Nigeria (1979-80); University of Zimbabwe (1989); and University of Zambia (1973-4), among others. He was a member of the Commonwealth Scholarship Commission from 2002 to 2009, and serves as Editor of the International Political Economy of New Regionalisms Series (Ashgate Publishing) and International Political Economy Series (Palgrave MacMillan). Some of his recent publications include *New Approaches to the Governance of Natural Resources: Insights from Africa* (co-edited), and *Africa and International Relations in the Twenty-First Century* (co-edited).

W. Andy Knight is Chair of the Department of Political Science and Professor of International Relations at the University of Alberta, Canada. He also serves as Advisory Board Member of the World Economic Forum's Global Agenda Council on the Welfare of Children. Until recently, he was Director of the Peace and Post Conflict Studies Certificate Programme in the Office of Interdisciplinary Studies (OIS). In March 2007, Dr. Knight was appointed by the Canadian Foreign Minister to the Board of Governors of the International Development Research Centre (IDRC) and continues to serve in that position. He co-edited the international journal, Global Governance, from 2000 to 2005, was Vice Chair of the Academic Council on the United Nations System (ACUNS), and is currently a member of the Board of Directors of the John Humphrey Centre for Peace and Human Rights, the Canadian Association for Security and Intelligence Studies (CASIS), the Canadian Consortium for Peace Studies (CCPS), and the Education for Peace Academic and Research Council (EPARC). Professor Knight has written and edited several books, book chapters and journal articles on various aspects of multilateralism, global governance and peace, and United Nations reform. His recent books are: *Global Politics* (with Tom Keating); *Routledge Handbook of the Responsibility to Protect* (with Frazer Egerton); *The Ashgate Research Companion to Political Leadership* (with Joseph Masciulli & Mikhail A. Molchanov); *Adapting the United Nations to a Postmodern Era: Lessons Learned; A Changing United Nations: Multilateral Evolution and the Quest for Global Governance*; and *Building Sustainable Peace* (with Tom Keating). In 2010 he was awarded the National Harry Jerome Trailblazer Award, and in 2011 he was elected as a Fellow of the Royal Society of Canada.

Wang Guo-An is Professor of international trade at Zhejiang Gongshang University, Hangzhou City, close to Shanghai in the east of China. His research interests encompass international trade, foreign direct investment, and e-commerce. As a visiting professor, he has visited over 60 universities in 20 countries and regions around the world, including the USA, Australia, New Zealand, South Korea, the UK, Canada, Japan, Turkey, Pakistan and the Philippines. He has held more than ten years of administrative positions including serving as Foreign Assistant to the university president, Director of the International Affairs Office, Director of the e-Trade Training Center, and Chairman of the Department International Trade. He has actively participated in the World Innovation Summit for Education (WISE), the International Association of University Presidents (IAUP), the Association of Universities of Asia and the Pacific (AUAP) and the Association of International Educators (NAFSA). He has more than forty academic publications, principally on Chinese business, international trade and economics, and e-Commerce.

Winston Dookeran is the Honourable Minister of Finance for the Republic of Trinidad and Tobago. A former Governor of the Central Bank of Trinidad and Tobago, he was also a Visiting Scholar at the Centre for International Affairs of Harvard University and at the World Institute for Development Economics Research of the United Nations University. He served as Senior Economist at the United Nations Economic Commission for Latin America and the Caribbean (UNECLAC) and has served as a consultant to several Caribbean governments on the political economy for their development. He was Lecturer at The University of the West Indies' Department of Economics and in 1991 he was awarded a Doctor of Laws (honoris causa) by the University of Manitoba as recognition for his work. He is widely published on Caribbean economic development and has contributed articles and interviews to numerous professional journals including *the Economist* and *Latin Finance* and has made several speeches in and out of Parliament on the politics of economic change in a small state perspective. He has published several articles on economics, finance and development in international journals. Some of his books include *Choices and Change: Reflections on the Caribbean; The Caribbean Quest: Directions for Structural Reform in a Global Economy* (co-editor); and *Power, Politics and Performance: A Partnership Approach for the Development of Small States.*

Index

Q

R

S

T

U

V

W

X

Y

Z